De Basil's Ballets Russes

Other books by Kathrine Sorley Walker

Dance and its Creators
Eyes on Mime
Eyes on the Ballet
Brief for Ballet
Robert Helpmann
Writings on Dance 1938–68 by A.V. Coton
(edited, with Lilian Haddakin)
Ballet for Boys and Girls (with Joan Butler)
The Royal Ballet: A Picture History
(with Sarah C. Woodcock)
Raymond Chandler Speaking
(edited, with Dorothy Gardiner)
Saladin: Sultan of the Holy Sword
Joan of Arc
The Heart's Variety (verse)
Emotion and Atmosphere (verse)

De Basil's Ballets Russes

Kathrine Sorley Walker

ATHENEUM

New York

1983

Library of Congress Cataloging in Publication Data

Walker, Kathrine Sorley.
   De Basil's Ballets Russes.

   Bibliography: p.
   Includes index.
   1. Ballet Russe de Monte Carlo—History.
I. Title.
GV1786.B3W34   1983   792.8′0947   82-16339
ISBN 0-689-11365-X

418608

Contents

Acknowledgements

Writing this book would have been impossible without a great deal of co-operation. Given time, and unlimited funds for travel, I would have involved even more people than I have managed to do, but those with whom I have established contact, either personally or by letter (some letters were unanswered), have been generous in their response.

I list below my main sources, but I would like to extend specially warm thanks to two ladies who have been continuously helpful and encouraging throughout the many months of preparation: Mme Irina Baronova-Tennant-Severn and Mme Olga Morosova de Basil.

People associated with the de Basil Ballet in various capacities:

Anna Adrianova, Lorand Andahazy, Thomas Armour (letters to the late Mrs Margaret Power);
Robert Barnett, Irina Baronova, Maria de Baroncelli;
Douglas Coudy (D. Kydine);
Alexandra Danilova, the late Mme Felia Doubrovska, Sir Anton Dolin, Vladimir Dokoudovsky;
the late André Eglevsky;
Vsevolod Grigoriev, Gerald Goode, Nina Golovina (Gladys Marvel);
the late Arnold Haskell;
Roman Jasinsky;
Boris Kochno, Diana Kelly;
Moussia Larkina (Moscelyne Larkin), Irina Lavrova (Valrene Tweedie);
Tatiana Leskova;
William McDermott, Herida May, Olga Morosova;
Vera Nelidova (Betty Cuff);
April Olrich;
Dimitri Rostov;
Maria Sanina (Brigitte Kelly), Anna Severskaya (Anna Northcote), Natasha Sobinova (Rosemary Deveson), Jack Spurgeon, Kyra Strakhova, Nina

Stroganova, Tatiana Stepanova (Gardner), Deane Schultz and her daughter Barbara Lloyd, Marina Svetlova;
John Taras, Tamara Toumanova, Tamara Tchinarova (Finch), Xenia Tripolitova, Joan Tucker, Oleg Tupine;
Nina Verchinina, Pat Vaughn, Anna Volkova;
Hilda Yussem, George Zoritch.

Organizations and individuals who have responded particularly helpfully to enquiries, assisted with research, or lent material for consultation, are:

Jack Anderson, Ben Arnott, Harold Atkins, The Australian Ballet Archives (Edward Pask), Bibliothèque de l'Arsenal, Paris (Marie Françoise Christout);
Peter Bellew, Oscar Beuselinck (for Jack Hylton (Musical Plays) Ltd), Douglas Blake, P. Bessand-Massenet, Bischoff & Co. Solicitors (B.C. Bischoff and R.J. Proudfoot);
Esther Corsellis, Esther Clifford;
Jerry Davidson, the late Baron Leo d'Erlanger, Janet Rowson Davis, George Dorris, Philip Dyer, *The Dancing Times* (Mary Clarke);
Angel Alberto Fumagalli (Archives of the Teatro Colón), Kathleen Fahey;
Mimi Grey, Mme Galina Gauthier;
Dr Lilian Haddakin, Dr James Harding, Doris Hering, Geoffrey Hutton, Alan Hutchinson;
Fred James, Alan Jefferson;
Leo and Janet Kersley, Alexandra Kirsta;
Carlos Maria Losasso (Cordoba, Argentina), Delfino Larrosa, The Law Society (London);
Monte Carlo Theatre Archives (Francis Rosset and Daniel Aubry), Rose Mary MacIndoe, P.W. Manchester, Eugenio Eloy Martinez (Cordoba, Argentina), Betty June Myers, Carlos Manso;
Claudia Ottley;
Noël Pelly, Walter E. Prude, the late Mrs Margaret Power;
Dame Marie Rambert, Laurie Rentoul, Nancy Reynolds, The Royal Opera House Covent Garden Archives;
Harvey Simmonds, Sir Robert Southey, Barbara Sullivan, Dorothy Stock, Simmonds & Simmonds (Solicitors) (Peter Richardson), San Francisco Dance Archives (Russell Hartley), Sydney Opera House Archives of the Performing Arts (Paul Bentley);
Harold E. Tidemann, Metropolitan Toronto Public Library (Theatre Section), John Travis;
Ward Lock Editorial Department (Suzanna Osman Jones), G.B.L. Wilson, Leland Windreich, the late Miss Isabel Wallace;
Iris Zinoviev.

ACKNOWLEDGEMENTS

I would like to thank specially:

Dr George Jackson, Washington, for editorial help and advice;
Dr George Verdak, Indianapolis, for trusting me by post with an entire file of correspondence relating to the Fortune Gallo period;
Lieut. Colonel Peter Davis, RM Retd, for help in research relating to Colonel de Basil's military career.

In London, I have relied considerably on research material available in the Theatre Museum and where illustrations are concerned on the specialist knowledge of Sarah Woodcock, who also read the proofs.

Additionally, I am deeply indebted to Adrian Ryan of Melbourne, who has given me invaluable help in research over the Australian seasons, in studying the Ringland Anderson films, and in finding photographic illustrations.

Nomenclature

The question of the names by which various Russian Ballet companies were known is at best complicated, and the fact that companies were described differently in different parts of the world aggravates the confusion. Most encyclopaedias and books of reference contain errors. My contribution to the definitions is as follows.

Companies associated with Colonel W. de Basil from 1932

1932

In Monte Carlo: Les Ballets Russes de Monte-Carlo

In Paris: Ballets Russes de Monte-Carlo, direction René Blum et W. de Basil

1933

In Monte Carlo and Paris: as before

In London: Ballets Russes de Monte-Carlo, director general W. de Basil, artistic director René Blum

In New York: Monte Carlo Ballet Russe

1934

In London: Ballets Russes du Col. W. de Basil, director general W. de Basil, artistic director René Blum, maître de ballet and artistic collaborator Leonide Massine

In New York: Monte Carlo Ballet Russe

1935

In London: Ballets Russes du Col. W. de Basil or Col. W. de Basil's Ballets Russes, founder and director general W. de Basil, maître de ballet and artistic collaborator Leonide Massine

In New York: Monte Carlo Ballet Russe

1936
In London: as 1935
In New York: Col. W. de Basil's Ballets Russes
In Australia: (II Company) Ballets Russes de Monte-Carlo (Col. W. de Basil's) or Col. W. de Basil's Monte Carlo Russian Ballet

1937
In London: as 1935
In New York: Col. W. de Basil's Ballet Russe (de Monte Carlo)
In Europe: (II Company) Ballets Russes de Léon Woizikovsky or Ballett des Zaren

1938
In London: Russian Ballet presented by Educational Ballets Ltd, directors Victor Dandré (chairman), W.G. Perkins, G. Sevastianov (managing director)
In Australia: Covent Garden Russian Ballet presented by Educational Ballets Ltd

1939
In London: Covent Garden Russian Ballet presented by Educational Ballets Ltd
In Australia: Original Ballet Russe Ltd's Col. W. de Basil's Ballet Company

Thereafter: Original Ballet Russe, except for one season at the Teatro Colón, Buenos Aires, April to November 1943, when the two companies of de Basil and the Colón were temporarily merged and billed as the 'Cuerpo de Baile del Teatro Colón', Director General Col. W. de Basil.

Principal other companies based on Russian dancers in the 1930s

1933 Les Ballets 1933, artistic director Boris Kochno, maître de ballet and choreographer George Balanchine
1928–34 Ida Rubinstein Ballet, various maîtres de ballet
1932–4 Théâtre de la Danse Nijinska/Les Ballets de Bronislava Nijinska
1931– Les Ballets de Boris Kniasev, artistic director Boris Kniasev
1934–5 The Levitov Russian Ballet (often called the Levitov-Dandré), artistic manager Alexander Levitov, organizer Victor Dandré, maître de ballet Paul Petrov (not the Petrov known from the de Basil Ballet)
1935 Les Ballets de Léon Woizikovsky, artistic director and maître de ballet Léon Woizikovsky
1935 Théâtre des Ballets Russes, director Mme S. Epstein, joint maîtres de ballet Lubov Egorova and Theodore Wassiliev
1937– Les Ballets de la Jeunesse, director Lubov Egorova, artistic director Jashf Crandall

1930–35 National Ballet of Lithuania, maître de ballet Nicolas Zverev

1935 Ballets Russes de Paris, directors E. Iskoldov and B. Daschevsky, maîtres de ballet Alexandre Fortunato and Thaddeus Slavinsky

1936–7 Ballets de Monte-Carlo, director René Blum, maître de ballet Michel Fokine. This company was succeeded in 1938 by Ballet Russe de Monte Carlo, artistic director Leonide Massine, managing director Serge Denham, founder and director of the Ballets de Monte-Carlo René Blum

Transliteration note

In accordance with current practice, Russian names such as Grigoriev or Rostov have been transliterated with a final 'v'. All such names used to be transliterated with 'ff'. Stage names of non-Russian dancers, e.g. Paul Petroff and Marc Platoff, were always written in this way. Colonel W. de Basil, where the W. represents Vassily, would now be written V. de Basil. An even more awkward inconsistency comes with Léon Woizikovsky – usually then written Woizikowsky. Now, the second 'w' seems more appropriate as a 'v' (as in Tchaikovsky) but the first 'W' would seem disturbingly unfamiliar as a 'V'. Consistency would be a praiseworthy goal at which to aim, but there is really no way it can be achieved in writing about the Russian Ballet.

Illustrations

Choreartium: Hélène Kirsova (Sasha/BBC Hulton Picture Library).
Choreartium: Tamara Toumanova (Sasha/BBC Hulton Picture Library).
Schéhérazade: Lubov Tchernicheva (Merlyn Severn/Theatre Museum).
L'Oiseau de feu: Alexandra Danilova (Gordon Anthony/Theatre Museum).
Symphonie fantastique: Tamara Toumanova and Leonide Massine (Gordon Anthony/Theatre Museum).

Between pages 174 and 175

Prince Igor: Nina Raievska and Léon Woizikovsky (photographer unknown).
L'Oiseau de feu: Hélène Kirsova and Igor Youskevitch (Jack Cato).
Les Présages: Tamara Tchinarova (Hollywood Studios).
Francesca da Rimini: group including Lubov Tchernicheva and Paul Petrov (Hugh P. Hall).
Protée: David Lichine with Alexandra Denisova, Natasha Sobinova, Sono Osato, Geneviève Moulin and Marina Svetlova (Hugh P. Hall).
Le Coq d'or: Irina Baronova and Marc Platov (King Dodon) with Galina Razoumova, Olga Morosova, Sono Osato, Tamara Grigorieva, Roman Jasinsky and Paul Petrov (Gordon Anthony/Theatre Museum).
Le Fils prodigue: Irina Baronova and Anton Dolin (Baron/BBC Hulton Picture Library).
Icare: Roman Jasinsky (Hugh P. Hall).
Les Femmes de bonne humeur: Tamara Grigorieva and Marian Ladre (photographer unknown).
Les Femmes de bonne humeur: Olga Morosova (Nanette Kuehn).
Le Beau Danube: Yura Lazovsky (Gordon Anthony/Theatre Museum).
Graduation Ball: Tatiana Riabouchinska and David Lichine (Hugh P. Hall).
Graduation Ball: Nicholas Orlov (Duncan Melvin/Theatre Museum).
Paganini: Dimitri Rostov (Baron/BBC Hulton Picture Library).
Irina Baronova with her husband Gerry Sevastianov (*The Bystander*/Theatre Museum).
Sir Thomas Beecham with Alexandra Danilova and Yurek Shabelevsky after premiere of *Les Dieux mendiants*, Covent Garden, 1937 (*The Sketch*/Theatre Museum).
Bronislava Nijinska with Baronova and Lichine after premiere of *Les Cents Baisers*, Covent Garden, 1935 (*The Bystander*/Theatre Museum).
Tatiana Riabouchinska, Vera Zorina, Olga Morosova, Irina Baronova, Alexandra Danilova, Roman Jasinsky and Yurek Shabelevsky, Santa Monica, California, 1936 (*The Bystander*/Theatre Museum).
Natasha Sobinova, Alexandra Denisova and June Roper, Vancouver, 1938 (Alfred Krause).
Tatiana Riabouchinska, David Lichine, Vsevolod Grigoriev, Natasha Sobinova, Lubov Tchernicheva, Galina Razoumova, Tamara Grigorieva, Maori

guide, Alexandra Denisova, Lina Lerina, Irina Kosmovska and Serge Grigoriev, Rotorua, New Zealand, 1939 (Moore & Thompson).

Toumanova, Baronova, Riabouchinska and Danilova, off stage (*The Dancing Times*/Theatre Museum).

Cain and Abel: Carlota Pereyra, Nancy Milton, April Olrich, Oleg Tupine and Kenneth MacKenzie (photographer unknown).

Le Mariage d'Aurore: Tatiana Stepanova and Oleg Tupine.

Serge Grigoriev, Vladimir Dokoudovsky and Colonel W. de Basil, Covent Garden, 1947 (photographer unknown).

Every effort has been made to trace copyright-holders of the photographs reproduced in this book. Author and publishers apologise if they have unwittingly used photographs still in copyright without obtaining permission.

Foreword

The legend of the Russian ballet, as disseminated worldwide on film by *The Red Shoes*, is made up of rivalries, temperaments, intrigues, romance, mystery and obsessive dedication. Legends are not always myths. Not one of these qualities is missing in the complex story of the companies connected with Colonel W. de Basil.

The chronicle of their fortunes recalls a firework flourish: brilliant at its height, beautiful in dispersal, fading as it falls to extinction.

The theatrical experience of ballet, the brief living moment, is always difficult to recapture. Every ballet-goer knows how his first feelings as part of an excited audience become diffused when they are assailed by countless separate shades of opinion from press, commentators and his own acquaintance. The picture that is finally established as ballet history is created out of many written and spoken statements, dominated not so much by majority vote as by the most forceful voices. However much an individual may be convinced that the accepted record is untrue, its testimony will stand for later generations.

The ballet historian is at the mercy of this state of affairs. The facts that he has to flesh out are often hard to establish. Written records may be non-existent, programmes undated or uncorrected, and personal memories are inevitably angled or inaccurate. One powerful statement can establish a fact for the records that research reveals as an error – and the faulty fact is picked up and perpetuated by later books of reference so that it seems disturbingly well documented. Worse still, beyond the facts lies even more debatable ground, the quagmire of personal opinion where no one can find a solid foothold. This is the area where, for current events, one relies totally on one's own view, however divergent this is from other people's. The historian, however, as opposed to the critic or contemporary ballet-goer, has no personal experience to act as yardstick in the checking of reported opinion. In dealing with the recent past, a writer may be part historian, part observer. For my own part, I have some sketchy juvenile memories of performances by the de Basil ballet in London in 1938 and 1939 and later ones of the 1947 London season. I am naturally very conscious that plenty of my readers remember it all . . . in their own way.

The raw material of this book has been varied: books, newspaper articles, programmes, correspondence and documents, interviews with some of the protagonists and some of the worldwide audience. Many of the principals are dead. No affidavits can be taken from René Blum, or Colonel de Basil, from Serge Grigoriev and Lubov Tchernicheva, from Michel Fokine, from Sol Hurok or German Sevastianov. The resulting assessment is obviously open to error and bias, and where views conflict there is no way of establishing with any certainty which of them represents truth. Sometimes the reader will have to make up his own mind on the evidence offered. More, and possibly conflicting, evidence will go on emerging long after the book is in print.

One thing is certain. Because of the marvellous array of personalities who contributed to this company and the wide range of human emotions that motivated its daily life and eventual death, its story will look different to each one of us. We will all see it in the light of our tastes, temperaments and prejudices. There can never be one definitive view either of Colonel de Basil or of his company.

1
The Company, 1931 to 1952

January 1932 to August 1934

ON 5 July 1933, the traditionally anonymous critic of *The Times* in London wrote:

Sir Oswald Stoll has certainly secured that the Alhambra, soon to be demolished, shall go down in a blaze of glory. For the company of dancers directed by Colonel de Basil and styled Ballets Russes de Monte-Carlo, who made their first appearance there last night, is the most splendid that has been seen in London for many years.

It was a verdict little questioned at the time or at any time since. The evening stands as one of the historic performances of ballet, in line with the first night of the Diaghilev Ballets Russes in Paris in 1909 or the *succès fou* of the Sadler's Wells Ballet at the Metropolitan Opera House in New York in 1949. It could also be termed the launching-pad from which the company went into orbit.

What were the ingredients of that unforgettable occasion? First of all three ballets, one old – Fokine's *Les Sylphides* – and two new: Massine's delectable *Le Beau Danube* and his first striking and controversial symphonic ballet, *Les Présages*. Second, a group of dancers of mixed experience and promise led by the splendid former Diaghilev stars, Alexandra Danilova and Leonide Massine, and introducing two of the phenomenal 'baby ballerinas', Irina Baronova and Tatiana Riabouchinska. The third, Tamara Toumanova, would only rejoin the troupe, after a term with Les Ballets 1933, later in the year. Another contributory factor was what *The Times* terms 'a first-rate orchestra conducted by Efrem Kurtz'.

Combined, these dancers and ballets proved stimulating to a degree it is impossible to overestimate. The wonder and excitement remained,

1

and if anything increased, as the weeks went by, and a season intended to finish on 25 July continued to the first frosty days of November.

It was an ecstatic season for London theatre-goers, a season in which one marvel followed another, in which a habit of going to the Russian Ballet was formed by many young people who had never seen the Diaghilev Ballet. These new enthusiasts found the Ballets Russes a company worth spending time and money on, a West-End-of-London company (and it must be remembered that London's theatrical West End in the 'thirties had a special aura, its extraordinary glamour playing a vital part in the brilliant society scene) that would give them an evening full of colour and music. If the bait were escapist enjoyment, however, the hook was far more enduring – the compelling alliance of music, design and superb dancing and mime that was offered in the ballets by Fokine, Massine and George Balanchine in the repertoire at the Alhambra Theatre.

These audiences were on the whole composed of young or youngish people, drawn largely from the educated middle classes rather than the elite society to which the Diaghilev Ballets Russes had originally appealed – the emphasis had begun to change with his postwar seasons – and representing both sexes to a greater degree than is sometimes the case with ballet. The Alhambra was a spacious, gracious theatre with a warm atmosphere. Performances were given every evening, with matinées on Wednesdays and Saturdays. Prices were not exorbitant, especially in the upper, unreserved part of the house for which, in the custom of the time, people could buy stools in a queue outside earlier in the day. Friendships (and enmities) emerged from this queue and are remembered even now, when some of the ballet-goers have turned into critics and museum curators. There were no dissentient voices as to the overall effect of the company, however much debate went on about individual ballets and dancers; and, looking back, many remember it as an important milestone in their aesthetic development.

To estimate the effect of this remarkable debut in London, it must be looked at in context. Although the Ballets Russes de Monte-Carlo had been actively planned from October 1931 and given its first performance at Monte Carlo on 17 January 1932, with subsequent seasons in Paris and elsewhere in Europe, it was the London reception that established its position as the most important ballet company of the time.

2

The diaspora of artists following Diaghilev's death on 19 August 1929 had very drastically scattered the available talent. In 1931 Fokine was in New York, Massine at La Scala (Milan), Balanchine in Paris, Bronislava Nijinska in Vienna. In England Ninette de Valois and Marie Rambert were at the beginning of their work. Soviet Russia was isolated and uncommunicative, represented in the world scene by the handful of dancers who had moved out to the West. There were cumbersome and reputable organizations at most of the European opera houses, but none of them would ever start international fires. The Royal Danish Ballet maintained its beautiful August Bournonville repertoire but was known only on its home ground. Ida Rubinstein had a ballet company, Boris Kniasev had a ballet company, small groups associated with artists like Nijinska, Serge Lifar or Boris Romanov appeared from time to time. In the USA, in spite of a good deal of dance activity, there was no major company.

One of the key figures for the future of ballet proved to be a man about whose qualities of culture and humanity everyone in the opinionated world of the dance is in agreement – René Blum. In 1931 he was already 53 years old and had been associated with the theatre for some time.

Blum was born in Paris in 1878 to a family of well-to-do Jews from Alsace. His elder brother, Léon, the famous French socialist leader who became premier in 1936, was initially a brilliant academic and a popular literary and dramatic critic; and René's early life was also spent in literary and artistic activities. From 1910 to 1914 he was co-editor and art critic of the literary journal *Gil Blas*, and he was decorated for his contribution to the protection of French works of art and national monuments in World War I. His friends included Marcel Proust, whom he first met at the turn of the century, and it was on his advice that Proust contacted Bernard Grasset in connection with the first publication of *Du Côté de chez Swann.*[1] The theatre, however, was Blum's special love and he became director of plays and operettas at Monte Carlo in 1924 after organizing a pilot season in 1923.

When Diaghilev died in August 1929, leaving an unexpired contract with the theatre at Monte Carlo for his Ballets Russes, the director of the Monte Carlo Opera, Raoul Gunsbourg (whose marathon tenure ran from 1893 to the end of the 1951 season), hoped to carry on the company. René Blum was appointed director of ballet. However, the debts were heavy. Diaghilev's company was disbanded, costumes and decors dispersed and sold.

Blum, like Gunsbourg, was eager to revive Russian ballet, and while he booked various dance or ballet groups to appear at the famous theatre he sounded out possibilities for collaboration in starting a new Ballets Russes company to be based on Monte Carlo. He wrote to Massine, Balanchine, Lifar, Boris Kochno and Diaghilev's *régisseur général,* Serge Grigoriev.

Nothing was resolved. Blum planned an excellent programme for the spring season in 1931, including the Boris Kniasev Ballet, the Paris Opéra Ballet, the Indian dancer Uday Shankar and the Spanish flamenco dancer Vicente Escudero, and on 25 April the visiting company at the Théâtre de Monte-Carlo was the Ballet de l'Opéra Russe à Paris. At this point one of the main protagonists of our play, Colonel W. de Basil, makes his appearance.

De Basil, Cossack officer turned emigré impresario, is an infinitely more controversial figure than Blum and his background and character must be looked at in more detail later on. While everyone liked and admired Blum (Toumanova sums him up in the phrase *'un vrai monsieur'*[2]), by no means everyone liked or admired de Basil. Yet it was de Basil who was mainly responsible for the worldwide impact made by the Ballets Russes in the 1930s, de Basil who publicized its new image and steered it into new worlds, and who somehow kept a company in existence, albeit eventually lowering standards, through the years of the Depression and World War II.

Totally unlike Diaghilev (but why should he have resembled him?), never influencing artists in their work for ballet or initiating artistic achievement, because he had no deep knowledge of the involved arts, he was still capable of persuading all kinds of people to make contributions, material, emotional and intellectual, that would enable his ballet company to dance into history. Where ballet was concerned he was a man of destiny by virtue of his flair for leadership, his unfailing vitality and determination, and his infectious and vigorous enthusiasm.

All these qualities had been apparent in his colourful military career in Russia, where he had been aide-de-camp to General Bicherakov in the Persian campaign of 1916. He also featured in the negotiations that took place between the Allies and the Bolsheviks in the Caspian Sea area towards the end of 1918. As an emigré Russian, he simplified his real name of Vassily Grigorievitch Voskresensky to W. de Basil and settled in Paris, working at first as a lorry driver. His wife, Nina Leonidova, was a stage dancer and when she and his cousin Valeria Ellanskaya joined him he started a small dance group with which he toured variety theatres in France, Switzerland and Italy.

4

Through this he came in touch with the Georgian impresario Prince Alexis Zereteli, who had been manager of the People's Theatre in St Petersburg, Zereteli, de Basil and Ignaty Zon, the one-time owner of a theatre and *café chantant* in Moscow, opened an artists' agency in Paris about 1925 which they called Zerbason. A few years later Zereteli and de Basil, in partnership with Michel Kachouk, the personal manager of Feodor Chaliapin, became directors of L'Opéra Russe à Paris. This large opera company was formed by Maria Kousnetsova, the Russian soprano who had appeared with the Diaghilev Ballet in 1914 as Potiphar's Wife in *The Legend of Joseph*, and her second husband Alfred Massenet, a nephew of the composer Jules Massenet. It was based on the Théâtre des Champs-Elysées, Chaliapin was star artist, and Fokine was engaged to re-stage his Polovtsian Dances in the production of *Prince Igor*.

In June 1930 Nijinska became maître de ballet and choreographer, and her first work for them was the dances in *Sadko*. Then, for their Paris season at the end of January 1931, she composed ballets for the operas *Russlan and Ludmilla* and *Russalka*. In the former there were Turkish, Arabian and Caucasian dances and a men's ensemble. In *Russalka* the dance scenes included a Slav dance, a Bohemian or Gypsy dance and a *corps de ballet* arrangement for water nymphs. The Slav and Bohemian Dances were later to be incorporated into a *divertissement* ballet, *Danses slaves et tziganes*, staged by her for the de Basil Ballet in 1936.

Nijinska's engagement made it possible for the company to present their first evening of ballet. For this she produced a new version, *Etude*, of a work to a selection of music by Bach which she had sketched out in Margate, England, in 1925 as *Holy Etudes* and developed in Buenos Aires in 1926 as *Un estudio religioso*. She composed a ballet to Rimsky-Korsakov's *Capriccio espagnol* and staged, with choreographic embellishments, Fokine's *Petrouchka*.

At the end of the Paris season Nijinska left to form her own company, the Théâtre de la Danse Nijinska. When the Ballet de l'Opéra Russe à Paris appeared at Monte Carlo in April 1931 Boris Romanov was their new maître de ballet. Romanov, who made his choreographic debut with *Salome* for the Diaghilev Ballet in 1913, had later been associated with the Russian Romantic Ballet, a company that toured widely in western Europe in the early 'twenties. Financed by a German millionaire, Gutchov, for a variety dancer called Elsa Krüger, it employed about fifty dancers. Krüger was not the prima ballerina: she appeared, for

5

instance, as Bathilde in their production of *Giselle*, in which Alexandra Smirnova and Claudia Pavlova alternated in the leading role with Anatole Oboukhov as Albrecht. Most of the other ballets in the repertoire were by Romanov.

When Romanov went to the Opéra Russe he staged his own versions of *Chout, Pulcinella* and *El amor brujo*. The programme at Monte Carlo included these ballets and *Le Rêve de Ratmir* (a scene from *Russlan and Ludmilla*), Fokine's *Polovtsian Dances* and a short *divertissement*. Only six performances were given. The company had been strengthened by Felia Doubrovska, a prima ballerina of great style and technical ability, and by an excellent English character dancer, Eleonora Marra, who had also been with Diaghilev. Romanov and Oboukhov danced the male leads.

Meeting de Basil for the first time, René Blum was impressed by his energy and initiative, and began to discuss with him the cherished scheme of forming a Russian Ballet at Monte Carlo. Blum had the most to offer the new venture – the Monte Carlo connection, with its theatre as a headquarters, its rehearsal rooms and storage space, its financial backing. He had some dancers and so had de Basil, but everything depended on their being able to recruit good choreographers and principals.

Matters were left temporarily unresolved, and de Basil, with the Opéra Russe, went to London for an important season at the Lyceum Theatre. Sir Thomas Beecham was the artistic director and chief conductor, and they opened on 18 May 1931 with *Russalka*. *The Times* wrote guardedly in advance that 'this company consists of Russian artists trained at or in the traditions of the late Imperial Opera of Petrograd' (an oddly mixed phrase). 'Its most famous member is M. Chaliapin, who will sing twice a week.'[3]

The ballets in *Russalka, Russlan and Ludmilla* and *Sadko* were now credited to Romanov and the company in London, as in Monte Carlo, was led by Doubrovska, Marra, Romanov and Oboukhov. Later in the season guest artists appeared: Vera Nemtchinova, Anton Dolin and Léon Woizikovsky.

The new ballets were given short shrift by *The Times*. *Pulcinella* was 'even more obscure than in Massine's original without the countervailing advantage of an imaginative invention.'[4] In *El amor brujo*, which had not been staged previously in London, 'Romanov's choreography brought out the dramatic quality but hardly succeeded in giving full value to the rhythmic vitality of the music.'[5]

The public however approved of the ballet evenings and Doubrovska remembers discussions with de Basil, Beecham and Lady Cunard for their extension and enlargement. The three Romanov ballets continued to be given (conducted on at least one occasion by the young musician Eugene Goossens) but sizeable *divertissements* were staged. Doubrovska and Valentin Froman danced the Adagio from the Snowflake scene of *The Nutcracker*, while Nemtchinova and Oboukhov danced the Aurora *pas de deux* from *The Sleeping Beauty*. Most of the leading dancers contributed their current party pieces, such as Dolin's *Espagnol* (Albeniz) and Algeranov's *Bogey Man*. Towards the end of the season Woizikovsky staged Fokine's *Petrouchka*, presumably in a purer version than Nijinska's, for himself and Nemtchinova, and Balanchine's *The Gods Go A-begging* for himself and Edna Tresahar.

Arnold Haskell saw the company and was unimpressed. He reports how he spoke to de Basil during an interval. 'Well,' said de Basil, 'what do you think of it?' 'Rotten,' Haskell told him. 'We can do much better than that in England' – an interesting remark in 1931, when English ballet was very much in its infancy. 'Perhaps', replied de Basil, 'I have only just begun. But I will learn . . .'[6]

Meanwhile, in Monte Carlo a pattern was beginning to emerge. By the end of 1931 de Basil had signed contracts, following up Blum's earlier approaches, with Balanchine as maître de ballet for an initial term of four months from 4 January 1932 and with Kochno for six months from 15 December 1931 as *conseiller artistique*. The conductors were the Monégasque Marc César Scotto, Diaghilev's orchestral director Roger Desormière, and Pierre Kolpikov. Serge Grigoriev was appointed *régisseur général* – an important acquisition. Diaghilev, in a famous remark, had said, 'He is the only one of us who is indispensable', and although this was hyperbole it was certainly true that Grigoriev was to be invaluable to the new company in establishing (along with his wife Lubov Tchernicheva and a few former Diaghilev dancers such as Jean Hoyer and Nathalie Branitska) a centre of continuing discipline and tradition to counterbalance fresh choreographic ideas and an unusual reliance on very young and inexperienced stars.

This policy of featuring extreme youth was as firm as it was novel. Child dancers in themselves were nothing new, but they had never been the dominant theme of a company. It was Balanchine's idea – for him, as a choreographer, youth and a degree of unconditioned temperamental flexibility had an appeal. Blum and de Basil approved, knowing that

7

instead of limping along as a poor descendant of Diaghilev their company should find its own personality, and de Basil, in particular, with his instinct for audience reaction, must have recognized immediately what excellent publicity such a policy would attract.

The idea and the policy, however, stemmed not from romantic hopes but from realistic fact – already Balanchine had seen his potential stars. The Paris studios of two great emigrée prima ballerinas from the Imperial Russian Ballet at the Maryinsky Theatre, St Petersburg, Olga Preobrajenska and Mathilde Kschessinska, had produced three outstanding little dancers. There was Tamara Toumanova who, in March 1929, just before her tenth birthday, had caught the critics' attention in a student performance of *L'Eventail de Jeanne* at the Paris Opera. There was Irina Baronova, of equal age and equally prodigious technique. There was Tatiana Riabouchinska, their senior by a couple of years, who was already touring with Nikita Balaiev's avant-garde Franco-Russian revue, the *Chauve-Souris*. Toumanova and Baronova were pupils of Preobrajenska, while Riabouchinska had been trained by Kschessinska.

This trio promised to be inspiring choreographic material for Balanchine, and for Blum and de Basil an assurance that their company had a new image to offer.

With these strong cards in hand it was possible to go ahead. In addition Massine, although still engaged at La Scala, had promised to produce a ballet for the first season. Blum and de Basil decided to found a shareholding company (this was first mentioned, a little prematurely, in October 1931[7]); and the Société des Ballets Russes et Ballets de Monte-Carlo was formally registered in Monaco on 20 April 1932 – postdating the company's first performance on 17 January – with a capital of two million francs. The two men were equal founders, each receiving 120 shares worth 5000 francs each, leaving 160 for outside shareholders. Blum made over to the Société his existing contracts, including the one with the Théâtre de Monte-Carlo which still had four seasons to run. De Basil, who with Zereteli, controlled some ballets from L'Opéra Russe à Paris, contributed the bulk of the repertoire.

The two-towered Casino Theatre in Monte Carlo (often called Salle Garnier after its architect, Charles Garnier) was an admirable headquarters. Its underground rehearsal room was deep in memories for the former Diaghilev artists, but for the rest of the new company the associations were mere hearsay and there was little time for looking

8

back. One change, not very acceptable to the older artists, was the presence of a good many ballet mothers – not, of course, a new species but certainly with a new dominance.

Parents had signed the contracts for under-age artists (and the 'baby ballerinas' were not the only ones in this category). Naturally the mothers were ardently enthusiastic for their children's rights and careers and protective about their health and morals. They were, moreover, emigrées themselves, already uprooted and prepared to reverse the Ruth-Naomi tradition by saying to their daughters, 'whither thou goest I will go . . .' These mothers would have their uses in terms of work and support but they were also, often and inevitably, a source of conflict and time-wasting trouble. Time, however, meant one thing for Russians, something different for their western collaborators – a factor of no little importance as they travelled more and more throughout the world – and they throve on emotional conflict.

The first new creation, Balanchine's *Cotillon*, went into production. It was to be primarily Toumanova's ballet. With music by Emmanuel Chabrier, designs by Christian Bérard – the costumes were the first made for ballet by the later famous Karinska – and libretto by Kochno, *Cotillon* has haunted the memory of everyone who saw it. Many feel that it should be revived, and although its choreographic detail is apparently forgotten, critics who enjoyed it did much to record its quality.

Haskell compares it to a dream that leaves a vague disturbing impression. 'When the curtain goes down on the light-hearted fun . . . one asks oneself, has it all happened? What exactly has happened?'[8] Cyril Beaumont speaks of its atmosphere, which 'emanates a curious bitter-sweet perfume, a mingling of elegant sophistication with the shyness of adolescence'[9] and the ballet has been vividly memorialized in words by A.V. Coton. Atmosphere again is his theme. He writes of its identification with the world of 1933 (which was when he saw it):

Only the air of the world today . . . acting indirectly on the acute observation of a master choreographer, could produce this vehicle of decadence. The aura of the fatal ballroom, the loveliness of corruption, the sense of sweet sin implicit in every move and gesture is the triumph of atmosphere – building by indirection . . . As creation of atmosphere – in the absolute sense, not an atmosphere of a time or place – nothing else in ballet compares with *Cotillon*.[10]

This was something new, a territory that would be explored rewardingly as the century wore on, not only by Balanchine but by other choreographers.

There was no story. The ballet opened with Toumanova putting the finishing touches to her toilette. The guests arrived, the Conductor of the Cotillon (oddly abbreviated in English programmes as 'the Conductor') received them. There were dances by harlequins, jockeys and Spaniards (represented by hats), an intriguing *pas de deux* called 'The Hand of Fate' that developed into a fortune-telling sequence and an excitingly choreographed finale.

This remarkable ballet was given its premiere at a gala in honour of Prince Louis II of Monaco, for the Fête Nationale de la Principauté de Monaco, on 17 January 1932, and Toumanova was immediately admired. Now twelve years old, she was a beauty as well as a virtuoso and added to these qualities the ineffable charm of early girlhood and exciting potential. The finale of *Cotillon*, when with a spectacular series of *fouettés en tournant* she moved into the memories of a generation, was an expression of her impact at that crucial beginning of her career. Coton writes:

The Young Girl walks slowly into the centre stage, as the music winds into a fugue-like figure she spins a series of *fouettés* madder and swifter than any of the earlier movement in the work. The guests suddenly reappear, run to her, sweep into circular formation round her as she slows her spinning, then rises on to the pointe, and eases her movement exactly as the music slides from fugue to the final bars. The revolving circle slows and slows, precisely counterpointing her moves in an alternate direction; the visual and aural images are perfectly fused, and the final bars sigh away and the curtain gradually creeps down . . .[11]

For the one opening performance Balanchine himself danced the role more identified with David Lichine. The Introduction, later taken by Riabouchinska, was created by Valentina Lanina-Blinova (more usually known as Blinova). Blinova had not been a pupil of the Imperial School in St Petersburg. She was the product of a course founded after the Revolution in an attempt to reform teaching methods, went to Germany with Vera Trefilova and Pierre Vladimirov and then danced at the Théâtre de Monte-Carlo in April 1931. Later in the 'thirties she made a partnership with a fellow Russian, Valentin Froman, and with him joined the second de Basil company, which went to Australasia in 1936. Woizikovsky, one of Diaghilev's great Polish *demi-caractère* dancers, was the Conductor of the Cotillon, and another of the company's young discoveries, 16-year-old Lubov Rostova (Lucienne Kylberg), danced the Hand of Fate.

The Monte Carlo opera season began on 21 January 1932 with *Tannhäuser*. The production followed the Paris version of 1860 which had enlarged the first scene to include a substantial Venusberg ballet. At Monte Carlo this was led by Blinova and Woizikovsky, and in the next couple of months the ballet company appeared in a long series of operas.

In some, of course, the dance element was much more important than in others. Extended ballets were featured in *The Tales of Hoffmann, Le Prophète, Une Nuit à Venise, Turandot* and two modern pieces: E. Paladilhe's opera-ballet *Patrie* and Joseph Redding's *Fay-yen-fah*. Blinova, Froman, Marra and Woizikovsky were usually the principal dancers, but Toumanova danced leading roles occasionally. Dancers also appeared in a mime scene in René Blum's play *Les Amours du poète*.

When operas were given their Monte Carlo premieres, as in the case of *Le Prophète,* Balanchine obviously created new choreography. He maintains (in conversation with Nancy Reynolds) that because the dancers, decors and staging varied from one year to another, he composed new dances even for operas with which he had already been associated. *Le Prophète* had a number of danced episodes but the most substantial was the skating scene in the third act, to music used in 1937 by Constant Lambert for Ashton's *Les Patineurs*.

Paladilhe's *Patrie* was a *pièce d'occasion*, created for a gala in honour of the French colony in Monaco. Balanchine choreographed a series of regional dances – Neapolitan, Indian, African, Flemish and Spanish – and a Ballet Classique, before a Monégasque finale. Blinova, Toumanova and Froman were the principals in the classical section.

Fay-yen-fah, described as 'an American opera', had first been given in 1925. The book, credited to Charles Templeton Crocker, dealt with a love story in Old China. The heroine was destroyed by the Fox God, the hero set fire to 'the temple of bigotry and ignorance' and the apotheosis found them both 'lost in a shower of blossoms'. In *Invitation to the Ballet*, Ninette de Valois recalls appearing in this work when she was with the Diaghilev Ballet:

I had an entrance with Danilova, both of us completely hidden in lotus leaves which, upon the slight pulling of strings inside loosening the walls of our prison, fell about us as a form of extra skirt. On we both came, whirling, and on I

11

continued to whirl until the end, like a mad white cabbage, for my leaves had refused to fall, and so I remained imprisoned for the entire performance, guided about the stage by the frenzied whispers of Danilova . . . [12]

In 1932, the ballet scene composed by Balanchine had dances for lilies and poppies (Toumanova led the poppies), gold and white peacocks, and a flying ballet on which five of the Ballets Russes dancers (Branitska, Chamié, Slavenska, Tresahar and Valenska) bravely embarked.

The opera-ballets must have meant a good deal of work for Balanchine but in addition he completed another new ballet, *La Concurrence,* for the opening of the regular ballet season on 12 April 1932. With a score by Georges Auric and designs by André Derain, *La Concurrence* was a tale of rivalry in the rag trade. Two tailors and their wives competed over the display of fine clothes, and the amusement lay in the characterization of their customers and neighbours. The most remembered section is Woizikovsky's brilliant solo as a flea-bitten Vagabond. That opening programme included a repetition of *Cotillon* with Lichine in place of Balanchine and a performance of *Les Sylphides*. In this Blinova danced the *valse* and the *pas de deux* (with Lichine), Toumanova the mazurka, while Riabouchinska made her first appearance in a role that has ever since been considered her masterpiece, the prelude.

April 14 saw the premiere of Massine's *Jeux d'enfants*. During this first year of the company, waiting in the wings, Massine was very much the once and future king. *Jeux d'enfants*, like *Cotillon*, had a book by Kochno, and like *Cotillon* it was a new direction and a perfect unity of dance, music and design. Kochno had approached Alberto Giacometti, who had doubted his ability to create ballet designs, but the second choice, Joan Miró, was totally successful. Where Bérard had dressed the *Cotillon* dancers in brilliant light shades and softly romantic styles, Miró recreated the bright primary colours of the nursery toy-cupboard. Massine, like Balanchine, made superlative use of the daunting technical capacity Toumanova had acquired under Preobrajenska's eye, employing her facility for single and double *fouettés* in either direction for legitimate and telling stage effect. Toumanova created the Top, but this was a role Baronova stole from her. Adrian Stokes writes of Baronova:

[She] comes in on her points, moving sideways, facing the front. She is dressed from head to foot in tight woollen bands of colour that convey a most vivid

12

memory of the ricochetting, hard-used nursery top. The music makes a sudden utterance; the top is wound and poised; she is loose, she spins, twenty-three *fouettés en tournant* with double ones mixed in . . . The music itself seems to become visible.[13]

The Top was the most spectacular role in the ballet but two others were equally important. The theme was of a child who wakes in the night to find that her toys and games are alive. Riabouchinska was the Child, in a performance Beaumont aptly describes as having 'a fascinating artlessness all her own, at once ingenuous and all-understanding'[14] and Lichine was the Traveller with whom she falls in love whom Coton called 'a joyous figure of adventure with the dash and grace of every Ballantyne and Stevenson hero.'[15]

Lichine was one of the talents that would expand in the conditions supplied by the Ballets Russes de Monte-Carlo. He was twenty-two, a latecomer to dancing who had been born in Rostov-on-Don but brought up in Paris. Trained by the Imperial Russian Ballet prima ballerina Lubov Egorova and by Nijinska, he appeared with L'Opéra Russe à Paris, while Nijinska was maître de ballet, under his own name of Lichtenstein, dancing leads in *Etude* and *Capriccio espagnol* as well as the Bohemian dance in *Russalka,* during their Paris season at the beginning of 1931. He then went to the Ida Rubinstein Ballet and later in the year joined Massine at La Scala. A volatile personality, darkly handsome, full of animal magnetism and highly susceptible to women, Lichine was even more strikingly temperamental offstage than on. He was more a *demi-caractère* dancer than a classicist. This, however, was symptomatic of the period. The trend of the time was to *demi-caractère* ballets rather than pure classical or neo-classical. The repertoire of the 'thirties, vastly popular all over the world, reflects the fact; every dancer in the company was versatile, every one a distinctive character – and often capable of technical virtuosity in the classroom that was never demanded on stage.

The prevailing conception of ballet, derived from Fokine and Diaghilev, and completely opposite to the fashions of today, was of an initial book or scenario and of the expression, through dance, music and decor, of a story or at least a thematic development. The creation of character, the grasp of period style, of dramatic inflection and mimetic comedy, were stressed as more important than mere technical perfection. Virtuoso dance technique, where it contributed to the artistic whole, was highlighted; but it was always a means to an end, never an

13

end in itself. Audiences then, unlike those of today, happily accepted its subservience or even near-absence because they delighted in the ballets they saw.

This meant of course that ballet was far nearer the legitimate dramatic theatre than it is now, that dancers were more actors than athletes, that their performances meant more to the general public in emotional and intellectual terms as opposed to sensual response. Productions had a clearly defined individuality far more difficult to achieve in plotless work, and as part of each dancer's stock in trade was his personal ability to characterize, artists developed and matured their emotional expressiveness as they now work on trimming their physiques to conventional perfection by exercise and diet. Dancers of the Ballets Russes came in many shapes and sizes, and no one bothered too much about streamlined physical standards.

If the company was short of *danseurs nobles* – and this would remain a weakness – it had strong male *demi-caractère* talent headed by Lichine, the masterly Woizikovsky, and later Massine. Woizikovsky, a warm, humorous, life-loving man – he could never, apparently, resist an attractive woman, nor a game of poker – had a marvellous ability for keeping on terms with most people, of not taking sides. For anyone to contrive *not* to take sides in this world of pitched and tossed emotions, he had to possess exceptional balance and tolerance.

Some people recall him as impressive mainly in rather unpleasant roles like the Vagabond in *La Concurrence* or speak of him with limited enthusiasm as 'a bouncy little dancer'. The other side of the coin is much more deeply engraved, however. Beaumont declared that:

He radiated vitality . . . You always had the impression that he danced not simply because it was his profession but because he enjoyed dancing, revelled in dancing.

That is a quality one always treasures in a dancer and relatively few have it to any outstanding degree. He pays an even greater tribute, which crystallizes Woizikovsky's value more particularly:

No matter how difficult, how elusive the rhythm of the sequence, he always reproduced the details of its choreographic colour with an infinite precision and delicate appreciation of style.[16]

Other male dancers of the 1932 season were to become world-famous. Yurek Shabelevsky and Roman Jasinsky had similar origins. Both were

14

Polish, trained at the Warsaw Opera, and made their professional debut outside Poland with the Ida Rubinstein Ballet in 1928 when Nijinska was maître de ballet. Both appeared with Olga Spessivtzeva (Spessiva) at the London Coliseum in May 1930 and with the Kniasev Ballet in 1931.

Ballet-goers of the time, when asked about Shabelevsky, speak with rapture of his physical beauty and brilliantly vigorous dancing. As the years went by, he graduated from roles such as the King of the Dandies in *Le Beau Danube,* in which his footwork was superbly precise, to the great Fokine leads of Petrouchka, the Golden Slave in *Schéhérazade* and the Warrior Chief in *Prince Igor*. Gordon Anthony writes of him as having 'an astonishing capacity for characterization plus tremendous vitality and athleticism'. He compares him to a wellbred whippet – 'he certainly had the muscles and velocity of one'.[17]

Jasinsky had also danced with Lifar in France and with Massine at La Scala before joining the Ballets Russes de Monte-Carlo. He spent the early part of 1933 with Les Ballets 1933 and appeared with Lifar in the United States. After his return to de Basil, however, he stayed with the company through all its vicissitudes until 1947, establishing an admirable reputation in both *demi-caractère* and classical roles.

When *Le Mariage d'Aurore* was revived in 1935, Jasinsky alternated with Lichine as the Bluebird – and his perfectionist attitude to dance led him to sharpen the finer points of this bravura piece until he was an outstanding exponent of it – but he shared the Aurora *pas de deux* with the third of the young male principals of the early seasons, Paul Petrov. Petrov, whose adopted Russian surname was invariably transliterated Petroff (most names at the time were given the 'ff' ending), was a Dane, Paul Pedersen. Born in Elsinore, he studied in Copenhagen with the teacher Katje Lindhart, and the Ballets Russes de Monte-Carlo was his first engagement with a ballet company although he had taken part in concert performances with Violet Fischer in Denmark in 1930.

This professional name of Paul Petrov constitutes a trap for the unwary ballet researcher, as there is another older and totally unrelated Paul Petrov who appears in contemporary references. The older Petrov was a Russian, a Maryinsky character dancer and maître de ballet who toured in the 1930s with the Levitov-Dandré Russian Ballet. Petrov the Dane, a dancer of classical style, considerable range and aquiline good looks, was a developing asset to de Basil.

Lichine, Shabelevsky, Jasinsky, Petrov, and a brilliant American

15

from Flat Rock, North Carolina, Roland Guerard, balanced and complemented the trio of ballerinas. Guerard had quit accountancy studies to learn dancing, and studied with Fokine, Egorova and Alexander Volinine. He came to the de Basil Ballet by way of a company called the Ballets Franco-Russe and the Folies-Bergère in Paris.

It was the little girls, however, in whom Blum and de Basil were putting their faith. Both felt a proprietary fatherly interest in their schoolgirl stars. From the earliest, de Basil also recognized how valuable the 'baby ballerinas' were in terms of publicity – although publicity in the early 'thirties had a simplicity and naivety totally lacking today. He would make much of them and the sentimental appeal of their youth to the press and public with an eye to pulling in audiences and with them the essential money, the lifeblood of an organization that had only its Monte Carlo subsidy (applicable to the Monte Carlo seasons) and had to find all supplementary finance by the use of its wits. Using its wits involved among other things publicity, and de Basil never lost faith in the publicity value of the really young dancer. He launched a succession of them over the years and even in 1947, the last London season with which he was personally associated, it was about the 15-year-old April Olrich that he spoke to the press.

None however equalled the 1932 trio. They were exceptional, even if they were exceptionally lucky in their opportunities, and worthy of the superlatives that immediately began to be showered on them. Hardened critics in France (but how susceptible to youthful femininity, as well as to beautiful female legs, are most hardened critics!) such as André Levinson and Pierre Michaut were captivated from the beginning. Michaut wrote of them as *'véritables étoiles-enfants... Leur jeunesse, leur brio précoce, leur virtuosité, leur tempérament déjà affirmé, emerveillèrent les spectateurs'.*[18]

The year 1932 was a honeymoon year for the company. The dancers were eager, happy, never stretched unbearably. They pleased Monte Carlo, they pleased Paris, where they appeared at the Théâtre des Champs-Elysées, and they went on an undemanding tour of Belgium, Holland, Germany and Switzerland. For this they had cut-price transport by bus, as Lichine's uncle was manager of a transport company in Paris. The anonymous critic of *L'Illustration* wrote of the Paris season that the company were the true heirs of Diaghilev. He

16

praised *'cette précision rythmique, ce synchronisme parfait que fait songer à un dessin animé sonore'* and declared that the new company was *'un foyer rayonnant qui rechauffera le zèle de nos étoiles nationales'.*[19]

At Monte Carlo the creations *Cotillon, La Concurrence* and *Jeux d'enfants*, which were to provide three of the most perennially popular ballets of the de Basil repertoire, were augmented by some revivals. Fokine's *Les Sylphides* and *Polovtsian Dances* (given as part of the opera *Price Igor* or with the short opera *Samson et Dalila*) were staged, as was the Woizikovsky production of Fokine's *Petrouchka*. There were the three Boris Romanov ballets which had been in the programme of L'Opéra Russe à Paris, *Chout, Pulcinella* and *L'Amour sorcier* and two more new works by the indefatigable Balanchine.

Suites de danses (5 May) used music by Glinka and opened with a Jota Aragonaise led by Marra and Woizikovsky. A Tarantelle followed, danced by Nina Verchinina, Hélène Kirsova, Lichine, Metek Borovsky and Shabelevsky. The important central section was a classical Valse, in which the principal dancers were Blinova, Toumanova and Riabouchinska, with Baronova among the six girls of the ensemble. The finale, Komarinskaia, was danced by eight couples with Irène Kervily and Woizikovsky in the leading roles.

The other new work was *Le Bourgeois Gentilhomme* (3 May), another Kochno ballet, a delicious affair with decor and costumes by Alexandre Benois and a score by Richard Strauss, originally composed as incidental music for a production of the play. This score was its downfall. Strauss took exception to its use for a ballet and prohibited further performances. In 1944 when the music was technically free, because of World War II, as an enemy copyright, Balanchine staged a new version for Denham's Ballet Russe de Monte Carlo in America, and he rechoreographed it for Nureyev in 1979, in collaboration with Jerome Robbins.

In the 1932 version the action concerned the scene in which Cléonte presents himself at the house of M. Jourdain disguised as the son of the Grand Turk in order to trick M. Jourdain into accepting him as Lucille's fiancé. Lichine, as Cléonte, had an introductory dance with his friends disguised as slaves and a final *pas de deux* with Toumanova as Lucilla. Blinova and six girls presented the classical ballet staged by M. Jourdain in honour of the occasion. The Turkish *divertissement* began with a *pas de trois* for Olga Morosova, Shabelevsky and Leonide

Katchourovsky, continued with a *pas de deux* for Natalie Strakhova and Borovsky and ended (looking ahead, perhaps, to *Night Shadow*?) with a quartet of acrobats: Kirsova, Hélène Slavinska, Kervily and Jasinsky.

The remaining ballet was *Le Lac des cygnes* in the version of Act II that was described in programmes as 'a choreographic poem in one act'. It is worth remembering that discounting the 1907 version staged in Prague and Diaghilev's in London in 1912 the full-length production with its challenging double role of Odette-Odile was not familiar outside Russia until the Vic-Wells Ballet staged it in London in November 1934. The de Basil ballerinas identified with *Le Lac des cygnes* – Doubrovska, Danilova, Baronova, Toumanova, Nemtchinova and others – were seen only as Odette in the one-act ballet. A solo for Siegfried was usually included – not always the same one – and his slaying of the Evil Genius manufactured a dramatic curtain.

One of the most important members of the cast of this twenty-year touring spectacular was Serge Grigoriev. He was the constant factor over the years, bringing continuity from the Diaghilev Ballet, carrying it on to the future, weathering storms of division, disagreements, walkings-out and walkings-in, disbandment and reconstruction, and still *régisseur général* when the last curtain came down at London's Adelphi Theatre in January 1952.

An incredible record! Here, obviously, was a man absolutely fitted for his life's work. No one without his abilities and dedication could have attended to the countless details that were his responsibility: overseeing and adapting productions to theatres all over the world, advising on casting and understudying, staging revivals, supervising scenic and wardrobe staff, arranging timetables of performance, rehearsal and class. He knew the capabilities, temperaments and daily problems of the dancers and most of them thought of 'Papa Grigoriev' as standing *in loco parenti*. He was the co-ordinator of the company's life and without him the whole mechanism would have disintegrated.

Immensely valuable must have been the characteristic Beaumont describes:

Grigoriev had many unusual qualities for a Russian. He was punctual and exacted punctuality from others . . . He was business-like and to the point.

It is almost a relief to find that:

18

... if annoyed, he could easily lose his temper, when he would shout, beat his brow and shake his arms aloft with a flourish almost too reminiscent of the theatre to be genuinely intimidating.[20]

Plenty of shouting, both masculine and feminine, punctuated the daily doings of the Ballets Russes . . .

Grigoriev was of course a remarkable mime, who continued for years to perform cameos with which he was completely identified: Shariar in *Schéhérazade*, the Russian father in Massine's *La Boutique fantasque*, the Rich Merchant (often, in those days of innocence, called the Gay Merchant) in *Petrouchka*. He had his family around him (there was even a brother, André) and in fact this was part of his strength. His son Vsevolod (Vova), who had early dance training but no wish to make a career as a dancer – mathematics were his passion – began as de Basil's secretary. Vova married within the company, Tamara Sidorenko, better known as Tamara Grigorieva. She and her sister, Galina Razoumova, were trained by Preobrajenska and appeared with Les Ballets 1933 before joining de Basil. Grigorieva was one of the company's outstanding talents and beauties, but for those days she grew too tall to be considered for ballerina roles. A slight similarity between the name of Tamara Grigorieva and that of her contemporary, Tamara Geva (Gevergeva), has occasionally confused people but Geva, one of the small group of dancers who left Russia with Balanchine, never danced with the de Basil Ballet.

Serge Grigoriev's wife had a role as important as her husband's. Lubov Tchernicheva, a Maryinsky ballerina, had been with the Diaghilev Ballet from 1911 until 1929. She had begun to dance leads in 1913 when that company toured South America, and created roles in later Diaghilev productions. She is remembered for her classic beauty and magnificent interpretative powers.

Tchernicheva became ballet mistress for Diaghilev in 1926 and when she (with Grigoriev) joined the Ballets Russes de Monte-Carlo in 1932 it was as the company's resident teacher that she was engaged, to take daily class and coach the dancers. Baronova praises her ability for helping them over interpretation and the creation of character, and this is echoed by a later ballerina, Tatiana Leskova. Her son, Vova Grigoriev, says that although she had no interest in teaching young children to dance, she loved teaching professional, 'formed' dancers. Her vital role in developing the talents of the young dancers in the company and maintaining standards in a constantly nomadic pattern of existence

19

must be stressed. Daily class was held, often under extraordinary circumstances. When they travelled by road, Baronova recalls how they all piled out of their coaches and into a roadside field, using the wire fences as *barres*, to the astonishment of cows and passing motorists.

Dormant in Tchernicheva the teacher, however, lay a vigorous performing artist and although by 1935 she was in her forties she came eagerly out of retirement to dance Zobeide in *Schéhérazade* when Fokine's ballet was revived. Thereafter she danced the title role in his *Thamar* with enormous effect and occasionally the Miller's Wife in Massine's *Le Tricorne*. In 1937 she created the title role in Lichine's *Francesca da Rimini*, in which she was still appearing in 1948.

The sense of honeymoon in Monte Carlo was implemented for the young artists by the personality of Balanchine. Twenty-eight years old, Balanchine had emerged from Soviet Russia in 1924 with Danilova, Tamara Geva and Nicolas Efimov, and very quickly been engaged by Diaghilev. For Diaghilev he had produced a mixed handful of works beginning with *Barabau* (1925) and including two ballets that survive triumphantly in the contemporary repertoire: *Apollo* and *Prodigal Son*. The period he spent as maître de ballet with the Ballets Russes de Monte-Carlo had little to do with the mainstream of his career, which would flow in America.

His short reign at Monte Carlo was, however, a halcyon time for the little budding ballerinas. He was enormously attractive, easy to talk to, liable to punctuate serious work with popular music on the piano. They all fell deeply in love with him, as girls at a finishing school might universally fall for a good-looking music master. When he left for Les Ballets 1933 they would have flocked after him *en masse*, like the sailors' wives after Captain Belaye in John Cranko's *Pineapple Poll*, but not all the mothers thought this the best idea. Toumanova, Rostova and Tamara Tchinarova went with him, and so missed the July 1933 opening night at the Alhambra. Baronova, Riabouchinska and Morosova stayed at Monte Carlo.

The reasons for the replacement of Balanchine by Massine for the 1933 season vary – as do many accounts of ballet's past – according to who is giving them. Kochno told me that he and Balanchine began to find Blum and de Basil too dictatorial over artistic matters and decided to leave for that reason. That it was *their* decision is borne out by a letter of de Basil's which suggests that he was dismayed at the news. Pierre

Michaut presents it another way, suggesting that Blum wanted 'to re-establish his independence',[21] fearing that Balanchine's influence might narrow the company's repertoire too much. Bernard Taper combines the elements of the situation. He says that Balanchine, for whom de Basil's determination to 'peddle nostalgia' by emphasizing Russian 'glamour' was 'most uncongenial', had considered resigning but was forestalled by dismissal.[22] Whatever the facts, it has to be remembered that long-term contracts had not been negotiated – Balanchine's original agreement expired on 4 May 1932, at the end of the Monte Carlo social season – and that it was probably a question of not renewing agreements rather than of resignations or firing. The actual change inevitably involved on both sides the misunderstandings and hurt feelings that usually attend such events in the ballet world.

The appointment of Massine was a natural one. Massine, at this time, was in possession of the costumes and decors of a number of Diaghilev ballets (he himself put it at fifty-five,[23] although this seems rather many). They had been acquired with the help of Diaghilev's lawyer, Maître Aaron, in 1930 when Raymond Goetz, the American theatrical agent, intended to back Massine in an American Ballets Russes, a plan that came to nothing because of the Wall Street crash. Massine also possessed notated records of his choreography, and had an important name as a choreographer. In addition he was a star performer, unlike Balanchine who, because of a knee injury, was no longer dancing. Certainly if Blum and de Basil wanted a widely-based repertoire which could draw on many Diaghilev revivals, Massine was the man for them.

The next step for Balanchine was Les Ballets 1933, Edward James' project for his wife, the Viennese *demi-caractère* and modern dancer Tilly Losch. There were seasons in Paris and London but the company failed. It opened the way for Balanchine however, through the championship of an influential American enthusiast for ballet, Lincoln Kirstein, to later fame in the States. His sole continuing connection with the de Basil story is as the choreographer of the two lasting successes, *Cotillon* and *La Concurrence*. Only years later, in 1941, did he choreograph one more ballet for the company and for Toumanova: *Balustrade*.

Massine took up work at Monte Carlo at the end of 1932 and there was an immediate change of pace and mood. Nothing was easy-going any longer. Many people who have worked with Massine describe him as aloof, withdrawn, self-centred, hard, authoritarian. Others speak of him as even-tempered, courteous, friendly (within the limits of his reserve) and encouraging to all hard workers. Certainly he could always command rehearsal room and stage, and this counterbalanced for them the difficulty of making contact with someone who was universally found to be a very private person. Baronova, in spite of loving Balanchine and regretting his departure, feels that Massine's qualities of dedication and discipline were a vital factor in creating the stimulus and tension that this predominantly very young group needed to keep them on their mettle. He had a strong reserve of creative ideas and his engagement with the de Basil company was exactly the one to suit their development. He was not, of course, content with the position he had acquired. His ambition was to be sole artistic director; but with Blum in that capacity the best Massine could hope for initially was to compose ballets, dance leading roles and get programme billing as artistic adviser.

He was the ideal person to make the young company triumph; and although his ballets dominated the repertoire they never excluded the works by Fokine, Balanchine, and later Nijinska, Nijinsky and Lichine, or the two classics *Le Lac des cygnes* and *Le Mariage d'Aurore*.

For Massine in his prime as a performer the word has to be charisma – anachronistic though it may be. Never used in the 1930s, its present connotation is exactly right for the impact he made on an audience. His magnetism, his vitality, his absorbed concentration and total conviction generated a blaze of light whenever he appeared on stage.

His work was firmly based on the vigorous tradition of *demi-caractère* dance in which he had been trained with the Imperial Russian Ballet in Moscow, but out of his association with the Diaghilev Ballet and his exposure to Western European artistic influences he had developed a fresh and personal style of presentation. His audiences adored him. They found his comedy dancing in *La Boutique fantasque* and *Le Beau Danube* excitingly novel and entertaining. In fact, the unique character of his performances in the roles he created for himself has meant that they have never had the same effect when tackled by other dancers. Those who worked with him, like Lichine or Jasinsky, came nearest to success.

As a choreographer, Massine was admired by his public for his versatility, through which the enormously popular comedies contrasted with the revolutionary development of the symphonic ballets to make him the talking point of season after season. When he launched his copyright cases against de Basil in 1936 and 1937, public feeling was very much in his favour. A less involved assessment of the situation is inevitably greyer all round but the world of the Ballets Russes had a childlike propensity for seeing everything in strong blacks and whites. To Massine's devotees, de Basil was a ruthless exploiter and an unscrupulous schemer.

Another great star, Alexandra Danilova, joined the company at Monte Carlo in 1933. According to Taper, she had been excluded from the company originally because Balanchine wanted only the teenagers. When she heard he was going to Monte Carlo she had asked him when she would be needed. He had replied flatly that, at twenty-five, she was too old.[24]

During 1932, while Doubrovska had danced the Swan Queen and Blinova *Les Sylphides* for the Ballets Russes de Monte-Carlo, Danilova had been appearing in the London musical *Waltzes from Vienna*, but towards the end of the year she was approached by de Basil about joining the company as their chief ballerina. She went to see him and was dismayed to be shown up to his London hotel bedroom. He suggested that she 'dance for nothing' – Vova Grigoriev, although he was not present, feels that this phrase should perhaps not be taken literally. She thought the matter over and finally decided to accept on terms that were to be renegotiated a year later.[25]

The character of the Ballets Russes de Monte-Carlo or, as it was known from 1934, the Ballets Russes du Col. W. de Basil – already relations between Blum and de Basil were under strain – emerges sturdily during the *grande saison* of 1933 at Monte Carlo. This led with an ace on its opening night of 13 April, when the first of Massine's symphonic ballets, *Les Présages,* to Tchaikovsky's 5th Symphony, was given its premiere.

With Toumanova absent, *Les Présages* belonged to other principals. It belonged to the 14-year-old Baronova, expressing in the *pas de deux* with Lichine the deeply lyrical and loving nature of a passionate relationship. It belonged to Riabouchinska, the essence of light-heartedness and gaiety in her Frivolity solo, and to Verchinina, a major discovery, as Action. Verchinina pointed to the future. She was trained in classical ballet by Preobrajenska but strongly drawn to the study of modern dance, and in *Les Présages* she interpreted, and probably

23

influenced, Massine's choreography with a sure touch. Coton, who was himself a keen admirer of Kurt Jooss and Central European modern dance, speaks of her performance as being a

... perfect fusion of Central European free arm and head movement allied to the physical freedom of leg extension that ballet technique offers. Remarkable combinations of ever-developing arm and leg movements created plastic pattern of a richness hitherto unknown.[26]

Another significant discovery in *Les Présages* was the 15-year-old André Eglevsky, who had a breathtaking ability to control pirouettes and *doubles tours en l'air*.

Les Présages was not only effective and marvellously danced, it was controversial. It played safe to some extent by using a symphony that allowed of a programme, but it laid on the symbols heavily and there were cuts in the music. Coton claims that 'its success was out of all proportion to its absolute worth – as dancing'[27] but it had the ability to capture audience imagination by its emotional commitment.

André Masson's decor, too, was astounding, hated and admired almost equally. One who admired it was the theatre design critic of *The Dancing Times*, G.E. Goodman. He acknowledged that opinions would be sharply divided about it, but stated his own view firmly, that 'it is in the fullest possible harmony with the magnificent choreographic interpretation'. He described it evocatively:

Comets, stars, flames and waves surged stridently in a wild swirl of crude greens, garish reds and vivid purples – the whole gamut of a childlike delight in colour. From one high corner of the backcloth stared the huge symbol of an ever-watching eye, dominating the whole stage ... the decoration of the dresses also contributed to the vitality of the movements of the dancers. Costumes of lavender were whipped to life by the inclusion of a sudden motive of yellow or red, gowns of petunia were made stern by the introduction of dead black.

How significant was the contribution of decor to the effectiveness of the ballet was wonderfully demonstrated at the entrance of M. Woizikovsky. Suddenly into this riot of savage colour leapt the batlike figure of Fate, costumed in tones of light grey and pink. So finely balanced was the colour scheme that these usually mild and innocuous tints took on a decided sense of unpleasantness by virtue of their contrast with the surroundings.[28]

By following Balanchine to Les Ballets 1933, Toumanova had left the field clear for Baronova. Although Baronova too had been chosen by Balanchine, who had also worked with her, after the Ballets Russes contract had been signed, in a production of *Orphée aux enfers* at the Théâtre Mogador in Paris during the summer of 1931, she had been surprisingly little employed during the Monte Carlo season in 1932. She was listed as a sylph and a swan and a young girl in *Concurrence*. She danced in the Valse in *Suites de danses*, in a *pas de quatre* in *Chout* and – her most important role – the Shuttlecock in *Jeux d'enfants*. The slow start may have been helpful. Certainly her creations in 1933 were triumphant.

Three more Massine ballets were premiered that season: *Le Beau Danube* (7 March), *Beach* (the English word was used on the original programmes) (18 April) and *Scuola di ballo* (25 April). *Beach* was to prove the most ephemeral. It had a score specially composed by a young French composer, Jean Françaix. The working title had been *Les Dieux au beach*, and the starting-point of the scenario was the temporary transfiguration of the Sea King Nereus and his court into modern bathers on the beach at Monte Carlo. The set and costumes – typically jolly seaside designs by Raoul Dufy – were based on the latest Riviera fashions and as early as 1935 they were looking dated. By 1935 also, the programme synopsis had simplified the story by abandoning all mention of a Sea King. Baronova and Lichine had the leading roles as the Rose Maid and the Handsome Swimmer, while Riabouchinska created a cheeky Messenger Boy. It was a frolic comparable to Ashton's ballet *Les Sirènes* which amused Sadler's Wells Ballet audiences in 1946 but never established itself in the repertoire.

Le Beau Danube was a shortened and revised revival of a ballet created on 17 May 1924 for the series of performances known as Les Soirées de Paris, organized by Count Etienne de Beaumont at the tiny Théâtre de la Cigale. Desormière had arranged a score, mainly from pieces by Johann Strauss the younger. The set was based on a charming aquatint of old Vienna by Constantin Guys, recreated for the stage by Vladimir and Elizabeth Polunin, and the costumes were by de Beaumont. In 1924 the lighting was credited to Loie Fuller. The bustling scene of young salesmen and dressmakers, soldiers, dandies and ladies of the town at leisure in the Prater in the 1860s was created and sustained by Massine with a typically lively sense of period, and the leading roles were choreographed with charm and brilliance.

Where *Scuola di ballo* is concerned, its appeal over the years should not be underestimated. The ballet public loves 'classroom' ballets, as can be seen with the Bournonville *Konservatoriet*, the Harald Lander *Etudes* or the Asaf Messerer *Ballet School. Scuola di ballo* differed from these others because it used the classroom basis for a complicated and humorous plot based on Carlo Goldoni's comedy of the same name. The cross-currents of rivalry between a favourite pupil, a talented newcomer and a hopelessly clumsy but physically beautiful dancer read like an opera synopsis, but it was a popular work with a delightful score arranged by Jean Françaix from Luigi Boccherini, and it stressed the company's positive talent for comedy and character. It was eclipsed to some extent by *Le Beau Danube* mainly on account of the easy charm of the Johann Strauss score and the irresistible vivacity of Danilova and Massine as the Street Dancer and the Hussar.

Danilova was not the first Street Dancer in the Monte Carlo version of 1933. The Diaghilev Ballet ballerina Lydia Lopokova had created it in 1924 and when it was premiered at Monte Carlo, at a gala for the Fédération des Invalides de Guerre Russes à l'Etranger, the role was taken by Nina Tarakanova, another Diaghilev Ballet ballerina, who often danced it later. However, from the moment Danilova took the stage in the famous wine-coloured frock with its massed underfrills she made the role her own. This young veteran of the Diaghilev Ballet had a personal style, both in classic tragedy and brilliant comedy, and brought to ballet what Marlene Dietrich represented in cabaret or cinema – elegance, sophistication, wit and glamour. 'Saucy, sexy and scintillating' is Gordon Anthony's phrase for her . . .[29] She had problems to face at Monte Carlo, plunged into a world of teenage ballerinas and redoubtable mothers who saw in her a threat to their daughters' success, and immediately a pattern was set which eventually led to her resignation in 1938. She felt an alien in a company run very differently from the Diaghilev Ballet – where, of course, she had been one of the youngest and most promising and favoured. Now most of the publicity and attention went to children over ten years her junior. She was faced with the bitter fact that in ballet there are always younger dancers treading on one's heels. In fact, what she felt at Monte Carlo these baby ballerinas would themselves feel all too soon – nor had she any real need to worry. Lionel Bradley spoke for the majority when he wrote in his unpublished diaries:

Brilliant as the babies of the company may be, experience – and an experience that goes back to the Diaghilev company – still tells. Danilova has all her own the grand manner, like Edith Evans', which can shine equally brightly in the comedy of wit and in romantic comedy, and can scale the highest points of drama.[30]

Danilova was safely provided with an adoring public to whom she would always be their beloved and incomparable Choura.

None of the dancers, nor their mothers, could accept it at the time but there was room for them all. In a company that performed night after night, instead of in repertoire with opera, and almost all the year round, ballerinas, principal male dancers and soloists could all find their place in the hearts of the audience.

Danilova initially danced *Le Lac des cygnes, Les Sylphides, Le Beau Danube* and the Doll in *Petrouchka*, but steadily extended her repertoire. Her first creation for the company was in the first ballet composed by Lichine, *Nocturne*. This work, which was given its premiere at the Châtelet in Paris on 30 June 1933, had a libretto by Count Etienne de Beaumont based on Shakespeare's *A Midsummer Night's Dream*. De Beaumont also contributed the designs and Roger Desormière orchestrated a score from Jean Philippe Rameau.

Danilova's role was Titania, with Massine as Oberon and Lichine as Puck. During the same season she danced in a revival of Massine's *Les Matelots* with Massine, Woizikovsky and Lichine as the three sailors.

In the Paris audience that June was Gerald Goode, Sol Hurok's publicity manager, on holiday in Europe with his wife Ruth. He was no balletomane – it was in fact his first taste of ballet – but he was so thrilled, personally, that he sent an effusive 200-word cable to Hurok (who had seen their first Paris season in 1932) advising him strongly to book the company for America. Anton Dolin, the English-born dancer who had made his name with the Diaghilev Ballet, had agreed to dance *Les Sylphides* for them (23 June) and he was also, from a very different angle, impressed. He wrote to Hannen Swaffer of *The People*, one of the influential columnists in London:

It's a marvellous company – Danilova, Massine, Woizikovsky, a new boy called David Lichine who is grand. I am dancing alternately some of his roles. He welcomed me with open arms. Apparently I have always been his ideal of a dancer. Tchernicheva gives the lesson each morning. There is a young enthusiasm about the company. Two marvellous new dancers, Baronova who dances with me tomorrow, and Riabouchinska . . .

He was enthusiastic about Massine's choreography, too:

My whole and most vivid impression is the return of the ballet to the *dance*. No longer is it a succession of acrobatics. The choreography of the ballet is founded on the technique of the dance. Steps that one works and works to accomplish will now find their inclusion in the ideas of the choreographist thereby giving a sense of a dancer's virtuosity that was so lost or overshadowed before.[31]

As early as November 1932, de Basil had begun negotiating with Sir Oswald Stoll for a London season. He had also had an offer in April 1933 from B.F. Howell of the Lyceum Theatre for a four-week season from 15 May, but the deal with Stoll was the one that was concluded. It left one lady with a grievance.

Stoll had been in Monte Carlo in 1932, as had an Australian known as Daphne Deane, whose real name was Theodora Robinowitz. Miss Deane acted as an impresario, and there is some confusion about the part she played at this moment. In December 1933 she started proceedings against de Basil, claiming commission on the season at the Alhambra Theatre as having acted for him in the negotiations with Stoll.

In a long letter to the lawyers de Basil repudiated the claim and set out his side of the story. Daphne Deane, he said, was introduced to him in Monte Carlo in November 1932. She was full of enthusiasm for the company, and said she knew other people, some in Australia, who would help financially. She proposed forming a large committee who would guarantee a tour in Australia, but this had come to nothing.

De Basil had then met Stoll, who of course was already acquainted with Massine and Grigoriev and needed no intermediary, and they began discussions about bringing the company to London. It was he who had introduced Miss Deane to Stoll as a friend of the ballet, not the other way round.[32]

A hearing was scheduled for February 1934 but the case appears to have been settled out of court. Amicable relations were re-established, and Daphne Deane implemented her original promises by acting as impresario for the de Basil company that toured Australasia in 1936–7.

Dolin again danced *Les Sylphides* on 4 July 1933 at the opening performance of the Alhambra season. Had he settled into the company's life, Dolin would have provided an important influence as a *danseur noble*. He had other interests and commitments, however, and in addition always found it difficult getting along with de Basil. In 1933 he stayed a little over a month, appearing with Danilova in *Le Lac des cygnes* and *Les Sylphides* and dancing the Blackamoor in *Petrouchka*.

28

De Basil asked him to teach Baronova and Riabouchinska the Swan Queen and, recognizing Baronova's true ballerina quality, he was glad to agree where she was concerned. He was not scheduled to dance it with her, but when he found her in tears because Lichine and Petrov had refused to partner her he not only agreed to share her debut performance on 2 August – to her lasting gratitude – but kissed her hand at curtain call. This generosity from a famous dancer was something a 14-year-old debutante would never forget. As in his connection as guest artist with the Vic-Wells Ballet, Dolin was a stimulus and an example without becoming part of the regular life of the company.

The production of *Petrouchka* (19 July) was a great success. This was one of Woizikovsky's outstanding interpretations. In October 1935, when he danced it in London with his own company, *The Dancing Times* described him as 'superb . . . I can never hope to see a better study of this by no means simple part'. In the de Basil performance at the Alhambra the crowd scenes were also praised for their vivacity and for the sharply defined thumbnail sketches of minor characters such as Verchinina's chief nurse and Shabelevsky's head groom.

In August and September the contingent which had gone with Balanchine to Les Ballets 1933 rejoined the Ballets Russes de Monte-Carlo. Leading this, of course, was Toumanova, the third trump card that de Basil had hoped to play from the beginning. He and Blum had felt her loss, and before Les Ballets 1933 opened in Paris de Basil had sued Balanchine for taking her away but had lost the case. When the Savoy Theatre season of Les Ballets 1933 ended, Toumanova went back to Paris, 'to work and get thin,' as Haskell reports.[33] He, like other critics, had commented unfavourably on her 'childish weight' that summer. De Basil went over to Paris to see her and her parents and told them firmly that Balanchine was signing a new contract with him and wanted Toumanova to do the same. As she writes: 'Mama and I then went to London and found *no* Balanchine. It was a clever bluff . . .'[34] However, they were delighted to find that Massine was preparing *Choreartium* to Brahms' 4th Symphony.

Toumanova's initial appearance at the Alhambra (14 September) was in her created role of the Top in *Jeux d'enfants*. Lubov Rostova, Tamara Sidorenko (Grigorieva) and Tamara Tchinarova joined the company at about the same time, and Sidorenko was immediately cast

29

with Massine in a revival of Vaslav Nijinsky's *L'Après-midi d'un faune*. Fokine's *Carnaval* was staged by Woizikovsky, with Danilova as Columbine; and Danilova, in Baronova's absence for a month, danced Passion in *Les Présages*. A bewildered Eglevsky found himself dancing *Les Sylphides, Présages* (in Lichine's role) and *Beach*, as demands on Lichine became heavier.

Although this season launched Eglevsky on a fine career, it was not a happy time for him. A serious, solitary, shy teenager, he had responsibilities beyond his years. His father had emigrated to the USA, leaving his family in Nice, and from the moment André began to earn a salary he was expected to provide for his mother and sister. Dancing represented for him simply a method of earning money. He did not enjoy it. He was lonely in a company that brought him no real friendships. Above all, he felt that he was insufficiently developed as an artist. Only in England, where he went to another Maryinsky Ballet teacher, Nicholas Legat, did he begin to understand dancing beyond the fine technique he had acquired in Paris with Egorova and the Bolshoi Ballet dancer Volinine, and to enjoy it as an art.

The hundredth performance at the Alhambra was proudly billed on 28 September 1933 and there was still more to come, including *Choreartium*, on 24 October. Another lost ballet, although it was revived at Nervi in 1960, *Choreartium*, for many people, was the best of the symphonic ballets. It was rehearsed through a heavy programme of performances and in one of the hottest London summers – and although London never reaches the extremes of temperature experienced in other parts of the world, it is arguably as trying to work in London heat as in cities more used to coping with it. When the first night came the excitement was intense. Coton, who had found *Les Présages* 'an experiment of vaulting ambition which had o'erleaped itself', was totally enthusiastic.

An absolute balance between musical line and choreographic score was achieved; every external factor which could intrude on the development of pure balletic movement . . . was eliminated . . . As fully as knowledge of his medium allowed, Massine scored the dance progression in line, mass, unit, group and the combinations and permutations of these elements, exactly with the musical score . . .[35]

From every account, the striking development of *Choreartium* lay in Massine's masterly use of mass movement, of lifts and acrobatic throws that have become normal in choreography and have been surpassed in

30

difficulty since World War II but which were at the time exhilaratingly novel. It showed as well an ability to relate movement in depth to music, so that a total visual-aural experience emerged, and an eagerness to employ and invent steps and sequences new to classical ballet.

For Haskell, *Choreartium* was 'the birth and the triumph of pure dancing . . . now no music is beyond the reach of ballet'[36]; and the music critic Ernest Newman conceded:

We are bound to grant, I think, that there is nothing *a priori* incongruous in the mating of 'pure' music, whether that of Brahms or any other composer, with the lines and masses and movements of the ballet . . . The only question is to what extent the choreography has succeeded.[37]

He then speaks of parallelisms between music and dance and accepts those in *Choreartium* wholeheartedly. Adrian Stokes, the English art and music critic, asserted that 'two different yet related plastic forces, orchestral music and dancing, may enliven and enrich each other'.[38] But everyone was not of the same mind, and there was still opposition to the whole question of ballets set to symphonies – opposition from ballet-goers as well as music-lovers.

Choreartium was much delayed in reaching America. *Les Présages,* considered an easier ballet for audiences to accept, was given at the first programme in New York but it was far from a success. No one took a risk on *Choreartium* until 1935.

The New York opening was the next milestone in the company's progress. Before then there was a drama at Bournemouth – the company undertook a short English tour in November – in which Lubov Rostova almost followed the nineteenth-century ballerinas Emma Livry and Clara Webster into the annals of ballet history through a death by fire. It was the last Saturday evening, and *Le Lac des cygnes* had begun. In the wings, Rostova (a 17-year-old, and Lichine's bride of three months) moved too near to one of the lighted candles at which the girls melted eyeblack, and her dress caught fire. She ran out on to the stage to reach Lichine. Jean Hoyer (one of the huntsmen) and Serge Grigoriev managed to put out the flames, getting slightly burnt in the process, but Rostova was unharmed. Danilova made her entry and the interrupted performance continued: not surprisingly, as the *Bournemouth Daily Echo* comments in a graphic account, 'The incident was the talk of the building in the interval which followed'.[39]

31

The company, with the devoted Haskell and a newly-recruited associate conductor, a young Hungarian, Antal Dorati, sailed for New York on the *Lafayette* on 12 December from Plymouth. Sol Hurok had acted on Gerald Goode's advice. This active Russian-American impresario, obviously sincerely devoted to the artistic enterprises he sponsored for as long as he sponsored them, is a vital factor in the life and death of the de Basil Ballet. He has written, more than once, his account of his dealings with it and of the people involved. His relationship with de Basil is worth later investigation. Although he was far more concerned with music in the 1930s and even the 1940s, his activities on behalf of the Ballets Russes de Monte-Carlo – the Monte Carlo Ballet Russe, as it was known in the USA – sprang from initial enthusiasm and an instinct that this was something which might, if cleverly handled and determinedly pursued, prove a very worthwhile investment in the long run. He would have liked even more famous names, and there was a suggestion that the company might be expanded to include the small group headed by Serge Lifar and the former Diaghilev Ballet ballerina Alice Nikitina which had been presented by Edward James at the Savoy Theatre in London in the summer of 1933. This de Basil sturdily opposed, asserting (with justification) that it was quite unnecessary and that the standard of production of the Lifar group was too low.

Hurok and Gerald Goode then initiated an intensive publicity campaign to try to ensure the success of the Ballets Russes. Hurok, with an eye to the press boys, was down on the quay when the *Lafayette* docked to offer a traditional salt-and-bread Russian welcome. Goode worked in conjunction with an expert on the New York social scene. There, as in London during the 'thirties, the importance of the wealthy socialite or society-business influence was paramount. There were the strongest links between business, banking, the social world and the international wealthy, who constituted a closely woven and exceedingly powerful factor where the arts were concerned. Behind theatre productions and ballet premieres lay intricate safety-nets of private sponsorship and financial commitment impossible at this distance to analyse completely. It was imperative for artists and impresarios alike to play a part in the social scene, to foster vital contacts, to give and attend parties, to dine out and flatter the patrons. Before the Ballets Russes' New York debut at the St James Theatre on 22 December 1933, the Hurok organization had plotted a very thorough campaign to appeal to significant people. A list of the 'wealthy and literate' (then, as

32

now, presumably, some of the wealthy were far from literate) was compiled and kept informed of developments. A Sponsors' Committee was set up, headed by the Grand Duchess Marie of Russia and Otto H. Kahn. Kahn, who was chairman of the Board of the Metropolitan Opera House as well as being a partner of the banking firm of Kuhn, Loeb, was not only one of the most affluent devotees of music, opera and ballet – he had sponsored the first visits of the Diaghilev Ballet and Anna Pavlova – but a man who loved publicity. Stephen Birmingham in *Our Crowd* speaks of his 'long love-affair with the press'.[40] This suited Hurok admirably. He arranged, to follow the opening programme, the first of his gala ballet suppers at the Savoy-Plaza, and at this Otto Kahn and Paul Cravath sipped champagne from a brand-new Fifth Avenue-made ballet slipper. Everyone was delighted with the baby ballerinas, who, according to Hurok, 'looked as though they should have been put to bed in the nursery instead of staying out late drinking champagne – actually they had not yet learned to drink it – they ordered milk!'[41] Their news value sadly eclipsed Danilova, Massine and Woizikovsky off-stage.

The ballet supper set the tone. The ballets themselves, and particularly the dancers, made the success. As John Martin pointed out, it was the finest classically trained ballet to present a season in New York for a generation.[42] Everyone was in agreement with him about 'the delightful youngsters' – that they were talented and excellently trained – but that it was the work of Danilova, Massine and Woizikovsky that gave the company its stability. Where the ballets were concerned, only the amusing ones appealed. *Les Présages* plummeted sadly, in striking contrast to its London popularity – Martin put this down to the fact that America had the Isadora Duncan modern dance tradition and England had not, but this is to simplify too much. It is enough here to remark that *Les Présages* had an 'early demise' in New York and although it was tentatively put into the programme now and then, in Boston or Chicago or Philadelphia, it was never the attraction in the United States that it remained in London, Canada and Australia. One strongly adverse reaction came from Alfred Frankenstein, the noted music and dance critic in California, who described it as 'an incoherent and paranoic breast-beating of its choreographer'.[43]

There was of course no possibility that the lengthy Alhambra Theatre triumph could be repeated. In London there was already a responsive audience and the Alhambra itself was a friendly and suitable theatre. The St James had a small stage, the New York public were slow to make

33

bookings, in spite of the 'human stories' in the press and fetching photographs of the ballerinas. At the end of a month Hurok was faced with a problem. The 'stop clause' in his contract with the St James, which ensured that the theatre would not lose an attraction earning over a specified weekly figure, had been fixed at too low a rate and prevented the company from leaving New York, but he had booked a short tour. So he divided the company into two and sent Massine, Danilova, Toumanova and most of the repertoire out of New York. Three ballets continued to be given at the St James, *Les Sylphides, Petrouchka* and *Prince Igor*, danced by Baronova, Riabouchinska, Lichine and Woizikovsky, with a hastily implemented *corps de ballet* of American dancers whose identities were concealed under contrived Russian names. A few of these have been revealed, among them Leon Barté, an American who toured with Pavlova; Nicolas Daks, a Russian born in Istanbul who became associate producer at Radio City Music Hall; George Kiddon, a Russian-American dancer; Léon Fokine, Fokine's nephew; and Allan Wayne, who, as P. Weine, danced Fate in *Les Présages* later on tour. It was a fair compromise which was not needed very long. Soon the reunited company opened in Chicago, where *Le Tricorne* was added to the repertoire.

Wherever they went, over the years, young dancers would be brought to the theatre for auditions or watched in class at important ballet schools. Such talent was often engaged in the specific category of student-dancer. These student-dancers received a minimal salary, tuition and a chance to learn the repertoire. Sometimes their parents would pay towards tuition, sometimes just contribute to their child's keep. It was not a new idea – Pavlova used to make similar arrangements with promising young people (Robert Helpmann, for one, toured in that way with her company in Australasia).

In Chicago in February 1934 de Basil auditioned and engaged as a student-dancer Sono Osato, a gifted 14-year-old who had been born in Omaha, Nebraska, of Japanese and Irish parents. She had studied with Adolph Bolm in Chicago and with one of his students, Berenice Holmes. She was to spend seven years with the company, establishing herself as a dancer of great style and expressiveness with enough oriental character to add piquancy to her classical work.

Le Tricorne was presented in New York, with Massine as the Miller and Toumanova as the Miller's Wife, at a second gala opening at the St James Theatre on 9 March 1934. The evening included *Le Lac des*

34

cygnes and *Les Matelots* (which flopped). On 16 March however the company staged what John Martin felt to be choreographically one of their strongest programmes: *Carnaval, Cotillon* and *Le Tricorne*. Massine in *Le Tricorne* earned superlatives – 'one of those electrifying achievements which elicit bravos from an audience almost as an irresistible reaction'. *Carnaval* Martin loved, and *Cotillon* was immediately a prime favourite: 'Though it is witty and impudent in large part, there are moments in which the surface is pierced, and extremely substantial dance composition is allowed to shine through.'[44]

By now de Basil had a problem over Monte Carlo. Things were going very differently from plan. The agreement which he and Blum had made envisaged a company based on Monte Carlo, which would fit into the annual schedule of opera and ballet. There would be a work period before a spring season at the Casino Theatre. Touring would take only the remaining months. The unexpected extension in London had altered the emphasis. It had made it obvious to de Basil that his company had the potential to be a world success. Living and travelling with it in a way that Blum, with his commitments at Monte Carlo and as artistic director of the Théâtre Pigalle, could never do, de Basil was already looking on it as 'his' company. He thought of it very much in the way a commanding officer might regard a regiment as his own.

The link with Hurok opened up the wide horizon of the United States and Canada. It would have been madness not to have signed with him but the acceptance of the New York season had meant that there could be no appearance, as there had been in the two previous years, for the anniversary gala at Monte Carlo, nor any involvement in opera-ballets there. Blum spent the appropriate funds on engaging other dancers to provide these – confusingly enough, they were also called the Ballets Russes de Monte-Carlo – with Nijinska as maître de ballet. Nijinska's own company had closed and, after acting as ballet mistress for Max Reinhardt's spectacular production of *The Tales of Hoffmann* in Berlin she had renewed her association with L'Opéra Russe à Paris in 1932. Kousnetsova had continued the company after de Basil left and for them Nijinska staged *Etude, La Princesse cygne, Les Biches* and *Bolero* as well as two new creations, *Variations* (Beethoven) and *Les Comédiens jaloux*, at the Opéra Comique in Paris in June 1932.

Now, in March 1934, with the ballet season at Monte Carlo imminent, de Basil tried the split personality policy Hurok had adopted in America in February – perhaps on Hurok's suggestion – and sent to Monte Carlo a contingent of dancers led by Danilova and Woizikovsky, Tchinarova, Jasinsky and Guerard, to join the company recruited by Blum which included an American, Ruth Chanova, a young Yugoslav ballerina, the red-haired Mia Slavenska (Corac) and Boris Kniasev.

They fielded a mixed repertoire, presenting some Nijinska ballets that were never otherwise staged by the de Basil Ballet. Danilova danced in *Bolero, Variations* and *Les Comédiens jaloux. Etude* was led by Chanova, Kniasev and Jasinsky. *Variations* – Vladimir Pohl had arranged and orchestrated a number of piano pieces by Beethoven for this – fell into three curiously selected scenes: one in ancient Greece, featuring Diana (Danilova) and Idomène (Jasinsky); one of Russian peasants of the time of Alexander I, led by Chanova; and the third in Paris during the Directoire, in which Danilova headed the Merveilleuses and Woizikovsky the Incroyables.

Les Comédiens jaloux had a story about a troupe of Commedia dell'arte performers, a simple tale of young lovers told in a singularly complicated manner. Gunhild Schüller, in her monograph *Nijinska*, quotes the critic E. Vuillermoz, writing in *Excelsior* of 13 June 1932 when the ballet was first produced in Paris:

Vingt danseurs exécutant en même temps, dans tous les coins du plateau, des prouesses différentes qui exigent toutes un examen attentif. Cet écalement de l'oeil devient vite insupportable.[45]

Danilova danced the leading role of Clarisse with Jasinsky as Flavio, Guerard as Arlecchino and Woizikovsky as the valet Pedrolino.

Back in the USA, in March 1934, *Union Pacific* was in preparation, obviously angled to the American market. The idea for this ballet originated with the American poet Archibald Macleish. Massine had spent three years, from 1926 to 1929, at the Roxy Theatre in New York, and become interested in the possibility of staging a ballet with an American theme. Now, when he was back in America and working with the de Basil company, seemed a good time to develop this. Hurok heard from Nicolas Nabokov, who had composed the music for the Diaghilev Ballet *Ode*, that Macleish wanted to write a scenario about the Union Pacific railroad. Railroads might, by European standards, be a dull subject, quite unappealing as a basis for a ballet, but the tale of their development is of course one of the big romances of North American history. Massine liked the idea and a collaboration began.

36

The score, eventually composed by Nabokov in twenty-three days, was based on a treasure trove of songs and dances recorded on cylinders at the turn of the century, and old jazz and black music from Chicago and New Orleans. Finance was found, with some difficulty, and a ballet emerged with what seems, on paper, to be an unwieldy and unpromising libretto about Chinese and Irish workmen, Mormon missionaries, capitalists and surveyors, slightly leavened by a lady of easy virtue (the Lady Gay), a barman, and a trio of Mexicans in which Toumanova danced a Massine version of the Hat Dance. Caryl Brahms describes it as 'a rather raw ballet, manifestly made for an American public' and says that it

achieves ballet three times in its long action. Once when Baronova takes the floor as the Mae of the Golden West, and when the Barman does his ballet-transposed cake-walk, and the short sequence in which the corps de ballet are used as sleepers and riveted to the line.[46]

Not only the *corps de ballet* were so riveted. Friends of the company and ballet mothers, if standing in the wings, were liable to be thrust into one of the brown jumpsuits and helmets that characterized the sleepers and carried on stage as hasty replacements for missing dancers.

In performance, *Union Pacific* had a good many amusing moments, a delicious role for the ballerina created by Eugénie Delarova (at the time Massine's wife) which Baronova and Morosova also later turned to good advantage, and an outstanding solo danced by Massine himself as the Barman. For this he had studied black dance in New Orleans and Harlem, cleverly combining step dance and cake-walk, strut and shuffle. Beaumont describes the result as

just the mixture that an uncouth, half-demented, half-inebriated creature might be expected to contrive . . . A little masterpiece of characterization.[47]

A tiny role as the Barman's Assistant singled out Sono Osato. All this emerged out of a chaotic period of creative work that Nabokov describes vividly and during which he quite forgot to insist on a royalty contract – no doubt much to the relief of the man he calls 'the crooked Colonel'.[48] Probably no one who ever worked for the de Basil Ballet ended up without a financial grievance. Everyone was cheated, one way or another, or at least *felt* cheated, which comes to much the same thing. Dispassionately considered, it seems impossible that the company could have kept going if it had attempted to pay its way honestly. For survival, it needed a director who was ethically undisturbed by conning or cheating – and it was lucky to find this in de Basil. It is the Falstaff credo, 'Can honour set a leg?',[49] transposed into 'Can honour keep a ballet company in existence without subsidies, grants or industrial funding?'

Immediately after the *Union Pacific* premiere at the Forrest Theatre, Philadelphia on 6 April 1934, the company paid its first visit to Boston, where *The Transcript* observed that 'Next to New York, there is probably more money in Boston to spend on such pleasures and more disposition to spend it than in any other American city'.[50] Certainly the papers were confident that their readers would be sufficiently interested to enjoy detailed advance information, running to columns of newsprint. On the first night (9 April) the Boston Opera House was filled by 'an audience that was as representative of youth as of middle age and silver-haired seniors'.

The Transcript's critic wrote:

Perhaps to the technicians they miss some of the finish and polish of their Diaghilev predecessors. But what may be lacking on that side they atone for in their gayety [sic], their zeal, their lively imagination, the pleasure that they obviously take in their work, and that they communicate to their audience. This was primarily an evening to be enjoyed for its warmth, its color, its display of youthful graces.[51]

An excellent picture indeed of the company's special character . . . The *Globe* critic had no reservations about technique: 'Technically their dancing was of a high order. All of the principals were so expert that they made amazing leaps and leaping turns seem simple.'[52]

Union Pacific was briefly brought into New York to the St James's Theatre on 27 April and then became the new attraction for Europe – without being a great ballet, it made an appeal and survived for a number of years. It even succeeded in Australia without Massine, where Lazovsky danced Massine's role of the Barman.

It had its Paris premiere at the Théâtre des Champs-Elysées on 4 June 1934, a season in which the company broke all attendance records for the theatre. L. Franc Scheuer regretted Balanchine's departure, but found great pleasure

in witnessing a company that really dances, that plays its role in choreography consciously and seriously . . . Nor does any other ballet boast a like homogeneousness. One no sooner selects a favourite dancer than another puts the whole choice into question again.[53]

The company opened in London on 19 June. This time they danced at the Royal Opera House, Covent Garden, beginning an important association. Instrumental in this union was Captain Bruce Ottley. A product of Eton and Balliol, who had seen war service in France and in the Far East, Ottley was a first-rate musician who had composed several suites for the piano. His piano improvisations at private parties are remembered with delight. As well as his connections with the de Basil Ballet and with Covent Garden, he was a director of the banking firm of Erlangers Ltd, and his enthusiasm for the ballet was shared by more than one of the Erlanger family.

In 1933 Covent Garden was in the first year of a new period in its history. Sir Thomas Beecham, helped by Lady Cunard, formed an organization to take over the lease of the theatre, and Geoffrey Toye was appointed managing director of the new company. Toye, who had been manager of the Sadler's Wells Opera Company, was also a conductor and composer – two of his ballets, *Douanes* and *The Haunted Ballroom*, were staged with choreography by Ninette de Valois by the Vic-Wells Ballet. Beecham of course knew de Basil from the season of L'Opéra Russe à Paris in 1931, and he conducted occasionally at Covent Garden during the ballet's 1934 summer season.

The de Basil Ballet was well provided with its own conductors however – this was one of its strengths. Efrem Kurtz, whose association with ballet included a season when, as a young pianist, he played for the group of Soviet dancers that included Danilova and Balanchine, now had Dorati as associate. The dancers appreciated them both, finding Kurtz the more orthodox and predictable and Dorati the more lively and amusing. Many other conductors, including some very eminent names, were given temporary engagements at various times and in various localities.

The London audience was thrilled to welcome the company again and the company was thrilled to be back. London, after the Alhambra season, was even more home to them than Monte Carlo and was to remain so during the 'thirties. They loved the city and its social life, the supper parties, weekend house-parties, charity balls. They were feted and pampered by well-off admirers, they were chaffed and complimented by Covent Garden fruit-market porters. Lesley Blanch, in *Journey into the Mind's Eye*, writes of them living 'in small, dingy hotels round the British Museum, their narrow bedrooms stacked with steamer trunks',

39

but constituting 'a world of their own, turbulent and magnetic, glittering Harlequin figures for whose public and private lives the British public were soon avid'.[54] Toumanova later recalled that she 'lodged in a Seven Dials attic, lived on fish-and-chip meals, shopped warily in street markets and cooked for herself over a gas ring on Sundays'.[55] Inevitably, the press gave them publicity – illustrated magazines, like *The Bystander, The Tatler, The Illustrated London News* and *The Sketch* printed splendid pages of pictures month by month, and they featured in the society and gossip columns as well as in the critics' reviews.

Critical notices were full and constant. Haskell wrote in *The Daily Telegraph* as, later, did Beryl de Zoete. Horace Horsnell was critic of *The Observer*, Ernest Newman of *The Sunday Times*. Edwin Evans wrote in the *Daily Mail*, Francis Toye (brother of Geoffrey) in *The Morning Post*, Adrian Stokes in *The Spectator*, the conductor and composer Constant Lambert in the *Sunday Referee*. These were only some of the critics dealing seriously and often at length with the company's work. The audience included plenty of devoted enthusiasts, some of them later to become well known themselves as ballet critics, authors or archivists. Others, like the remarkable Margaret Power, became closely identified with the dancers and their careers. Margaret, who was later to do so much for the Nijinskys,[56] was a young widow with two small daughters when she was taken along to rehearsals of *Choreartium* in 1933 and became a friend and helper of Toumanova, Riabouchinska and Lichine. She represented the element always important in ballet – the knowledgeable and caring members of the audience who unselfishly devote time and thought to bridging the gap of the footlights and acting as liaison between dancers and public.

Most of the regulars sat in the upper part of the house. Stalls, stalls circle and grand tier (then called dress circle) (priced from 9s. to 15s.) were filled out of the society columns, and full evening dress was customary. On gala nights this was embellished with tiaras and decorations. The amphitheatre and balcony stalls (3s.6d. to 8s.6d.) looked down to splendour or up to the gallery (unreserved, 2s.) full of excited, chattering and applauding young people. They had queued on stools outside in Floral Street and chased upstairs when the doors opened, in an extraordinary artistic marathon, to scramble for the best places on the bench seats, exactly as film-goers can still watch them doing in *The Red Shoes*.

The pros and cons of dancers' performances, of emerging dancers and new productions, opinion against opinion, were avidly discussed, and night after night, after each ballet, the stage was filled with enormous floral tributes that jammed dressing-rooms and corridors after the curtain came down. Admirers of the rival ballerinas outdid each other over bouquets and baskets, laurel wreaths regularly arrived for Massine, and soloists or even *corps de ballet* would have surprise gifts of flowers. Philip Dyer recalls how the ballerinas, too poor to have jewellery, used these flowers with endless invention as ornaments when they went on to post-performance parties. Toumanova's glossy dark head would be wreathed with lilies, or roses might be tucked gypsy-style behind an ear.

The 1934 London season provided pleasure for a Committee of Friends of the Ballet organized by Bruce Ottley, who now reaped a reward from their generosity. These influential socialites had moved into action as fund-raisers to acquire for the company, probably from Massine, costumes and decors of many Diaghilev ballets. Now, *La Boutique fantasque* and Fokine's *L'Oiseau de feu* were revived; with *Le Tricorne*, they made a strong trio of proved works to show a new generation of the public.

Inevitably the productions seemed less good than previously to those who had seen the originals. Constant Lambert began his notice of *Boutique* by saying 'There is no character more irritating than the man who has always known everything in its palmy days . . .' but he continued:

La Boutique Fantasque is the most successful of the various revivals staged by M. de Basil, peculiarly suited to a company whose strong point is the number of dancers who can fill a secondary role with brilliance and intelligence.[57]

Looking down the cast list, one realizes how true this is. The Shopkeeper and his Assistant were Edouard Borovansky and Vania Psota; the Snob and the Melonhawker, Shabelevsky and Jean Hoyer; Eglevsky was the Cossack chief with Delarova as the Cossack girl; Rostova, Verchinina, Petrov and Guerard were the Court Cards; Toumanova and Jasinsky danced the Tarantella.

Borovansky and Psota both came from Czechoslovakia and had memorable careers as character dancers with de Basil as well as making important contributions to ballet later on as directors. Borovansky was the elder by some half dozen years. He was a leading dancer with the Prague National Theatre and then toured with Pavlova from 1928 until

41

her death. It was Victor Dandré who put him in touch with de Basil in 1932, and in London in 1933 he married Dandré's niece, Xenia Nicolaeva Smirnova, who had also danced with Pavlova. Among the roles he created for de Basil were the Athlete in *Le Beau Danube* and Girolamo in *Francesca da Rimini*, and he had an additional responsibility in recruiting and rehearsing the large numbers of extras employed in many productions. Modern stagings of *Petrouchka* or *Schéhérazade,* with ensembles limited to dancing roles, give no idea of the intricate and busy crowd backgrounds implied by such programme lines as the one in *Petrouchka*: 'Pedlars, Officers, Soldiers, Aristocrats, Ladies, Children, Maids, Cossacks, Policemen, Animal Trainers, etc.'

Psota too was a product of the Prague National Theatre although he was born in Kiev of Czech parents. He never completely lost contact with his native country, particularly with the city of Brno. He had danced there before joining de Basil in 1932 and he went back as maître de ballet in 1937 when he married the Colonel's former wife, Nina Leonidova. They rejoined de Basil in 1941. After the end of World War II he returned to Brno as maître de ballet and choreographer, where he did much to foster a love of classical ballet in dancers and audience.

As choreographer, none of the works he produced outside Czechoslovakia had any critical praise but he seems to have worked more successfully on his home ground. He choreographed the first production of Prokofiev's *Romeo and Juliet* in Brno in December 1938, for the Czech ballerina Zora Semberova. As a dancer with de Basil he became firmly identified with roles such as the Eunuch in *Schéhérazade* and Pantalon in *Carnaval*.

One of the senior character dancers with the company was Jean Hoyer, who had been with the Diaghilev Ballet. Once he settled in with de Basil – he was, in fact, with L'Opéra Russe à Paris in 1931 – he remained there, as did his wife Nathalie Branitska, until 1947. His performance of roles such as Pierrot in *Carnaval* is remembered with great pleasure.

L'Oiseau de feu, unlike *Boutique*, depended on only four principal roles, but those roles were marvellously interpreted. Lionel Bradley, writing of the same cast a couple of years later in his diary, describes Massine's 'fineness of carriage' as Ivan, Grigorieva's 'superbly simple and stately Tsarevna', Lichine 'at his very best' as Köstchei, and Danilova 'who must be as good a Firebird as there has ever been'.[58] Her ability to conjure up brilliant supernatural authority, true theatrical magic, which would enable her later to be one of the finest interpreters of Myrtha in *Giselle*, was augmented by the clarity of her technique. She told Eric Johns that she found the Firebird one of the most difficult roles to dance 'with so many sustained flying leaps and so many intricately timed entrances'.[59]

In *Le Tricorne*, Toumanova scored a success as the Miller's Wife, although this was spoiled for her when she realized that Grigoriev and Tchernicheva had been hurt that she, and not Tchernicheva, had been chosen by Massine for the revival. Because of this she persistently refused – to ballet's loss, one feels – to dance the roles of Zobeide and Thamar which were revived for Tchernicheva.

Another Diaghilev revival, *Contes russes*, proved successful. Baronova danced the beautiful adagio solo 'The Lament of the Swan Princess', and Riabouchinska contributed a haunting performance as the little girl lost in the forest. The final peasant dances were led with enormous style by Danilova and Shabelevsky.

The failure of the summer was Lichine's second ballet, *Les Imaginaires*, which had been premiered in Paris on 11 June. A score by Auric, costumes by de Beaumont and a set by Lesley Blanch and Freida Harris promised reasonably well, but looking at the scenario it is easy to see why it failed, however novel and exciting it may have seemed to its creators when they embarked on it. At least, as it was about geometrical figures on a blackboard and a sponge erasing them, it was a gift to any critic feeling like a wisecrack. Ernest Newman commented: 'a sponge passed over the whole production would have led to no passionate protest on my part';[60] and Lambert said that the geometrical subject made him think of a geometrical proposition: 'nought + nought = nought . . .'[61]

By now some homegrown competition was beginning to make itself felt from the Vic-Wells Ballet. This company had in its repertoire three Fokine ballets, *Les Sylphides, Carnaval* and *Le Spectre de la rose,* and revivals of *Casse-noisette*, two acts of *Coppélia, Le Lac des cygnes* (Act II) and *Giselle*. Their prima ballerina was Alicia Markova, the English girl who had danced with the Diaghilev Ballet, and they were nursing along various young dancers with an eye to the future. As resident choreographers they had Frederick Ashton and Ninette de Valois.

Overall, however, the de Basil season was another triumph; and it kept Covent Garden, without precedent, open until the middle of August – 'the London Season may now be said to end when Colonel de Basil's troupe leaves London and not before'.[62]

August 1934 to April 1936

The next American tour began in October 1934, when Hurok booked the company to open the newly re-modelled Palacio des Bellas Artes in Mexico City, where no one knew how to operate the elaborate lighting system and they had to make do with spotlights.

From there they were due to go to Canada, by the Ward Line ship *Roosevelt* to New York and rail to Toronto, a journey that made news, at least in the Toronto press.

Delayed at sea for more than forty hours, tossed about on the stormy stage of the Atlantic when nature in gleeful mimicry arranged an unexpected symphony of the elements and the waves performed a ballet all their own, the Ballet Russe de Monte Carlo reached Toronto from New York by special C.P.R. train last night less than two hours before the curtain was scheduled to rise on the opening performance of their three-day appearance at Massey Hall.[1]

The headlines really said it all:

> Wild Race Against Time
> But "the Show Goes On"
> As Ballet Russe Arrives
> Company Finally Reaches
> Toronto and After
> Lengthy Assembling of
> Intricate Scenery
> Starts Program at 9.50
> P.M., Concluding at
> 12.45 A.M. – Perform-
> ance Gets Sympathetic
> Reception

A long delay at the Customs had been predicted but was avoided. De Basil praised the Canadian Customs officers – 'not a single bit of trouble'. He 'admitted that some members were very ill during the voyage but they would appear, sick or well'. There was no need for any fuss – all had been organized during the train journey as much as it could be and the performance would be a little late but not too late – two hours from now all would be well. He was an accurate prophet.

The local critic found that the performance showed 'an enviable technique and skill from both a terpsichorean and histrionic standpoint'. The symphony orchestra, not surprisingly, 'revealed a suggestion of anxiety'.

Prior to taking their places in front of the stage, the musicians had taken part in a hurried rehearsal in the vicinity of the dressing rooms where difficulties were aggravated when one of the main fuses failed to function.

The conductors were, as usual, Kurtz and Dorati. Similar problems faced them with many orchestras in many parts of the world.

In Philadelphia in November, the company revived *Le Mariage d'Aurore* (the abbreviated version of *The Sleeping Beauty*) and Danilova rejoined them after an abortive engagement in *The Great Waltz* (*Waltzes from Vienna*) in New York.

Le Mariage d'Aurore was an important event. As Lillian Moore wrote: 'Apart from the abbreviated *Lac des Cygnes* in New York, this generation in America has had no previous opportunity of seeing ballet of the pre-Fokine era'.[2] It was, of course, similar to the Diaghilev *divertissement* staged in Paris in 1922. It opened with a polonaise and continued with the 'dance of the seven ladies of honour and their partners'. Then came the ballerina variations from Act I, Scene 1, of *The Sleeping Beauty*, usually now thought of as the Fairies' solos. These varied in number, sometimes five, sometimes six, and in the later years from 1938 often only three, but they always included the Sugar Plum Fairy solo (from *Casse-noisette*) danced by the evening's Aurora, the Lilac Fairy variation and the 'Finger' variation. The dance of the duchesses followed, then the farandole from the Vision Scene. The fairytale section was made up of Florestan and his sisters (with an occasional alternative of Ariane and her brothers), Red Riding Hood, the Bluebird *pas de deux*, the Porcelain Princesses (a *pas de trois* for a man and two girls to the Danse Chinoise, again from *Casse-noisette*) and the Three Ivans in Nijinska's choreography, with the Aurora *pas de deux* as the penultimate delight before the final mazurka.

'The cream of the Social Register'[3] turned out in force, and in pouring rain, to the Boston Opera House to see the revived ballet on 13 November 1934, when the critic of the *Post* termed it:

an elaborate, stylized, slightly old-fashioned ballet with regular alternation of chorus dancing, solo dancing, duets, trios and quartets, all costumed with an eye for colour and effect.[4]

He much preferred *Le Beau Danube*, praising its grace and charm, artistry and smoothness, and in particular the brilliance of Massine. The classical conventions took some getting used to.

The tour was a major one, covering 20,000 miles in seven months with performances in ninety towns, many being one-night stands. The company reached California in January 1935 – a first taste for some of the dancers of the state they would eventually make their home – and had a marvellous engagement in Hollywood where the movie stars came out in strength and Marlene Dietrich, memorably, even stood in the wings to watch. Hollywood at that time had as much glamour for the dancers as they had glamour for the general public.

The next month they appeared at the Vancouver Theatre for the first time, and, as Leland Windreich writes, *Les Présages*

became the model for every piece of choreography created locally for several years and June Roper's ballet classes [Roper was a Texas American who became head of the British Columbia School of Dancing in Vancouver in 1935] became crammed with aspiring Terpsichores who now had tangible role models in the persons of de Basil's "baby ballerinas".[5]

The initiative in booking the company had been taken by a remarkable Scots-Canadian entrepreneur, Lily J. Laverock, who established International Celebrities in Vancouver in 1921.

It was an unlucky tour from the health point of view. Baronova suffered from the altitude in Mexico City (in fact some dancer fainted at every performance there), Massine strained a knee, Rostova had an operation and Riabouchinska scarlet fever. Tragically her mother, Mme Riabouchinska, died in a Chicago hospital.

Chicago was visited both going and coming, and during the March 1935 season they gave premieres of Massine's *Le Bal* and *Jardin public*. *Le Bal* was a new version by Massine of the Diaghilev *divertissement* ballet choreographed by Balanchine and composed by Vittorio Rieti in 1929 – three months before Diaghilev's death. Giorgio de Chirico's designs had dominated that production and Massine proved even less successful in giving the work stage vitality.

Jardin public, which was one of the necessary new attractions Hurok always had to provide for the New York season, was the kind of work that never comes right but nags at its creators so that they keep on trying to improve it. Its composer, Vladimir Dukelsky (Vernon Duke) and Massine worked out a scenario from a section of André Gide's *Les Faux Monnayeurs*, an analogy between human life and a day in a public garden. It concentrated on contrasts – between rich and poor, age and youth, innocence and depravity, those who wish to live and those who wish to die – but the points seem to have been laboured too heavily for balletic success.

Dukelsky approached de Basil, who responded (as no doubt he did to all brainwaves by creative artists): 'Wonderful, Dimotchka, you get the money, I'll put it on.'

The money was found, the score was written and sent to Paris for copying. Massine put the ballet into rehearsal and it was scheduled for a Chicago premiere on 8 March 1935. The orchestral score and parts only reached Chicago at 4.30 pm that day, so it was hardly surprising that everyone felt the ballet needed revision. The score, moreover, was not popular. De Basil protested to Dukelsky: 'The moment you start a tune, and I say to myself, good, very good, you go off completely as though you were ashamed of yourself . . . Then I feel like howling like a dog, I grit my teeth and suffer. But maybe I am not qualified to judge . . .'[6] Qualified or not, he was not alone in this reaction. Even Massine wanted the score to be less harsh and strident and when it was heard in London, in July, Ernest Newman wrote: 'Dukelsky apparently still thinks we are likely to be impressed by a profusion of discords without any distinction or continuity of ideas to justify them.'[7]

Both *Jardin public* and *Le Bal* fell very flat in New York where Hurok could find no suitable theatre except, for five performances at the end of March 1935, the Majestic, another small house. Only *Le Mariage d'Aurore*, of the new items in the repertoire, pleased. Russell Rhodes reported that the season 'began poorly after a long cross-country tour and ended in a blaze of virtuosity.'[8]

A new dancer was beginning to be featured – Vera Zorina, whose real name was Eva Brigitta Hartwig. She had danced in Max Reinhardt's *Tales of Hoffmann* in Berlin in 1931 and in 1933 had starred with Dolin in London in a play, *Ballerina*. Zorina was born in Berlin of

Norwegian parents and studied with Eugenia Eduardova and Victor Gsovsky. She joined the de Basil Ballet in August 1934 and by January 1935 was dancing the Street Dancer in *Le Beau Danube.*

In New York there was also a debut of interest to English balletomanes – that of Prudence Hyman (Paulina Strogova) in the Bluebird *pas de deux.* One of the most forceful personalities among the English dancers of the time. Hyman joined de Basil along with two other girls from Marie Rambert's Ballet Club – Betty Cuff (Vera Nelidova) and Elizabeth Ruxton (Lisa Serova) – at the end of 1933. Hyman and Cuff had danced with Les Ballets 1933, and then Elizabeth Ruxton, in a spirit of 'nothing venture, nothing win', suggested auditioning for the Ballets Russes de Monte-Carlo. They were all accepted, and on the way to New York were given their new Russian names.

All three did well, but like other non-Russian/Polish dancers found it hard to advance without friends at court. Hyman, probably the most ambitious, moved on to the Markova-Dolin Ballet in 1935, but the others stayed, dancing certain soloist roles regularly. Among Serova's staples were the American girl in *Boutique* and Red Riding Hood in *Le Mariage d'Aurore*, although she occasionally danced the Child in *Jeux d'enfants* and the Daughter in *Beau Danube.* Nelidova's roles included the Florestan *pas de trois* and one of the Fairy variations in *Le Mariage d'Aurore* and, in contrast, the Polovtsian girl in *Prince Igor.* Fokine altered this for her completely, making it much stronger and more masculine in movement, with big jumps and landings on the knees.

Over the years a good many English, Canadian, American and Australian dancers became known under Russian names and were a source of strength to the company. Some integrated more successfully than others. Some always felt partially shut out from the Russian-Polish front – and all of them felt, too, that they were left far more to fend for themselves, while the Russian and Polish girls would always be looked after. Perhaps this was not unnatural. The stateless dancers, travelling on their Nansen passports,[9] constituted a large family headed by the Grigorievs and de Basil. The English dancer and teacher Leo Kersley, who knew a good many of them, has described them as 'travelling around like Holy Russia on tour', and they certainly had the bonds of shared origin, heritage, language and experience to unite them. Inevitably the others, who had national identities and, somewhere in the world, settled family homes, were felt to be different. There was also an underlying notion that most of them had rich parents and could send home for money, while the emigrés had nothing behind them. It was in no way true. Only in a couple of cases had wealthy parents bought a passage, as it were, for a not-very-talented daughter. Most of the Western recruits were not from well-to-do homes but were so dedicated to the ballet that they were glad to make any sacrifices to learn and dance the great repertoire. They learnt it in many odd ways. Natasha Sobinova (the Canadian Rosemary Deveson) recalls a crash course in *La Concurrence* in a hotel bathroom in Cincinnati, with Baronova humming the music. Observation and emulation were the basic necessities of daily work. Wits had to be quick and memories retentive. Where ensembles were concerned, new recruits were often 'talked through' the first time by experienced members of the *corps de ballet.*

The creators of *Jardin public* clung tenaciously to the hope of making it succeed. Dukelsky was taken to Europe to work on revisions and it was given half a dozen performances in London. Then it was allowed to slip out of the repertoire. The critics probably made its fate inevitable. *The Times* wrote that it was difficult to understand why Massine had been at pains to revise the ballet: 'We can imagine no other form of entertainment at all in which such triviality, alternately boring and ugly, would be tolerated.'[10] All that was left were some magnificent photographic studies by Gordon Anthony to record the touching performances of Massine and Toumanova as the Poor Couple. Similar pictures of Massine and Nini Theilade in his 1938 *Nobilissima visione* (*St Francis*) for Denham's Ballet Russe de Monte Carlo suggest a relationship of mood and style between the duets.

During the winter of 1934–5, Blum had once again made independent arrangements for the provision of the opera-ballets. The maître de ballet and leading dancer of his group was Nina Kirsanova; her partner was Aubrey Hitchins, both of whom had been with Pavlova. The local press looked forward to the opening of the Ballets Russes on 4 April 1935, taking considerable pride in their achievements. A reporter in the *Riviera News* wrote:

This superb organization has been an enormous success in London and in America and Canada. Only a few days ago we received a rapturous letter from Vancouver . . .

It should be scarcely necessary to say that René Blum is the artistic director and M. W. de Basil the general manager. Many of us here resent the way in which René Blum's name is always omitted in London newspapers, for we know that this wonderful revival is primarily due to him. Honour where honour is due, and in this case the credit should be "René Blum and M. de Basil".[11]

The association of Blum and de Basil had never been a happy one. In every way they were opposites – in temperament, background, taste, methods and intentions. They had come together purely from temporary necessity, deliberately ignoring their obvious dissimilarities in the hope that a collaboration would serve their different ambitions for Russian Ballet.

Blum withdrew from the administrative management as early as the end of 1933, remaining as Artistic Director, and on 16 August 1934 he and de Basil signed a new contract, annulling the previous one, for the short period until 15 May 1935 – a 'sorting-out' period, presumably – after which they would each have 'entire liberty'. Blum was to receive a compensatory fee of 250,000 francs. De Basil managed to find this by 30 April 1935, when Blum signed a receipt declaring that their individual independence would be from that date.

Blum's protests were two-fold – a continuing one as to the omission of his name in publicity concerning the company, and a dissatisfaction that he had eventually become more an unpaid publicity officer than an artistic director.

René Blum easily gains one's sympathy. Here was an understandable man in the context of artistic Western Europe, cultured, humane, modest, knowledgeable, ethical – a man whose parallel is recognizable in establishment posts in the arts and sciences, as curators of museums and art galleries, throughout the civilized world. He has sometimes been misinterpreted, by being credited with a softness and naivety that were obviously no part of his nature. He would not have been a true scion of his family, nor consulted on artistic affairs, nor appointed as organizer of exhibitions and theatrical seasons, had he been lacking in business acumen, judgement of character or decision. His modesty, moreover, was not so excessive that he did not finally make public protest about receiving insufficient credit, not only in connection with the de Basil Ballet but with the Massine-Denham Ballet Russe de Monte Carlo.

This was in a long letter to *Dance Magazine* (US) published in April 1940. In it he declares:

It is a well-established and indisputable fact that I was the founder, the first director and, for a time, the only backer of the original Russian Ballet [i.e. the Ballets Russes de Monte-Carlo founded in 1932]

50

He goes on to point out that the Massine-Denham company had been created by him as the Ballets de Monte-Carlo while Massine was still with de Basil and that Massine had 'simply broadened it, adding a few new stars and making some general changes'.

He continues:

Though my contracts are very clear and specific as regards my part and my title in the company the reading of posters and programmes is somewhat misleading! The search for my name is a most delicate task, reserved, it would seem, to those who are wont to decipher puzzles . . .[12]

Blum's outlook and principles were diametrically opposed to those of the man he terms 'the gangster Colonel'[13] and, having gone along as far as he could with the company they had mutually created, it must have been with considerable relief that he severed connection with it in 1935. It is tantalizing to know that he dealt with the whole period in a book of memoirs and that not only was this never published but the manuscript itself was a casualty of World War II.

That April 1935 season was the last in Monte Carlo for the de Basil Ballet and they had little that was new and good to show. *Union Pacific* was given on 4 April and *Jardin public* on 13 April. There was more publicity, in the international press at least, for a real-life drama involving Rostova. Contradictory stories exist as to details, including references in newspapers to ghosts and sleep-walking,[14] but the central fact was that she fell from a window in her hotel and was badly injured on railings. Fortunately the injuries healed and she continued her career, staying with the de Basil Ballet until 1937. Her divorce proceedings against Lichine were completed; he married Riabouchinska and Rostova, later, became the Comtesse de Dampierre.

Marriages, love-affairs – sometimes of long-standing fidelity and sometimes open to a reasonably cheerful periodical re-shuffle – were a natural feature of nomadic tribal life involving a large number of young, healthy, physical human beings. Some of the men gained quite a reputation as womanizers. The girls, although they might dispense with marriage, were, like most girls of their time (and possibly more girls even now than is sometime suspected) concerned with love and romance as much as with sex. When they fell for one of the boys, their emotions were involved every bit as much as their senses. Their career ambitions and vagrant status meant that abortions were all too often the result.

Among the long-term alliances were the Hoyers (Jean Hoyer and Nathalie Branitska), the Ladres (Marian Ladre and Lara Obidenna) and of course the Grigorievs, the Riabouchinska-Lichine and Baronova-Sevastianov marriages. There was relatively little homosexuality.

De Basil had now lost the Monte Carlo connection which had provided headquarters, rehearsal and try-out facilities as well as some financial support. However, in London he was closely linked to Covent Garden and Erlangers Ltd, and there was Hurok in America.

The Ballets Russes opened their second season at the Royal Opera House in London on 11 June 1935. It was the summer of King George V's Silver Jubilee, with all that a royal jubilee in Great Britain entails in the way of social and community celebration, and the Russians were everywhere entertained and feted. One favourite rendezvous, the Savoy Grill, advertised in the Covent Garden programmes 'special Russian dishes prepared for the Russian Ballet Season' – blinis, bitkis of volaille smitane tsarsky, pirojky moscovite, varenikis . . . To some extent, however, the artistic climate had changed. Feelings of pride in local endeavour and criticisms of the Ballets Russes began to emerge.

The Dancing Times' review of the opening night's performance of *La Boutique fantasque, Les Présages* and *Le Mariage d'Aurore* included some significant strictures:

It is just two years since this company made that wonderful debut at the Alhambra . . . To some extent the triumph was repeated last year, but in the meantime we had grown more critical . . . Our own ballet at the Vic-Wells has made immense progress and whereas, at the Alhambra two years ago, the Russians appeared to be on a plane far above that occupied by any English ballet company, we found last month at Covent Garden on the opening night that they occasionally presented work far below the standard that the Vic-Wells Company have accustomed us to expect.[15]

It went on to deplore broadened and even vulgar humour, raggedness in the *corps de ballet*, and compared the Bluebird *pas de deux* of Riabouchinska and Guerard adversely with a performance of it by Markova and Harold Turner of the Vic-Wells Ballet.

The Vic-Wells Ballet had certainly consolidated their position a great deal. In November 1934 they had added to their repertoire a production of the four-act *Le Lac des cygnes* staged by the former Maryinsky *régisseur* Nicolas Sergueev, in which Markova had danced the dual role of Odette-Odile and the young Australian Robert Helpmann, who had studied with Pavlova and Novikov, was praised for his dancing and mime as Prince Siegfried. In March 1935, Margot Fonteyn, nearly sixteen and a contemporary of Baronova and Toumanova, achieved her first important role in Ashton's *Rio Grande*, and other young dancers, including Pamela May and Elizabeth Miller were beginning to be noticed. Just before the de Basil season the Vic-Wells Ballet, with private backing, and led by Markova and guest artist Anton Dolin, appeared with great success for the first time in the West End of London at the Shaftesbury Theatre (not the present one of that name) for two weeks.

London was very well provided with ballet in 1935. First came the National Ballet of Lithuania, which appeared at the Alhambra from 18 February. Its asset was the former Diaghilev prima ballerina Vera Nemtchinova, known to the popular press as the lady who insured her legs for £50,000 in the 1920s. She was credited by *The Dancing Times* for 'the purity of her line, the softness of her arabesques, the brilliance of her work *sur les pointes* . . . Her personal charm and ability to act'.[16] This company presented two novelties, the full-length Petipa *Raymonda*, which was generally considered a colossal bore, and the then rarely performed third act of *Coppélia*. Original ballets by Nicolas Zverev proved uninteresting and the Lithuanian soloists and *corps de ballet* work were mediocre.

As the year went on the Ballets Russes repertoire was closely echoed by two other visiting companies and in both cases de Basil resorted to legal action.

In July a company called the Ballets Russes de Paris, directed by E. Iskoldov and B. Daschevsky, opened at Daly's Theatre. They included in their repertoire *Les Sylphides, Prince Igor* and *Le Spectre de la rose* (a ballet due for revival that summer by the de Basil Ballet). This company was presented by Michel Kachouk, and possibly in view of the old association of de Basil and Kachouk over the Opéra Russe à Paris the Colonel was fairly tolerant of the competition. It was not in fact serious, as the standard of production was not high. The only one of its productions to prove embarrassing was Alexandre Fortunato's *Danube au printemps*, which not only had a Johann Strauss score arranged by Pierre Kolpikov but featured hussars, flower-sellers, aunts and a young niece. It was obviously perilously close to *Le Beau Danube*, and de Basil was awarded an injunction on Massine's behalf to prevent its further performance in England.

In September, the Ballets de Léon Woizikovsky opened at the London Coliseum. This season only got under way because Sir Oswald Stoll was able to get a legal discharge of an injunction applied for by de Basil on Fokine's behalf to restrain Woizikovsky from producing *Prince Igor, Petrouchka, Les Sylphides, Spectre* and *Carnaval*.

Woizikovsky had left de Basil in 1934, largely because he was upset that Massine danced all the important performances of the Miller in *Le Tricorne*, and formed this company of his own with which he toured Europe. He liked staging ballets, both as a choreographer (for which he had little talent) and, because of his exceptional memory for choreography, as a producer. He was exceedingly good to work with, and never seems to have been at odds with his dancers. It was over business matters that he had problems.

The Coliseum season was a great success. Woizikovsky's leading ladies included Tarakanova, Blinova, Ruth Chanova and the *demi-caractère* dancer Nina Raievska. The men were led by Woizikovsky himself, Froman, Eglevsky and a young protegé of Woizikovsky's, Igor Youskevitch. Youskevitch was twenty-two, born in Moscow but brought up in Yugoslavia. He was an athlete before becoming a dancer, competing with the famous athletic group Sokol. He took up ballet, appeared as partner of a Yugoslav ballerina, Xenia Grunt, and then studied with Preobrajenska.

The Woizikovsky repertoire was made up of old favourites, with especially strong productions, as might perhaps have been expected, of *Petrouchka* and *Prince Igor*. Anatole Fistoulari was orchestral director.

The de Basil season at Covent Garden ran from 11 June to 24 August and included, apart from the revival of *Le Spectre de la rose* danced by Baronova and Petrov on the penultimate night, two important events. Lubov Tchernicheva returned to the stage, in revivals of *Schéhérazade* and *Thamar*, and Nijinska choreographed *Les Cent Baisers* for Baronova.

Photographs of Tchernicheva confirm tales of her exceptional good looks. A patrician profile was matched with a great range of facial expressiveness that made her an outstanding dancer-actress and for the roles she now took she had still, in her mid-forties, sufficient flexibility and technical command. Fokine is hard on her Zobeide. He found it 'grossly exaggerated'; she 'added so much "tragedy" to it that for me it destroyed the whole originality and charm of the part'.[17] Choreographers' views on such matters have to be respected but it is only fair to Tchernicheva to recall Fokine's dislike of her husband, Serge Grigoriev, and to underline how marvellous her performances as Zobeide and Thamar seemed to other people. Lionel Bradley was a great admirer. In 1937, when he saw her as the Miller's Wife in *Tricorne*, he wrote:

All her dancing and miming has breeding in it. The imperious stance, the subtle economy of gesture, the sudden flashing eye and quick movement, all made up a portrait of distinction. This conception has a fineness and an inner dignity which needs no artificial or meretricious fire.[18]

Ernest Newman found her Thamar 'flawless in every respect, in repose no less than in action'[19] and Gordon Anthony, remembering the performances from 1976, captured an essential element of their appeal: 'In *Thamar* she gave a hair-raising performance of a sensual, homicidal queen of nymphomaniacs' while her Zobeide was 'exotic, remote and imperialistic, difficult to explain but thrilling to see . . . A fully matured and astoundingly arrogant, almost erotic, performance.'[20]

The advent of Nijinska, who had a year's contract from July 1935 to July 1936, was, as always for the dancers she worked with, an outstanding experience. No one found her easy to begin with – but none of the great choreographers of those days was easy. They were hard, they made cruel and demolishing remarks about dancers, they expected unremitting work and unquestioning commitment in rehearsal. Once Nijinska was convinced of an artist's serious purpose her guidance was invaluable. She created difficult choreography but they found it worthwhile applying themselves to it. Baronova, creating the role of the Princess in *Les Cent Baisers*, premiered at Covent Garden on 18 July 1935, was stretched technically and interpretatively, and enjoyed it. She found Nijinska remarkably helpful in showing how to work out a part, a fine teacher for artistic detail. Her admiration was such that when, the following April, *Les Noces* was revived (and given only four performances) in New York, she asked if she might work in the *corps de ballet* simply to have the experience of learning the ballet under its choreographer. De Basil was amazed – 'Everyone asks me all the time if they can dance the Swan Queen . . .' In the end she danced the role of the leading woman guest.

Les Cent Baisers had a score specially composed by Baron Frédéric d'Erlanger. In 1933, when the de Basil Ballet had stormed London, d'Erlanger, who was already sixty-five, was taken to the Alhambra by Lady Galway in the hope that it might help him through a difficult period of mourning. They saw *Les Présages* and that ballet, and Baronova, gained his allegiance. It was an important evening for the company, not only because he was to provide them with two scores but because it consolidated the Erlanger connection. He and Bruce Ottley were to play a part in the big re-shuffle in 1938.

Frédéric d'Erlanger however kept totally separate his family banking interests (he was vice-chairman of Erlangers Ltd) and his creative life, to the extent of adopting an anagrammatic pseudonym (Ferdinand Regnal) for his early compositions. According to Edwin Evans, his score for *Les Cent Baisers*, written to a programme carefully worked out in detail by Kochno from Hans Andersen's story *The Swineherd*, reminded one of his birth in Paris 'by its French elegance, clarity and effective scoring – qualities invaluable for the purposes of the ballet'.[21] Another music critic, Ernest Newman, wrote: 'The music flows along smoothly and always effectively.'[22] The score has not survived in performance, nor of course has the ballet, but they had a reasonable life and the recorded music is surprisingly pleasant. It is light in texture, well varied and reflects clearly the dramatic sequence. The designs by Jean Hugo, in apricot, cherry and black, were as much admired by some as disliked by others, and certainly forcefully memorable. The ballet provided an excellent role for Baronova and some complex solos for the men, danced by Lichine, Jasinsky and Shabelevsky.

The action followed the fairy-tale closely. A spoilt princess rejects the rose and the singing bird offered her by a princely suitor. The prince acquires from a swineherd a magic crock that plays delightful music, disguises himself as the swineherd and trades the crock to the princess for a hundred kisses. Andersen ends the story bitterly, leaving the princess discarded by both father and suitor, and Kochno and Nijinska were faithful to the unhappy ending.

Nijinska's contribution had all the ingenuity and strength one might expect – and this was one ballet that she did not manage to revise persistently, as she did so many works. Coton calls it 'a ballet with great beauty of structure'. 'The story', he writes, 'was unfolded in impeccable sequences of pure dance idiom . . . The choreography was neat and graceful with absolutely no looseness or hiatus of action.'[23] Caryl

Brahms insisted upon the close links Nijinska maintained with academic technique, stressing that the charm of the *enchaînements* lay in her use of conventional classroom steps and exercises to depict a wide range of emotion. As an example, she cites the moment when the princess is finally banished from her palace – 'her despair is caught and expressed in a single slow extended *rond de jambe tendu* – one of the loveliest crystallizations of situation within *pas* that the ballet can boast.'[24]

Another revival that season was *Les Femmes de bonne humeur* – a further case where the depth of good *demi-caractère* dancing available in the company was evident. Beaumont, not unnaturally, found it lacking in the wit and sparkle of the original production[25] but others got immense pleasure out of it. Bradley adored it – its charm never faded for him – and he wrote of Danilova 'every little coquettish movement is so exactly in keeping and so justly fitted to the music'.[26] She was supported by a delicious trio in Morosova, Grigorieva and Tchinarova.

The London season finished on 24 August 1935 and after a holiday the company once again arrived in New York. For this third season from 9 October, Hurok had managed to book them into the Metropolitan Opera House and, as he says:

Now for the first time New York really saw the ballet. This was a house of the proper size to create illusion. The stage was a dream of spaciousness, big enough and wide enough and high enough to give a ballet company room to breathe. And there is the atmosphere of the glamorous old house itself, the faded gilt and red plush, the monumental chandelier, the diamond horseshoe of boxes with their little three-leaved clovers of lights dimming long after the house lights have gone out. There are the big lobbies and the foyers. And there is Sherry's, where a proper continental custom can be observed with a drink in the entr'acte . . . New York embraced us at last.[27]

There were only sixteen performances but the season included Tchernicheva's debut in the USA in *Schéhérazade* and *Thamar*, the New York premieres of *Choreartium* and *Les Cent Baisers* and the revivals of *Les Femmes de bonne humeur*, *Le Spectre de la rose* and Massine's *Le Soleil de nuit.*

Midnight Sun (as *Le Soleil de nuit* was alternatively programmed), revived in February 1935 at the Academy of Music, Philadelphia, was Massine's first ballet (1915) for Diaghilev. It used part of Rimsky-Korsakov's music for the opera *The Snow Maiden* and was very much a

57

character ballet, with boldly patterned and coloured costumes by Michel Larionov.

Although de Basil was probably unaware of it in the excitement of a Metropolitan Opera House season, a shift in emphasis was beginning in the USA where ballet was concerned.

Balanchine had gone to America at the end of 1933 on the invitation of Lincoln Kirstein and Edward Warburg with the purpose of founding a school and company of American ballet. The school came first. Then, in December 1934, a group of Balanchine students appeared in Hartford, Connecticut, for a three-day season as The American Ballet. This was followed by a two-week season at the Adelphi Theatre in New York from 1 March 1935 and a few months later the group were engaged as the opera ballet at the Met. Some of the repertoire was new, some revived from Les Ballets 1933. The dancers included Ruthanna Boris, Annabelle Lyon, William Dollar, Eugene Loring, Lew Christensen and Paul Haakon. The foundations of American ballet were being laid.

The Ballets Russes season at the Met in October 1935 was followed by an even more ambitious cross-country tour of 25,000 miles. Boston was included early (29 October) and the *Globe* found that *Le Mariage d'Aurore* had established itself – it 'brought the crowd to a most un-Bostonian pitch of enthusiasm'. Baronova, 'now apparently developing as the most brilliant ballerina of the company', was 'called upon for an encore'.[28] It was Baronova who brought the company unexpected publicity some months later, in February 1936, by her runaway marriage to German Sevastianov. Sevastianov has a place of his own in ballet history, not only with de Basil but later with Ballet Theatre. A nephew of Konstantin Stanislavsky, born in Moscow, he had been educated in Yugoslavia at the University of Ljubljana. He emigrated to Paris and in 1934 was given an introduction to de Basil, starting to work for him as a chauffeur – a status symbol only for the Colonel, who was notorious as a reckless driver of his own cars.

An able, charming, sophisticated, good-looking young man with a sense of humour and an attractive manner, Sevastianov soon metamorphosed from chauffeur into executive secretary, learning the wiles of directorship from the Colonel and in return teaching him something of society style and acting as liaison officer for those who found de Basil difficult. He would do the same later for Sol Hurok, when he became his promotion manager.

Baronova fell in love with him quite early, but Gerry, a debatable dozen years her senior, had other attachments at the time and thought of her then, understandably, as still a child. However, by February 1936 she was seventeen and, against the wishes of her parents and of de Basil, she and Gerry walked out, leaving a note of their intentions, and were married by a magistrate in Cincinnati. A couple of years later they had a church wedding in Sydney, Australia, with Dolin and Dandré as witnesses. Headlines were made by the elopement, and even more a few days later when a lady in Paris filed a charge of bigamy against Sevastianov, claiming a previous marriage of 1928 which had in fact been dissolved.

Baronova returned to the company for the next New York season, which began at the Met on 12 April 1936. The talking point of the first night among the audience was the musical that had opened the previous evening at the Imperial Theatre. This was *On Your Toes*, produced by Dwight Deere Wiman and choreographed by Balanchine, with Tamara Geva as a temperamental Russian ballerina, Vera Barnova.

Russell Rhodes, writing about its burlesque ballet *Princesse Zenobia* in which Balanchine satirized all the popular Near Eastern dramatic ballets like *Schéhérazade* and *Thamar*, praises Geva's talent for satirical dancing and speaks of the ballet's 'impious but good-natured raillery'.[29]

Schéhérazade was in the de Basil repertoire at the Met, providing a splendid comparison with *Princesse Zenobia*, but the important event of the season was Nijinska's staging of her ballet *Les Noces* on 20 April. The production of this exciting revival was made possible by the Art of Musical Russia Inc., who provided the four singers, four pianists, mixed chorus and six percussionists. This group had rehearsed the musical side of the work for many months, performing it as a concert piece. Inevitably with *Les Noces* people felt strongly for or against it. Edwin Denby was among the enthusiasts. He wrote of it as 'one of the finest things one can see anywhere . . . It is noble, it is fierce, it is simple, it is fresh, it is thrilling'.[30] It was magnificently performed, and Nijinska was given an ovation on the first night; but because of the difficulties of providing the full complement of musical performers anywhere except at that time and in that place it never established itself in the repertoire and New York had the sole benefit of a distinguished occasion.

At the same time however Nijinska staged *Danses slaves et tziganes* (17 April). This was a two-part *divertissement* from the opera *Russalka* (succinctly described as *Gypsy* on Grigoriev's rehearsal calls) dating from the time when Nijinska was maître de ballet for L'Opéra Russe à Paris in 1931. It proved popular worldwide, and it was in this work that two celebrated guest artists interpolated solos at a Covent Garden gala on 14 July 1936. Lydia Sokolova's contribution was a Danse Russe while Mathilde Kschessinska, in an unforgettable return to the stage, danced a traditional Danse Boyard. Wearing the long embroidered sarafan and pearl-decorated headdress, she presented what was basically a simple solo with incomparable elegance and nobility of gesture and expression.

In the New York premiere and later, the *Danses slaves* were a triumph for Danilova. David Maclay reported that it suited her exactly 'for she brought life, colour and a subtle meaning to the simplest *pas de basques* and folk steps'. For the rest, he recorded the emergence of a 'most promising classical talent in young George Zoritch as the Poet in *Jardin public*'.[31] Zoritch, Moscow-born, had trained in Kovno and with Preobrajenska before joining the Ida Rubinstein Ballet. Shabelevsky was back and dancing the leading male guest in *Les Noces*. He had injured an ankle badly in *Schéhérazade* the previous October, in the famous leap from the stairs which was afterwards discontinued.

Maclay was enraptured with Baronova's Aurora – 'at each performance this lovely dancer seems to endow it with a new and yet purely classical beauty of dancing', and he liked the vigour and enthusiasm of Vera Nelidova as the Polovtsian Girl.

April 1936 to April 1937

After his break with de Basil, René Blum created a new ballet company for Monte Carlo which he called the Ballets de Monte-Carlo, with Fokine as maître de ballet and choreographer. He took this to London in 1936, settling into the Alhambra Theatre in May for a two-month season.

The company's prima ballerina was Nemtchinova but Blum had other excellent *danseuses* to offer. They included Hélène Kirsova from the de Basil Ballet, Nathalie Leslie (Krassovska) from the Ballets Russes de Paris and Maria Ruanova from the Teatro Colón in Buenos Aires. Kirsova was Danish – her real name was Ellen Wittrup – and she began her career with the Ida Rubinstein Ballet in 1931 before becoming a founder member of the Ballets Russes de Monte-Carlo. She had danced the waltz in *Les Sylphides* on the opening night at the Alhambra in 1933. P.W. Manchester, recalling her 'glorious back', speaks of that performance as 'better than anybody I ever saw, except Karsavina. It was a totally different way of doing it, but magnificent'.[1] Leslie was Russian, trained by Preobrajenska and Legat in Paris and London. She had appeared with Nijinska and Lifar and been a member of Les Ballets 1933. Ruanova was new to Europe although she had been a ballerina at the Colón since 1932.

Blum's principal male dancers included Anatole Vilzak, Maryinsky-trained and a former Diaghilev Ballet dancer, who had appeared with Ida Rubinstein and worked as maître de ballet and choreographer at the Riga Opera in Latvia, and Nemtchinova's principal partner, Anatole Oboukhov, who was also maître de ballet. They were joined by Eglevsky and by Nicholas Zverev, a Moscow *demi-caractère* dancer who had also been with the Diaghilev Ballet.

In spite of all these dancers, Sir Oswald Stoll obviously thought some additional 'known' names were needed and he hired, over Blum's head and to the great dissatisfaction of Blum's dancers, Woizikovsky, Raievska, Tarakanova and Youskevitch from the Ballets de Léon Woizikovsky, to appear with the Ballets de Monte-Carlo as guest artists in June. It was a season of prestige success which left London ballet-goers with many treasured memories and showed them new Fokine ballets in *L'Epreuve d'amour* and *Don Juan.*

Native English ballet continued to build up its challenge. The Vic-Wells Ballet constantly gained new support, and a new company, the Markova-Dolin Ballet, began with a tour towards the end of 1935, presenting a season in London at the Duke of York's Theatre in January 1936.

De Basil's star however continued to be in the ascendant. Despite all rivals London was still in love with his dancers and repertoire, and Massine was rehearsing with Toumanova the next symphonic ballet, *Symphonie fantastique*, premiered on 24 July 1936.

Symphonie fantastique was, of course, set to a programmed work by Berlioz and the ballet followed the composer's scenario – the Young Musician's vision of the Beloved, the Ball, the Pastoral scene, the nightmare of murder and judgement, the witches' sabbath. There were superb sets and costumes by Christian Bérard, the designer of *Cotillon*.

61

An outstandingly inventive artist, Bérard had the ability to create magical theatre by simple means and to emphasize a feeling of space on a stage, transfiguring the familiar into the mysterious. He co-operated closely with the makers of his costumes and was constantly concerned with the effect in movement of the materials used.

Symphonie fantastique had magnificent central roles for Massine and for Toumanova as the Beloved, which ensured the work's popularity with the audience, but the critics were very much divided. To Coton it was a grave disappointment – he was ahead of his time in craving pure dance ballet, and had almost found what he was looking for in *Choreartium*. He blames the public:

the peculiarly ovine audience . . . the abstract is strong meat and drink, much too heady for an audience carefully guided to admire correctly the limited inventiveness of the general run of popular works.

Massine, he felt, was, in *Symphonie fantastique*, 'offering them an apology for his disturbance of their mental equilibrium' in *Choreartium.*[2]

Very different views were held by other critics. Haskell wrote: 'Massine has undertaken the most extensive and complex production known to choreography and has been fully successful, attaining a greater unity of purpose than ever before.' He felt, moreover, that this work confirmed that there was now a 'Massine School' in ballet[3] – and, following through this theme in a later notice, he judged that Toumanova and Verchinina were 'the interpreters most in tune with this evolution'.[4] Verchinina certainly found her fame through the Massine symphonies. They were not the only ballets she danced – she was a stylish Chiarina in *Carnaval* and her roles included the Snow Maiden in *Soleil de nuit* and even the Street Dancer in *Beau Danube* – but she much preferred the freer, more modern movement that Massine let her introduce in the symphonies. Considering her exceptional talent, she was content with a singularly circumscribed career as a dancer, but her authority and individuality ensured her reputation. She can be seen as a pioneer, the prototype of the ballerinas who now unite classical and modern dance techniques in works by similarly catholic choreographers. One never-fulfilled project de Basil had for her was an exciting one – a revival of Massine's *Sacre du printemps* in which she would have danced the Chosen Virgin.

By a curious coincidence, *Symphonie fantastique* had close parallels in mood, theme and style with a ballet produced by the Vic-Wells Ballet five months before (February 1936) – Ashton's *Apparitions*, for which Constant Lambert had adapted Berlioz's programme for the *Symphonie fantastique* to an arrangement of Liszt music. This had been designed by Cecil Beaton, and Beaton was also the designer for a new ballet by Lichine that summer, *Le Pavillon* (11 August). Lichine was still feeling his way, still very badly needing – and well aware of needing – the kind of artistic guidance and discussion on which the Diaghilev choreographers had thrived. The book of *Le Pavillon*, a simple theme about a poet, a young girl and the spirits of the garden, was by Kochno and the music an arrangement by Dorati of Borodin piano pieces.

For Beaton it was not a happy assignment. He wrote:

There was no feeling of co-operation and at the conferences beforehand everyone would suddenly burst into Russian amongst themselves, leaving me quite in the dark as to what decisions they might be making without my knowledge.[5]

There were casting problems too. Lichine rehearsed the ballet with both Danilova and Baronova, and Danilova rather naturally expected to create the leading role. At the last minute Baronova was chosen to dance the first night and Danilova only came in on the third.

Right through the summer of 1936 the ballet world had been full of rumours about the likelihood of a second de Basil company being formed to go on an Australian tour. Thomas Armour, an American dancer from Miami who was with the Ballets de Léon Woizikovsky on the continent, wrote to Margaret Power as early as April:

I have been told de Basil really plans this year to have two companies and that Nijinska will be in charge of the second . . . It should relieve the problem of giving good roles to so many *premières danseuses*.[6]

In July he wrote that he had heard Woizikovsky had signed with de Basil to use their company as the nucleus of a second de Basil Ballet, and by 20 July contracts were being made with the dancers.

Contracts with de Basil dancers were legally detailed and covered a great deal more than the length and terms of the engagement. A typical one of 1937 mentions various company disciplines, including obligatory class with fines for non-compliance and approved rehearsal clothes ('ladies in a black Greek tunic, men in black trousers, white shirts and white stockings'); there is an undertaking by the artist to keep himself in a good and fit physical condition, to shave his beard and moustache according to instructions, and not to smoke, drink or gamble in the theatre. In 1938, during de Basil's absence, there was an additional clause – was it perhaps introduced by Victor Dandré? – stipulating that the artist should 'maintain by his behaviour that standard of dignity and conduct laid down by Educational Ballets . . .' (the company's name at that time).[7]

In August 1936 the recruited dancers were assembled in London for a three-week crash course in the repertoire, held in the Tavistock Hotel ballroom – this particular Tavistock Hotel was in the Piazza right behind the Royal Opera House. They were drawn mainly from two sources. Blinova and Froman, Nina Raievska and Woizikovsky, Sonia Woizikovska (Léon's daughter) and Igor Youskevitch, with most of the male *corps* and half the female *corps*, came from the Ballets de Léon Woizikovsky. Tchinarova, Guerard and a delightful young newcomer from Paris, Nina Youchkevitch, with the other girls, had all been with de Basil at Covent Garden during the summer. Kirsova returned from the Ballets de Monte-Carlo to be joint prima ballerina with Blinova, and Jean Hoyer was appointed *régisseur général*. The repertoire included most of the popular de Basil ballets as well as two of Woizikovsky's own, *Port Said* and *L'Amour sorcier*. The conductors were Jascha Horenstein and Ivan Clayton. There was a good deal of resentment among members of the main company, who were already under severe pressure owing to the number of performances and rehearsals and who therefore objected to giving up even more time to teaching roles to the newcomers.

This second company sailed from Tilbury on the SS *Moldavia* at the end of the month. The impact of the three de Basil tours on Australia will be described in greater detail later. They were tremendously popular in the Antipodes and their existence of course freed the main company for the most ambitious USA tour of all – seven months of mainly one-night stands reaching almost every state.

Before going to America they went to Berlin. Eduard Duisberg, the artistic director of the Scala Cinema, was interested in booking ballet, so from 1 October 1936 the de Basil Ballet appeared there for a sensationally successful two-week season. The emphasis on modern dance throughout Germany had caused a complete decline of interest in classical ballet and the season proved a triumphant and historic reversal of this trend. Joseph Lewitan, ballet critic and editor of *Der Tanz*, wrote:

People of all classes, from the most sophisticated to the man in the street, filled the theatre, with its 3000 seats, to capacity every night.[8]

and the dancers won attention both from the Nazi leaders and the ex-Crown Prince and Princess of Germany. Hitler proposed to attend, although this visit was cancelled, and he was later reported to have a painting of Riabouchinska – a regulation beautiful blonde – hanging in his Berlin apartment. Goebbels was of course something of a balletomane. A pupil of Eduardova's, Irina Kosmovska, signed a contract to join the company in July 1937 and proved to be one of their most gifted comediennes.

The opening of the US tour of 1936–7 came with an eleven-day season at the Met beginning on 28 October 1936, during which *Symphonie fantastique* was given its New York premiere. Russell Rhodes was enthusiastic, describing it as 'Massine's finest work as a choreographer . . . immeasurably a finer contribution than his *Les Présages* . . . and theatrically more exciting and imaginative than his *Choreartium*.' *Le Pavillon* was shown and Rhodes was kind in his comments. He found that 'many little twists, gestures and positions' of a novel character made it 'a sheer delight as well as a matter of technical interest'.[9] Another revival, which for many people had considerable charm, was Massine's *Cimarosiana*. A *divertissement* ballet with designs by José Maria Sert, it had originally been part of Diaghilev's production of Cimarosa's opera *Le astuzie femminile* in 1924.

Coton describes its stages – an opening *pas de trois* for 'a male dancer with unusual fluidity of line' and two girls with 'enough elevation to help create the illusion that the dancing is a transposition of music into water-forms, as in the counterpoint of fountains'. This was danced, when he saw it on the opening night of the Covent Garden season in 1937, by Grigorieva, Rostova and Zoritch. Then came a Sicilian *pas de six* followed by a Tarantelle (Marra and Lazovsky) – 'one of Massine's best miniatures of speed and gaiety'. The *pas de quatre* (Nelidova, Tresahar, Bouslov and Ismailov) was an 'exercise in support work' and led to a second *pas de trois*, 'a beautiful demonstration piece of fine character work built around a maze of lifts' and danced by Danilova, Jasinsky and Petrov. The ensemble Contre-danse prefaced the leading *pas de deux* (Riabouchinska and Lichine) which had 'a Petipa-like quality in its rigorous simplicities of pattern based on the circle and triangle and was followed by a joyous finale'.[10]

The New York season included an Election Day on 3 November, and to avoid poor houses Hurok made a special announcement: 'Sol Hurok invites you to spend an afternoon with the Ballet.' This began at 12.30 pm with a luncheon (vodka, a talk by Irving Deakin and a copy of his book *To the Ballet* all included) followed by a matinée of *Le Lac des cygnes, Schéhérazade* and *Le Beau Danube*. Election results were to be announced from the stage – and the total cost was $3.75.

After New York the company set off on the road again. First stop was Philadelphia, on 9 November. By now they had a special friend there – Henry Clifford, the Curator of Paintings at the Philadelphia Museum. Clifford is remembered, by Baronova among others, as an extremely cultured, charming and brilliant European-American – he kept a summer home in Italy, near Florence. He and his intelligent and witty wife Esther (Rowland) had always been keen followers of ballet. Now he became in effect the company's artistic director, supplying guidance and advice from which Lichine and others greatly profited.

That winter tour was the longest and most arduous the company ever undertook in North America. Their circus caravan was a special ten-car train which carried the dancers, hairdressers, wardrobe personnel and caterers. It would arrive at some city (Cedar Rapids, perhaps, Amarillo, Texas, Mobile, Alabama or Spartanburg, South Carolina) in the late afternoon and everyone would go straight to the auditorium. While the stage staff moved the sets in and the wardrobe was sorted out Tchernicheva held class on stage and Kurtz or Dorati united locally recruited players with the travelling nucleus orchestra. Papa Grigoriev saw to it that the performance was prepared. Always he stressed the importance of the paying public: 'The main thing is that when the curtain goes up we present the ballet to the audience.' After the performance the dancers found a coffee shop or drugstore and ate hamburgers, then went back to the theatre for an all-night rehearsal. Sleep had to be fitted in during the next day's journey. Card-playing was the chief entertainment on the train, endless games of gin rummy or poker for low stakes. Money was always short. Everyone was on half pay while travelling by train – on a sea journey no one was paid at all – but some managed to wheedle extra cash for tips. There were impromptu concerts, with singing and guitar-playing. Some of the mothers worked for the wardrobe and were kept busy sewing, darning, laundering. There were pets to look after – dogs and cats, rabbits and tortoises, and the occasional more exotic parrot or marmoset. De Basil had two monkeys. Occasionally a dog or cat sauntered on to the stage during performance and proved difficult to dislodge. Massine's affectionately remembered dog Smokey took part in *Prince Igor* one night and a terrier puppy of Rostova's gambolled happily through *Les Sylphides*. When that happened, fines were imposed and paid without question. Puppies or kittens were frequently left with ballet fans when a tour came to an end, particularly when the next stop was a country with quarantine regulations. Smokey, to everyone's grief, disappeared forever one night in Philadelphia in November 1936.

There were physical ailments and emotional crises to be sorted out on these journeys – quarrels, reconciliations and much laughter in between. The company moved in and out of different weather conditions and in February 1937 faced up cheerfully to an 'act of God' that worked out as excellent publicity. About 150 miles from Eugene, Oregon near Delta, California the special train was snowbound for 52 hours. Food supplies ran low, but the dancers kept their morale high, playing snowballs and having contests for snow sculpture. The Cuban Alberto Alonso, small in stature, delighted with his first sight of snow, leapt on to it and completely disappeared.

Wherever they went, the zest for life and experience possessed by these dancers was undimmed. Performances, however, were what counted most. Valentin Zeglovsky declares that personal grievances were forgotten when dancers went on stage: 'Seldom have I known an indifferent performance through anything but extreme fatigue or illness.'[11] There was camaraderie as well as rivalry, loyalty as well as intrigue. Disappointments and grumbles could always be shared with fellow dancers. There were always shoulders to cry on, just as there were always friends ready to celebrate a success.

The company's devotion to the dance triumphed over everything. This is a point that cannot be overstressed. The commitment of dancers in the 'thirties, dancers of all nationalities, to ballet was total. Their belief in it as a vocation affected every aspect of their lives and temperaments. Where, as an historian, one accepts the universal importance of religion as a motivating force in the medieval and renaissance world, one must also accept the overriding importance of the ballet to the dancers of the 'thirties and 'forties. They cared so passionately about ballet that to dance, even in small roles, in the *corps de ballet*, the great ballets of the repertoire, was a privilege. To work with choreographers such as Fokine, Balanchine, Massine or Nijinska they were willing to forgo financial return, to scrape along on a pittance, to work all hours of the day or night, well or ill, in any conditions. Because of this they fought each other for roles, they clung with all their might to the roles they had acquired, they intrigued for places, wept over unkind words or inadequate billing or lack of publicity, quarrelled over partners who stole their limelight or failed to show them off to their best advantage, or with conductors who, they felt, ruined their performances by adopting unsympathetic tempi. Because of this the mothers squabbled and jockeyed for the positions of their daughters. Also because of this they produced performances that were glowing with vitality, capable of infecting audiences with their own passion.

April 1937 to March 1938

The winter tour of 1936–7 made very great demands on Danilova. After an operation in Berlin in October 1936, Baronova had not been able to dance. Toumanova shared the first part of the American tour with Danilova but remained in California, partly for health reasons, partly, in her own words, 'to devote more time to my education and artistic development'.[1] Danilova carried the weight of the repertoire from then until Baronova returned (at the Met on 9 April 1937). This time the company gave only five performances in New York, but these included one that was billed as their thousandth.

Changes, new beginnings and re-shuffles were in the air. In New York Massine was approached by David Libidins on behalf of a new company that was being set up. This was being organized by a Moscow-born financier, Serge Denham (Sergei Dokouchaiev), with backing from World Art Inc., a company belonging to the wealthy Julius Fleischmann of Cincinnati (Yeast) who had a particular admiration for Massine as an artist. Massine was offered, and accepted, the position of artistic director, the title he had always coveted but never wrenched out of de Basil. The company was to be an enlargement of René Blum's Ballets de Monte-Carlo which Blum was finding it difficult, financially, to continue. He sold it to World Art Inc. for $30,000 and the new organization was therefore able to use the title Ballet Russe de Monte Carlo.

De Basil was meanwhile announcing to the press in New York that Fokine had signed a two-year contract with him and would join the company at the end of June. Obviously de Basil must have been aware that it was unlikely Massine would extend his contract beyond its expiry date in September 1937. It was of paramount importance that the ballet should not be left without an experienced and respected maître de ballet and choreographer. There had been a preliminary legal skirmish between Massine and de Basil the previous year. In August 1936 the Vacation Court in London had heard an application for an injunction on behalf of Massine against de Basil to restrain the performance of his ballets in Australia by the second company. The case came to nothing, as everyone left England. The second company went on happily pleasing Australian audiences with *Boutique, Présages, Beau Danube, Scuola di ballo, Contes russes* and *Soleil de nuit*. The issue was unresolved however and de Basil knew that Massine, with his notable persistence and determination, would resume the case when they returned to England. This was the background of his invitation to Fokine and no doubt he was delighted at Fokine's acceptance. It gave him a famous replacement for Massine.

Fokine's ballets had been a vital part of the de Basil repertoire from the beginning but none of them had been supervised by Fokine himself. They were staged by Grigoriev with assistance in some cases from Woizikovsky. Fokine had obviously had mixed feelings about this, particularly in view of his long-standing animosity towards Grigoriev. When the company first appeared in the USA, however, Vitale Fokine declared that although his father's ballets were somewhat altered and even mutilated they were nevertheless superior to anything New Yorkers had seen in many years.[2] This, naturally, did not displease their choreographer. Also, some of the de Basil principals went to Fokine's studio whenever they were in New York and he admired their talents. As time went on, he began to feel that he should in some way profit by the great success his ballets were having worldwide and decided to sue de Basil. Litigation is a recurring theme not only in the affairs of the de Basil Ballet but throughout the history of Russian Ballet abroad. The rare exception, such as Vova Grigoriev, might disapprove, maintaining that court cases were demoralizing for the dancers, who neither liked nor understood what was going on, and bad for the reputation of a company whether or not it was in the right. The majority of directors and choreographers however flew to their lawyers in the way people later flew to their analysts, often with the same kind of inconclusive results. It was an escape valve for emotions. Once they were assured that legal sniping had begun they could get on with the day-to-day business of producing ballet. The Fokine-versus-de Basil case was resolved amicably, and when Fokine and de Basil met, they found enough common ground to become friends. Out of this friendship came their agreement: that Fokine should join the company to revise his older ballets and create new ones. He would join some six months before the end of Massine's term.

There was a Paris season in 1937, because the Théâtre des Champs-Elysées, one of the few suitable houses for ballet in the city, was open again. Then the company made its Italian debut with four performances in Florence for the Maggio Musicale. Riabouchinska and Lichine stayed at the Cliffords' villa near Florence. Esther Clifford's first meeting with the company – before, she had 'been content to be *audience* and have the beautiful show put on for *me* and not know about their aching toes and aching hearts' – was when she and Henry arrived on Russian Easter Eve, and found celebrations going on.

David had found a Russian teashop in Florence, had ordered *koklitch* and *paska*, and we discovered that we were giving a party after the Easter service. So the first time I saw them, *en masse* out of costume, was when I was walking round the Russian church with a candle in my hand and then up at our house, where I was shocked to see the gods of my idolatry dancing plain ballroom dances to the music of our little wind-up gramophone.[3]

Russian festivals were always kept. As Highland Scots people worldwide quote nostalgically from the *Canadian Boat Song*:

> and still the blood is strong, the heart is Highland,
> and we, in dreams, behold the Hebrides . . .[4]

so Russians never lose identity. Many at that time still lingeringly hoped for a return to Imperial Russia – it was, after all, barely twenty years since the Revolution – but even without that they were deeply involved with their origins. Their native food and drink, their native songs and music, their native customs and traditions, remained always dear to them.

After the Florence performances, which were a great success, the company went to London. It was Coronation Year for George VI, who had inherited his brother's coronation arrangements after the Abdication, and Beecham organized an opera and ballet season at Covent Garden. The ballet first appeared in two operas during June 1937: *Prince Igor* and a production of Gluck's *Orphée*. This last, apparently, was an extraordinary mixture, in which the music critics much preferred the ballet's contribution to the opera's. Richard Capell wrote, about the third-act ballet arranged by Lichine and danced by most of the company's principals, 'here, suddenly, the production became finely distinguished. Gluck's conventional set of dances was rendered in a properly chilly way with an agreeable taste of rococo classicism.[5]

The staging of the opera, from the design point of view, was dull and dowdy, but the ballet appeared wearing exotic Karinska costumes in layered shades of colour, new and glamorous and wildly out of keeping with the rest of the production.

It was also an evening when the audience was fairly equally divided between opera and ballet enthusiasts, alternately bored and interested at different moments. But the ballet won (and presumably the opera audience left) when the short *Orphée* was followed by *Le Beau Danube*. As *The Times* reported:

After an interval the orchestra struck up the cheerful strains of Johann Strauss, and the dancers could have the stage to themselves in *Le Beau Danube*, and the gallery could greet each of its favourites on his or her entry with a round of applause as they do at the Halls.[6]

'Only Russian dancers', wrote the *Evening News*' critic, W. McNaught, 'could rise to the delicious effrontery of giving us Johann Strauss on top of Gluck . . .'[7]

The amount of ballet on show in London continued to be substantial. This Coronation year of 1937 saw additions to the Vic-Wells Ballet repertoire by both Ashton and de Valois. Margot Fonteyn danced Giselle, partnered by Robert Helpmann, and the virtuoso soubrette Mary Honer received considerable praise. Ballet Rambert, enlarged from its Ballet Club beginnings, staged a West End season at the Duchess Theatre in February and March. Ballets by Antony Tudor and Andrée Howard had been added to its earlier Ashton repertoire.

The Markova-Dolin Ballet appeared in the suburbs, at the King's Theatre, Hammersmith, near enough for all ballet-goers to visit. Nijinska had joined them as maître de ballet and their repertoire included her rarely danced ballets *Les Biches* and *La Bien-aimée*. Blum's Ballets de Monte-Carlo were again in Great Britain. This time they appeared at the Coliseum in London in May and June, with more new ballets by Fokine, particularly *Les Elements*, and an outstanding new principal in the Texas American Nana Gollner. Gollner had danced briefly in the *corps de ballet* of the de Basil Ballet in 1936. Now with Blum she was acclaimed for her interpretations of Odette and Swanilda.

Fokine joined de Basil as arranged at the end of June 1937, so the ballet season that began at Covent Garden on 1 July saw the beginning of his work with the company. He himself felt that the dancers were unco-operative in his attempts to re-burnish the revivals:

It was extremely difficult for me to inspire them. For many years everything had gone along successfully and with seeming correctness; then suddenly Fokine appeared and began to change, criticize, and force them to re-learn their roles.[8]

From the beginning, however, the difference seemed noticeable to the critics. *Schéhérazade* was the first to benefit. Ernest Newman wrote:

The company rises brilliantly to the occasion . . . No flaw slurred the timing or blurred the harmony of the corps de ballet movements . . . Gentility was almost banished from their part in the amorous orgy.[9]

Papillons had been revived in America and proved popular. For the benefit of stage-hands, who got thoroughly confused between sets marked *Pavillon, Papillons* and *Cotillon*, it was dubbed *Butterflies*. A revival of *Cléôpatra*, for Tchernicheva, Danilova and Shabelevsky, had been tried out occasionally during the American tour, in Philadelphia, Newark or Indianapolis, and was staged in London on 27 July. This was its only performance, although Bradley felt it had dated less than he expected.[10] Its failure was perhaps due to the amorphous score attributed to Arensky, Glazounov, Glinka, Moussorgsky, Rimsky-Korsakov, Tanaiev and Tcherepnine . . .

Over *L'Oiseau de feu* Fokine was in some despair. The choreographic version was surprisingly accurate:

In spite of the fact that everything was transferred without any written directions from one generation of dancers to another by word of mouth or to be more exact from feet to feet, I recognized all my steps. Only the groupings had disintegrated and the climax seemed to be entirely different.

The interpretation was the real trouble:

Everything seemed to have lost its former force, characteristics and expressiveness and its former consistency.

The performance was lackadaisical, it had no gaiety – 'the smile had left the ballet'.[11]

Again, Fokine's presence was acknowledged by the critics. *The Times* found that:

Under Fokine's guidance the magic works again ... There is no suggestion of staleness or routine ... It was as it should be, all poetry and fairytale ... In the details, the company have recaptured the original inspiration. Köstchei's monsters are once more terrifying, the maidens have found their old simplicity.[12]

The second performance however brought disaster for Danilova, when Massine accidentally let her slip in the opening scene and she landed awkwardly on point. Eric Johns described it:

She collapsed in Massine's arms. He carried her off, limp as a corpse ... The stage was empty. The curtain was still up ... the orchestra continued playing to the end of the first scene and then the princesses came on ... The ballet proceeded until the cue drew near for Danilova's reappearance ... Massine produced the magic feather and waved it to summon the aid of the Firebird ... Danilova stepped out onto the stage and was greeted by a shout of welcome and relief.[13]

Danilova herself thought she would never dance again, but fortunately it was a matter of torn ligaments rather than broken tendons and was healed in about six weeks.

Fokine was preparing a new ballet, *Le Coq d'or*, but it was planned for later in the year. The premiere on 15 July 1937 was Lichine's *Francesca da Rimini*, a ballet for Tchernicheva that owed its existence to Henry Clifford's devotion to Italian art. The music was an obvious choice, Tchaikovsky's Fantasy Overture, and Clifford worked out a libretto from the tale of Paolo and Francesca. This was probably based on Gabriele d'Annunzio's tragedy, which was adapted for an opera by Riccardo Zandonai. Certainly the scenario reads like opera: it is a melodramatic tale of love, rivalry and tragic death. Francesca has been promised to Gianciotto Malatesta but falls in love with his handsome brother Paolo, sent to woo her by proxy. The marriage with Malatesta goes forward but Paolo and Francesca, following the example of

Lancelot and Guinevere, betray Malatesta by becoming lovers. The brothers fight and Paolo dies. Francesca kills herself by falling on her husband's sword.

The story suited Lichine's creative talents best in the wronged and vengeful character of the ugly Malatesta (Marc Platov), in the grotesque dances of his dwarfs and in the final duel between Malatesta and Paolo (Petrov). However, he achieved an effective lyrical duet for Francesca's vision of Guinevere and Lancelot, expressively danced by Danilova and Jasinsky. The feeling and dramatic power of the ballet derived greatly from the artistic discoveries that Clifford had helped Lichine to make in the art galleries of Florence and the churches of the Tuscan hill towns. The set and costumes, by the young English artist Oliver Messel, who had designed the costumes for the historic film of *Romeo and Juliet* with Norma Shearer and Leslie Howard produced by Irving Thalberg in 1936, were very beautiful to look at although stylistically vague.

It was a controversial production and ballet is never the worse for an element of controversy. Horace Horsnell spoke of its visual splendours, compulsive music, magnificent dancing.[14] Bradley found it 'tremendously exciting and alive. Lichine has at last found himself and produced something which he obviously really felt to be worth doing.'[15] Coton disliked it intensely, although allowing that the finale 'came near to atoning for the earlier sterility of the work.'[16] Newman quarrelled with it from a musician's point of view: 'It costs [the musician] a violent mental effort to follow the music in conjunction with a totally different literary idea.'[17]

What was never in question was Tchernicheva's creation of Francesca, a role completely identified with her over the rest of her performing life. It was a total contrast to Zobeide and Thamar, and she was able to infuse it with rapture, tenderness and terror. Coton found that 'she elevated the action into poetry' in the second movement,[18] where she mimed her secret love for Paolo, and a fellow dancer, Zeglovsky, corroborates this, describing her as 'pure magic'.[19]

In July 1937, although Massine continued to appear for the sake of his public and his contract at Covent Garden, he was featuring as the plaintiff in what *The Times* described as 'a dispute over copyright of the Russian Ballet'. This was a case that confused everyone connected with it. Ballet was not a subject understood by those outside, however professional they were in legal matters. They tried, all the same, to work it out in recognizable legal terms, according to English law.

The dispute of course followed on from the previous summer's writ, which had been before the Vacation Judge when 'the parties left the country, and it was hoped that they might come to an agreement, but they had not done so . . . The plaintiff [Massine] has now asked for damages in respect of the presentation of the ballet last autumn.' De Basil, the defendant, 'had applied for an injunction to restrain Massine from asserting that he was the owner of the copyright of the Russian Ballet at present being performed at Covent Garden'.[20]

The eminent Sir Patrick Hastings, K.C., appearing for de Basil, divided the ballets in question (without naming any of them) into three epochs: those before 1932, when Massine was 'not in the defendant's employment'; those from 1932 to 1934, when he was 'under contract with the defendants, the terms being sufficiently clearly, but not very clearly, defined in writing in the form of two letters'; and those from 1934 onwards, when he was 'under very clearly defined terms of contract with them'.[21]

Judgement was given on 30 July, by Mr Justice Luxmoore. First, he tried to clear legal minds about the construction of a ballet. It was composed of four or five parts. The elements were music, the story or libretto, the choreography or notation of the dancing, the scenery and the costumes. No copyright existed in the ballets as composite entities. He then worked out the relationship that existed at various times between Massine and de Basil. They had been associated from January 1932 but there was no agreement between them until November 1932. Then two letters had been written which confirmed that Massine would render services from 15 January to 15 June each year as maître de ballet, choreographer and chief dancer, and produce new ballets as needed. This arrangement continued until 10 August 1934, when a more formal contract was signed. This specified that Massine had agreed to give his services as choreographer, *collaborateur artistique*, maître de ballet and dancer. Four of the pre-1932 ballets were presented before that date and four afterwards. De Basil had paid for the right to perform the first four, but not for the copyright. He had also paid for the right to present the four pre-1932 ballets which had been staged after 10 August 1934, for three years from the date of first performance or until Massine ceased to be employed by him. That term would finish in September 1937 but de Basil had an option to buy and intended to exercise it.

The judge ruled that the agreements between Massine and de Basil were legally 'service agreements'; that the first four pre-1932 ballets were Massine's copyright; that the copyright in the next four pre-1932 ballets was vested in Massine subject to de Basil's right to acquire it on option payment; and that the copyright in the remaining ballets was vested in de Basil.

This verdict would seem to have meant that de Basil owned, without question, those ballets created by Massine for him from 1932 onwards, i.e. *Jeux d'enfants, Beach, Les Présages, Scuola di ballo, Choreartium, Union Pacific, Le Bal, Jardin public* and *Symphonie fantastique*. He could continue presenting until 1937, and later if he paid the option fee, the pre-1932 ballets which had been staged for him after the agreement of 10 August 1934, i.e. *Les Femmes de bonne humeur, Cimarosiana* and *Le Soleil de nuit*. (Four ballets were mentioned in this category, and perhaps the fourth was *Contes russes* which, however, was staged on 7 August 1934, just before the contract date.)

He would lose, when he lost Massine, the other pre-1932 ballets; four were mentioned: *Le Beau Danube, La Boutique fantasque, Le Tricorne* and *Les Matelots.* Some ballets of course were already not being performed, e.g. *Beach, Le Bal, Jardin public, Contes russes* and *Les Matelots.*

For de Basil, *Le Beau Danube* was the real problem. Without Massine, *Le Tricorne* was of little interest to him. *Boutique* he could, reluctantly, do without, especially if Danilova, as seemed likely, left at the same time as Massine. *Beau Danube*, however, was enormously popular, and very much associated with artists such as Baronova, Riabouchinska and Lichine who were still with his company. Certainly Danilova was the most famous exponent of the Street Dancer but it had never been exclusively identified with her; Tarakanova, Zorina, Baronova, Tchinarova, Kirsova, Blinova and even Verchinina had all danced it. Obviously some thought had to be given as to how to circumvent its loss, if that were at all possible – but for the present the legal ruling was followed.

The day after the verdict came the last performance of the summer season, and with passions well aroused it was a heartbreaking twenty-four hours for Massine's public. They knew that Massine would not reappear in the September season – he was going on a diplomatic holiday until he had to rejoin the company under Hurok's agreements for the US winter season. For them it was the end of an era, and for the de Basil Ballet it was a curtain on Act II – Act I had finished when

Balanchine left. At the matinée, when Baronova danced the Street Dancer in *Beau Danube* in lieu of the still injured Danilova, the gallery stayed, shouting and applauding Massine, until a fireman managed to clear them out of the theatre. In the evening Danilova, in the audience, was given an enthusiastic reception. *Boutique* was put first on the programme – with Riabouchinska in Danilova's role – and for Massine's admirers this naturally looked like a malicious reprisal on the Colonel's part. De Basil hardly helped matters when he took a curtain at the end of the evening, brought Massine on stage and insisted on shaking hands. Most people read the gesture as hypocritical. It may indeed have been dictated by a natural instinct towards putting a good face on a dispute with an eye to the press. It may even have had something in it of the professional soldier's respect for a worthy opponent; but with feelings running high it did him no good with the audience. They jammed Floral Street, into which the stage door opens, to see Massine leave, wishing him good luck and assuring him of their lasting loyalty.

The dancers went on holiday, but the Colonel had a date to meet the second company in Marseilles on 13 August. Their long and triumphant tour of Australia and New Zealand had ended in July, when they embarked on the *Strathnaver* on their return journey. Woizikovsky wanted to keep them together in Europe and de Basil was willing to arrange further contracts for the rest of the year.

Although they were all very tired, there was only a fortnight's break before they opened at the Scala in Berlin on 1 September for a month's season. They were advertised as the 'Ballett des Zarens', but Eduard Duisberg wrote a long introduction in the programme, linking them with the de Basil Ballet which had been so successful at his theatre the previous year and, through Woizikovsky, with Diaghilev and with Poland.

Kirsova had decided to settle in Australia and Guerard had gone back to the main company. Ruth Chanova was now engaged, and danced *Spectre* and Columbine in *Carnaval* very well. *Le Beau Danube* had had to be dropped from the repertoire because of the result of the copyright case.

The main company returned to Covent Garden in September, but under a different arrangement. Bruce Ottley had formed a syndicate, the Covent Garden Musical Productions, to sublease the opera house

77

each year from September to February from Beecham's London and Provincial Opera Company Ltd. One of Beecham's favourite recurring projects, however, was featured during the season in a production of *Les Dieux mendiants* (17 September) with choreography by Lichine. Beecham had arranged and orchestrated the Handel score for Diaghilev, and he conducted the de Basil staging. This was mildly successful, although it was very much a rush job, but the other new Lichine ballet, *Le Lion amoureux*, which had a score by Karol Rathaus and designs by Pierre Roy, was on the whole a failure. It was Fokine's *Le Coq d'or* (23 September) that triumphed, and was to be a staple in the repertoire for ever after.

Apparently there was a proposal, even before Fokine's engagement with the company, that de Basil should revive the opera-ballet version of *Le Coq d'or* (staged by Fokine for Diaghilev in 1914) for the Coronation Opera season. Nathalie Gontcharova prepared sketches for scenery and costumes with which Fokine was delighted. He first proposed to de Basil that they should try to follow the opera-ballet production with a straight ballet version which the ballet company could continue to perform, and then asked if de Basil could get permission from Covent Garden to shelve the opera-ballet idea altogether and let him concentrate on a new ballet.

This de Basil arranged with Beecham. Fokine started selecting from and editing the Rimsky-Korsakov score, first with Dorati and then with Nicolas Tcherepnine, and it was Tcherepnine who decided which musical instruments should be substituted for the voices of singers and chorus. This musical version came in for very heavy criticism from *The Times'* critic who, because of the cutting of words, vocal music, dialogue, recitative and the compression of the orchestral score, wrote: 'Can these ravages be called art? . . . The composer's intentions no longer count for anything if he is dead.'[22]

Fokine, bitterly hurt because of the care he and Tcherepnine had taken, replied:

I have altered the intentions of the composer less than he altered the intentions of Pushkin . . . and the suite upon which the present ballet is arranged is a much less curtailed version than the one which was made during the composer's own lifetime . . . [23]

However, from the point of view of ballet-lovers the work was a delight. The story, with its charming alliance of earthy humour and

ABOVE LEFT *Cotillon:* Tamara Toumanova
ABOVE RIGHT *Cotillon:* Lubov Rostova and Valentin Froman
TOP *La Concurrence:* posed rehearsal photograph, Monte Carlo, 1932
(foreground) Tamara Toumanova with Olga Morosova, Lubov Rostova,
Edna Tresahar, Doris Sonne and Natalie Strakhova
(background) Colonel W. de Basil, René Blum,
Boris Kochno, George Balanchine

ABOVE *Jeux d'enfants:* Tatiana Riabouchinska and David Lichine
TOP *Jeux d'enfants:* Tamara Toumanova, Lubov Rostova and André Eglevsky

ABOVE *La Boutique fantasque:* Tamara Toumanova and Roman Jasinsky
TOP LEFT *Le Beau Danube:* Alexandra Danilova and Leonide Massine
TOP RIGHT *Le Beau Danube:* Irina Baronova and Yurek Shabelevsky

Le Mariage d'Aurore:
Irina Baronova

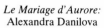

Le Mariage d'Aurore:
Alexandra Danilova

Le Mariage d'Aurore:
Tamara Toumanova

Les Présages: final tableau including Irina Baronova,
Tatiana Riabouchinska, Nina Verchinina
and David Lichine

ABOVE *Les Cent Baisers:* Irina Baronova and Paul Petrov
TOP *Union Pacific:* group including Leonide Massine,
André Eglevsky and Sono Osato

Choreartium
THIS PAGE:

ABOVE Second movement.
Group including Tamara
Grigorieva
LEFT Group including
David Lichine

OPPOSITE:

TOP Nina Verchinina
FAR LEFT Hélène Kirsova
NEAR LEFT Tamara
Toumanova

ABOVE *Symphonie fantastique:* Tamara Toumanova and Leonide Massine
TOP LEFT *Schéhérazade:* Lubov Tchernicheva
TOP RIGHT *L'Oiseau de feu:* Alexandra Danilova

supernatural poetry, suited balletic treatment admirably. The Astrologer, a cunning magician, gives old King Dodon an enchanted Golden Cockerel who is guaranteed to warn him of danger. In due course he has to go to war but finds that his opponent is the fabulous Queen of Shemakhan, who consents to become his wife. The Astrologer, promised a reward, asks for the Queen and when Dodon refuses the Golden Cockerel pecks him to death. Queen and Cockerel vanish, and the immortal Astrologer points the moral – that dishonesty and ingratitude will be duly punished.

For a strict supporter of ballet as dance, such as Coton, the work relied too much on mime, characterization and decor[24] – the interesting dancing was largely limited to marvellous roles for Baronova as the Queen of Shemakhan, which she indelibly stamped as her own, and Riabouchinska, equally perfectly cast as the Golden Cockerel. But those who were happy with dramatic ballet revelled in the gorgeous colour and unity of Gontcharova's settings and costumes, in the pageantry and comedy, all too rare in Fokine ballets, and in the superb character work of the young, red-haired American from Seattle, Marc Platov (Marc Platt), unrecognizable in a grotesque make-up as King Dodon. Fokine himself said: 'Only when Dimitri Rostov later took his place did it become apparent that it was possible to be still more Russian – Rostov I considered to be a great Dodon.'[25] Harcourt Algeranov, an English character dancer who had a distinguished career with many companies including Pavlova's, was equally striking as the enigmatic Astrologer.

During the summer of 1937 the company had not only the stimulus of collaborating on a new creation with Fokine. The great Maryinsky *danseur noble*, Pierre Vladimirov, also worked with them as a guest teacher. Vladimirov had danced the Prince in Diaghilev's *Sleeping Princess* in 1921 and settled in New York in 1934. A notable stylist, he was an excellent influence in a company that had been criticized as lacking strictly classical *premiers danseurs*, and Petrov and Jasinsky both benefited. His wife, Doubrovska, came to London with him but danced only twice, as guest artist, in *Les Sylphides* and the Bluebird *pas de deux*. She seemed to critics to be too nervous to do justice to her great technical accomplishment.[26] Another Diaghilev ballerina, Alice Nikitina, created the Queen in the unfortunate *Lion amoureux*. She was light and slight, according to Bradley, with an 'ugly but piquant

79

face' . . . 'if she could shed her mannerisms of the variety stage', he wrote, rather brutally, 'she might well alternate in roles with Riabouchinska'.[27] However, she did not add to the existing complications of too many ballerinas in competition for leading roles by remaining. She disliked the choreography she was given, deplored the brief preparation time and was upset that other dancers should learn the role she was creating.[28]

The autumn season of 1937 at Covent Garden ended on 9 October and for this last performance the queues started as early as 10 o'clock the previous morning. It was Danilova's last London appearance with the company and she danced *Le Lac des cygnes*. There was also a presentation to de Basil, of a cheque and an eighteenth-century silver cockerel symbolizing *Le Coq d'or*, which had been subscribed to by all sections of the house and, at its own request, by the company.

Immediately after, they sailed for New York where they opened at the Met on 22 October. New Yorkers enjoyed the splendours of *Le Coq d'or*. Russell Rhodes was delighted that Fokine had an ovation at curtain call, praised Riabouchinska's 'rare spirit and amazing pointe-work' and Baronova's 'vivacity, dramatic pantomime and flawless technique'. It was 'her own gala occasion'. Platov 'proved himself an admirable comic'.[29] *Les Dieux mendiants* was preferred to *Francesca da Rimini* because of the charming romantic dancing of Danilova and Shabelevsky. *Symphonie fantastique* and *Choreartium* succeeded, in spite of Toumanova's absence, because of Baronova's greatly improved acting.

The winter tour of the USA in 1937–8 followed the usual lines and is remembered principally for the company's emotional farewell to Massine. He gave his final performance in *Le Beau Danube* during the matinée at the San Francisco Opera House on Sunday 30 January 1938.

Meanwhile the second company was having a hard winter tour of its own in Europe. After Berlin it went to other German cities. During October 1937 it visited Cologne, Leipzig, Düsseldorf and Frankfurt and spent two weeks at Hamburg, appearing at the Ufa Palast Cinema. Its link with de Basil was its managing director, Jacques Lidji, who went backwards and forwards – his reappearances usually heralded arguments about salary cuts. The dancers hung on because of loyalty to Woizikovsky and the dangling carrot of a possible London season.

This did not materialize. Bruce Ottley's syndicate at Covent Garden had engaged an ice ballet show, *Rhapsody on Ice*. This was a new craze, linked with the ice-star of the cinema, Sonja Henje, and there had been a successful show, *St Moritz*, staged at the London Coliseum. *Rhapsody on Ice* elbowed out the second de Basil company and it continued its itinerant life in western Europe. Blinova and Froman left it and Nemtchinova arrived. Her repertoire included the works she still danced excellently such as *Le Lac des cygnes*; she was far less suited to the more romantic or modern ballets such as *L'Oiseau de feu* or *Les Présages*.

The company went to Scandinavia, appearing at the Stockholm Opera, in Helsinki and in Riga. In Helsinki, Chanova and Thomas Armour danced *Spectre* with notable success. Armour wrote to Margaret Power:

It surprised me all the more that two Americans could have a success in a Russian ballet in a theatre filled with Russians. There are so many of them here and they have turned out in full force for us.[30]

The weather was bitter, −15 degrees centigrade, but the buildings were well heated and taxis from one to another very cheap.

Nemtchinova left and once again Blinova and Froman led the company as it went on to appear in the south of France early in 1938. Froman was a tempestuous character, given to rows and quarrels. They danced at Nice, Cannes, Marseilles and then went on to Italy: Rome (where they appeared for a week at the Teatro Quirino from 4 March), Milan, Verona, Genoa, Modena and other cities. Chanova and Youskevitch danced the Bluebird *pas de deux*, Tchinarova, Armour and Savva Andreiev, the son of the Russian playwright Leonid Andreiev, were Ariane and her brothers. Soon afterwards the company disbanded.

March 1938 to September 1939

The winter of 1937–8 was a time of turmoil in the Russian ballet world. There was a widespread feeling that to run two major Russian ballet companies in competition, splitting the repertoire and leading dancers, might spell disaster all round.

In the spring of 1938 the new American company of Denham and Massine was still called the Ballets de Monte-Carlo, the title Blum had used for his own company from 1936. After the Monte Carlo season they would be known as the Ballet Russe de Monte Carlo.

It was in Monte Carlo that Massine rehearsed his new ballets. He had a starry selection of principals: Danilova, Markova, Toumanova, Tarakanova, Slavenska, Rostova and Krassovska (Leslie), with Lifar, Frederic Franklin, Michel Panaiev, Guerard, Platov and Youskevitch, besides himself, as leading male dancers. The new ballets were to be *Gaîté parisienne* and *Seventh Symphony*. 'There are so many stars', wrote Armour to Margaret Power, 'that I cannot see how there will be enough ballets to go round.' Those who got good roles were happy but there was considerable discontent and bickering over casting.

The American company had Serge Denham as director, Blum (programmed rather inconspicuously) as 'founder and director', and Massine as artistic director, maître de ballet, choreographer and leading dancer. Efrem Kurtz was musical director and David Libidins company manager. The company had the Monte Carlo connection and the financial backing of Fleischmann and World Art (later Universal Art) Inc. The Ballets Russes du Col. W. de Basil had the Colonel as founder and director general, Fokine as personal supervisor of his own ballets, Lichine as choreographer, Henry Clifford as artistic adviser for new productions, Grigoriev as *régisseur général* and Dorati as musical director.

Denham, according to Hurok, had descended to following the de Basil company around and making tempting offers to the dancers to change companies.[1] He approached Danilova in Chicago in December 1937, impressed her as being an excellent alternative to the Colonel, for whom she had little regard,[2] and she left de Basil early in 1938. Otherwise Denham's overtures do not seem to have been a particularly profitable exercise. Most of his other principals came from Blum's company except for Toumanova, who had not been dancing for some time, and Rostova. De Basil, who still had the backing of Covent Garden and Erlangers Ltd, retained most of his dancers – judiciously raising their pay a little and sharing out coveted roles amongst them.

Hurok had never liked the Colonel and he disliked even more three men who were concerned in the de Basil affairs. Ignaty Zon was de Basil's partner in the Zerbason agency. Where the de Basil Ballet is concerned he does not seem to have exercised any particular influence. Jacques Lidji (Lidjinov) was a Bulgarian lawyer trained in France. Alexandre Philippov was a very old friend of de Basil's who had toured with the second company as executive manager. He had been at one time the editor of a Russian-language journal with a French title, *Le Théâtre et la Vie*, published in Paris.

Hurok dismissed Lidji and Philippov as overbearing, rather pathetic: 'as a pair of characters they might have been mildly amusing in the *Spring Maid* type of operetta. As collaborators on behalf of ballet they were a trial and a bloody bore.'[3]

Philippov was short and fat and spoke only Russian. He had at hand a good-looking, competent, but for many people unsympathetic, interpreter in his daughter Olga. For de Basil he was someone to talk to, to criticize, someone with whom to have rows. Baronova recalls one 'clearing the air' row in London in 1937 when de Basil had an arm in plaster after it had been broken in three places in an accident with an elevator door. The tall, lean Colonel pursued the tubby little Philippov round the room and over the furniture. De Basil hit out at him, Philippov ducked, and de Basil broke the arm plaster. Like many other people, Philippov is believed to have cheated de Basil regularly, rather to de Basil's admiration. He vanishes from the picture in about 1941, the year before his death.

Lidji was in a different category from either Zon or Philippov. So many lawyers and legal firms were involved in the countless contracts and disputes, writs and injunctions associated with de Basil that it would be impossible to isolate Lidji's responsibility as resident legal adviser. No doubt he was operative in most of them. He played an additional role as managing director of the second company, by whom he was for the most part disliked and distrusted. Haskell supplied a little whitewash, saying that after an initial antipathy he found him a highly capable and sympathetic fellow, although with little experience of the theatre.[4] No one else has a good word to say for him.

Curiously enough, he appears in the New York City Ballet records as well as with de Basil. Round about November 1937, when the second company in Europe had largely reverted to Woizikovsky, Vladimir Dimitriev of the School of American Ballet recommended Lidji to Balanchine as a successor to Edward Warburg, and for a short while he was in charge of The American Ballet. Anatole Chujoy reports that Lidji had the idea of 'converting it into another Ballet Russe de Monte Carlo or de New York'[5] and spent his time on meetings, conferences, negotiations, and threatening legal action, which seemed to be his prime pleasure. Little wonder that with Lidji at his side the Colonel was always embroiled in court cases all over the world.

Partly because of his antagonism to the Colonel and his 'henchmen' but no doubt also because of the promising financial future of Denham's company, Hurok decided to drop his sponsorship of de Basil and adopt the Ballet Russe de Monte Carlo. This put the annual USA appearances in jeopardy and at this point an advisory committee, headed by Prince Serge Obolensky, was set up in New York to examine what could be done for the de Basil Ballet. De Basil had meanwhile been in touch with another American impresario, Fortune Gallo, well known as the manager of the (American) San Carlo Opera Company and later also as the general manager of a Chicago opera company. Gallo was prepared to back a tour and began making bookings. By now however the advisory committee had committed de Basil to discussing a merger with Denham's company.

These discussions dragged on. They were hindered by the intrigues of the opposing managements and pushed on by Obolensky and Baron Niki Gunsbourg. After much debate, a verbal agreement was reached in New York, at the St Regis Hotel. De Basil, who was obviously extremely reluctant to lose identity under the proposed blanket, left for Europe without either signing or appointing an attorney to sign for him. Eventually he cabled a power of attorney. Hurok and Denham thought all was well and an agreement was signed on 15 April 1938 that left Gallo to cut his losses over the bookings he had made. In May, *The Dancing Times* (London) featured an announcement made by Bruce Ottley (from a sickbed) to the effect that 'the basis of the amalgamation is absolute equality between the two entities forming the new company'.[6] De Basil, though, on his return to London, told Frédéric d'Erlanger and Gerry Sevastianov, emotionally and with tears, that the copy of the contract he had now received was quite different to the one he had understood he was signing. He did not read English easily, he said, and Obolensky, who had acted as interpreter, had not managed to make it clear to him what the contract actually contained.

What it did contain, apparently, was his agreement to 'turn over to Universal Art complete legal title to six ballets together with scenery, costumes and choreographic rights'. These ballets were *Le Coq d'or, Symphonie fantastique, La Boutique fantasque* and *Le Tricorne*, and two others to be agreed upon later.

Boutique and *Tricorne* had not in fact been in his repertoire since Massine's departure but de Basil had, presumably, exercised an option on them. He was also 'to assign a contract to Universal Art which he claimed to have with the Covent Garden Theatre, London, which would have assured Universal Art of twelve-week performances for four years at a guaranteed payment'. He relinquished in perpetuity the right to use the names Ballet Russe, Ballet Russe de Monte Carlo, Col. W. de Basil's Ballets Russes and similar names. He agreed 'that Universal Art might use for five years 125 ballets he owned upon payment of royalties'.[7] One is left wondering what possible advantages de Basil was supposed to gain from such a contract – presumably simply the right to USA bookings without competition or harrassment. It is inconceivable that he would have voluntarily agreed to these terms if he had fully realized their comprehensive nature.

Anyway, he now maintained that he had been tricked (the legal wording applied later was 'fraudulently induced') into signing the agreement. D'Erlanger, although he disliked the idea of going back on a contract, still wanted very much, as did Sevastianov, to maintain the de Basil Ballet's independence. They told the Colonel that if he were ready to state on oath that he had not understood the terms, they would 'be prepared to fight for the existence of the company we all love'.[8] On 8 June 1938, therefore, de Basil wrote to Universal Art Inc. repudiating the contract. Hurok, Denham, Fleischmann and Obolensky arrived in London to confirm the merger. The situation looked desperate, but the lawyers thought of a possible solution. The Colonel would have to be sacrificed. He would have to be eased out of all connection with the company and all properties, contracts and copyrights handed over to a new board of directors. This would be called Educational Ballets Ltd (a name believed to have been chosen to give it an advantageous tax status in the UK) consisting of Sevastianov, Victor Dandré (Pavlova's husband) and W.G. Perkins, who was Sevastianov's personal solicitor and a partner of the firm of Kenneth Brown Baker Baker.

Everyone scurried round getting the dancers, who were mostly in Paris, to sign documents transferring their contracts, which had been made with de Basil as director of the Ballets Russes, to Educational Ballets Ltd on terms to be discussed later. New agreements were not signed until August 1938. Sevastianov was the man of the moment. Dandré was elderly, and something of a figurehead: a non-combatant, esteemed and experienced man who brought with him not only the publicity value of an elder statesman to set against the untried young Sevastianov, but the rights and properties to the Pavlova ballets. These never proved of any use, as most of the costumes and decors were already disintegrating. It was Sevastianov, apprentice turned master,

85

who took on the mantle of de Basil – the Colonel was more than a little dismayed to find that his pupil could make such good use of his instruction. For Sevastianov it was a heaven-sent opportunity to accede to a position of authority, and one that stood him in good stead later as managing director of Ballet Theatre from 1941 to 1943.

Chaos was now complete. Covent Garden seemed about to sign up with Universal Art Inc. under the impression that this was to be what Hurok called 'the Biggest and Best of all Ballets'[9] for a season of ten weeks from June 20. Sevastianov, who had his own brand of firm and charming opportunism, decided on a coup d'état, arranging for the de Basil Ballet (now the Educational Ballets Ltd) to move physically into the opera house, into the dressing-rooms, wardrobe and prop rooms, presumably in the belief that possession was nine-tenths of the law.[10] It seems to have worked. Hurok took the Theatre Royal, Drury Lane, for Denham's company and London ballet-goers embarked on a never-to-be-forgotten dual summer season. They scuttled up and down Bow Street from one theatre to the other, sometimes seeing part of each programme in an evening as they tried not to miss either Shoura, Tamara and Alicia (Markova) at Drury Lane or Irina, Tania and Nemtchinova at the Royal Opera House. Energetically keeping up with both companies and no doubt ending up deeply 'in the red', they met for chats in the intervals, enjoying the stimulus of rivalry and faction taking. Everyone said, happily, that it was a good thing the famous Bow Street police station lay exactly between the two theatres to keep the peace. The managements if not the maîtres de ballet were on good terms, and after performances Sevastianov and Hurok met at the Savoy Grill to gloat over their equally excellent box office receipts. These exchanges no doubt laid the foundation for their later association when Sevastianov became Hurok's promotion manager. The Colonel had meanwhile withdrawn to lick his wounds in a small house in Shepherd Market.

The two repertoires complemented and balanced each other astonishingly well. The duplications meant exciting opportunities for comparing interpretations of great roles. In *Carnaval*, Nemtchinova and Shabelevsky were at Covent Garden, Danilova and Guerard at Drury Lane. In *Spectre*, it was a choice between Baronova and Petrov or Toumanova and Youskevitch. In *Schéhérazade*, Tchernicheva and Shabelevsky were set against Jeanette Lauret and Frederic Franklin. In

86

Igor, Franklin and Shabelevsky were in competition as the Warrior Chief.

There were popular old works on show at each house. Covent Garden had the older symphonic ballets, Drury Lane the new *Seventh Symphony*. Drury Lane had important cards in new productions of *Giselle* with Markova and Toumanova – and a dazzling Myrtha in Danilova – as well as the three-act *Coppélia* with Danilova and Michel Panaiev.

The creation of Educational Ballets Ltd and the shelving of the Colonel had happened just in time. When the merger was repudiated, Universal Art Inc. applied for an injunction to restrain de Basil from 'producing, performing, authorizing, advertising or otherwise announcing any performance or intended performance of certain ballets including *Le Coq d'Or*' and from 'representing that he had any right or interest in any of those ballets'. The case began to be heard on Friday 17 June 1938 and the Educational Ballets season was to open on Monday 20 June. 'The matter', stated Counsel, not without truth, 'was very urgent.'[11]

Judgement was given on the Saturday by Mr Justice Morton. It hinged finally on the fact that de Basil was no longer connected with the ballet company. The injunction was granted, restraining him from producing, performing or in any way dealing with the ballets named – but it did not of course apply to the new directors of Educational Ballets Ltd and for some reason no further case was brought by Universal Art Inc. in London.

Educational Ballets Ltd had its internecine troubles, however. Sevastianov and d'Erlanger were not in agreement about policies – perhaps youth and age had something to do with this – and Sevastianov suggested buying out d'Erlanger with money offered to him by the Aga Khan – always generous to the arts.[12] D'Erlanger had presumably had to compensate de Basil, although the Colonel was very little concerned about money for himself and much more hurt in his pride that Sevastianov was capable of running the company without him. He and Morosova went to live on a rather primitive farm property he had acquired and meant to improve at Sospel in the south of France, not far from where her parents had settled, but he never really lost touch with the people who had surrounded him for so long.

He was completely out of the picture of management however in

1938–9. The Covent Garden season proved extremely successful and both Lichine and Fokine produced new ballets. Neither was of major importance but both had appeal. Lichine's *Protée* (5 July) is generally remembered as a very beautiful cameo ballet that no doubt owed much of its stylish blending of music by Debussy and designs by de Chirico with Henry Clifford's knowledge and taste. There was little story. At a temple by the sea, five young girls pray to the god Proteus. He appears, dances with them, but returns to the sea without satisfying their curiosity about what the future holds for them. Charm was the operative word among the critics. Francis Toye said it was 'exceptionally charming. The whole pretty trifle was exquisitely danced'.[13] Horsnell wrote: 'This pelagian idyll is charming'[14] while the anonymous *Sketch* critic varied the wording by calling it 'enchanting'.[15]

The five maidens, five linked soloist roles rather than a *corps de ballet*, were a strong group of emerging dancers. Sono Osato had now been with the company four years, and was settling in well and dancing a wide range of ensemble and minor parts. Anna Adrianova (Shirley Bridge from Rochester, New York) had also joined at the end of 1933. As a dancer she particularly appealed to Massine, who was also interested in her spontaneous ability to 'invent steps instantaneously to music, responding to the style, mood and rhythm of the piece, even though I might never have heard it before'.[16] In February 1937, when the company were snowbound on their special train in Oregon, she showed him a choreographic project she had worked out to César Franck's Symphony in D Minor. They had a long and deep discussion about her ideas for this and Massine was sufficiently interested to suggest 'a collaboration'. Like many young artists, however, she was too wedded to the notion of independent creation to accept the proposal and so it came to nothing.

The remaining three maidens in *Protée* were very new recruits, all engaged in 1938. Lina Lerina (Jacqueline Leri) was from Paris, Alexandra Denisova (Patricia Denise Meyers) and Natasha Sobinova (Rosemary Deveson) from Vancouver.

The two Canadian girls were particular protégées of Lichine's. They were trained by an outstanding teacher, June Roper, who had studied with Preobrajenska and developed something of her flair for producing dancers with strong technical and turning ability. An audition in February 1938 when they were fifteen years old led to their joining the company the following month. Denisova, whose style was reminiscent of Baronova, danced the Top in *Jeux d'enfants* during the London season in 1938 and gradually gained other leading roles. In 1939 Baronova told a *Daily Mail* reporter:

I feel like a grandmother now that we have ten children in the ballet. They are aged from 14 to 17, and at 20, I tell you, I feel old![17]

Fokine's *Cendrillon* (19 July) had a score composed by Frédéric d'Erlanger, exquisitely elaborate designs by Gontcharova and delicate fairytale performances from Riabouchinska and Lichine with Grigorieva as the Good Fairy. The scenario was very like the one made familiar by Frederick Ashton's ballet to the Prokofiev score and, similarly, cast men as the Ugly Sisters – in this case Algeranov and Ladre. The principal difference was the introduction of Cinderella's Cat, a role delightfully created by Raisse Kouznetsova, who had joined the company from Blum's Ballets de Monte-Carlo.

In the absence of Danilova, Nemtchinova was recruited to share ballerina responsibilities with Baronova. There had been talk, as early as 1934, of the engagement of a celebrated young Italian dancer, Attilia Radice. She had instead married Dr Paolo Fabbri, the Italian critic who became *régisseur* of the San Carlo in Naples. The idea was revived in 1937 and *The Dancing Times* prophesied that she would join the Ballets Russes in the September 1938 season on a long-term contract and that Fabbri would then become an artistic and technical collaborator of de Basil's.[18] None of this happened.

During that summer season of 1938 at Covent Garden, certain ballets are programmed as having been conducted by Georg Solti. *The Times* mentioned him by name, critically, in connection with a performance of *Carnaval*:

Pierrot has grown violent. Borovansky hurls himself with such force across the footlights that his dangling sleeve struck the double-bass players . . . The conductor, M. Georg Solti, also was violent – too violent, for he lashed at the orchestra and flogged the music so that he endangered the delicate evocative atmosphere M. Fokine had been at such pains to recreate – but the company was not to be driven into disruptive courses and the fragrant charm of this period piece was preserved in spite of too much Florestan and not enough Eusebius in the music.[19]

This reference to Solti comes as a surprise. According to Harold Rosenthal, Solti refused Dorati's invitation to be assistant conductor this season, and his first appearance at Covent Garden was in December 1959.[20]

Solti however confirms that he was in London in 1938 and *did* in fact conduct performances of *Prince Igor, Le Lac des cygnes, Carnaval, Les Papillons, Danses slaves et tziganes* and *Scuola di ballo*. He was asked whether he would go to Australia with the company after the London season but refused, feeling that he and ballet were incompatible.

Given the rivalry of the two Russian Ballet companies in London that summer, it is interesting to analyse the two repertoires. Both were largely based on Fokine and Massine ballets, but the overlap occurred only in the ever-popular old Fokine works such as *Les Sylphides* or *Carnaval*, and over *Le Lac des cygnes*. In these, balletomanes had the joy of making comparisons between interpretations on show at Covent Garden and at Drury Lane, and between them the companies provided a wide range of unduplicated pleasures.

Without the Hurok backing, there was no USA tour for Educational Ballets Ltd in the winter of 1938–9. First, they appeared again at the Scala, Berlin, to appreciative and sophisticated audiences, and in Copenhagen. Then, Sevastianov arranged with the Australian management, J.C. Williamson Ltd, for an extensive Australasian tour. Under the title Covent Garden Russian Ballet, the company opened on 28 September 1938 at His Majesty's Theatre, Melbourne. Adelaide and Sydney followed, with seven weeks in New Zealand, a return visit to Melbourne and a farewell performance in Sydney's Theatre Royal on 27 April 1939.

It was all a brilliant success: again, it will be described in greater detail later. The public that had enjoyed the second company were even more enamoured of the first. There were many important ballets that had not been seen in Australia, including *Choreartium* and *Symphonie fantastique*, as well as substantial old favourites such as *Les Femmes de bonne humeur* and *Jeux d'enfants*. There was even a world premiere, of Lichine's *Le Fils prodigue* (30 December).

This, like *Les Dieux mendiants* (which was the first Lichine choreography shown in Australia) and Massine's *Le Bal*, was a question of new wine in an old bottle – new choreography for an old framework. For once it worked excellently. It had more dancing than the Balanchine version, a more seductive role for the Siren, and an effective final scene in which the homecoming was danced rather more than mimed. The leading role was created by Dolin, with Grigorieva as the Siren.

Dolin got on well with Sevastianov and had therefore felt it possible to join the company again. He especially loved partnering Baronova. Apart from the dancers it was Fokine and Sevastianov who counted in Australia. Dandré, who was there in a façade capacity, had to be flown home to England prematurely as he took ill.

Shabelevsky made his first appearances in Australia but left abruptly after the Melbourne season. His departure was an opportunity for a dancer who had been steadily progressing in his particular sphere, Yura Lazovsky, to establish a great reputation as a *demi-caractère* artist. Lazovsky was also Polish, born and trained in Warsaw. He danced with Ida Rubinstein during her company's 1934 season, and joined de Basil in 1935. The following year he began to be noticed among the Three Ivans and in the Scherzo in *Choreartium*, but although he was tried out in *Prince Igor* he was not yet up to the very high standard maintained for the role of the Warrior Chief. Now, in 1938, working with Fokine, he soared into prominence, dancing Harlequin and Petrouchka. He was equally brilliant as the Vagabond in *La Concurrence* and the Barman in *Union Pacific*.

Fokine was already deeply immersed in his great project for *Paganini*. This dated back to the summer of 1937 when he and Vera Fokina visited Serge Rachmaninov and his wife at Senar in Switzerland. They discussed a possible collaboration and Rachmaninov suggested his *Rhapsody on a theme of Paganini*.

Fokine was initially doubtful. He wrote to Rachmaninov:

I must hear it more often before I can feel that I know it. If after studying your Rhapsody I feel able to create a suitable and worthy setting of it for the stage, I hope you will allow me to do so and give me your blessing for it. I confess that I vaguely hoped that our meeting would result in the new ballet that I've dreamt about for so long. As yet this hasn't happened. You've become busy with something else and I haven't yet found a theme that seems *absolutely* suitable for you.[21a]

He went on to propose all kinds of themes – from Ovid, from Hans Andersen, from Pushkin, from Russian history (Peter the Great, the Empress Anna) – without any conviction that Rachmaninov would like any of them sufficiently to compose a new score for him.

He was right. Rachmaninov continued to urge the Rhapsody, but he supported this with a theme:

91

Consider the Paganini legend – about the sale of his soul to the evil spirit in exchange for perfection in art, and for a woman. All variations on the Dies Irae would be for the evil spirit . . . It would be good to show Paganini with a violin – not, of course, a real one, but some devised, fantastic violin. And it also seems to me that at the conclusion of the play the several personages [representing] the evil spirit should be caricatures, absolute caricatures, of Paganini himself . . .[21b]

This was enough. Fokine began to study the 'Paganini legend', as Rachmaninov termed it, and it soon became an obsession. Vitale Fokine talks of his father's close personal commitment to it, seeing in Paganini's career some parallel with his own. With the composer he worked out an all-too-complex scenario and from the Antipodes corresponded with both Rachmaninov and with the designer, Serge Soudeikine.

Fokine divided the ballet into three scenes: Paganini on the concert platform, Paganini in relation to his public, Paganini in solitude. He compared Paganini's own conviction that his gift was from God and the popular notion, widely spread by gossip (gossip, scandal and envy were personified in the ballet), that he was possessed by the Devil. In the leading role he cast Dimitri Rostov, the dancer who had greatly impressed him as King Dodon. In fact, when Grigoriev and de Basil had tried to persuade Rostov, inheriting Platov's role, to intensify the comedy and caricature, Fokine had supported him in his more human and dignified characterization. Now he repaid Rostov by giving him the role for which more than any other he is remembered by virtue of its powerful mime and superb make-up.

Rostov, whose real name was Kulcizky, was born in Kharkov and became a junior officer in the White Army on the German front in 1918. He took part as a singer in army groups of music and dance and when he left Russia studied singing and violin with leading teachers in Berlin. He had been separated from his mother and sister but now found that they had also managed to emigrate and were in England. He joined them there, and as a singer appeared with an opera ballet company directed by Ileana Leonidov-Massera and led by herself and the Italian dancer Vincenzo Celli, which performed at Covent Garden in March 1924. Afterwards Madame Leonidov went to Rome and started a ballet school. Rostov, who had become interested in ballet, studied dancing there for four years while he also took a law degree at the University of Rome.

In 1934 he went with the Levitov-Dandré Russian Ballet on tour to South Africa, the Far East and Australasia, and joined de Basil in 1936. As a latecomer to classical ballet he was naturally strongest in *demi-caractère* and character dancing, and he was an outstanding mime.

A very different ballet, and one which had a longer life and a wider public, began to be planned on the ship that took principals of the company from Australia to Los Angeles, by way of Honolulu, where they gave two performances. This was Lichine's *Graduation Ball*, for which Dorati had gone to the Viennese archives for unpublished pieces of Johann Strauss music. Some of the choreography was composed en route, including the Drummer's solo. This, created eventually by Nicholas Orlov, was set for Dolin with the idea that it would be danced by him. War, the return of the Colonel, and Dolin's engagement by Ballet Theatre, prevented this.

In the summer season of 1938 at Covent Garden the Educational Ballets Ltd had been followed by the Ballet Russe de Monte Carlo. The same fair shares were to be allotted to the companies in 1939. The Covent Garden Russian Ballet, as it was now called, was to appear at the Opera House from 19 June to 29 July, while the Ballet Russe de Monte Carlo was scheduled to open on 4 September.

The event of the Covent Garden Russian Ballet season was the premiere of *Paganini* on 30 June 1939 to very conflicting reactions. Fokine himself allowed that it was an immensely complicated production, as far as sets, costumes and lighting were concerned, and that the dancing was difficult and virtuoso.[22] All the same he was delighted both with the performance and its reception on the first night.[23] Among the critics, Beryl de Zoete was one of the most enthusiastic. She declared *Paganini* to have been:

a remarkable demonstration of Fokine's great mastery . . . [It was] a *tour de force* to make a ballet on such a subject at all . . . What he has really done is to externalize the drama of a soul.

Particularly she praised the 'extraordinary beauty and dignity' of Rostov's performance, and Riabouchinska's dance in the second scene as the Florentine Beauty – *a tour de force* of fluent turning and dipping *enchaînements* – was 'perfectly composed, and the melody and lightness of her bending and fleeting body are indescribably lovely'.[24]

Fokine liked working with Riabouchinska – she had the kind of technique that suited his invention. De Zoete returned to the subject of Rostov's Paganini with the perceptive remark that 'he has qualities even rarer than his fine presence – a great musicality and an inner power which operates as much when he is still as when he moved'.[25]

Beaumont, whose deep appreciation of Fokine's choreography makes his opinion even more telling, gave a very balanced view:

Although *Paganini* has many moments of beauty, it has also moments of weakness . . . The figure of Paganini himself is finely conceived and dominates the ballet throughout. It is admirably played by Rostov . . . But I find certain of the subordinate characters less happily formed . . . The second scene radiates pure poetry . . . the final scene is the weakest . . . the choreography for the Divine Genius and her attendant Spirits is too formal. They are simply dancers. They do not succeed in radiating divinity, in making us conscious of a "breath of heaven".[26]

The season as a whole was a good one. *Le Fils prodigue* was admired in Dolin's performance although the *Times* found that Lichine's 'richer characterization, and one apparently more deeply felt than that which had been seen previously, much enhanced the dramatic effect of the whole work'.[27] In the same way, although Baronova made a tremendous impression as the Siren, there was also critical praise for Sono Osato's 'prodigious impersonation'.[28]

On 16 July, Horace Horsnell wrote:

The Russian Ballet keeps beauty in the theatre when beauty is most needed. These admirable dancers have their own gift for dancing their way into the heart of the dying theatrical season and giving it new life . . . even those carpers who, when the season opened, lamented the absence of Danilova and Massine, now take a more gracious view of the company and acknowledge its merits.[29]

It was not only the theatrical season that was dying. The years of peace were nearly over and with them would end a way of life. August however was the traditional holiday month for the Ballets Russes and no one was thinking particularly of international affairs.

The artists of the Ballets Russes were in fact remarkably insulated against the desperate divisions that faced the western world in the 1930s. When the de Basil Ballet appeared in Berlin in 1938, Sobinova, who had been brought up in a strongly socialist family in Canada, was astonished at the apolitical attitudes of the rest of the company. She herself was deeply conscious, as were most thoughtful young people outside Germany, of the sickening aspects of Nazi doctrine and the increasing inevitability of war.

The Ballets Russes spared little thought for them. This was no doubt due partly to the introverted world of ballet in which they lived, where trivial debates and conflicts occupy so much emotional energy, and partly to the fact that the Russian artists had no personal political stake in any country.

Neither Sevastianov, at the time very much in charge of arrangements, nor Fokine seems to have had any unwillingness to book a season in Berlin for September 1939, although in his unpublished memoir Sevastianov records an odd little story, which suggests that he did try to withdraw earlier in the year. He writes that he cabled the German authorities to the effect that he regretted, but he did not have enough Aryans in the company to fulfil the contract. He had a reply from Goebbels to the effect that it was for Goebbels to decide who was Aryan and from his point of view all members of the Covent Garden Russian Ballet were pure Aryans.[30]

Denisova recalls that Fokine began to rehearse a ballet for the Berlin season. This was set to Wagner's Venusberg music from *Tannhäuser*, to be called *Bacchanale*, and sounds like a revival of a ballet staged by Fokine at the Lewisohn Stadium in New York in 1935. The role of Venus was tried out first on Baronova, then on Verchinina, then on Denisova, but the project was dropped. Oddly enough, Massine was working with the Ballet Russe de Monte Carlo in America on exactly the same idea. Massine's *Bacchanale*, with Salvador Dali designs, was given its premiere at the Met on 9 November 1939.

For Europe, Fokine's idea could hardly have been less timely. Although the company had visas in their passports for Germany and Vova Grigoriev had sent the music ahead to Berlin, every emphasis was altered on 3 September 1939 when World War II began. In common with all other individuals in Europe the ballet personnel were at a loss to know what to do. Dancers were widely scattered on holiday, in France, in Switzerland, in Italy. Baronova and Sevastianov however were in England, staying at the Balmoral Hotel in Torquay, and within a short space of time they were joined there by some of the company, including Petrov. Danilova, who was supposed to open the new season (now cancelled) with Denham's company at Covent Garden, also arrived.

Vova Grigoriev began negotiations to get the music out of Germany and managed to do so via Italy, still at that time neutral. The same means were adopted for one of the dancers, a vague and dance-oriented young man who went to Berlin as scheduled without realizing there was a war on.

Now that it affected them personally, the rest realized it all too clearly, and also the fact that they would be lucky to get out of Europe before hostilities became too fierce. They were due to go to Australia but were no longer sure how they would get there.

At this point de Basil returned from his personal Elba to direct the company. There had been no quarrel between Sevastianov and Fokine on the one hand and the Colonel on the other. His absence had been a legal arrangement. Although there is no evidence to support the idea some people have put forward, that he remained an *éminence grise*, in secret charge of affairs, and a good deal of reason to presume that from the date of his retirement from the scene in 1938 Sevastianov, Fokine and Dandré had made their own decisions, de Basil had certainly stayed in personal touch. Baronova and Sevastianov visited him at Sospel. He was delighted, and told his sombre servant Vassiliev to set off some fireworks. In the sensitive political climate of the French Italian frontier at the time, the explosions brought out the military police to investigate, but the Colonel plied them with vodka and everyone was happy.

The Colonel's return can perhaps be accounted for by the real confusion of the outbreak of war. Perhaps, temporarily, even Sevastianov felt glad to consult with the older man. Obviously no legal proceedings were going to result if de Basil were once more installed as director general and he immediately moved back into complete control.

September 1939 to September 1940

Australia was suddenly popular. Lifar, in Paris, had a plan to take a French ballet company abroad on a propaganda tour and began working out a programme with the playwright Jean Giraudoux, who had become the French Minister of Information. When he heard that de Basil had a contract with J.C. Williamson Ltd he suggested that they should create a combined company with Franco-British backing, de Basil recruiting in England and Lifar in France. The only way, however, that any dancers were likely to reach Australia was by dividing into smaller units and taking ship or air passages as and when possible.

The *Washington*, the last big passenger ship to sail for the States from England, took Baronova, Sevastianov, Petrov, Dolin, Igor Schwezov and Sobinova. The *Orcades* from Tilbury to Australia carried others, including de Basil, Morosova and the Grigorievs, some joining in the south of France. The *Mariposa* from America took Toumanova, who was rejoining the Colonel, Riabouchinska, Lichine and Dorati.

The *Washington* also took Antony Tudor and Hugh Laing, who were going to America to join the new Ballet Theatre, directed by Lucia Chase and Richard Pleasant. Irving Deakin cabled Dolin to ask if he would stage *Swan Lake* and *Giselle* for that company. Sevastianov had been unsettled by de Basil's return. It is never easy to be demoted from authority, and by the time they reached America he and Baronova had decided to break with the Colonel and go on to Hollywood, where she had an offer to make a movie. Dolin, after an exchange of telegrams with de Basil – de Basil's declaration that 'owing to war conditions must ask you to reduce your salary in Australia by forty per cent'[1] was hardly encouraging – was released from his contract. Without Baronova and Sevastianov he would have lacked his favourite partner and had no buffer between himself and the disliked de Basil.

Even without Baronova and Dolin, the Australian company of 1940 was the largest and strongest of them all, augmented by one or two of Denham's principals who had been stranded in London. It was led by Toumanova, Riabouchinska, Nemtchinova and Tchernicheva, with Verchinina, Morosova, Grigorieva and Denisova. The men included Lifar, Lichine, Petrov, Jasinsky and Rostov, with Michel Panaiev and George Skibine from the Ballet Russe de Monte Carlo. Anatole Oboukhov was maître de ballet and teacher, Dorati and Max Goberman conductors.

There were new names, or names becoming prominent for the first time. Among the listed ballerinas were Marina Svetlova, Geneviève Moulin and Tatiana Stepanova.

Svetlova, French-born of Russian parents and trained with a galaxy of leading teachers in Paris, first appeared with the Ida Rubinstein Ballet. Moulin, another French dancer, studied with Egorova and appeared with Egorova's small company, the Ballets de la Jeunesse, in 1937 and 1938. She and her sister Thérèse both joined de Basil in 1939. They were both given Russian names: Geneviève was Lubov Zlatina, Thérèse Natasha Melnikova. Geneviève's *nom de théâtre* was only

97

briefly used. Stepanova had a long-standing association with the company. A child prodigy of Preobrajenska's, she was now, at sixteen, following Denisova as the next 'baby ballerina'.

Like Moulin, Oleg Tupine, who was born in the Caspian area of Russia and brought up in Paris, came to de Basil by way of Egorova's studio and the Ballets de la Jeunesse. As Moulin had a sister in the company, he had a brother (Vassily Nikolaiev). Oleg's main opportunities were to come later, in South America, but he joined the company at Covent Garden in 1938, appearing in the ensemble in *Cendrillon.*

Serge Lifar's association with the company was short and colourful. Not unexpectedly, he quarrelled with the Colonel, whom he described as having an almost insane self-centred mythomania. There had been problems about obtaining permission for dancers to leave France, especially young men of military age, but Lifar (whose unpublicized and generous help during the years of war and occupation is remembered by many dancers) managed to arrange for the French authorities to release Skibine, Orlov, Tupine and others so that they could go to Australia. Like Dolin in 1938, Lifar himself flew there. His temper was immediately aroused by the company's title, particularly by the revival of the description 'Colonel W. de Basil's Ballet'. As there had been, apparently, some French propaganda finance put into the project, he was also upset that this was not made apparent on the posters by terming the company a Franco-British Ballet – a title that would have mystified the Australian public and borne little relation to the character of the repertoire. As a result of his protest, the French authorities recalled him to Paris (somehow the Australian press imagined that it was for military service) so that he appeared only in Sydney, from 30 December 1939 to 1 March 1940. He danced *Les Sylphides* and *L'Oiseau de feu* with Toumanova, *Le Spectre de la rose* with Toumanova and Riabouchinska, *Le Lac des cygnes* with Nemtchinova and his own *Icare*, as well as staging his eight-minute *Pavane* (*Las Meninas*) – 'a veritable wisp of a ballet'[2] – for Lazovsky.

Lifar was also involved in a highly irregular project – a re-staging of *Le Beau Danube* to which he made choreographic alterations. This was given a new title, *Le Danube bleu*, and premiered in Sydney on 9 February 1940 without any choreographic attribution and with a programme description ('Scenes and dances arranged by Serge Lifar') which rather cleverly left the legal position in some doubt. The production was de Basil's questionable method of getting round the English court copyright ruling, but no one was fooled, and the Sydney critic commented simply: 'It has lost a good deal of point.'[3] Lifar's own appearances were not initially popular with the public. The critics spoke of his technical accomplishment and vitality, and admired his performance in *Lac*, but complained of an impression of 'visible effort' in other ballets – certainly a characteristic of his at that time when he had allowed himself to put on weight. He had a particular success, however, with *Icare*, which remained an admired piece in the repertoire for a good many years, giving Jasinsky one of his most striking roles. The company enjoyed working with him.

The triumph of the time was *Graduation Ball*, which right from its premiere on 1 March 1940 was a declared charmer. Apart from the obvious enjoyment everyone took in Riabouchinska and Lichine, it brought forward other dancers – 16-year-old Tatiana Leskova as the pigtailed girl – 'a magnetic little comedienne'[4] – Orlov's miraculously precise Drummer, Denisova and Moulin, sparkling and secure in the Competition Dance, and delicious character studies of the Headmistress and the General, played in a less caricatured style than has developed later, by Borislav Runanine and Igor Schwezov.

Leskova joined the company in London in May 1939. She had been selected from Egorova's studio by Tchernicheva and Dandré, and set off from Paris eagerly, confident in the knowledge that she had strong technical qualifications. She recalls her first day of rehearsals. It began with Grigoriev, for the first movement of *Choreartium*.

Not much was really showed to me and I just had to follow the other three girls. The music was beautiful and so was Massine's choreography and my colleagues were helpful. I remember Lara Obidenna pushing me around, somehow I made it till the end of the movement thinking that in the afternoon it will come out better . . . But to my surprise the [afternoon] rehearsal was with Lichine and instead of *Choreartium* it was *Francesca da Rimini* . . . I still had another rehearsal in some other place and I heard it was with Fokine. So I felt scared stiff (everybody was) . . . The rehearsal started by *Prince Igor* (the third ballet to learn in the same day) and Fokine was in a frantic mood, giving hell to Lorand Andahazy who was replacing Lazovsky in the male lead. We followed as the Polovtsian girls. I thought it was wonderful and I could give all my temperament (what for!) but again Fokine gave hell and I was the chosen target . . . Life was not easy, but how wonderful was that experience, that electric shock I received, to be alert and learn the quickest possible way.[5]

99

Schwezov, too, was new to the company in 1940. Born in St Petersburg, he had left Russia in the late 1920s and written a prize-winning autobiography, *Borzoi* (1935), about his experiences. His life outside Russia had been widely itinerant, but he established a school in London in 1937. Now he worked with the de Basil Ballet for a year.

Boris Runanine was a dancer of considerable range and a sparkling technique. A Yugoslav, he had trained and appeared with the Belgrade Opera Ballet but joined de Basil in 1937. He danced one of the Spirits of the Toy Cupboard in *Jeux d'enfants* and Temptation in *Les Présages* but revealed a new comic talent with the Headmistress.

The company was in trouble, however. Harold Bowden of J.C. Williamson at last announced that the New Zealand tour would have to be cancelled. The group was much too large and very expensive, and travelling would have to be reduced to a minimum. Even with the success of *Graduation Ball* to help, the financial outlook was bad. The dancers would have to be asked to accept substantial salary cuts, some 25 per cent, others as much as 50 per cent or more. Seventy dancers were far too many, and some of the principals had had very little to do. Nemtchinova had danced only two roles. Grigorieva had been little seen.

Looked at in the context of the overseas situation of course there were reasons for the very large company. Obviously more dancers had actually turned up in Australia than were needed. Had some of them not managed to get out of Europe, however, there could equally easily have been too few.

There were three other new productions in Australia. Igor Schwezov's *La Lutte eternelle* (29 July 1940) was a re-working of a ballet called *Elckerlyc*, set to Schumann's Etudes Symphoniques, that he had staged in Amsterdam in 1936. Dennis Stoll praised it then as 'a choreographic symphony which a musician can watch without feeling alternate pangs of fury and sorrow'[6] but it was not particularly liked either in Australia or later in North and South America. Its cast included Toumanova as Illusion, Osato as Beauty, Svetlova as Truth, Tupine as Will, while the leading roles were created by Verchinina and George Skibine, a young Russian who had been discovered by the Ballet Russe de Monte Carlo and, like Panaiev, only joined de Basil because of the war.

Verchinina had made her choreographic debut with the San

Francisco Opera Ballet some months before. Now she produced a work called *Etude* in Australia and *Quest* when it was given in the United States. The designs were also changed. In Australia, the costumes were credited to the wardrobe mistress, Olga Larose, but in America Carl Kent produced scenery and costumes after designs by Francesco Cristofanetti. Verchinina took a line from Tennyson as her theme, 'I follow up the quest in spite of day and night', and the ballet was in three parts, Aria, Arioso and Sarabande. She herself headed an all-female cast and the choreography was based on her own fluent and forceful dance style.

Finally, Oboukhov put on a version of *Coppélia* in Sydney in which Toumanova, Riabouchinska and Nemtchinova alternated as Swanilda. This was in two acts, 'after Petipa' with the further credit 'arranged by Nuitter and Saint Leon'. Franz and Dr Coppélius were taken throughout by Panaiev and Sviatoslav Toumine, who had been dancing the roles with the Ballet Russe de Monte Carlo.

The company made its last appearance in Australia in a special midnight performance in Sydney on 19 September 1940. They left reluctantly, and the Australian audience was sad to let them go. J.C. Williamson Ltd however must have been relieved that such a heavy financial responsibility was again off on its travels.

September 1940 to November 1941

The company's route lay across the Pacific, on the *Monterey*, via New Zealand, Fiji, Samoa, Honolulu, but this time with no performances anywhere en route. They arrived in Los Angeles on 7 October 1940, where Hurok and the influential San Francisco manager L.E. Behymer (known as 'Bee') were to present them in the Philharmonic Auditorium.

Hurok's decision to pick up the threads with de Basil was not because he had forgotten his previous problems. He felt that Denham's company was deteriorating and he had heard pretty good news about the de Basil Ballet – the Original Ballet Russe as it was now called – from Australia. Because he had been wily enough to have the 'exclusivity' clause removed from his contract with Universal Art Inc. he was able to take on both companies backing, as it were, for a win or a place.

Los Angeles audiences got more than a little confused by this, and were by no means alone in doing so. From 1938 onwards, few people

101

have really been clear about the Ballet Russe identities and countless ambiguous or incorrect entries in encyclopaedias worldwide have made it all worse. The Los Angeles News gave a boldly mixed-up list of ballets the Original Ballet Russe were to present, including *The New Yorker, Poker Game, Vienna 1815, The Nutcracker* and *Serenade*, which were items in the repertoire of the Ballet Russe de Monte Carlo.

All the same there was a sufficient number of works new to the USA for the de Basil Ballet to show in an extremely successful Los Angeles season, in Chicago and later in New York. There were Fokine's *Cendrillon* and *Paganini*, and Lichine's *Le Fils prodigue, Protée* and *Graduation Ball.* Hurok claimed that he liked most of them; *Paganini* had 'a fine theatrical effectiveness', *Cendrillon* 'a distinct charm of its own'. *Prodigal Son* was 'a moving theatrical experience'.[1] *Graduation Ball* of course continued to be the biggest draw.

The de Basil Ballet followed the Ballet Russe de Monte Carlo into New York. Because the Met was closed for renovation they opened at the 51st Street Theatre on 6 November 1940 with *Le Mariage d'Aurore, Le Coq d'or* and *Graduation Ball.* For this season titles were anglicized so that *Jeux d'enfants* was *Children's Games, Les Présages* was *Destiny* and *Scuola di ballo, Ballet School.* For the last time, the three 'baby ballerinas' of 1932 were united. Russell Rhodes felt that the company was better than the rival troupe and 'acquitted themselves with spirit and grace'. Their weakness continued to be in male classical dancers. Rhodes was greatly impressed by *Paganini*, finding that Fokine 'had brought his genius to play with greater imagination, sense of theatre and youthful attack than in his earlier period'.[2] John Martin also approved of it, claiming that:

none of Fokine's other creations exhibits more powerfully the force of his genius. As a work of art it is tremendously evocative . . . Fantasy and psychological penetration are fused in its emotional substance much as dramatic action and choreography are fused in its outward forms. The intuition of a true theatre artist and a knowledge of the theatre's craft are evident here and the result is nothing less than a great occasion.

Martin also found *Graduation Ball* 'fresh in spirit, full of spontaneous invention and totally without swank or pretence', even though it was much too long. He saw in *Protée* (which Rhodes disliked) some of the merits that many of the audience and dancers found in it. He probably delighted de Basil by taking up the point of 'a veritable crop of new baby ballerinas': Denisova, who made the Divine Genius in *Paganini* 'a lovely figure', Leskova, who 'does a charming comedy bit in *Graduation Ball*' and Moulin, 'a wisp of a child', whose 'technique is crisp and fine'.[3]

Denby, too, liked *Graduation Ball*, writing perceptively of its humanity – 'Lichine's numbers, instead of being made up out of smug references to what is supposed to be funny, are the actions of real dance characters in a plausible situation, they are real dancers, with all the exuberance of dancing.'[4] This is the quality that even now, when most productions exaggerate and broaden the comedy quite beyond its original intentions, makes *Graduation Ball* a perennial pleasure.

Walter Terry, after a number of viewings, felt convinced that *Paganini* was 'a work of genius, brilliant and dramatic of surface and profound and adult in its understanding study of a great artist'. He praised Schwezov's choreography for *La Lutte éternelle* as foretelling the possibilities of 'further effective fusions of the brilliance of ballet with the potency of the modern dance'. Its execution however was faulty because the classically trained dancers were 'unable to move their torsoes with the strength and range which the modern dance requires'.[5]

Terry reiterated the need for stronger male classicists, for better *corps de ballet* work and for new ballets of maturity. Where the ballerinas were concerned, at this point Toumanova had the edge over Baronova, probably because she had been working consistently with the company in Australia while Baronova had been filming in Hollywood. Russell Rhodes wrote of her versatility, her 'extremely lovely performance in *Swan Lake*', her 'sense of comedy stylization' in *Petrouchka*, and her brilliant *Firebird*.[6] These Fokine ballets, and *Les Sylphides, Carnaval* and *Le Spectre de la rose*, she had personally studied and polished with their choreographer and the work was evident.

It was Toumanova's presence in that New York season that persuaded Balanchine to create another ballet, *Balustrade*, for the company. To the Concerto for Violin and Orchestra by Stravinsky, a score he was to use again as *Stravinsky Violin Concerto* for New York City Ballet many years later, he choreographed a controversial abstract work. The composer conducted, with Samuel Dushkin as violinist. *Balustrade* is remembered chiefly for an erotic trio, and for the fantastic designs by Pavel Tchelitchev. These included a setting of a low white balustrade that accounted for the title, and a stunning black jewel-

103

encrusted costume for Toumanova, with a fringed georgette skirt drawn between the legs, black silk tights embroidered with sequins and brilliants and long black silk gloves with pendant crystal drops at the finger tips.

The opening toccata was danced by Leskova and Jasinsky with eight supporting girls. In the second movement (Aria), Svetlova and Petrov were joined by Sonia Orlova and Irina Zarova (Yvonne Mounsey), and the trio for Toumanova, Jasinsky and Petrov came in the third movement (also called Aria).

Balustrade has achieved the posthumous reputation of resounding failure, apart from the haunting designs. It is hard to see just why this is so, except that some leading critics damned it – often a burden too great for a stimulating and original work to survive.

Irving Kolodin's notice shows the type of adverse reaction the ballet elicited:

[Balanchine] has exceeded himself in the designing of intricate weavings of hands and legs and stunty groupings. But if he has done any more than this, it has escaped the notice of this onlooker. To be sure, one is hardly so naive as to expect meaning or significance from a ballet, especially one that uses Stravinsky's acidulous and banal violin concerto as a point of departure.

He went on to comment on costumes 'that look vaguely like what a bat might wear if dressed by Hattie Carnegie' but allowed that the movement contained 'many sequences which were original in their viewpoint and full of crisply distinctive patterns'.[7]

John Martin was completely dismissive. He quoted the programme credits and continued:

Beyond the recording of these simple facts, the event need not detain us. Nobody involved in it can have been very serious about it, so there seems little reason for anybody else to be. The only thought that gives one pause is that while gifted American artists are starving in the effort to bring their work before the public, there is money available for the production of European importations of this caliber.[8]

The lobby in favour, however, makes a case that reads differently. Lillian Moore, while allowing that 'some of the patterns employed are so startling as to jar the nerves of those accustomed to more conventional design' spoke of Balanchine enlarging the scope of the traditional technique with 'effects of a decidedly acrobatic nature, without ever losing touch with the classicism which forms the true foundation of the work'. She described the celebrated trio in a way that certainly confirmed its novelty:

Here Paul Petrov, always a fine partner, is asked to perform miracles. He is obliged to support Toumanova in various difficult pirouettes and arabesques while impeded by the full weight of Jasinsky who is hanging with both arms from about Petrov's neck![9]

One critic produced an interesting commentary:

The choreography has its triplicate roots in the American jazz dance, post-Wigmanesque hauteur and out and out ballet. Strange to relate, the resultant growth is all to the plausible and, what is even more startling, wonderfully attractive as a spectacle . . . To say that there are irony, broad burlesque, austere dignity, a touch of the erotica, sheer insolence and grimacing contempt in the beautifully contrived pattern would be as right, perhaps, as to advance the idea that no such qualitites exist in it. That's the kind of ballet it is . . . It took some time before the music and the dancing became one to this auditor-spectator, however, but the unification was complete when it occurred. Beautifully costumed and boasting a scenic design of disarming simplicity, *Balustrade* is definitely one of the important new works in the repertory. Often may it be repeated.[10]

It was repeated exactly twice. One thing is obvious, *Balustrade* was far ahead of its time. Edwin Denby saw in

this new "undissonant", "undeformed", "one-at-a-time" way of dancing a kind of parallel relation to Miss Graham's new modern-school manner in *Letter to the World.*[11]

No doubt the blatant novelty of composition, the work's odd juxtaposition with programmes that contained ballets such as *Le Mariage d'Aurore* or *Petrouchka*, and the influential bad reviews accounted for its quick disappearance.

Two ballerinas were lost to the Colonel during the New York season, Osato and Denisova. With both, the crisis came because of overwork and emotional problems in their private lives. Osato was appearing in as many as seven ballets on matinée days. Although she had leading and featured roles in some, she was also still dancing in the *corps*. A long-standing relationship with Jasinsky was also reaching its climax. She put in an application to de Basil to have her salary raised from $60 to $75 a week and to be exempted from the ensembles of *Sylphides* and

Le Lac des cygnes. Her letter was ignored, and after twelve days she walked out of his company for ever.

Denisova was pregnant, but her schedule of performances remained intensive. She suffered a miscarriage after dancing six ballets in a day but received no sympathy or understanding from the management, so she and her husband Alberto Alonso left de Basil to direct the ballet school of the Sociedad Pro-Arte Musical in Havana. This society, of which Alonso's mother, Laura Rayneri de Alonso, was President, had from 1918 sponsored visits by international artists to Cuba. The ballet school dated from 1930.

Hurok, once more bothered by the Colonel, Philippov and Lidji, also recognized that the de Basil Ballet finances were precarious. He was still committed to both Russian ballet companies, and claims that trying to cope with intrigues on two fronts made him turn with some relief to the prospect of managing Ballet Theatre. He was of course no novice in the matter of intrigue himself and there were contributory reasons for his action.

Charles Payne suggests that this swing of Hurok's was largely dictated by his desire to keep clear of entanglements with warring Europe, to which both Russian ballet companies were linked. This, he maintains, was also a prime motivation for Sevastianov at the time.[12] Sevastianov, who had been Hurok's promotion manager from 1939, was proposed to Ballet Theatre by Dolin as a possible business manager. Discussions began late in 1940, when Baronova also made a direct contract with Hurok Attractions. Hurok had agreed to sponsor de Basil until March 1941.

The company went north, after the New York season in February 1941, to Montreal and Toronto, where they were given a great welcome. In Toronto they appeared at the Royal Alexandra Theatre, and there were long lines at the box office. The *Globe and Mail* talked of 'ballet fever' and said: 'This city is now showing the same enthusiasm for this delightful form of entertainment as London and New York.'[13] Although Denisova and Sobinova had left, there were still Canadians in the company – Kira Bounina (Jean Hunt of Vancouver), Ludmila Lvova (Betty Low of Ottawa) and Boris Belsky (Robert Bell of Montreal).

A feature-writer of the *Globe and Mail*, Thelma Craig, contributed a word picture of the company in its ante-performance time on stage which typified every evening it passed in every theatre worldwide:

106

Every ballerine and ballerina was doing different exercises – "limbering" exercises. Every packing box, too, had someone clutching it with one hand while the human form shot out in all and different directions. In the centre of the floor solo artists did spins and whirls and gliding movements. In the wings, on the stairways, even in the dressing rooms there were human forms – doing limbering exercises. The props move on and still they're doing their limbering exercises. Only some of them have scampered away, and come back with long, curled eyelashes and lips red as American Beauty roses and pretty wreaths of forget-me-nots about their heads and in those foamy white frocks that spell enchantment when the curtain goes up on the outside. They take turns in the box of powdered rosin, getting their satin ballet slippers sharpened for the moments that are ahead . . .

It never ceases. Wiggle an ankle, Shake a wrist, Bend a leg, Curl an arm, Dip, Dash, Spin, Whirl, Bend, Curl, Twist, Pose, Swing, Sweep, Swirl. It never stops . . .[14]

Boston followed Canada, and a few performances in Philadelphia, after which Toumanova left on the expiry of her contract. The next date was Mexico City. From there they were to go on to Cuba and South America.

Cuba however was to be written on everyone's heart, rather as Calais was on Mary Tudor's. In Australia, J.C. Williamson Ltd had, as we have seen, introduced salary cuts. In Boston, de Basil collected the company on stage and warned them about financial changes for the forthcoming South American tour. He told them that since Hurok had reduced the weekly monies allotted for payment of company salaries by more than $2000 weekly, the company could not receive the same wage scales as they had in the States. This reduction was based on lower costs of living in South America.

According to some of the dancers, the speech was too general. It failed to deal with them individually, and they felt this keenly. Payment with the Colonel was always on a more personal and flexible basis than could exist today. Contracts specified sums, but these could not always be paid. On the other hand, what money was available was often apportioned according to need. A dancer with a relative to support, or medical and dental bills to pay, could argue for, and get away with, a bit extra at times. Someone else had to do with less in consequence.

Seventeen dancers now signed a letter to de Basil dated 18 March 1941 – the tone is more of sorrow than of anger – giving him an ultimatum. It referred to 'individual conferences' which had, too

107

belatedly, been held in Mexico City in his absence on 13 March and stressed that the signatories found their last salary 'inadequate to sustain even food and hotel bills'. They stated the minimum salaries they would be willing to accept – $140 per month for the South American tour, $180 per month in Cuba – and declared that nothing should be deducted from these salaries towards the advances they had received in Australia until they were once again receiving the full AGMA (American Guild of Musical Artists) wages in the USA. Unless the conditions were accepted by 7 o'clock on 20 March on the Fausto Theatre stage in Havana, they would not perform.[15] There was no acceptance, and they did as they threatened.

The company as a whole did not support the dissidents. Many of them – Valrene Tweedie, an Australian who danced as Irina Lavrova, was one – felt that the strike had been engineered. The strikers had been guaranteed money and jobs with Ballet Theatre, although this did not in fact work out as forecast. The majority returned to de Basil later on. Valrene felt that de Basil had done all he promised for her. She was being paid, for *corps de ballet* work, roughly twice what older girls in other jobs than ballet were earning in Australia at the time.

The Cuban engagement, which had been arranged by the Sociedad Pro-Arte Musical, called for different programmes each evening and the contract would be considered broken if any programme were altered. This, plus Grigoriev's guiding rule that the paying public must never suffer, inspired the non-striking dancers to rehearse all day each day to cover all roles. Principals danced in the *corps* as well as in leads. Tchernicheva disguised herself as a Boyard in *Coq d'or*, Lichine danced one of the rivals in *Paganini*. Although the opening bill of *Sylphides, Coq d'or* and *Graduation Ball* was delayed by an hour, it was presented, as were all the other performances. Even *Symphonie fantastique*, which they felt to be impossible, was staged in a tremendous effort of loyalty on the part of the dancers.

Baronova, although she had not signed the letter, has often been included in the number that went on strike. Her position was rather different. Certainly she withdrew at that point, but as she was under personal contract to Hurok, and married to Sevastianov, she could hardly have continued once Hurok decided to drop the company. Sevastianov is quoted by Charles Payne as having written to Philip Richardson, the editor of *The Dancing Times* (London) on 2 April, saying that Baronova left after being insulted by de Basil.[16] The Colonel maintained that she 'summarily quit the company in Havana without notice after three performances'.[17]

She was replaced by Denisova who was of course working with the Pro-Arte in Havana at the time. De Basil made Denisova an offer, via her husband Alberto Alonso, to go to South America with the company as prima ballerina but Alonso refused it as he himself was not to be given equal rank as principal dancer.

Strike action by dancers was unprecedented, and everyone concerned would have been amazed to think that in the 1980s there would seem to be nothing strange about it.

The background of this affair, which proved disastrous to the company, was very differently described by Hurok and de Basil. Hurok's account, which is better known, lacks detail. He agrees that he undertook to send the company to Mexico and South America, but blames de Basil for not having enough money to pay salaries. Sevastianov, who was still connected with Hurok but negotiating with Ballet Theatre, was actually in Cuba and Hurok sent his secretary, Mae Frohman, to try to straighten things out. 'The mess', he writes, 'was too involved, too complicated, and the only possible course was for me to drop the whole thing.'[18] Mae Frohman seems to have been his ultimate reserve of power – if she failed, the implication is, who could succeed? Outside arbitration seems not to have been considered. It was fortunate for Hurok that the 'only possible course' for him was the one that best suited his future plans.

De Basil's account is more complicated. He says that for the South American tour Hurok 'reduced the weekly monies allotted for payment of company salaries by more than $2000 weekly', a sum based on what were considered to be lower costs of living in South America. The salary scale for the entire Western Hemisphere was approved by AGMA and it was these Hurok cuts that made it impossible for him to accede to the dancers' petition.

De Basil's statement then refers to the adverse publicity that had been released about the strike, and claims that this 'appears to have been designed to injure the international prestige and good standing of our company'. He believed that there had been 'deliberate sabotage'. He thought it was significant that Hurok seized on the strike as an excuse to withdraw, alleging breach of contract, and to cancel the agreement which had been made for two years of touring in North, Central and

109

South America. According to de Basil, Hurok notified him of this withdrawal only one day before the company was scheduled to sail from Havana to Peru, and did not pay for the last four Havana performances nor the return transportation of the company.[19]

At this point Sevastianov was apparently actively supporting the striking dancers. Payne says that, from New York, Sevastianov 'pressed the strikers' case with AGMA and continued through correspondence to direct their activities in Havana'.[20] This may have been from genuine sympathy with their cause but its effect was undoubtedly to weaken the Colonel's position, and as Sevastianov and Hurok were both turning to Ballet Theatre this was suspiciously much to their advantage. Hurok was already telling his local managers that 'as a patriotic duty he was rescuing and enlarging Ballet Theatre and would substitute it for the de Basil Company which he had booked with them for the 1941–42 season'.[21] In mid-June the contract between Ballet Theatre and Hurok was concluded.

De Basil filed a conspiracy suit against them, which Hurok and Sevastianov suggested settling out of court. Ballet Theatre, unaware of much that had been happening, pressed for defending the charge. In fact, it foundered on a technicality concerned with de Basil's absence in South America. When he returned to the USA after the war he was once more presented by Hurok, who had dropped Ballet Theatre in turn, and there was no resumption of the suit. From the Colonel's point of view this was possibly a pity. Charles Payne, in the light of his researches, is obviously in no way convinced that the court would have decided in favour of Ballet Theatre and Hurok.[22]

The dancers were now stranded in Cuba, almost penniless. They moved out of the Hotel Presidente into the cheapest possible lodgings and augmented the tiny sums the management contrived to hand out by organizing small recitals. Four or five of them would go out to various towns – Matanzas, Cienfuego, Santiago – and perform a programme of *divertissements*. Lichine choreographed a dance scene, *Congo Pantera*, which ran for three months at the Tropicana nightclub with Leskova in the leading role of the Panther. Leskova was the only girl sharing a big flat with four of the men, Lazovsky, Jasinsky, Petrov and Grisha Alexandrov, and her earnings helped to keep it going. While she shopped and cooked, they did the cleaning. 'We had the sea, the beach and the sun, and having no money we couldn't get too fat . . .'[23]

Some of the dancers left, as did Madge Lynch, an Australian who was acting as de Basil's secretary. She urged Valrene Tweedie and Phillida Cooper (another Australian who danced as Lydia Couprina) to go home with her but they refused. In spite of a real problem over their inability to learn Russian, which meant that they were dreadfully teased by most of the Russian and Polish boys who were extremely quick at languages, they had settled well into company life. Contracts always stipulated that dancers were due to get their fares home if the company were stranded, although often there were no funds to honour this. Valrene's travel money was borrowed back by the Colonel in July 1941 to pay the dues on scenery that had been impounded during the troubles. Pro-Arte had offered him the chance of staging two performances at the Teatro Auditorium and in these Denisova made her last appearance with the company, as guest artist in *Le Mariage d'Aurore, Les Cent Baisers, Petrouchka* and *Choreartium*.

Quite apart from initiating litigation in the United States, de Basil had been far from idle. Hurok had not been the only impresario to be impressed by the Australian successes. Offers had been made at that time to de Basil by Fortune Gallo, who decided to forget the disappointments of 1938. Now the Colonel went to Gallo in the hope that his company might be saved. At the same time he had talks with Nicholas Koudriavtzev in Montreal. Koudriavtzev, a Russian impresario who lived in New York but had close links with Canada – he was Hurok's representative there – had married the de Basil dancer Tatiana Lipkovska.

The outcome must have pleased de Basil greatly. He signed two contracts in May and June 1941, after visits to Montreal and New York. Frank Benedict was the Canadian signatory, engaging the Original Ballet Russe for a three-week tour in Quebec and Ontario. The second, and more substantial, contract was with Gallo. By this Gallo agreed to set up a shareholding corporation in New York, Ballet Art Inc., to present the de Basil Ballet throughout the United States.

Of this corporation de Basil was to be president and Gallo treasurer, secretary and chairman. Gallo would handle bookings, advertising and publicity. De Basil would engage the company, musical director, choreographers, dressers and others, with the proviso that Gallo should give written consent to each engagement. De Basil indemnified Gallo against all existing debts and claims. However, Gallo was to pay $3000 towards transporting the company and properties back from Cuba to New York. There was a supplementary letter-agreement in connection

111

with a South American tour which was to begin about 1 April 1942, for Brazil, Chile, Peru and Panama, Argentina and Uruguay.

Things were settled, and a temporary euphoria descended on everyone. Gallo set about disabusing people's minds of the ideas – which had somehow travelled rapidly through the States – that '(a) the company is busted, (b) the company is merged, (c) the Colonel has disappeared – cannot be found, (d) de Basil has no artists like Baronova/Toumanova.' He worked out some 'ammunition' for his representatives to counter these rumours. De Basil had not disappeared. He was in New York, working day and night on plans for his company. The company, including seven of the 'strikers', were all together and Baronova and Toumanova would be replaced by well-known leading dancers. Nijinska would be maître de ballet.[24]

De Basil was at the same time writing to Maurice Seymour a warmly appreciative letter asking for photographs of Moulin, Stepanova, Leskova and others for publicity purposes.[25] The two men had known each other from the first Chicago season in February 1934. Seymour, who had emigrated to the USA from Bessarabia in 1920, was standing in the lobby of the Auditorium Theatre – a striking figure with a great mane of hair. He noticed de Basil staring at him and finally the Colonel asked if he were an artist. 'Not exactly,' said Seymour, 'I'm a photographer.' 'Fine,' said de Basil, 'I would like you to photograph my ballerinas.' Next day they were at Seymour's studio, and he was launched on a famous career as a ballet photographer.

Gallo of course presented the story of the Cuban *débâcle* a third way, working out that when Hurok cancelled the contract he saved himself $38,500. He wrote:

Hurok had the Ballet Russe booked in this country twenty weeks according to his contract but only gave them seventeen weeks, thereby saving himself 5,500 dollars each of the three weeks, or 16,500 dollars. He was to pay the Colonel at the end of twenty weeks in this country 10,000 dollars according to the contract, so the Colonel could move his company wherever he wished, and this was not paid. Then again if Mr Hurok exercised his option for the season 1941–42, which he did, he was to pay the Colonel another 12,000 dollars, but this was not paid. The above 38,500 dollars Mr Hurok saved by making a new contract with the Colonel to take the ballet down to South America but at the end of three weeks he cancelled it, leaving the company in Havana and saving himself 38,500 dollars . . . The company is okay with AGMA. In addition, to my way of looking at it, the company is a real one, and this is admitted by all connoisseurs, critics and the New York public.[26]

Gallo however had problems where bookings were concerned. Hurok had made bookings far in advance via the affiliated National Broadcasting Company, but some of these had been taken over for Denham's company or Ballet Theatre. Confusions continued. Seattle for instance thought of suing de Basil for not appearing there in July. Gallo pointed out that the contract had been made by Hurok and, as de Basil would gladly have played the date if Hurok had not dropped the company, if Seattle were to sue anyone it should be Hurok . . .

Meanwhile Gallo was arranging for the reappearance of the de Basil Ballet in the United States. He had a commitment to Washington DC for the (American) San Carlo Opera to appear from 13 August 1941 and he proposed to follow the opera with 'Ballet under the Stars'. Performances were to be at Watergate – a name then known solely in its local sense as a part of Washington near an actual lock or watergate between the Potomac River and the Chesapeake and Ohio Barge Canal. There was no theatre, but a very efficient covered stage was constructed on a steady barge, with wings and dressing-rooms, space for minimal sets and orchestra. An audience of over eight thousand could be accommodated on shore. For seven days the company presented programmes that changed nightly and contained *Schéhérazade* – presumably the minimal sets included a staircase, gates and cushions – *Les Présages* and *Prince Igor* as well as, appropriately, *Le Lac des cygnes*. The Odette was Nana Gollner who, with Tchernicheva, Riabouchinska, Grigorieva and Morosova, led the ballerinas. There had been talk of signing Patricia Bowman too, but the American stars Gollner and Bowman were apparently mutually exclusive.

The men in this revived company were very much as before – Lichine, Shabelevsky and Lazovsky, Petrov, Jasinsky, Panaiev and Rostov. Alexander Smallens conducted.

The week was a complete success, even with unsettled weather and high humidity. The Washington Post interviewed Riabouchinska who, 'wringing with perspiration', declared 'You should have seen it in Cuba . . .'[27]

113

From Washington de Basil took his company to Canada. This contract had been carefully kept outside his agreement with Gallo, although there was apparently some promise that the corporation should receive four per cent of the gross. The exclusion was to prove one of the rocks on which the Gallo-de Basil ship foundered. The Canadian tour had been set up by Armand Vincent, president of the Wings for Victory campaign in aid of the British war effort, and it was under the patronage of the Canadian Governor-General and his lady, the Earl and Countess of Athlone. The ballet took part in a charity ball on 19 September 1941 and then opened a week's season at the Massey Hall, Toronto, on 22 September where, in contrast to the packed houses in February, the audience was 'disappointingly small but enthusiastic'.[28]

They then went to Montreal for two weeks and fulfilled some shorter engagements in the area. New names of two young Americans appeared on the programme: Leon Danielian in *Carnaval* and Kenneth MacKenzie in *Protée*. Danielian, New York-born, had made his debut with the Mordkin Ballet and became a soloist with Ballet Theatre in 1939. He had a considerable range of style, from classical to *demi-caractère* work, but he remained with de Basil only during the Canadian tour. Their association ran into litigation later on. MacKenzie stayed with the company for some years and became one of their principal dancers in South America. He was Chicago-born and trained with Novikov, making his debut performances with Ruth Page and Novikov and with the (American) San Carlo Opera.

Montreal was a triumph. *The Standard* called it 'the most successful stage event in Canadian history . . . The gross receipts shattered all Montreal records for any stage production', and the report added, 'they will leave behind in eastern Canada vivid memories of brilliant performances, glittering spectacle, superb technique – and all in a magnificent patriotic cause'.[29]

The Gallo tour was resumed in Chicago on 20 October 1941, but already the end of the collaboration was in sight. Gallo had been nettled by de Basil's behaviour over the Canadian engagement. Probably *The Standard*'s remarks about gross receipts had excited his expectations. He considered that $15,000 should have belonged to the corporation, and began to take a tough line in his letters to lawyers, publicity representatives and to de Basil himself. As early as August he had been complaining that the Colonel originally told him the company would cost $3500–$4000 a week, and this had gone up to $5000. All the same he went on with a massive correspondence regarding future bookings – setting up a Pacific coast tour and other dates to follow engagements in Chicago and Detroit.

Gallo's nephew Mario (Edward M. Gallo), who was acting for him (and had been appointed company manager), achieved a very friendly relationship with de Basil. Gallo himself, on the evidence of his correspondence, was an irascible man and became increasingly irritable when de Basil failed to answer letters, failed to provide essential information regarding dates and repertoire, failed to sign documents, failed, indeed, to be in any way a co-operative partner. Gallo wrote to Walter Socolow, de Basil's current New York attorney:

Since the company left I have heard nothing, received nothing, and what is more could not even get the programmes necessary for the exploitation of the engagement in this city [Chicago] where the company appears October 20 to 25. In order to receive a programme I had to make three long-distance telephone calls at my expense. Finally the programmes were sent by telegraph, which as you know is very costly . . .[30]

The Russian ability to postpone, or procrastinate, or behave as if time were non-existent, had no charm for men of affairs in the western world.

De Basil had however already put up a defence against the accusations. Gallo wrote him in September saying:

It is important that the finest opening programme you can assemble be scheduled for presentation [in Chicago] and this should be sent immediately . . . They are interested in having a Polish night on Friday October 24, featuring Shabelevsky and any other Polish artists in the company.[31]

To that, de Basil replied promptly:

We sent to Chicago a programme of the opening night, *Swan Lake, Paganini, Graduation Ball*. As regards the programme for the entire week, before planning such it is indispensable for us to know what days there will be matinées. [This obviously referred to scene-shifting as well as apportioning of roles for the dancers.] Concerning the Polish night, I doubt very much whether we could have a Polish ballet, as some time ago you declined the offer of the Polish manager who had all the ready material for such a bill. We have four Polish members in our company and of course they will take part in the performance. We have nothing specifically Polish. Re Nijinska – you know the situation and the question of her presence depends entirely on whether we can afford to pay her the salary she wants . . . Kindly let me know what orchestra we are going to have in Chicago besides the nineteen musicians we are bringing

115

with us, as this must be considered in the planning of the programme. Several of the important ballets are impossible to give without an adequate orchestra.[32]

The Polish group mentioned was a Polish company presented by Marian Brunszwig (Mariano Norsky, twin brother of the well-known European impresario Julian Braunsweg) who had proposed two works, *Harnasie* and *Country Wedding*, to be included in the de Basil repertoire during the 1941–2 and 1942–3 tours. He would have organized Polish audience groups to sell tickets, and at the end of the contract the scenery and costumes of the ballets would have become de Basil's property.

The reference to Nijinska is interesting. There has often been speculation as to why she did not continue as maître de ballet after the end of her contract in July 1936 or indeed after the brief Washington engagement in August 1941. Reasons put forward, such as the likelihood that she did not co-operate easily with de Basil or needed more rehearsal time because of her perfectionist temperament, may well be true. Obviously however a contributory reason was that the company was not able to offer her sufficient money.

Money is frequently forgotten when people talk of dancers and choreographers joining and leaving companies. Usually the reasons given are artistic or personal ones. Naturally, if an artist feels particularly happy with artistic conditions in some company he or she will make financial sacrifices to stay there. If however he has to choose between relatively parallel and in no way ideal artistic conditions in two companies, money will sway the choice.

Among the Russian ballet artists, especially as they got older, money inevitably became a more vital factor in decisions about where and with whom they would work. De Basil's frail financial background, as time went on, was unlikely to tempt any of them to work with his company.

By this time neither Gallo nor de Basil felt that the other had any understanding or sympathy for him. Gallo was also worried about blocking tactics being directed against de Basil which only adroit handling might circumvent. Even after his split with the Colonel he was still hinting in letters to Lily Laverock in Vancouver of 'conspiratorial machinations against the Colonel in an effort to limit the number of ballets in the field to "one management".'[33] He was not however innocent of such dealings himself. Round about mid-October conferences began between Gallo, Hurok, de Basil and their various attorneys,

116

discussing the possibility of either a merger of the competing ballet companies or an agreement for some non-competitive booking arrangements. Gallo's advisers were suggesting a cartel arrangement between Hurok and Gallo, with mutually agreed territories and/or joint presentations of performances. The two companies might undertake separate tours, each 'presented by S. Hurok and F. Gallo'. Some of the advisers, on the other hand, reverted to the idea of a complete merger. The strongest ballets from each repertoire could be used and the best members of each company placed under contract, achieving that alluring daydream of 'the finest ballet company in the entire world'.[34] The Colonel was the stumbling-block in this picture and undoubtedly they would have been very content to edge him out.

Meanwhile there was a brilliant opening audience in Chicago on 20 October 1941. Gallo had worked hard on this, as he invariably did, writing to influential people in poetic vein:

If you would like to view the equipment of the Original Ballet Russe and glimpse the effervescent ballerinas and coryphées of the dance backstage, I will take you on a personally conducted tour . . .[35]

Knowing your proclivities for the dancing excellence of the Original Ballet Russe, I want you to know that you are as welcome as the flowers in May to ask for anything you wish during the engagement here this week.[36]

The company's performance did not disappoint them. He admitted that the first night in Chicago was excellent, while commenting: 'This ballet proposition should be a toy for a millionaire . . . They have enough equipment that if it was piled before the defences of Moscow, Hitler couldn't take the town in 43 years.'[37]

Gallo and de Basil were now basically more opponents than partners. They each had, ranged behind them, assistants and attorneys. Gallo had his nephew Mario, although he was seconded to de Basil, and his attorney Max Schoengold, who disapproved of the whole venture. Schoengold had pointed out right at the beginning that they must get the corporation set up within the agreed term of one week after the execution of the contract, to avoid starting business relations with a default. It was preferable, if possible, to put the Colonel in such a position that *he* was the defaultor. Gallo also had regional representatives such as Tom Girton in San Francisco, Bill McCurdy in Portland and Charles Burke in Seattle (with whom he frequently had epistolary battles). His office staff included Charles Strakosch and Mary Toye.

De Basil was less well attended in numbers. He relied on Alexandre Philippov, at this time designated executive manager, on Lidji, on his attorney Walter Socolow and his company manager Vova Grigoriev. He had no office staff as such, nor particularly well organized files, and this probably contributed to his unsatisfactory character as a correspondent. When spurred into it, however, he counter-attacked, as in a letter to Gallo of 28 October, referring to enquiries from 'the London company'. This was the Original Ballet Russe Ltd, a holding company run by solicitors which had been registered in London in October 1939 and remained in existence until October 1972. They were asking for information regarding future bookings and he pointed out that Gallo had not sent him the itinerary. He complained that lack of information about the itinerary had created

an extremely unhealthy condition with the company and its personnel, causing only mental confusion. Each hour the situation becomes graver, and in addition the rumours emanating from your office regarding the disbandment of the company only hurt the situation. Your definite plan for a complete and definite state of understanding between us is vitally necessary, so that the company can complete its successful tour.[38]

Four extra performances were given in Chicago, in association with the highest-paid ballroom dance duo of the time, Veloz and Yolanda, who, with their guitarist Vicente Gomez, were sandwiched between *Les Sylphides* and *Aurora's Wedding*. The company then moved on to Detroit, where they opened on 2 November and played nine performances. At the end of these Gallo informed them that he had cancelled the already publicized tour to the Pacific Coast and would return them to New York the next day.

Gallo's decision seems to have been precipitated by a letter from L.E. Behymer. Because of the confused bookings by Hurok and Gallo for the two Russian ballet companies, Behymer advised Gallo on 7 November 1941 to 'forget California'.[39] On 10 November, Mary Toye in Gallo's New York office was besieged by telephone calls from people who had heard by telegram from the dancers that they were returning that day. Gallo explained his action, to her and to various other correspondents, by saying that there were important letters which de Basil had not signed. They reached a confirmatory agreement on 31 October for 'the maintenance and the continuance of the American Tour of the Ballet

Russe'. The tour was envisaged as beginning on approximately 15 November 1941 with four weeks on the Pacific coast and a guaranteed further four weeks, returning to New York where 'the scenery and other paraphernalia and accoutrements' of the ballet would be stored. A supplementary letter dealt with the executing of a bond regarding the scenery, and possibly this was what de Basil had slipped away, in characteristic style, without signing.[40] Gallo also raised his earlier grievance, that the Colonel had not paid him 'one single nickel' of the Canadian receipts and that day-to-day co-operation was impossible.[41]

De Basil was astounded at the collapse of the tour and maintained that he had kept his part of the bargain. He pointed out what must have been obvious to everyone, that the action had 'placed the company in a desperate plight'.[42] He stressed that to keep the company together and provide them with a living – which is a good summary of his life's work – it was essential for bookings in the Eastern states to replace the Pacific Coast tour.

There were losses all round, as money for advance bookings had to be returned. Gallo prepared other outspoken press statements about de Basil's 'complete lack of co-operation', but may not have issued them. Charles Burke dealt inventively with the press of Vancouver and Victoria and cabled Gallo: 'newspapers through my direction handled debacle beautifully dignifying you and Colonel.'[43] Indeed the *Victoria Daily Colonist* had reported as a result:

Because Colonel de Basil has had to seek a realignment of capital since his London committees are unable to maintain subsidies under which the American tour was operating, the Ballet Russe has postponed its Pacific Coast tour . . . The company has now gone back to New York for reorganization.[44]

A few days later Burke was writing to Mario Gallo:

It is most fortunate that I was on the ground here to be the official undertaker. The corpse at least had flowers on the casket . . . It is very evident to me, through practical experience, that had the OBR been booked properly and solidly from the inception of the tour results would have been productive of pleasure and profit, since the company was in actual demand by the public and their heralded appearances were welcome to the public. However, with insecure bookings; limited time for advance publicity and exploitation; and inability to have given the contracting managers sufficient time to sell the attraction properly – all these factors combined to obstruct reasonable and favourable results.[45]

119

'Reorganization' was perhaps a polite word for what was going on in New York. Mario Gallo wrote to his uncle:

Since the return from the coast of Colonel de Basil last Friday there has been quite a bit of activity round the Park Central, at present ballet headquarters. A place was arranged for rehearsal of the company but the railroad company made it very difficult for us to reach the baggage cars for the music so that rehearsal has been postponed to Monday December 15. Mr Stanton finally agreed, upon payment of 100 dollars in cash, to have the baggage cars placed at the platform . . . I am working out a railroad movement to Mexico City for about 60 people and three baggage cars, where the company open in the near future, sometime after Christmas. The Colonel desires that I should go with the company to Mexico but I did not accept. If you think that the San Carlo might not go on tour on account of the war situation during this last week, then I could take a trip with the ballet. Going to Mexico City is not official yet. The Colonel is the only one to know the fact.[46]

Although all was really over between Gallo and de Basil from 9 November 1941, Gallo still wrote of the company as being 'under his management' on 19 November;[47] and on 21 November about 'gradually approaching an understanding in the conglomeration of differences which obliged me to cancel the Pacific tour of the OBR' and emphasizing that he had the highest regard for the company from the artistic point of view.[48] He was still hoping that de Basil would sign the unsigned bond, and it is not clear when or whether the Colonel ever complied.

Such matters must not be overstressed, however. The real difficulties lay in Hurok's opposition and de Basil's quixotic ideas of co-operation.

Mario Gallo continued to try and sort out company problems with reasonable cheerfulness. The dancers settled down to rehearse at the Park Central Hotel and Vova Grigoriev took on the complicated arrangements for transferring the company and its baggage to Mexico City.

Eventually Fortune Gallo and the Colonel reinstated a friendly relationship on paper, and de Basil wrote Gallo from Mexico City in the warmest terms, by hand, thanking him for 'kindnesses' and referring to possible future collaboration.[49]

They were all keeping their options open. For the Original Ballet Russe, however, the South American years were about to begin.

November 1941 to March 1947

To the rest of the world these years in South America from 1942 to 1946 possess something of the aspect of the Children of Israel's wanderings in the desert. It looks very different from a Latin American standpoint. Little has been known about the tours and no one outside the sub-continent has previously really bothered to work out even where and when they performed. For the company it was a period of incredibly hard work, often in impossibly difficult conditions, punctuated by the two long periods when they were based on the Teatro Colón in Buenos Aires. Wherever they went they made a lasting impression. Their influence was important and widespread.

Even then these years were compounded of melodrama, fantasy, fun and farce and they lose nothing in reminiscence. Often in fact they gain that gloss of nostalgia inherent in times when life is lived intensely and insecurely.

Russian ballet was not new to the main centres in Latin America. The Diaghilev Ballet twice toured there, in 1913 and again in 1917, and Anna Pavlova's company visited more than once. Many individual dancers and maîtres de ballet from Europe fulfilled terms of service with the leading theatres.

In 1942 the Viennese maître de ballet Margarita Wallmann was principal choreographer at the Teatro Colón, where she had been since 1937. The Russian Maria Oleneva, choreographer and principal dancer at the Teatro Municipal in Rio de Janeiro from 1927, left there in 1942 to direct the school at the São Paulo Teatro Municipal, while the Czech maître de ballet and choreographer Vaslav Veltchek, who had been in Brazil from 1939, moved in the opposite direction from São Paulo to Rio. In 1939 the American dancer Kaye Mackinnon, who studied classical ballet in Paris and modern dance with Mary Wigman and Harald Kreuzberg, dancing in Nijinska's ballet company in 1934, married the Peruvian composer and conductor Luis Pecheco. They settled in Lima where she directed a ballet school. In Chile, classical ballet was less important than modern dance as one of Kurt Jooss' dancers, Ernst Uthoff, was teaching in Santiago.

The de Basil Ballet spent the opening months of 1942 in Mexico City and Guadalajara. De Basil obviously managed to re-negotiate with the various South American theatres part of the tour forecast in June 1941 in his supplementary agreement with Gallo. This was probably done through Mario Gallo's good offices, and began at the Teatro Municipal in Rio in April, going on to São Paulo in May.

The impresario concerned was Ernesto de Quesada of the Sociedad Musical Daniel, which had been established in 1908 and operated through South and Central America. It was very much a family concern, with members of the de Quesada family as president, vice-president, treasurer and secretary of the company.

The journey from Mexico to Brazil was eventful. Leskova recalls how they arrived in Vera Cruz and found a little ship, the *Rio de la Plata*, which was already full of Spanish refugees on their way to Argentina. The dancers had to sleep four to a tiny cabin – she shared with Tchernicheva, Grigorieva and Anna Volkova. They had an alarm a few days out, when a destroyer and two cruisers surrounded them, but they turned out to be ships of the Allies, not part of the German fleet. Then a tremendous storm blew up in the Caribbean and the ship had to circle for four days off Barranquilla until the Spanish refugees and some of the sailors were on the point of mutiny. In Guaira, a Venezuelan port, Leskova caught measles and spent the rest of the voyage in the ship's hospital. The dancers worked as well as they could in the ship's saloon and before she fell ill Leskova was asked to teach the second movement of *Paganini* to Marie-Jeanne, the American dancer who had just married into the Quesada family and was to appear briefly with the company.

On 12 June 1942, the company made a triumphant Argentinian debut at the Teatro Politeama Argentino in Buenos Aires, opening with *Le Lac des cygnes, Paganini* and *Graduation Ball* and continuing with a full repertoire until 12 July. From there the dancers went to La Plata, which boasted Argentina's oldest opera house, the Teatro Argentino, dating from 1890, and played their first date in Uruguay (the Teatro SODRE in Montevideo) from 15 July to 2 August. Other cities in Argentina (Rosario, Cordoba and Mendoza) and Chile (Santiago and Viña del Mar) followed, before their return to Buenos Aires and their first appearance at the Teatro Colón.

On 28 August 1942 de Quesada signed a long and comprehensive contract with the directorate of the Colón on behalf of the Original Ballet Russe, for a season lasting from 15 October to 15 November – extended eventually to 28 November. In this Vania Psota, who had just rejoined de Basil after some years in Czechoslovakia, appears as *régisseur* and choreographer. Grigoriev remained *régisseur général* and

Eugene Fuerst was musical director and conductor. The dancers included Gollner, Tchernicheva, Grigorieva, Morosova, Stepanova, Leskova and Moulin; Petrov, Jasinsky, Orlov, Tupine, MacKenzie, Rostov and Algeranov. New names featured were Nina Stroganova, Moussia Larkina and Vladimir Dokoudovsky.

Stroganova was Danish, and had danced originally under her real name of Rigmor Ström. Trained by teachers from the Royal Danish Ballet and later with Preobrajenska, she appeared first with the Paris Opéra Comique. In New York she danced with the Mordkin Ballet and the Ballet Russe de Monte Carlo. Moussia Larkina was a stage name for Moscelyne Larkin, who was born in Tulsa, Oklahoma, of a Russian mother and an American Indian father. Her first dance studies were with her mother, Eva Matlagova, but she went on to Vincenzo Celli, Mordkin and Vilzak in New York.

Dokoudovsky, born in Monaco of Russian and Italian parents, also studied with Preobrajenska. His sister Tatiana Dokoudovska and his father's half-sister Kira Abricossova were with de Basil at different times. He appeared with the company at Monte Carlo in 1935 when he was only thirteen, and became a leading dancer with Nijinska's Polish Ballet in 1937 at the age of fifteen.

Before joining de Basil in 1941 he danced with the Ballet Russe de Monte Carlo and with Ballet Theatre. He inherited a wide range of roles with the Original Ballet Russe. His strong technique and great dramatic and comic talent fitted him for parts as divergent as Paganini (learnt from Rostov, for whom he had a great regard as an artist) and the Junior Cadet in *Graduation Ball*.

The repertoire at the Colón was selected from the ballets performed in Australia, and programmes were shared, in a two-to-one ratio, by the home and visiting companies. The Colón was a splendid, cumbersome old house, metaphorically full of establishment dust and cobwebs, with a stage bigger than that at La Scala. In the rotunda rehearsal room the dancers listened to Papa Grigoriev's reminiscences of Nijinsky's great leaps round the pillared hall, and in their dressing-rooms found the cohorts of dressers almost an embarrassment after their usual co-operative routines. Under Wallmann the *corps de ballet* had increased from 26 to 110 and *Le Lac des cygnes* was always given with 32 swans plus leaders and cygnets. Built in 1908, the theatre was used as a home for opera and ballet from 1925. After that date Bolm, Nijinska, Boris Romanov, Fokine, Balanchine and Wallmann all worked there, and this

123

was reflected in the large repertoire of the home ballet company. Wallmann versions of *Le Tricorne, Casse-noisette* and *La Valse* were listed, as well as Balanchine's *Apollo*, for the 1942 season. Perhaps the longest and most consistent influence on the resident company had been the English *régisseur* and ballet mistress Esmee Bulnes. Having gone there as assistant to Fokine in 1931, she stayed eighteen years before moving to La Scala, Milan.

This 1942 de Basil Ballet at the Colón is immediately seen to have only dwindling links in personnel with the pre-war company. Not even Riabouchinska remained from the familiar roster of prima ballerinas; Anna Volkova inherited, and danced brilliantly, roles such as the Golden Cockerel, the leading girl in *Graduation Ball* and Frivolity in *Présages*. Volkova, only slightly younger than Riabouchinska and like her born in Moscow, was another of Preobrajenska's pupils. She joined de Basil in 1933 and worked her way up in roles such as the Street Dancer in *Petrouchka* and Papillon in *Carnaval*. She quit the company in 1943 when she married and settled in Australia. Tchernicheva continued as a guest artist, mainly in *Francesca da Rimini*, astounding audiences and fellow-artists alike. Grigorieva danced Zobeide, a very fine performance – Rostov, who was the Shariar, remembers with delight her moving appeal in the final moments, when he often wished he could forgive rather than condemn. She also appeared as Action in *Présages*, in which role for some years she had alternated with Verchinina with notable success. Gollner was the main classical ballerina, dancing the Swan Queen and Aurora with brilliance and delicacy. Morosova, who, under the inspiring guidance of the great teacher Elisabeth Andersen-Ivantzova in New York, had gained in range from the days when she was loved primarily for her sparkling vivacity and her talents as a comedienne, was the Queen of Shemakhan or Mariuccia in *Les Femmes de bonne humeur*. Moulin danced the Bluebird *pas de deux* and Passion in *Présages*. Stepanova and Stroganova were young dancers of strong technique, capable of very varied work, and Larkina was emerging as an able and attractive soloist. Leskova danced a great range of roles, some, such as the Florentine Beauty in *Paganini*, inherited from Riabouchinska, some, such as the Street Dancer in *Danube bleu* or Columbine in *Carnaval*, taken over at short notice when Morosova broke an elbow in Canada in 1941. Petrov and Jasinsky were joined by Tupine and Dokoudovsky as *premiers danseurs*, Tupine in the romantically princely roles, Dokoudovsky as Harlequin, Bluebird and the Golden Slave. The dramatic elements in *Coq d'or* and *Francesca da Rimini* were ensured of effectiveness by Algeranov and Rostov, two of the most outstanding mimes in ballet history.

Wallmann, in her autobiography, says that she agreed gladly to the proffered hospitality of this contract but that it produced countless problems.[1] This could easily have been envisaged by everyone concerned. Two performances were given each week and each company began learning the other's repertoire. Violent multilingual arguments ensued about the use of the main rehearsal room. No one could resolve them and she longed, rather naturally, for the collaboration to end.

Although the de Basil repertoire was fresh to South American eyes, a new production was planned as a compliment to the Colón. The Colonel no longer had any outstanding choreographer, however, as Lichine had elected to stay in the USA. Vania Psota had composed ballets in Czechoslovakia and, in 1941, for Ballet Theatre, *Slavonika*, which Hurok described as 'an almost total loss from every point of view'.[2] He wanted to do more choreography. De Basil had already in Australia worked towards getting backing for a ballet on a local theme. There had also been a scheme, inspired by the sponsorship of the Canadian tour in 1941 by the Wings for Victory organization, by which he hoped to get money from the Bundles for Britain charity. In September 1941 he had put up to them a project for a ballet that Lichine had 'conceived, designed and executed, which he has called "Victory". The sense of the action depicts the valor of the British in the prosecution of the victory drive.' Lichine was one of the few in the Ballets Russes who took a close interest in world affairs. Although it might have been instructive, and would no doubt have been amusing, to have seen a White Russian counterpart of the Soviet propaganda ballets ('the valor of the Soviet workers in resisting capitalism'), this proposal, fortunately, came to nothing.

Now, in Argentina, de Basil obtained local patronage for a new work which was staged on 27 November 1942, *Fue una vez ... (Once upon a time...)*. It was set in Buenos Aires in 1830, the music was by Carlos Guastavino and the designs by Ignacio Pirovano. The choreography was credited to an Argentinian dancer, the wife of a politician, Silvia Pueyrredon de Elizalde, who studied with Volinine in Paris. The company gossip was that she was pregnant, and believed that if she worked on a ballet her child would be a choreographer. Production was by Psota, and according to the dancers – who had a low opinion of the ballet – it was he who took all rehearsals.

Fue una vez . . . was a love story, and the leading roles were created by Gollner and Jasinsky. One performance of it, remembered by Valrene Tweedie, was at the President's Palace in Buenos Aires, where the company, who had travelled by train from Cordoba where they were appearing at the time, danced it on an open-air stage in the gardens. Afterwards they were furious to discover that although there were splendid tables set for the guests with silver and expensive food, the dancers were served with sandwiches on tin trays. Some of them put this right by crawling under the tables and pinching better food when they got the chance – before getting the train back to Cordoba.

Valrene was now in love with one of the Cuban dancers in the company, Luis Trapaga (Trefilov), and they wanted to marry. They were under age, and as they had no parents in Argentina to stand sponsor they asked the Colonel. Typically, he asked why. There was no need, he thought, for a wedding. However, the Argentinian government appointed guardians for all foreign-born boys and girls under twenty-two, to check on where they stayed and how late they stayed out, because of the dangers of the white slave traffic, and their guardian agreed to give formal consent.

The use of local tales and legends seems to be a dominant theme in ballets staged in Argentina and Brazil, and it is hardly surprising to find the Original Ballet Russe during its Latin American years staging five of the kind: *Fue una vez . . .* was followed by *El Malón* (1943), *La Isla de los ceibos* (Montevideo, 1944), *Yx-Kik* (Guatemala, 1945) and *Yara* (Brazil, 1946). Much later, in the 'fifties and 'sixties, choreographers were still producing ballets locally with titles such as *The Discovery of Brazil* (by Leskova and Eugenia Feodorova), *Estancia* (Michel Borovsky) and *The Legend of Impossible Love* (Aurel Milloss). It is not usually a very fruitful genre.

The company had been a success in Cordoba and returned there for a longer season from 5 December 1942 to 3 January 1943, giving a special 'workers' programme' on 19 December which was shared with an actress, Angelina Pagano. It was also shared, over Christmas, with a nativity play. Sharing was very much part of the pattern of theatrical life in Latin America.

The next stop was at Viña del Mar in Chile, from January to February 1943. In Lima, Peru, in March, a Chilean conductor, William McDermott, was engaged. McDermott was a man with the right humorous approach and adaptability for the extraordinary itinerant months that were to follow. Apart from the welcome break of a seven-month stay at the Colón the company were for the next couple of years on the roads – and what roads! Most of their journeys were long-drawn-out and tedious, where they were not positively full of discomforts and dangers.

One of the first of McDermott's memories is of their arrival at La Paz, Bolivia, in April. As their train climbed in to the city, 12,000 feet above sea-level, the local dignitaries and the town band were waiting to receive them. McDermott, unaffected by the height, was able to appreciate the scene as one by one the expected stars staggered on to the platform, their faces various shades of green, hardly able to hold up their heads, while de Basil, typically unruffled, shook hands with the official party. Somehow they managed to get acclimatized, somehow they managed to dance *Le Lac des cygnes* and *Prince Igor*.

On tour the orchestras were largely recruited locally. Players rarely knew the scores of the ballets and, worse, they often could not sight-read. Often the conductor had to make enormous compromises – by cutting, for instance, all timpani in *Francesca da Rimini* in order to ensure the exactness of the final role of drums. Then there was the risk that someone might pull a wrong switch backstage and plunge the orchestra pit into darkness, or someone might confuse the scores and play *Schéhérazade* against the rest of the orchestra's *Prince Igor*. Sometimes a key player had to be temporarily borrowed on parole from a lunatic asylum or prison and sometimes the orange box that occasionally served as podium would collapse under the conductor.

After La Paz, however, they embarked on another and longer season at the Colón, on a different footing, as Margarita Wallman had returned to Europe. This started on 22 April 1943, but the contract, signed this time by Psota and not by de Basil, although de Basil remained director general, is dated 2 May. It laid out terms for a much more integrated existence between the Original Ballet Russe and the Colón Ballet. In fact the programmes temporarily shelved the title 'Original Ballet Russe' and referred to 'The Colón Ballet, director general Col. de Basil'.

The repertoire was drawn from both companies, but although Argentinian dancers performed in the de Basil ballets the de Basil

127

dancers did not appear in the Colón repertoire. The exception to that rule was a couple of performances of Wallman's version of *The Sleeping Beauty* in which Stepanova danced Aurora with Alberto Siccardi, replacing the injured Maria Ruanova. Of the Colón principals, Leticia de la Vega danced Columbine and Zobeide, Dora Del Grande Thamar, Maria Ruanova *Sylphides,* Lida Martinoli *Cimarosiana*, Angel Eleta Petrouchka and the Golden Slave, Louis Le Bercher Harlequin. The season lasted from 22 April to 28 November. Ballet alternated with opera, as usual, and dancers from both companies appeared in the operas *La Traviata* and *Armide* with choreography by Psota.

To many in the audience the Russians and their repertoire were a revelation. One small girl of eleven, a ballet student with a leg in plaster, sat in a stage box entranced by the dancers and the ballets. This was April Olrich, born in Zanzibar of British parents, who now had her home in Buenos Aires. Her first memories of the company she was to join two years later are of the impact of the three symphonic ballets (particularly *Choreartium*), of the wit and style of *Les Femmes de bonne humeur* or *Cimarosiana*, the splendours of *Coq d'or* and the tempestuous excitement of *Schéhérazade* and *Prince Igor*. By the end of the season, when her leg was better, she was turning *fouettés* endlessly in the theatre corridors. 'I hear you do a lot of *fouettés*,' said de Basil, meeting her in the audience. 'Will you show me what you can do?' And when he had watched her, thinking back no doubt to Toumanova and Baronova in 1932, he said, 'You must join our company when you are a little older.'

A second local folktale ballet was staged on 16 July 1943. *El Malón*, with choreography based on Indian and samba rhythms by Psota, in association with Antonio Barcelo, had music by Hector Iglesias Villoud and decor by Hector Basaldua. Basaldua was the resident scenic director, who designed most of the decors and costumes for operas and ballets at the Colón during the years 1930 to 1956. '*Malón*' means a surprise attack by Indians and the cast list featured an engaged couple, Rosario and Lorenzo, and a rich landowner, Hilarion. Without knowing the story one can guess at it . . . The score was conducted by the composer and the cast was an 'integrated' one, with Esmeralda Agoglio, a 17-year-old who had joined the Colón Ballet two years before, in the lead and Angel Eleta as the fiancé. Kenneth MacKenzie was Hilarion and Lara Obidenna the girl's mother.

Montevideo followed, a long season at the Teatro Municipal de Verano from 29 November 1943 to 31 March 1944. Like Buenos Aires, Montevideo wanted a new ballet with which it could identify, and so the hardworking Psota choreographed *La Isla de los ceibos*. Again the libretto, by Roman Vignoly Barreto, was from a legend, this time about the indigenous scarlet-flowered silk cotton tree. Eduardo Fabini composed the music, Jacob Anchutin, who travelled with the company as a scene painter, was the designer. It was danced by Stepanova as the Flower, Volkova as the Bird, Tupine as the Branch and MacKenzie as the Wind. The ensemble were flowers, branches, winds and roots, with extra personnel pressed into service as part of the scenery as blossoms perched on a giant tree.

From Montevideo the company returned to Brazil (São Paulo and Rio, which most of them loved). They were back in Uruguay from June to July 1944, and then appeared in Buenos Aires at the Teatro Avenida from July to October. Wallmann had returned to the Colón, so there were no further contracts with that theatre.

At this point Grigorieva left, having decided to work at the Teatro Municipal in Rio. It was a considerable loss. She had made an indelible mark in both lyrical and dramatic roles and would have had an even wider range if she had not been, for those days, rather too tall. Petrov and Gollner also fled, borrowing back on some excuse the passports lodged with de Basil. As usual when someone pulled off a successful coup, the Colonel laughed and admired them for having outsmarted him. Stepanova and Tupine inherited their roles, Stepanova at last attaining the status of prima ballerina foreseen by Massine, Haskell and de Basil in the mid-'thirties when she was ten years old. She and her parents had shown great loyalty to the Colonel, who had paid Preobrajenska for her continued tuition on the understanding that she would join his company, in refusing an offer from the Ballet Russe de Monte Carlo in 1938. Now she reaped some reward in the acclaim of enthusiastic audiences in every Latin American country.

In October the company danced at La Plata, Santa Fe and Rosario and from 11 to 17 October in Santiago, Chile. Here they were joined by April Olrich, now thirteen – de Basil's last 'baby ballerina' – not yet a ballerina of course but a dancer of considerable promise. Like the earlier 'babies' she was accompanied by her mother, and '*la madre di April*' became a feature of the ballet's daily life. To begin with things were difficult. April's mother, unused to the company's raggle-tagglegypsy method of travelling, carried no food, and the dancers, wary as any other tribe might be of newcomers, made no overtures of friendship. Professionally, too, April was unwelcome, until she established with Grigoriev that she was a quick learner. The men, and the topliners, were kinder than the *corps de ballet* girls, but the topliners often travelled separately. The antagonism gradually broke down, particularly as it became apparent that April's mother would share the advantages her husband arranged in the way of rooms with baths or showers, or offer medical advice. Like so many of the mothers of former years she turned her hand to all kinds of work. Also like those other mothers, she guarded jealously her daughter's health and virtue – and, because she was an academic lady, saw that April did her lessons and even took examinations, in solitary state at British consulates.

From Chile the company were due in Peru and Vova Grigoriev had the problem of getting a boat to take them from Valparaiso to Lima. He found one, with pretty poor conditions but the right number of places – and no worse, perhaps, than those Dolin recalls in their journey from Australia to New Zealand in 1938 when they travelled on a 'far too small boat, stinking of rotten wood and seaweed'.[3] The Chile-to-Peru boat-trip was shared with a circus troupe, lots of cattle, and gunpowder. Roman Jasinsky and Moussia Larkina, who had married the previous Christmas Eve in Buenos Aires, had a cabin directly under the part of the deck on which the cows were housed, and a leaking cabin roof. Meat was fresh, they remember. Each day a cow was killed . . . Despite everything, Papa Grigoriev took rehearsals, and the company did class holding on to the deck rails. It was the boat's last trip. It sank on the return voyage.

Travelling conditions were often just barely tolerable. Although South America was neutral, the wartime shortage of spare parts for the repair of vehicles was acutely felt. The company travelled by worn-out buses or tiny planes, by coastal ships or old-fashioned river paddle-steamers. On one of these, Larkina and Jasinsky recall, there were ants all over the boat. They bought a sausage at a market – everyone, including the Colonel, shopped by barter at local markets – and hopefully hung it from the ceiling. When they woke next morning it was thick with ants.

Everywhere, the audiences compensated for the hardships. There were full, and predominantly enthusiastic, houses after each journey. The Lima engagement lasted from 16 December 1944 to 16 January

1945. From Lima the company embarked on its roughest year of touring. All the time, as soon as he settled them in at one theatre, the Colonel would disappear to the next possible city or state to charm the local authorities into providing the next booking. He would then fly back, like a parent bird with a beakful of food, to report a six-week engagement coming up. No one looked further ahead than the next journey.

As they progressed, scenery and costumes suffered. Wallmann records that the Colón had re-made and repaired these in 1942[4] but by now they were again showing the strain. However, in a world where workmen and needlewomen could not only be hired but would work for their money, carpenters, painters and seamstresses patched things up reasonably well. More difficult were tights, which were often improvised from stockings and pants, and shoes, which were hardened with shellac and kept in service as long as possible.

In January and February 1945 they were in Ecuador (Guayaquil and Quito) and went on to Colombia (Bogotà, Medellin, Barranquilla and Cartagena), reaching Venezuela (Caracas) in July.

In Guayaquil there were tropical floods. A heavy truck with scenery stuck in the mud and all the male dancers had to help extricate it. McDermott remembers the Teatro de 9 Octubre surrounded by water, the orchestra pit gradually flooding. The audience, arriving in evening dress, found its own solution to the problem of stepping out of transport into a moat. The men took off their evening trousers and carried them and their long-skirted ladies into the theatre, where they dried off and dressed up again. In Quito four performances were extended to twenty-six, by public demand.

From Ecuador to Colombia the transport was by a caravan of buses and trucks over the back country towards the frontier. The road deteriorated at times into a path. When darkness fell, the boys had to get out of the buses to guide the drivers by flashlight, so that they would keep to the path and not take a wrong turn accidentally and plunge over a cliff. Eventually they reached an airstrip on the Ecuador side of the border. From there they were ferried in relays in a ten-seater plane into Colombia.

The ranks of the company were thinning and locally recruited dancers were brought in to fill the gaps. 'These Russians all have Spanish names', McDermott heard someone say. Some of the South American dancers were given temporary Russian aliases – usually a surname once familiar with the company whose previous owner had left. Thus Elsa Garcia Galvez was programmed as Alexandra Golovina, Nelly Laport as Kyra Nelidova.

Leskova, the creator of the pigtailed girl in *Graduation Ball* five years previously, left the company in São Paulo. She had become a fine and versatile ballerina, dancing many leads, and one of her unique assignments was to create a role in Balanchine's *Balustrade* in 1941. She found him easier to work for than any of the other choreographers associated with the company. He knew exactly what he wanted from his dancers, explained movements clearly, in a way that made the most difficult combinations emerge fluently.

Balanchine was instrumental in helping her make up her mind to quit de Basil. In 1942, when the Original Ballet Russe was appearing at the Teatro Politeama in Buenos Aires, Balanchine was staging his *Mozart Violin Concerto* at the Colón. He went to see a number of de Basil performances and then, over supper with the Ladres to which Leskova had been invited, asked her to dance in the first and third movements of the new ballet.

She went to rehearsal with Shabelevsky (at that time a guest artist at the Colón – he was never a member of the de Basil Ballet after 1938) but kept it a secret from the Colonel. At last she broke the news to him and he seemed to take it calmly, but the day after she received a lawyer's letter pointing out that as a minor, whose father had entrusted her to the Colonel, she could not leave the company. Balanchine tried and failed to get her released, and she refused an offer of marriage from one of the Colón's directors, a 75-year-old bachelor who thought he could solve the problem. Reluctantly, she missed the chance of dancing the Balanchine ballet.

Had the Colonel been more generous about leave of absence then he would probably not have lost her in 1945, when she and Anna Volkova were offered an excellent six-month contract to appear at the Copacabana Casino. De Basil again refused. This was hardly surprising, as the war was coming to an end and he must have been alarmed to think how few of his leading dancers were going to be with him when he returned, as he obviously wished to do, to New York and London. The director of the Casino was determined not to be defeated and a clever scheme was put into play. It was arranged that the two girls would be stopped in the street in São Paulo and asked for identification papers, which they could not produce as these were always lodged with de Basil. They were kept overnight at the police station, and when the Colonel arrived from Rio with the passports and his lawyer they told him they were going to stay in Brazil. They were in an awkward position, however, because their visas were part of a collective one granted to the company, and the company was due to go on to Uruguay. De Basil went to presidential level to try and get the girls extradited from Brazil. They in turn appealed to influential friends. At last they got individual visas to take them to Paraguay and the Colonel had to admit defeat.

It was a bad miscalculation on his part. Both dancers loved the repertoire and were infinitely grateful for the opportunity they had to work with Fokine (in spite of the fact that he scared them), with Massine (whom they greatly admired), with Balanchine, Lichine and Nijinska. They were proud and happy to be part of such an organization.

The company arrived in Caracas during a typical small South American revolution, which everyone took very much as a matter of course. Olrich and her mother, travelling ahead, checked in at the apartment booked by her father but found a machine gun mounted outside. When they went out to buy food they were sent back by a friendly man who said, in answer to their questions, 'We're the rebels – but don't worry, it won't be long until we're the government.'

Quite apart from revolutions, Venezuela had a bad reputation in South America as a graveyard of theatrical companies. The reasons are obvious if one looks at a map: it was extremely difficult to get any forward or backward engagements. De Basil solved the problem with the kind of flair that proved his quality as a leader. Panama was a military zone and normally an insurmountable barrier. He went to talk to the commander, soldier to soldier, and came away with an invitation for the company to give free performances for the troops in return for military transport out of the Canal Zone after shows in Panama and Colón. This would take them to Costa Rica, thence to Honduras (Tegucigalpa), San Salvador, Guatemala and back, no doubt with a big sigh of relief, to Mexico. From there he could arrange for them to travel by boat to Brazil (Rio, São Paulo and Recife) via Havana.

The Forces concerts went well but some of the other engagements had their difficulties. In Tegucigalpa there were no musicians at all to be had, not even in the prisons or asylums. The town band was offered but McDermott felt it would be better to dance to a piano, only to find that pianos were almost as scarce as musicians. At last one was run to earth,

133

an old lady's pet Bechstein – but to his further dismay there were no expert removers. The piano suffered badly for its sudden spell in the limelight and is still on McDermott's conscience.

In Guatemala, Psota rapidly ran up a ballet, *Yx-Kik*, based on a Maya-Quiché legend by Ricardo and Jesus Castillo, of which all other recollection seems (perhaps mercifully) to have slipped from people's minds. In Mexico they supplemented their main performances at the Palacio des Bellas Artes by dancing in the bull-ring. The girls changed in the matadors' hospital, where the blood of the last gored matador still stained the floor. They went out and danced *Les Sylphides* and *Danube bleu* to an audience of Mexican Indians who sat in stolid silence and torrential rain. The performance was called off only when the musical instruments became waterlogged.

At last, in Mexico, however, a new ballet was prepared of a different calibre to the earlier productions of the South American years. Lichine was now a citizen of the USA – the dream of most stateless dancers – and living in California. In 1945, when Sevastianov was managing director of Ballet Theatre, they implemented a project for a ballet first mooted by Educational Ballets Ltd in 1938 – *Fair at Sorotchinsk* – and Lichine and Riabouchinska appeared as guests with that company. Now he began working with the de Basil dancers on *Cain and Abel*.

McDermott orchestrated and arranged for him *Siegfried's Rhine Journey* from Wagner's *Götterdämmerung*, and the decor and costumes were by Miguel Prieto. Like Lichine's early work *Les Imaginaires*, it was an easy target for critics. When it came to New York, Denby wrote:

Cain and Abel stressed manly Body Beautiful poses by two rugged boys in tiny trunks, and sexy entanglements with two girls called Good and Evil; Cain and Abel also bumped around together on the floor a good deal and perspired freely. A wit called it "Tarzan in a Turkish Bath" . . .[5]

Plenty of ballets since then however have featured sweaty, sexy entanglements with rugged boys in tiny trunks . . .

However unpopular it was with the New York critics, *Cain and Abel* was enjoyed by a good many audiences, before and after New York. In the early days in Central and South America it was enthusiastically received. It was strong and dramatic and worked well in theatrical terms. There had been trouble over its preparation. De Basil had thought – hoped? – that it was ready to launch, but Lichine was not satisfied. There was the inevitable row, and Lichine vanished back to California. Kenneth MacKenzie got permission from him by telephone to finish the ballet but almost immediately Lichine changed his mind. He returned, and completed the work, which was given its premiere on 8 March 1946 in Mexico with Olrich and Carlota Pereyra, Tupine and MacKenzie in the leading roles.

Gioia Vanni, who had watched it from its first rehearsal, reflected the view of its admirers:

Into the character of Evil Lichine has woven all the sinuosity and allure of the snake; she belongs to the strange exotic women, akin to his siren of *The Prodigal Son*. The character of Good has in her dance with Cain a gaiety and carefree charm, and always the movements are possessed of a striking originality. But the chief interest centres round Cain. This part is played by Kenneth MacKenzie; it is one of those tremendous creations which hold one fascinated throughout. Despite the essential egotism of Cain, he succeeds in gaining our sympathy; in the agony of his remorse, he leaves one strangely moved and elated.[6]

De Basil went back to New York after Panama and was once more in touch with Nicholas Koudriavtzev. Koudriavtzev had settled in Montreal, where he created Canadian Concerts and Artists. He began to make some bookings for the company, but decided that they would get nowhere without trying to repair the Hurok connection. De Basil was ill – he had a heart condition as well as constant ill-health from old war wounds. He was living (according to Hurok) at the home of a friend on upper Fifth Avenue. Koudriavtzev phoned Hurok and opened negotiations.

The picture of these discussions as given by Hurok[7] is typical of theatrical autobiographical style: in other words, his side of the proceedings is portrayed amusingly, as a case of a warm heart winning over better judgement. In fact he needed a ballet company. He had given up the Ballet Russe de Monte Carlo at the end of the autumn season of 1942 and had now also given up Ballet Theatre. He had taken on a new company, the Markova-Dolin Ballet (America), but this small venture was hardly a replacement for the larger groups. It was to his advantage to make a deal with de Basil.

The deal he eventually made included another outsize character of the time, the Marquis de Cuevas. This was on de Cuevas' own initiative.

De Cuevas, whose wife was a granddaughter of John D. Rockefeller, had already survived one balletic financial catastrophe. In 1943 he had set up the Ballet Institute and subsequently established Ballet International, taking and renaming the Park Theatre on Columbus Circle, New York, for a two-month season that exhausted him financially but resulted in some interesting choreography. The ballets were physically in store, and the dancers dispersed. He wanted to begin again so, like Hurok, he could now find a use for de Basil and his Ballet.

De Cuevas went to Mexico in March 1946 to see the Original Ballet Russe and then approached Hurok. Lengthy negotiations took place, mostly in de Basil's temporary home in New York. At last Hurok was able to travel to Europe and report to de Cuevas, who was now in France, that something was settled. They would give a season at the Met. This would bring the de Basil Ballet back to the States (which suited de Basil). They would revive some ballets from Ballet International's repertoire and name de Cuevas on the programme as artistic director (which suited de Cuevas). They would then go on a tour, which would fulfil Hurok's promises of a ballet company to his States-wide contacts (which suited Hurok). As an additional bonus for Hurok, de Basil now naturally dropped his long-standing conspiracy suit.

At this point it was realized that the de Basil repertoire, both in terms of costumes and decor and in terms of performance, needed a thorough overhaul. This was hardly surprising. The surprise was rather that a company existed at all, after the battling nomadic months that had followed the final Colón engagement. The dancers who had seen it through, and would come to New York, were the indomitable Tchernicheva, Morosova, Stepanova, Stroganova, Moulin, Larkina and Olrich with Jasinsky, Dokoudovsky, Tupine, and Kenneth MacKenzie. Rostov was leaving, having decided to work with Kaye MacKinnon who had recently founded her own school, Escuela des Ballet Peruano, in Lima. Psota would stay, although as the war in Europe had ended on 7 May 1945, he planned to return at some point to Czechoslovakia with his wife, Nina Leonidova.

Hurok engaged John Taras, who had been with The American Ballet, Ballet Theatre and the Markova-Dolin Ballet, as maître de ballet to the amalgamated company and sent him down to Brazil in July 1945 with some additional dancers. Meanwhile Psota, as his last choregraphic assignment for the company, was staging a Brazilian ballet, *Yara*, premiered at the Teatro Municipal in São Paulo (5 August). With an excellent score by Francisco Mignone (de Basil had tried for Villa-Lobos, who was not well enough) and fantastic surrealist decors and costumes by an important Brazilian painter, Candido Portinari, *Yara* was an exotic tale of the love-affair of the water goddess Yara and the sun god Guaracy and its influence on earth and its inhabitants. The leading roles were created by Stepanova, Tupine and MacKenzie and featured spectacular travelling lifts. It was the only one of Psota's de Basil ballets to be shown in the United States but it failed to repeat there the success it had in Brazil.

Psota's choreography, although dealing with folk subjects, was firmly classical. Stepanova recalls it as often effective but distinctly old-fashioned, and this probably explains why his reputation was so much higher in Czechoslovakia than in America and Western Europe. His position as principal choreographer in the South American years, when other members of the company like Dokoudovsky and MacKenzie very much wished to create ballets, probably owed something to the continuing influence of his wife Nina Leonidova with her ex-husband de Basil. She took a keen interest in performances and remained to some extent operative in company life.

Leaving from Brazil was not a simple matter. Not only were there problems about quittance of debts and transport arrangements. There were political ones, in the shape of a general strike and social unrest. Olrich again remembers a violent situation, with bombs being thrown and cars set on fire. Again the combatants were gentlemanly, and she got home safely from the theatre to find that her mother, in their fourteenth-floor apartment, would hardly believe her when she pleaded that a revolution had made her late.

The season in Rio finished on 31 August 1945, shortly after World War II had ended with Japan's capitulation on 14 August. The New York season was due to open on 29 September, but the personnel and properties of the de Basil Ballet were stranded in Brazil. Hurok flung himself into emergency arrangements. Taras was flown back from Brazil, where he had got on well with the Original Ballet Russe. An alternative sets of dancers was engaged so that the season could, if necessary, start with the de Cuevas ballets, but two days before the opening the de Basil Ballet arrived at a South Brooklyn pier. The dancers were naturally out of condition after eleven days in a cramped boat, and both the sets and the costumes were in a parlous state.

Hurok, who prided himself on the spick and span appearance of his companies, set about a hasty refurbishing, but the season was fatally prejudiced for the Original Ballet Russe by bad opening performances. It had to compete not only with a rival season from Ballet Theatre which opened on 30 September 1945 at the Broadway Theatre – a situation known locally as the Battle of the Ballets – but with its own past history. The repertoire that had been dragged from pillar to post over four years in South and Central America was made up of ballets that were now part of legend. Much had changed in the war years. Famous works, even if splendidly performed – and the company was in no state to perform them splendidly – now looked old-fashioned. Without financial backing or the presence of a first-rate artistic director and choreographer de Basil had been quite unable to stage new ballets that could in any way compare with the productions that Denham's company or Ballet Theatre were offering the public. *Yara* and *Cain and Abel* brought him no prestige although the latter had a small *succès de scandale*; some of the press found it shocking that the 14-year-old Olrich should be involved in a blatantly erotic duet and as a result the public queued to see it.

As for the dancers, they desperately needed a period of stabilization and disciplined classwork and rehearsal if they were to show themselves at their best. On the evidence of their performances either earlier (in Australia, Canada and the USA in 1941) or later, with other companies, there is no question but that this group of leading dancers had great technique and talent. It was their misfortune that no one made it possible for them to be rehabilitated before they were exhibited to the New York critics and public.

It would seem to have been merely sensible for Hurok, who always seemed able to find money somewhere if he made sufficient effort, to have arranged things differently. Naturally in his book he blames the late arrival of the company in New York, but in his determination to keep his commitment to a date at the Met it was hardly realistic to have left the short gap of one month for transporting and rehearsing a company known to be in need of an extensive wash and brush-up.

From reports, this seems to have been one occasion where the celebrated and very real Grigoriev discipline and standards were unable to operate. There are many independent statements about raggedness in the *corps de ballet* which, according to one witness, was 'of every shape,

138

age and ethnic origin known to man', and lack of style in the performances. There were also plenty of invidious comparisons made between the Original Ballet Russe and the New York recruits who were well drilled and pleasing in the de Cuevas ballets. Even if the Russians had been at their best, they would have found that an inevitable reaction had set in against them. Local pride in American ballet had been nourished during the 1940s by the growth of American companies and the emergence of American star dancers and choreographers, and now an element of chauvinistic prejudice entered into the judgement of audiences and critics.

They were *not*, however, at their best. Unsatisfactory standards are always inexcusable but, without making excuses, it is possible to account for them. Stylistically the two sets of dancers must have been incompatible and they were too equally balanced numerically to integrate. In the great days of the de Basil Ballet, dancers of many nationalities merged excellently, but there had always been a majority of Russian and Polish artists to set the style. Equally important, at that time the influence of Russian and Polish teachers was predominant throughout the profession. By 1946 there were definite schools of American or English ballet which could never have blended harmoniously with the eastern European manner.

The repertoire, too, was brought together in the wrong way. New ballets, modern ballets, can fit in with older works, but not if a handful are forcibly grafted on to a repertoire whose character has developed over years. The ballets salvaged from Ballet International, although they had a better press than the old stalwarts in their fatigued condition, were none of them outstanding. The most unusual was Antonia Cobos' *Mute Wife*, her first ballet, which had been considered an intelligent comedy when it was given on 22 November 1944. Edward Caton's *Sebastian* had, for its time, a certain melodramatic impact and the fashionable cachet of a Menotti score. William Dollar's *Constantia* was easily forgettable although it is by no means forgotten.

Of considerable help from a popularity point of view was Hurok's decision to engage guest artists: Markova, Dolin, Eglevsky and Francisco Moncion. This meant however that a third strong and unco-ordinated element was introduced.

Markova and Dolin were the *raison d'être* for the only new ballet, John Taras' *Camille*, premiered on 1 October 1946. The production, backed by Ballet Associates in America, had a Schubert score and typically romantic designs by Cecil Beaton. It was not greeted with any wild enthusiasm by the critics. Denby found it 'an agreeable though an excessively slight ballet',[8] Walter Terry described it as 'pretty as a picture and just about as flat',[9] and John Martin called it 'a veritable nothing'.[10] It lasted through the subsequent tour and then slipped quietly out of sight.

Dolin staged two additions to the repertoire. The first, on 11 October, was *Giselle*, for which the Benois settings were adapted by George Dunkel. This was a good choice, as not only was Markova's Giselle already legendary but there was a fruitful rivalry (did Hurok remember Covent Garden and Drury Lane in 1938 and their satisfying box office receipts?) as Ballet Theatre was currently staging *Giselle* with Alicia Alonso. Rosella Hightower, an emerging American dancer who had been with Denham's company and with Ballet Theatre, was the Myrtha in the Original Ballet Russe production, alternating with Marjorie Tallchief, while Skibine played Hilarion.

In 1941 Dolin had choreographed a version of the nineteenth-century *Pas de quatre* for Ballet Theatre. The first reconstruction of this lost Jules Perrot work, originally danced by Taglioni, Lucile Grahn, Carlotta Grisi and Fanny Cerito, was made by Keith Lester for the (English) Markova-Dolin Ballet in 1937. Lester could not get to the United States in 1941 because of World War II, and Dolin's was an independent creation. Now it was put on by the de Basil company with Markova as Taglioni, Stroganova as Grahn, Hightower as Grisi and Morosova as Cerito.

Dolin also resumed some of the roles, like the Young Musician in *Symphonie fantastique,* that he had danced in Australia in 1938–9. Eglevsky opened the season, partnering Hightower in *Le Lac des cygnes.* In addition he danced *Schéhérazade, Spectre,* and the Black Swan and Don Quixote *pas de deux.* The striking Francisco Moncion repeated two parts he had created for Ballet International – the Doctor in *Mute Wife* and the title role of *Sebastian*, the Moorish slave who sacrifices his life for the Courtesan he loves.

That New York season was disastrous for the basic de Basil Ballet but the tour that followed was better. There were still many people bitterly disappointed, but sometimes the company made converts to ballet among young people who saw them in Boston or Chicago, Philadelphia or San Francisco. Markova and Dolin continued as guest artists on a long tour, including Georgia, Florida, the Carolinas and Indiana and reaching California in February 1947.

In March 1947 the company returned to the Met briefly for what everyone still thinks of as a continuation of the Fall 1946 season. The two seasons run together, perhaps not surprisingly, in people's memories. This time there were two new ballets. One was yet another revival, Nijinska's *Pictures at an Exhibition*, a production which Denby had admired, but not greatly enjoyed, in November 1944 when it was premiered by Ballet International. Scenery and costumes were by Boris Aronson, and Cesar de Mendoza was guest conductor. *Pictures at an Exhibition* was an essentially peasant Russian interpretation of the score, linking village festivals, fairy-tales and activities – an ensemble work with two principal roles. The male lead was Serge Ismailov, who had danced it for Ballet International but was no stranger to the de Basil Ballet. He had been with them from 1933 to 1940. The ballerina was a beautiful newcomer, Sirène Adjemova, much publicized as the first principal dancer to reach America from Europe after the war. She had been born in Paris of Armenian and Russian parents and studied with Kschessinska before joining the Nouveau Ballet de Monte Carlo. For de Basil she danced, without any striking success, Zobeide in *Schéhérazade* and the Girl in *Spectre*.

The second new ballet was a witty send-up, *Pas de trois*, by Jerome Robbins. It was set to extracts from Berlioz' *Damnation of Faust* (the minuet of the will-o'-the-wisps and the dance of the sylphs) and danced by Rosella Hightower, Dolin and Eglevsky. Lillian Moore called it 'an irreverent and diverting bit of nonsense, a not too subtle but uproariously funny satire on classical ballet and the affected stage manners of ballerinas and premiers danseurs' and it proved immensely popular.

Hightower was replacing Markova because of illness, and for the same reason she made her debut in *Giselle* which proved the sensation of the season. She danced it at five hours' notice and some critics felt she had suddenly emerged as a full-ranking ballerina. Lillian Moore however, praising her as 'a brilliant, strong, resourceful dancer' felt that she was 'more at home in bravura roles than in that of the elusive night spirit'.[11]

March 1947 to January 1952

The uneasy alliance of Hurok, de Cuevas and de Basil was disintegrating. De Cuevas, who had never been more than nominally artistic director, was already in Monte Carlo discussing with Lifar the future of the Nouveau Ballet de Monte Carlo. They would all, once again, have liked to acquire the historic repertoire controlled by Colonel de Basil, preferably without the Colonel. Once again he was reluctant to co-operate, determined to remain as independent as he could.

He talked with them interminably, in Europe and in America. In London in March 1947 he gave an interview in which he spoke of a possible merger resulting in two companies, one based on New York and one on Paris. The European company, and it sounds as though this was the one he hoped to control, would tour Lisbon, Barcelona, Paris, Monte Carlo and the Scandinavian capitals. It would reach London in the late summer, play six weeks in the British provinces and then go to New York. He had been discussing with Beecham the idea of staging *The Great Elopement,* a Handel score adapted by Beecham and dear to his heart.[1] Springes to catch woodcock . . . But Beecham no longer controlled Covent Garden and it was difficult then, as now, to find other theatres in London suitable for large ballet companies.

Not unexpectedly, nothing came of the merger. De Basil stayed in Europe, renewing old contacts. He met Nadine Bouchonnet and her husband in Paris – Madame Bouchonnet had been the Paris representative of the Zerbason Agency and later of the de Basil Ballet. He met Mariano Norsky, who had frequently booked the company in European countries, and in London saw Bruce Ottley, George Kirsta the theatre designer and Julian Braunsweg. Like de Basil, Braunsweg had been connected with ballet since the early 1920s, when he managed Boris Romanov's Russian Romantic Ballet. The small man and the tall man had a good deal in common and had known each other for many years. Once back in the United States, de Basil cabled Braunsweg asking him to arrange a European tour for the company.[2] In London, Braunsweg contacted David Webster, the new general administrator of the Royal Opera House, Covent Garden, which had been re-opened in February 1946 with a season by the Sadler's Wells (later Royal) Ballet. Webster, rather reluctantly, agreed to book the Original Ballet Russe for a summer season. Braunsweg, with a realistic view of the situation, suggested that the Colonel should bring his dancers to Paris and recruit more there. He went over himself, and together they made plans.

De Basil had always taken a keen interest in his dancers. If Grigoriev was the company's papa, through the years de Basil was perhaps like an affectionate uncle – not always at hand, but always very much concerned. When he had money he gave them presents, when he thought they needed it he gave them vitamin injections, sometimes against their will, and often he stood sponsor at weddings and christenings. During the South American years he developed a friendship for his new principals, Dokoudovsky and his wife Stroganova.

Dokoudovsky was, with Jasinsky, the leading male dancer available in 1947 and Orlov too came to Europe. Tupine and Stepanova had both elected to stay in America – Stepanova had agreed to marry a long-standing admirer, George Peabody Gardner, and settle in Boston – but Morosova, Moulin, Larkina and Olrich were with the company (Stroganova was pregnant). Riabouchinska and Lichine promised to join for part of the London season and rehearse *Graduation Ball, Le Fils prodigue* and *Protée*. Grigoriev and Tchernicheva began to get the company into shape, and de Basil and Braunsweg engaged Renée Jeanmaire, not yet metamorphosed into Zizi by way of Roland Petit's *Carmen*, as the season's Aurora. They also engaged a young American of Russian parents, Hélène Komarova, who danced Action in *Les Présages* and Zobeide, the Chicago-born Hélène Constantine who, as Hélène Muselle, was in the *corps de ballet* in 1941, and a fluent young classical dancer of excellent elevation, Vladimir Skouratov from the Nouveau Ballet de Monte Carlo. Taras danced some important character roles such as the General in *Graduation Ball* and was titular maître de ballet. As he did not know the full repertoire Dokoudovsky and Larkina, who had good memories, assisted Grigoriev in rehearsal.

Most of the scenery needed re-painting. Some had been renewed by Hurok but other ballets had not been done since South America and some had remained throughout the war in Paris. These were restored by Michel Larionov, and costumes were re-made in material bought by Braunsweg and de Basil in Paris street markets at about a third of the shop prices – the sort of measure that would have won the firm approval of Lilian Baylis of the Old Vic and Sadler's Wells.

There was very little time, as the season was due to open at Covent Garden on 22 July 1947. A large repertoire was scheduled, including some ballets not performed in New York – *Les Présages, Carnaval, Le Coq d'or, Protée* and *Le Fils prodigue*. De Basil, according to Braunsweg, began for the first time to lose his nerve, no doubt remembering all that London had meant to the company in the pre-war years and how audiences must have changed since 1939.

They had changed more, in fact, than he probably realized. The war years had seen an unprecedented growth in the popularity of ballet throughout Britain, but it was very largely the popularity of the Sadler's Wells Ballet, led by Margot Fonteyn and Robert Helpmann who were both idolized. There were faithful audiences too for Ballet Rambert and for Mona Inglesby's International Ballet. Now visitors were bringing London back into the world scene, and the Original Ballet Russe was preceded by Roland Petit's chic and inventive Ballets des Champs-Elysées, and a season at Covent Garden in which Ballet Theatre showed vigorous creations by Jerome Robbins and Agnes de Mille. The new generation of enthusiasts, and the newer critics, had only snapshot memories, if any, of the Russian ballet repertoire. The Original Ballet Russe had also, once again, to face competition with its own early fame.

The reflex reaction of most people who saw the season, when it is mentioned to them, is of acute and quite natural disappointment. Those who remembered the pre-war company of course knew exactly how much had been lost. They felt, in the words of P.W. Manchester, that it was 'like taking away the entire foundation of those who had grown up with this company'. All the same, they were able to keep clear in their minds the definition between past and present. Those who were new to the repertoire suffered bitter disillusionment and took it in a less balanced fashion. Their imaginations had been nourished on panegyrics from their elders and they were unwilling to allow that these could even have been true at the time. The state of affairs is reflected in the conversation between P.W. Manchester and Dale Harris and David Vaughan of *Ballet Review*, in such exchanges as this:

BR: We were able to see *Présages* and above all to see *Symphonie fantastique* in 1947 and it seemed a ballet of no interest whatsoever.
PWM: But I think that you cannot compare what de Basil brought in 1947 with what he had had in the 'thirties. I think that's very unfair to do that, because there were sprinkled through the corps de ballet half a dozen who knew the ballets and the rest just followed, and this is really how those things were brought on in that season. By then he was almost bankrupt and he just brought the basic number of dancers he needed and he picked up English dancers or anybody who wanted to join . . .[3]

In 1947 de Basil was also bereft of the good advice and vigorous help he used to get from Bruce Ottley. Ottley had suffered for some time from high blood pressure, probably accentuated by the pre-war pressures and long working hours implicit in coping with the problems and dissensions of the de Basil Ballet. He took ill on 17 July 1947 at a pre-season party at the Savoy and died in hospital on 22 July.

The first programme was unfortunately chosen, a very usual state of affairs with companies visiting London. *Les Sylphides* was boringly familiar. It was in almost every British repertoire as the hackneyed opening ballet, but it was also very much better done by British dancers than by the de Basil Ballet. Jasinsky, admittedly, was a fine male lead and one of Fokine's own favourites in the role, and Riabouchinska produced much of her old form in the prelude but Jeanmaire was never greatly liked in London in the classical or Fokine repertoire.

The revival of *Paganini* fell very flat indeed. It did not march with the mood of the time. Fortunately *Graduation Ball*, given its London premiere, won hearts. Here Riabouchinska and Lichine were a delight, a new recruit, 16-year-old Barbara Lloyd from California, was enchanting as the pigtailed girl, and Orlov's Drummer will always be remembered as the definitive performance. The Dutch dancer Paul Grinwis and John Taras were excellent as the Headmistress and the General. 'Thank God for *Graduation Ball*,' said de Basil to Braunsweg...[4]

There were many good performances throughout the season. Obviously the company had a much greater homogeneity, in spite of its short period of rehearsal and a largely new set of dancers, than the de Basil-de Cuevas combination had achieved in New York. It was nevertheless still a rough ensemble. It was in the individual contributions that the potential of the troupe was apparent, something that, given better conditions of rehearsal and a longer performing life together, might well have resulted in a renaissance. Moulin danced a distinguished Bluebird *pas de deux*, Morosova was delightful in *Graduation Ball* and *Les Femmes de bonne humeur* and Dokoudovsky became a favourite with the audience. Richard Capell wrote: 'he has really won the out-and-out admiration of the London ballet public.'[5] He did this by his versatility – splendid mime as Paganini contrasted with such roles as the Warrior Chief in *Igor* and the Cadet in *Graduation Ball*, in which Beryl de Zoete found his 'ecstasy of movement' irresistible.[6]

The measure of the company is best taken from an article by Beaumont in Richard Buckle's periodical, *Ballet*. As a critic, Beaumont supplemented his length of experience and profound historical knowledge with unusual fairness of judgement. As far as is humanly possible he achieved unprejudiced assessments. His detailed analysis, which inevitably dwelt on deficiencies in view of his vivid memories from the past, can be summarized in his preamble:

In justice to "times past", I must state that this company is not the equal of what it was in 1933–39. The ballet-goers of recent adherence must rid themselves of the impression . . . that they are now seeing the ballets, familiar to them by name, as they were presented then.[7]

Unfortunately, very few of them seem to have been capable of taking his advice.

Beaumont examines the differences between then and now fully, both in detail and in standard of performance. Of the revivals *Le Fils prodigue* comes off best, with *Le Coq d'or* and *Paganini* as runners-up.

An interesting overall view came from a younger man. Peter Brook, now celebrated as a director of plays, was temporarily writing criticism for *The Observer*. For him there were certain highlights, including *Coq d'or, Prince Igor*, and especially *L'Oiseau de feu*, which he found 'very much alive . . . risen triumphantly from its ashes'.[8] He admired *Protée*, which he considered very much underrated. After censuring a 'mediocre' *Carnaval* and a 'strangely dated' *Présages* (over which *The Times'* critic disagreed), he revelled in *Le Beau Danube* – 'suddenly alive and gay, stylish, witty and infectious, typically Massine in the verve of its movement, with the company enjoying itself'.[9] This was of course the debatable version of the ballet staged by Lifar with which the Colonel had tried to circumvent the copyright case and keep a popular work in the repertoire. No one was deluded into thinking it was anything but Massine's ballet in a debased form. *The Times*, with cool decision, said it was 'not by Lifar, to whom the programme wrongly attributed it'.[10] There were five performances before a protest from Massine made the Colonel withdraw it.

The casting of the ballets remained largely unaltered throughout the season. It had been hard enough teaching everyone the roles without introducing alternate dancers, but there were a few exceptions. Nina Tarakanova danced Columbine a couple of times – she had settled in England on her marriage. Skouratov added *Les Sylphides* and *Protée* to his roles. He had been praised by critics as 'a classical dancer of unusual beauty and nobility of carriage',[11] and Richard Buckle had written:

There is a flow in his movements. He leaps high and lands lightly. In *Aurora's*

146

Wedding he soared above the heads of the other men performing *entrechats* in the background. It is his reticence I chiefly admire.[12]

This question of alternate casting had never been a problem in earlier days, when the company had enjoyed a long familiarity with the repertoire. Although certain dancers had very much of a monopoly of certain roles, usually because the public expected it that way, there were always others capable of replacing them at a moment's notice. Dancers of the de Basil Ballet were trained to adapt to the styles of all the different choreographers in whose ballets they appeared. Nowadays many companies are dominated by the work of one choreographer, or closely related choreographers, and although it is easy for dancers to alternate with each other in such a repertoire it is more difficult for them to interpret ballets created in other choreographic styles. The one-style company is unlikely to develop versatility in its dancers whereas versatility was one of the outstanding qualities of the Ballets Russes.

New works appeared only right at the end of the Covent Garden season, when two ballets by Boris Kniasev were staged, with only a fortnight's rehearsals – and these took place under difficulties. These productions were discussed in *Ballet* by Doris Langley Moore, who found the company uneven and unpolished in comparison with its pre-war state but also thought that there was 'a marked improvement between the first and the last performance in London'.[13] This is of course a theatrical commonplace. The first nights are the ones covered by the press, and those inevitably unsettled and patchy performances are the ones that are perpetuated by the written word and give a season its character. One of the Kniasev ballets, *The Silver Birch*, was no real newcomer to the ballet repertoire. The Kniasev Ballet at Monte Carlo in 1932 had featured a work called *Légende de berioska* and the Ballets de Léon Woizikovsky included a version called *Biroska*. The 1947 production was an excursion into a dated world of balletic natural history which tested Geneviève Moulin rather beyond her technical capacity. *Piccoli* had more originality and strength, although its character as a danced French farce did not greatly recommend it to London taste. It suited excellently the expressive and technical ability of Renée Jeanmaire, an ex-pupil of Kniasev, and Dokoudovsky.

From London the company moved to Paris, to the Palais de Chaillot. On the other side of the Atlantic de Basil was in legal trouble again, with a belated American sequel to the English court case of nine years before; on 17 September 1947, Federal Judge John Bright ordered him to pay $52,250 plus costs, a sum one cannot imagine he possessed (and which he presumably never met), to Universal Art Inc. for breach of contract.

The Paris season, which opened on 10 October 1947, was presented by Jules Borkor and Nadine Bouchonnet. Mme Bouchonnet was now an impresario herself. A few years later she and her husband were to die tragically, murdered by burglars who broke into their Paris home. At the Chaillot in 1947 the atmosphere was cool to begin with. The critic of *Arts*, Maurice Pourchet, who remembered the Diaghilev Ballet as well as the pre-war de Basil Ballet, suggested that lack of rehearsal and travel fatigue accounted for poor performances. In the second week he felt they were beginning to pull together well and the audience was warming to them. *Le Fils prodigue* was a tremendous success. Jasinsky's dancing in this work impressed him, very much, as having great emotional force, and he found the ensembles fine and memorable. He praised Morosova in *Carnaval* – '*alerte, spirituelle, simple mais charmante*'. By the end of the season he decided they had provided one of the most arresting visual experiences seen in the Paris theatre since World War II.[14] Another writer, Pierre Tugal, was completely censorious. The only ballet he enjoyed was *Piccoli* – 'much more complicated in choreographic execution than it appeared on the surface . . . fresh and gay and aesthetically reposing'.[15]

From Paris the company went to the Alhambra Theatre, Brussels, first for one week and then for a return fortnight. John Taras was left in hospital in Paris, seriously ill with meningitis. He never rejoined them, returning to the USA via England where he staged *Designs with Strings* for the Metropolitan Ballet.

In the spring of 1948 the Original Ballet Russe set off on a lengthy tour of Spain, Spanish North Africa and Portugal. It was to be their last journey in the Colonel's lifetime. De Basil had always had good connections with Spain, following in Diaghilev's footsteps and annually visiting Barcelona (Gran Teatro Liceo) as well as other cities. In Frank Salter's *Borovansky*, he quotes from Borovansky's memoirs about the opening night of the first de Basil season there on 12 May 1933:

The audience greeted us with a terrific ovation. Although we realized how much people looked forward to our performance we did not expect such a wonderful welcome. No one could possibly imagine how inspired we felt nor how we danced. The most wonderful moment of all came in the finale of the

Polovtsian dances from *Prince Igor*. The audience began to applaud and shout; they even threw flowers and bouquets on to the stage. Another surprise had been arranged for us by the staff of the stage management. During the day they had secretly prepared rose petals and filled the theatre flies with them. At the same time as the audience threw flowers to us, these rose petals were released and floated down over us like snow. We finished the finale practically covered with flowers and rose petals.[16]

Later in the 'thirties, the composer Vladimir Dukelsky (Vernon Duke) went there with the company and wrote that although he had always considered the Colonel a dyed-in-the-wool monarchist, he was on the best of terms with 'highly placed Catalan politicians of extremely progressive tendencies'.[17] Asked about this, de Basil said he always admired ability and success, whichever side it was on.

Both sides, apparently, enjoyed Russian ballet. In May 1936, during the Spanish Civil War, opposing parties temporarily ceased hostilities to sit side by side in the Liceo in Barcelona.

In 1948 the ballet was still welcome, the audiences warm and enthusiastic. The company played in about twenty-two cities, including Barcelona and Madrid, Seville, Valencia, Granada and Lisbon, Tetuan and Tangier. There had been many changes, again, among the dancers. Riabouchinska and Lichine appeared only at the beginning of the tour. Lichine had many disagreements with de Basil, and the two dancers left the company in Lisbon. The principal ballerinas for the tour were Morosova, Stroganova and Verchinina, who was in Europe with a few dancers from Brazil, the Groupe de danses de Nina Verchinina, backed by her husband Count Jean de Beausacq. Her group had given some independent performances, but she now appeared regularly with the de Basil Ballet, dancing Zobeide, the Polovtsian Girl, prelude in *Sylphides* and Chiarina in *Carnaval*, while de Beausacq had the title of Assistant to the Director General. The principal male dancers were Dokoudovsky and Paul Grinwis.

Pupils of Lichine and Nijinska from California were an important factor in the company's new look. Their forerunner, Barbara Lloyd, had of course appeared during the London season in 1947. Now she danced the waltz in *Sylphides* and Papillon in *Carnaval*, and was joined by Dolores Starr, Robert Barnett, Richard Adama, Betty Scott and Joan Damen. English dancers included Marita Kern, Jeanne Artois, Glen Gordon, Raymond Farrell and Stephen Warwick, some of whom had joined at Covent Garden.

149

The repertoire was astonishingly substantial. *Symphonie fantastique* and *Les Présages* were given, *Francesca* (with Tchernicheva), *Paganini* and *Le Coq d'or, Graduation Ball* and *Protée, Carnaval, Igor, L'Oiseau de feu* and *Sylphides, Le Lac des cygnes* and *Le Mariage d'Aurore*. In addition, Verchinina staged two ballets. *Suite choréographique* had music by Gounod. Dolores Starr and Richard Adama danced the adagio and variations, Barbara Lloyd had a solo, and there was a duet for Mary Jane Shea and Sandra Dieken. *Valse triste*, to Sibelius with designs by Manuel Muntanola, had a theme – Melancholy reigns among the shadows in the garden of a ruined castle, but is put to flight by the arrival of New Life. Verchinina danced Melancholy and Sandra Dieken Life, with an ensemble of four couples.

Another, totally different, production was staged, Anatole Joukovsky's *Danzas eslavas*. This colourful and spirited folk-dance ballet began with a Macedonian warrior dance. A *pas de deux* for Verchinina and Dokoudovsky was based on a Serbian religious ritual. There was a Croatian women's dance leading into a final Kolo Sinfonico featuring dances from Serbia, Macedonia, Croatia and Bosnia. Joukovsky later taught folk and character dance at San Francisco State University, but during this tour he was assistant to Grigoriev. Robert Bell was *régisseur*, and the indefatigable Georges Georghiev, who had been with them throughout, was still wardrobe master. There were three conductors: Joaquìn Gasca, Steven Candael and Janis Suchovs.

Barbara Lloyd's parents travelled with the company. Initially, her mother, Deane Schultz, had been with her in London, Paris and Brussels. There had then been a complete break in activity. Deane Schultz writes:

None of the top management were to be seen nor heard of. The dancers from the States plus England and other countries had to get home the best way they could. We were very bitter, to say the least, and never wanted to go through all that again. We were home for about three months when the Colonel phoned Mr Lichine and told him about starting the Company again in Spain and he wanted Barbara back again. Lichine phoned me and told me to think about it and how I couldn't stand in the way of her career; when Barbara heard about the Colonel wanting her back, she wanted to go very much, the hardships we encountered the first time seemed to vanish.[18]

This time Barbara's father joined them, bringing camera equipment to film the repertoire – a splendid project that never got off the ground because of the dissension between Lichine and de Basil. Deane Schultz did her best not to be a 'typical ballet mother', keeping out of everyone's way as much as possible, but observing a good deal of jealousy and infighting over roles. She found Verchinina and de Beausacq 'two of the nicest people to be associated with in a company' and, all in all, she felt the experience valuable. 'To have been part of that era, good and bad, was a schooling in itself and can never be duplicated. Even though there are some good companies now, the dancers don't have the discipline of working under someone like Serge Grigoriev.'

The company reached Palma de Mallorca at the end of October 1948 but the Colonel was ill and failed to negotiate onward dates. When the season ended at Palma on 6 November 1948 the company returned to Barcelona and was disbanded.

Life in post-war Europe was not easy for anyone. The combatant countries were equally exhausted, either by victory or defeat. Theatrical activity was considerable but conditions and tastes had changed radically since the 'thirties. There was enthusiasm for local companies which had shared the community life of wartime and were identified in the public mind with its dangers and difficulties. Any spare funds were rather naturally allocated to them. Public taste was also turning away from the past towards the novel and experimental. Everything had moved on, in a way that must have been hard to accept by artists and directors more familiar with conditions in the Latin American countries.

De Basil was too much a man of the theatre not to realize this and too much of a fighter to give up without a struggle. He had bent his energies to keeping things going somehow in the hope that he could get enough backing to establish some headquarters, engage new artists and begin to commission new ballets. He was well aware of the need to find choreographic talent and stage fresh works. Had he been in a financial state to tempt Lichine back into his fold he would have had a choreographer for the future and Lichine himself would have benefited from a stable connection.

The Colonel did however discuss projects for new ballets with John Taras (a ballet to Tchaikovsky's Theme and Variations) and Dokoudovsky. Dokoudovsky had composed a number of successful *divertissements* in South America, including a *pas de trois* to the polka from Shostakovitch's *Golden Age* and a tremendously popular Can-can for himself and Stroganova to the last part of the *Orpheus in the Underworld* overture. Now he suggested a ballet on the strongly dramatic and, for the time, daring theme of rape contained in Leonid

Andreiev's story *The Abyss*. De Basil, at first unsure of this, was won over and approached Alexander Tcherepnine to compose a score. Tcherepnine proved interested and lived and worked with Dokoudovsky for some time. The ballet was entirely set, but by then the company had been dispersed so the work had to be put in cold storage. Another project was for a ballet on the myth of Niobe, for which de Chirico completed designs. The idea was to have three acts set by three different choreographers.

De Basil was now constantly battling against ill-health but would not give in. He had arterio-sclerosis, and pieces of shrapnel in his leg, mementoes of World War I, increasingly disabled him. He was occasionally hospitalized, but never for long, and he had no thought of giving up work.

Dokoudovsky, whom he began to call his 'spiritual son', was a constant companion in Paris. De Basil never slept very much – dancers complained that he always summoned them to sign contracts at night when they were too tired to read the terms – and he would telephone Dokoudovsky in the small hours of the morning or meet him to walk to and from the Opera and the Etoile deep in talk. The talk was always of the future. One of the projects got under way early in 1949. This was for a series of thirteen films to be directed by Boris Zatourov and produced by a company called Tadié-Cinéma. Thirteen proved an unlucky number. The principal backer, a Rumanian, was killed and some of the other backers withdrew on hearing this. Eventually two films only were made, on a shoestring budget. One was of *Le Lac des cygnes,* the other of *Graduation Ball*. The hope was that they would earn a television contract and funds for more.

Dokoudovsky and Vida Brown were in charge of the group of dancers engaged for the films. Vida Brown, an American dancer who was with the Ballet Russe de Monte Carlo from 1939, had just left them for a short freelance period. A small contingent of British dancers, who never appeared with the company on stage, arrived in Paris on 3 April to join dancers stranded from the previous year's touring, including some Americans who had no money to pay their fares home. Pat Vaughn recalls that she auditioned for de Basil on 12 April, and then foregathered with the rest two or three times a week at de Basil's hotel to hear when rehearsals would start. Always there were excuses as to why rehearsals were being delayed. They would be called up to the Colonel's room in twos and threes, where he was invariably in bed, surrounded by Serge and Vova Grigoriev, and he would make soothing speeches in Russian and then lift up a corner of his mattress – like a miser trying to conceal the actual amount of money hidden there – and hand each of them 1500 francs (which then represented about £2 10s. in sterling) with a great flourish saying, with tears in his eyes, 'It is the last monies I have!'[19]

Rehearsals began on 19 May, with classes every day at 9 am, and the ballets they rehearsed – not only for the film but with a view to another Spanish tour – were *Graduation Ball, Le Lac des cygnes, Petrouchka* and *L'Oiseau de feu*. Everything went slowly and confusingly, as some of the really old Russian dancers insisted on arguing every step, and the arguments went on in a wide range of languages.

When it came to the point of filming, other elements of confusion were added. Like most film directors, Zatourov had his own ideas about filming ballet and knew little about dance and dancers. The conditions of filming were bizarre. Pat Vaughn noted in her diary that they started filming *Graduation Ball* on 10 June at the Musée des Arts Décoratifs. Dokoudovsky recalls a session at the Club de Gaulle. The club was being used the next day for the Diamond Ball and already the staff were encroaching on the sets in their efforts to prepare. Scenes were taken from extraordinary angles, even from behind, entrances altered, and there was no room to dance properly. Cameras were rented and one broke down. On 15 June they adjourned to the Parc de Bagatelle in the Bois de Boulogne for *Le Lac des cygnes*, where men running round with 'bombs' of fog almost stifled the dancers with sulphur fumes.

During April and May de Basil went to England to discuss possible participation, with Markova and Dolin, in Tom Arnold's London Ballet Festival. This was to be held in August 1949 at the Harringay arena in North London. Two new ballets, to be choreographed by Dokoudovsky, were mentioned by the Colonel. These were *Istar,* based on Assyrian Babylonian mythology, and *Celestina*, a melodrama written by Alexander Rojas with music by Pedrell. In the end nothing was concluded and Ballet Rambert supported Markova and Dolin at Harringay.

Nothing came of the Spanish tour either. The dancers in Paris were called to see de Basil, who told them an incredible tale about the Spanish backer having sent a man on horseback across the frontier with cash for fares and expenses. En route he had been attacked and robbed of his saddle bags . . . Could this have had any grain of truth in it? Far more was done in the way of handouts of untaxable cash in those less bureaucratic days and it might not be realistic to dismiss such an event as a fairy-tale, however unconvincing it sounds.

The dancers stayed around however, always hoping, until 15 July. The British girls earned a little money by teaching English and baby-sitting, and seven of them met a lady called Madame Kovno who arranged for them to do a television show up the Eiffel Tower on the *quatorze juillet*. They discovered that they were meant to dance topless, and refused; a furious cameraman had to wait around while Madame Kovno fetched some scanty tops so that they could produce a high-kicking routine.

After that there was nothing to be done but go home. Embassies were besieged with requests for assistance to pay hotel bills and fares – but Pat Vaughn comments: 'It was remarkable though how loyal everyone was to de Basil himself despite everything and how desolate everyone felt when the company finally folded up.'

De Basil had one major new interest. He had always admired and enjoyed Spanish music and dance. Vicente Mariero says that the Colonel found it had '*un gran afinidad con el espiritu de los bailes rusos*'.[20] In 1948, during the ballet's Spanish tour, he had seen a large and excellent group of amateur dancers and musicians from every province of Spain, the Coros y danzas de España. Two years later he decided to accept an invitation to become their administrative director. In spring 1951 they had a very successful Paris season at the Palais de Chaillot. De Basil, talking to those who congratulated him in the interval, disclaimed any credit, saying it was a company of people who danced and sang naturally and all he had done was to transport them direct from their villages. When they eventually appeared in London in February 1952, six months or so after his death, Beaumont was enchanted: 'The panorama here offered is so rich that in something over two hours you can travel the length and breadth of Spain.'[21]

From Paris the Spanish dancers went to Belgium, and there de Basil called in at the opera house in Ghent, where Dokoudovsky and Stroganova were guesting. He was unwell and very lame, and was allowed to sit on a chair in the wings to watch them dance *Le Lac des cygnes* and, later, their Can-can. Dokoudovsky reports:

We were both strong technicians, and I had put just about everything into my choreography except maybe the chocolate sauce on top, and we were pretty exhausted. But the applause was great and they asked for an encore. We felt we couldn't. But the Colonel wanted it too and said, "Of course you can do an encore! Come on, damn you, do it again!" And because we both loved him, we did what we could.[22]

It was the last time they saw him.

Toumanova too had a last glimpse of him, in May 1951, when he took the Coros y danzas to Italy. She was at La Scala creating a ballet, Richard Strauss' *Le leggenda di Giuseppe* for Margarita Wallmann. De Basil contacted her, and asked her and her mother

with great kindness to come with him to the theatre where his company were performing. Of course we went with him. He was like a young man, saying to everyone, starting from the box office people to the backstage electricians, musicians and of course the ballet: "This is my child, this famous ballerina dancing at La Scala, I knew her when she was only eleven years old, she was a star of my Ballets Russes . . ."[23]

The Colonel had not however given up the idea of resuscitating the Original Ballet Russe. He was in touch with his friend George Kirsta in England and now they began to make firm plans. Kirsta, who had been born in the Ukraine at the turn of the century, had worked as a designer in ballet from the days of World War I when he met Nijinska in Kiev. He had come to London from Vienna in 1937, when he designed her ballet *La Bien-aimée* for the (English) Markova-Dolin Ballet, and during World War II he was connected, as a designer, with ballet and opera-ballet in London. De Basil, recognizing his obsession with ballet and appreciating his artistic integrity, felt he could work with him.

In a letter, de Basil makes it clear that he thought of Kirsta as not only capable of looking after 'the improvement of the old standards of our established repertoire' (presumably a compendium phrase which really meant improvement *up to* the old standards) but as creatively strong enough to build up a fresh repertoire of new productions. He wrote:

I have not the slightest doubt that with your knowledge of the ballet's problems and your experience, your valuable collaboration will be at the base of our mutual achievements.

Later, realizing his own precarious state of health, he wrote:

155

I feel confident now because I have at last found in you a trustworthy successor who will doubtless continue my work should I vanish, and who will guide the Ballet Russe in the future.[24]

They planned to reconstitute the company and give performances in Paris and London the following autumn. In January 1951 de Basil wrote to Tom Bischoff, his London solicitor and friend, who was a director of the Original Ballet Russe Ltd, saying that his health was very much better. He had firm offers of engagements for the revived company for Spain, Portugal, the Scandinavian countries and also for Australia and New Zealand.

With regard to finances (and you know that is the most important part) we have hopes of securing some assistance from a group of persons who are apparently willing to help us . . . I do not want to hide from you the fact that this is going to be extremely difficult, but with God's help, and relying on my collaborators, I trust that we will finally succeed.[25]

He was conscious of the intrigues and opposition that had done so much to destroy his ballet. He was also concerned in case ballets that had been created for him on service contracts, or which he had acquired, were performed without permission by other companies – very naturally, as these were among his few assets. He wanted to be able to 'line them up as a basic attraction for any financier'. *Graduation Ball* was a case in point. Lichine had staged it for Ballet Theatre in October 1944, with new designs by Mstislav Doboujinsky, and again in September 1949 for Ballet Russe de Monte Carlo. It would seem that these productions had not been arranged with de Basil because he mentions 'the tendency of all ballet companies to copy, quite unlawfully and without our consent, productions which are our exclusive property'. He was now disturbed by a rumour that *Graduation Ball* was to be produced by the new London Festival Ballet. De Basil asked Tom Bischoff to look into this on his behalf, saying that this ballet 'was produced during the period of his [Lichine's] engagement with the OBR on a service contract (similar to the one Massine had when he created *Symphonie fantastique* and other ballets which are our exclusive property with all production rights)'. London Festival Ballet did not, in fact, produce *Graduation Ball* until July 1957, and its next staging, by the Royal Danish Ballet, was in March 1952, after de Basil's death.

De Basil and Morosova were now living in an apartment borrowed from a friend in the rue Jean-Mermoz in Paris. Another friend of long standing saw a good deal of them. This was Anthony Diamantidi, a charming and by all accounts unscrupulous Greek financier who had known them all since the 'thirties, when he lived in England and entertained them regularly at his home at Effingham in Surrey. Now de Basil recommended him to Morosova as someone who would look after her in an emergency.

The emergency came, on 27 July 1951. The Colonel had taken ill on 24 July. His doctor advised rest and, as he was himself going on holiday, left an injection prepared in case of another attack. De Basil would not stop working and three days later the second attack occurred. Both he and Morosova tried to give the essential injection but neither could find a vein. Morosova rushed out of the flat to get help. She returned with a substitute doctor to find de Basil on the point of death, which came unexpectedly even to those who knew him well and knew his state of health. That night Maurice Pourchet was talking to the Bouchonnets at the Gershwin Festival in Paris about the positive plans the Colonel had been making with Kirsta and their hopes for the future.

De Basil was buried in the Russian cemetery of St Geneviève du Bois. Morosova was in a shocked and confused state. Although she was over twenty-five years younger than the Colonel, she now had no home, no career and little money. Her parents were dead and her family consisted solely of her sister Verchinina, who lived in Brazil. They were close friends, and Verchinina suggested a move to Rio, but Morosova felt more at home in Paris than anywhere else. As de Basil had advised, she turned to Diamantidi for help and Diamantidi arranged a studio residence for her. She took pupils there until he suddenly sold the lease over her head.

Two separate holding companies had existed in London since 1939 – the Original Ballet Russe Ltd and the Russian Ballet Development Company Ltd. They supplemented, and later succeeded, companies called Ballets Russes de Monte-Carlo (Colonel W. de Basil) Ltd and Educational Ballets Ltd. De Basil had never been a director of either. They were run by solicitors with, for short spells as named directors, Sevastianov, Haskell, Captain Robert Jenkinson, Lidji and Philippov. Tom Bischoff of the reputable firm of Bischoff Coxe & Co. was the senior operating director. By a curious coincidence he died in London on the same day as de Basil did in Paris.

As a result, the solicitors remaining as long-term directors resigned.

Diamantidi took control of both companies, with co-operation from a new firm of solicitors, Fink Proudfoot & Waters.

Meanwhile George Kirsta went on with the plans to revive the Original Ballet Russe. On 16 August 1951 a new limited company, the Universal Ballet (London) Ltd, was registered as a subsidiary of Continental Opera and Ballet Entertainments Ltd. Ironically, looking back to the theme of *La Concurrence*, the two nominal outside subscribers were both tailors. The directors were Mr Middleton d'Este and Mrs Ellerie Fricker. Kirsta was appointed artistic director to the actual ballet company and recalled Grigoriev and Tchernicheva to recruit and rehearse the dancers, with Vova Grigoriev as general administrator. The conductors engaged were Joseph Horowitz and the 24-year-old Colin Davis.

This group was naturally unlike any previous de Basil company in personnel. Only a few names were the same, chief among them Stroganova, Dokoudovsky and Kiril Vassilkovsky, who joined de Basil as a 20-year-old in 1939. Many were English. Herida May and Joan Tucker had been soloists with Mona Inglesby's International Ballet and Anthony Burke with Sadler's Wells Ballet. Jack Carter and Norman McDowell were at the beginning of notable careers. Iris Holt was married to Vova Grigoriev and Maya Koumani, trained at the Legat School, was Middleton d'Este's stepdaughter. Jack Spurgeon, an English dancer of great experience with various Russian and Polish companies, was a principal male artist. Inge Sand and Poul Gnatt joined from the Royal Danish Ballet.

The small repertoire was sensibly chosen from old favourites. There were two classics, *Aurora's Wedding* and *Swan Lake* Act II; three Fokine ballets, *Le Coq d'or, Paganini* and *Prince Igor*; Lichine's *Graduation Ball* and Massine's *Les Présages*.

Even so, in a short rehearsal period of four to five weeks, it was impossible for Grigoriev and Tchernicheva to bring the group up to a satisfactory standard or inculcate a true Ballets Russes character. Few of the new company knew any of the works, even from seeing them as audience. The chance of learning them was greatly valued, but this was hardly enough to produce a successful performance.

The company opened at Wimbledon Theatre on 1 October 1951, and made the mistake of asking the critics along. Those who went out to see them were obviously making every allowance but the effect was hardly encouraging, and to make matters worse Dokoudovsky was suffering from a broken toe. Beaumont commented: 'To teach, rehearse and stage seven ballets in five weeks with a new company is a considerable achievement, but it cannot make for perfection of presentation.'[26] Richard Buckle wrote: 'It takes time to weld a company together and these dancers had only a month of rehearsals ... it was a grave error to open with *Aurora's Wedding*, which revealed the company's present limitations beyond possibility of argument.' However, he found *Paganini* 'a fine piece of theatre' in which Dokoudovsky 'dominated the evil spirits', Inge Sand 'whirled and span prettily' as the Florentine Beauty and Herida May 'gave a striking performance as Guile'.[27] He deplored 'the present plurality of companies' and wished it might be amalgamated with Festival Ballet for the general good. *The Dancing Times* was horrified. It found the *corps de ballet* 'lacking in even the most elementary rules of stagecraft such as how to put on and wear wigs and how to dress a stage'. However it praised Stroganova as 'a strong classical *danseuse*, technique assured and easy if a little hard' and found Inge Sand ideally cast in *Graduation Ball*. Her Aurora 'showed the disparity between the Danish and Petipa Schools only too vividly'.[28]

The company's next stop was Coventry Hippodrome, where the local paper preferred them to 'more established companies' who were sometimes 'rather angular and tired'. In contrast, the Original Ballet Russe had 'young and abundant life'.[29] At the Grand, Leeds, they were summed up by Ernest Bradbury of the *Yorkshire Post*. It was a 'standard but formidable programme from which their art emerged by no means unscathed. The ensemble was often loose and ill timed.' All the same, 'a sense of style is to be discerned, while the dancing certainly has its proportions of vigour and enthusiasm'. They felt they were floundering less and beginning to make progress. The two conductors, of whom the dancers preferred the sympathetic tempi of Horowitz to the less dependable ones (from a balletic point of view) of Colin Davis, were coping with small orchestras who 'battle gamely against symphonic odds'.[30]

They had a week at the Manchester Opera House after a week in Sheffield. Then it was Oxford, Bolton, and two weeks each in Newcastle and Glasgow. By this time *Les Présages* had been staged, with Stroganova and Dokoudovsky as Passion, Joan Tucker as Frivolity and Herida May as Action. It had not of course been seen in these regional areas. As the *Manchester Guardian* critic had pointed out, de Basil had always 'firmly refused to move his dancers beyond London', except for that brief tour at the end of 1933.[31] Now, Newcastle found that it 'scored an immediate and resounding success'[32] and Glasgow found it 'an appropriately impressive presentation'.[33]

The company returned to London at last on 26 December, Boxing Day, for a season at the Royal Festival Hall. As a setting for ballet, the Festival Hall has always had problems, and in spite of a specially constructed stage and the advantage of an augmented orchestra there was no hope of an artistic success. They opened with *Swan Lake, Le Coq d'or* and *Graduation Ball*. Sonia Arova, a Bulgarian ballerina who had trained with Preobrajenska and Lifar, and appeared with Ballet Rambert, the International Ballet, the Metropolitan Ballet and the Ballets des Champs-Elysées, had been recruited as guest artist to dance Aurora and *Swan Lake*. They were performing twice daily, something of a marathon, and competing with a glut of ballet companies – Duncan Harrison, in the *Evening News*, had even written a rather gloomy piece beginning: 'Is ballet in danger of becoming oversubscribed? New companies seem to be forming almost weekly. The public for ballet is undoubtedly a big one but I foresee a danger of too many companies vying too strenuously for favour . . .'[34] The Original Ballet Russe, at acting as maître de ballet under Grigoriev in rehearsing the repertoire.

On 3 January 1952 they staged a creation, *Femmes d'Alger*. This was Kirsta's idea, and based on the Delacroix painting with a score by Joseph Horowitz, designs by Kirsta himself, and choreography by Dokoudovsky. It was composed by Dokoudovsky under considerable pressure, as he had a full dancing programme and was, in addition, acting as maître de ballet under Grigoriev in rehearsing the repertoire. In the circumstances he was quite unable to cut and revise as he would have wished, and the production as shown was not a success. The story was the all-too-hackneyed one of sailors (three, naturally) ashore, this time in Algiers. Beaumont complained that it was banal, mixing character dancing, academic dancing and music-hall humour.[35] *The Times* found Stroganova scintillating and charming, praised its 'racy humour and the cunning invention of the sailors' antics' but agreed that 'the joke goes on far too long'.[36] Herida May, looking back without any great enthusiasm, nevertheless felt that the choreography of the duets was very much more advanced and interesting in practice dress than it looked when danced in costume.

From the Festival Hall the company transferred to the Adelphi

Theatre in the Strand, by arrangement with Jack Hylton (Musical Plays) Ltd, on 16 January 1952. It was not a particularly suitable theatre, although it is regularly used for musicals. The stage was small and the orchestra had once again to be diminished. The overall standard of the group was better, however. *Dance and Dancers* felt they had improved very considerably, although *Aurora's Wedding* remained 'on the whole undistinguished and at times embarrassing'.[37] Peter Williams in the *Daily Mail* found *Les Présages* 'incredibly dated, but Herida May as Action still brought strength and the right style to the first movement'.[38] Beaumont enjoyed Arova's engaging personality as Aurora – 'she is musical, has flowing *port de bras*, and dances with style and nobility'.[39] He also praised two other guest artists – Toni Lander from the Royal Danish Ballet as the Sylphide in *Graduation Ball* and Paula Hinton from Ballet Rambert as a dazzling Golden Cockerel. There was now a strong Danish bias, with Inge Sand and Toni Lander directly from Copenhagen, Stroganova Danish by birth, Poul Gnatt, and two very promising young Danish dancers, Werner Klausen and Anker Orskov, who was to die suddenly five years later at the early age of twenty-nine.

Money was running out, however, and audiences were not coming in. The backers became disenchanted and unwilling to hold on. Middleton d'Este told Jack Hylton that there would be no funds to pay the artists and Hylton took on this responsibility, feeling that it would otherwise look bad for his management. He impounded scenery and costumes against the debt.

It was to no avail, however. On Saturday 26 January 1952, Alexandra Kirsta, George Kirsta's daughter, as a very little girl, remembers a line of stony-faced dancers waiting to collect their last salaries. Vova Grigoriev, in his own words, 'paid people off and got out'. The last curtain had come down on Colonel W. de Basil's Ballets Russes.

There were various rumours of revival. *The Dancing Times* carried a report in May 1952 that the Original Ballet Russe would start rehearsing in June in Paris under a new director, Mr Mendoza, who had taken the Paris Opera Ballet to the Colón Theatre in 1950. Dokoudovsky was to be maître de ballet with Massine and Lichine as choreographer-directors (an unlikely combination); but Dokoudovsky never heard of the project.

The post-mortem period was not to be without its litigation and its mysteries, some of which are unlikely to be totally cleared up.

The litigation began immediately. Continental Opera and Ballet Entertainments Ltd sued Jack Hylton (Musical Plays) Ltd for recovery of the scenery and costumes left at the Adelphi Theatre. Bischoff and Co., representing the holding companies of the Original Ballet Russe Ltd and the Russian Ballet Development Company, intervened, saying that as no royalties had been paid, the rights had reverted to them, and they owned the scenery and costumes of these ballets. Before the main case against Jack Hylton could go forward, the case for settlement of title was heard. Master Clayton, presiding, found for Continental Opera and Ballet and then, whilst working out the judgement, changed his mind and found for Bischoff and Co. Middleton d'Este, for Continental Opera and Ballet, appealed to the Divisional Court and this appeal was heard by Lord Goddard, Mr Justice Slade and a third Justice, with a two-to-one result in favour of Bischoff. D'Este pursued it to the Court of Appeal where Mr Justice Singleton found in his favour.

After this play within a play, d'Este returned to the proceedings he had initiated in 1952 against Jack Hylton. This case came up at the end of January 1956. D'Este was represented by Stockton, Jack Hylton by Claude Duveen, QC, and Mark Littman. Jack Hylton won the case and costs were set at £1000, but there was no money to pay this and Continental Opera and Ballet went into liquidation. D'Este and Jack Hylton had initially had a heated encounter, and d'Este also sued Hylton for slander. This minor matter was settled out of court. Papers concerning these cases, and even official records, have been destroyed and this précis of the legal proceedings is owed to the memory of Oscar Beuselinck, the solicitor who acted for Jack Hylton (Musical Plays) Ltd at the time.[40]

Great mystery surrounds the activities of the Diaghilev and de Basil Ballets Foundation of Mr Anthony Diamantidi. This foundation is described in Richard Buckle's introduction to the catalogue of the Sotheby sale in July 1968 as being 'a non-profitmaking organization' with two purposes:

to assist and support in every way the maintenance, development and propagation of the knowledge, art and performance of classical Russian ballet, as the same was created, developed, directed or produced by Serge de Diaghilev and Colonel de Basil during the period 1909 to 1951[41] and to assist members of the profession, whether dancers, choreographers or other collaborators in the art of ballet who might be in need of financial support. Both were laudable aims.

Diamantidi, as chairman of the foundation, approached Buckle and Sotheby's after a sale of some Diaghilev Ballet material in June 1967. He suggested that all the surviving decors and costumes of the Diaghilev and de Basil companies should be put up for sale and invited them over to inspect property stored in a warehouse at Montrouge in south Paris. It was understood that very large sums of money were immediately required to pay storage debts over a long period of time. It seems unlikely that any warehouse would allow debts to accumulate to quite such an alarming degree, so the inference may be that Diamantidi had paid the warehousing and that the large advances which were forthcoming from Sotheby's on the prospect of a sale were to reimburse his expenses. The properties were of course a treasure trove and everyone was wildly excited at the richness that was revealed.

The sale went forward and was one of the unforgettable events of ballet history in London. The Scala Theatre was hired for the evening of 17 July 1968, students from the Royal Ballet School modelled the costumes in groups and poses arranged by Lydia Sokolova, and a considerable sum was realized and transmitted to the foundation. The emphasis not unnaturally was on Diaghilev rather than de Basil. The fourteen ballets represented had all originated with Diaghilev although most of them had been danced by the de Basil Ballet, and some were acquired for them by Bruce Ottley's Committee of Friends in 1934. Other sales followed, in December 1969 and March 1973. These were more specifically related to the de Basil Ballet. In the first, for instance, there was material from *Jeux d'enfants, Jardin public, Protée* and *Balustrade*. In the second, from *Cotillon, Beach, Choreartium, Les Imaginaires, Les Présages, Jardin public, Symphonie fantastique, Francesca da Rimini, Protée, Cendrillon, Paganini, Graduation Ball* and *Le Coq d'or*. These were all ballets created by the de Basil Ballet.

The background to Diamantidi's Foundation lies in the Russian Ballet Development Company Ltd, of which he became controlling director on the deaths of de Basil and Tom Bischoff in 1951, with only Morosova, who did not understand business matters, as co-director. Diamantidi had tabled a special resolution on 20 November 1964 to supplement the original 'objects' of the Russian Ballet Development Company, which were routine ones of raising finance for the promotion of performances of ballet and so on, by some interesting new clauses. One of these was the paragraph which Buckle quoted verbatim in the Sotheby catalogue. The others, couched in legal language, allowed Diamantidi not only to 'acquire, own, maintain or preserve' every kind of item relevant to 'the artistic heritage of the production of ballet in the classical Russian style directed or projected' by the companies of Diaghilev and de Basil but 'to buy, sell, hire out, exhibit, dispose of or otherwise deal with any of the said articles upon any terms'. It therefore constituted a *carte blanche* to cover himself in the eventual dealings with Sotheby's.[42]

There is now no way of establishing exactly who legally owned each item on de Basil's death. Too many factors contribute to the confusion – his habit of raising ready money against assets, his stateless condition, the lack of documents dealing with transactions. On the face of it, Diamantidi seems to have been the self-appointed owner of mate.ial that may well indeed have been his to sell for high prices.

After the December 1969 sale, he sent Morosova a detailed credit and debit statement full of unexplained items which she was in no position, in isolation in Paris, to check through. All it really conveyed was that she would receive no more money.

2
The Colonel

PERHAPS the first thing to say about Colonel W. de Basil is that he was indeed a colonel. A great deal of doubt has been thrown on his entitlement to the rank. Hurok, in the later edition of his memoirs – he is carefully kinder to his much-disliked colleague in *Impresario* (1947) than in *S. Hurok Remembers* (1953), which appeared two years after the Colonel's death and therefore outside the US libel limits – puts derisive quotation marks round the word 'Colonel' whenever he uses it. When I began researching this book, even some of the people who spoke well of de Basil suggested that the rank was self-conferred many years after World War I. One of the stories was that he suddenly said, 'If I had stayed in Russia I would by now have been a colonel,' and not only promoted himself but awarded himself decorations for gallantry.

In the 'thirties Haskell, among others, had always written of him as a much wounded Cossack colonel. The one asset that a refugee from a revolution possesses, however, is the freedom to create his own past and be reasonably sure that no one will be able to check it out very thoroughly. So it was perhaps not surprising that facts which were at first accepted widely began to be questioned. As time went on, and de Basil gained a reputation for devious dealing in the theatre, it became more difficult for people to believe that he had told the truth about his early life. The doubts about his army rank crept in and were eagerly fostered by ill-wishers.

He had not, however, lied. Vassily Grigorievitch Voskresensky – his real name – was formally referred to as a Cossack colonel in British military records in 1918, during an event known to military history as the Trans-Caspian Campaign. His promotion from captain had been accelerated by the Revolution. The Russian collapse of 1917 left a complicated situation around the Caspian Sea. There was the possibility of a German Turkish advance towards Persia and Central Asia which the Allies (mainly the British and Indian forces) were bound to oppose. The Bolsheviks had ordered the withdrawal of Russian troops to Baku and in consequence the British sent in a mission from Baghdad in January 1918. This was commanded by Major General L.C. Dunsterville – the original, as de Basil used to point out, of Kipling's character Stalky in *Stalky and Co.* – who later wrote an exciting account of his expedition, *The Adventures of Dunsterforce.*

One group of the retiring Russians decided to ignore the Bolshevik orders. This group was made up of several hundred Kuban Cossacks (the Kuban River area lies near the Sea of Azov) – 'fine-looking fellows on their shaggy horses' – under General Lazar Bicherakov. Dunsterville recalls Bicherakov as a 'truly heroic figure . . . an Ossietin Cossack, one of those semi-wild tribes that are typical of the North Caucasus . . . His men worship him as a fearless leader'.[1] This was Colonel Voskresensky's immediate superior.

Bicherakov talks of Voskresensky's background in an article he wrote for the military journal *Sentinelle*. The two men first met in 1916 in Persia, when Voskresensky became Bicherakov's aide-de-camp in the 3rd Kuban Division. They fought with the Tersko-Kuban cavalry in the interior of Louristan. By spring 1917, however, Voskresensky had become colonel of a special partisan detachment of Kuban Cossacks, one of two under the overall authority of Bicherakov and part of General Baratov's army, fighting the Turks in the Kurdistan mountains. A brilliant leader, according to Bicherakov, Voskresensky deployed his men with the flexibility of *'une liane des fôrets tropicales. Il ploie, mais ne se brise pas'.*[2] For a year, he and his detachment operated widely in Louristan and Kurdistan, always with distinction and courage.

In March 1918 the Russian army in Persia received the Bolshevik order to retire. They then set up a defence of Baku and the Caucasian oilwells against the Turkish German invaders. For six months Voskresensky played a leading part in this – Bicherakov terms him indispensable – and was heroic in his personal conduct during the ultimate evacuation.

During this period, as Major General Dunsterville describes, the territory was the scene of an adventurous ebb and flow of action by land and sea.[3] This involved cavalry, infantry, sailors and Royal Marines of the RN Caspian Flotilla. Negotiations cohered or disintegrated according to the whims of individuals. Relatively small units were concerned but the confusion was intense, and increased by the existence of a large number of minority groups, including Armenians, Tartars and Turkomans, whose allegiance to the main combatants was governed by their private interests.

In September 1918 Baku fell to the Turks. In his end-of-year report to his Commander-in-Chief, Captain B.J. Washington RN, Senior Naval Officer of the RN Caspian Flotilla, describes the ensuing events.

The Centro Caspian flotilla, he wrote, consisted of three gunboats, five auxiliary cruisers and a despatch vessel, 'nominally under the command of General Bicherakov, who has appointed Colonel Voskresensky – a Cossack – to be his Fleet Representative, and the latter is in position of actual command though having no naval or sea knowledge'.

This flotilla helped to recover Baku from the Turks by bombarding Turkish positions. In October Bicherakov despatched a mission headed by Voskresensky to confer with the British at Enzeli. Captain Washington continues:

On 12th October Voskresensky arrived in the Russian gunboat *Astrabad* and had a long conference with Brig. General Andrus and myself. Lieut-Colonel French [a Royal Marine Artillery officer, Russian interpreter and Naval Staff Officer] was also present . . . Voskresensky's main points were
(1) Fleet's absolute obedience to Bicherakov and their lately improved morale and discipline. Bicherakov is now dictator and committees have ceased to govern in ships.
(2) Intense suspicion still exists as to our arming ships.
(3) He ridiculed suggestion of his negotiating with Turks while he was off Nargen Island.
(4) He is short of ammunition and asked for this, or for British guns with ammunition . . .
Tone of conference was friendly but V. seemed doubtful of our present attitude.[4]

Colonel Voskresensky had arranged the release from Baku of 172 Russian officers and 1000 men and he brought with him to Enzeli nine British survivors from Baku.

A meeting between the British and Bicherakov in early November about the reoccupation of Baku included Voskresensky. He

had much experience of horses but none of ships, but on this occasion the horseman's verdict as to what the ships could do, or not do, was sound. He pointed out that the only assistance which could be given from the sea was by indirect fire and that of course steady gun platforms were necessary for this purpose. If his small gunboats were sent to sea in the weather which then prevailed, they would roll their guns under.[5]

A month later, on 20 November 1918, another meeting took place, and according to Captain Washington:

considerable progress was made. V. agreed to sending two ships north to take part in the Volga sweep . . . He agreed to send ships south to visit Lenkoran and Astrabad districts where there was unrest.[6]

Bicherakov and Voskresensky were however by now having trouble with some of the crews in the flotilla, who were 'showing strong Bolshevik tendencies'. Probably it was at that point that one of de Basil's theatrical, but quite possible, reminiscences fits in. He went on board one ship that was working up to a mutiny and harangued the men. What he said infuriated them further and they set on him and threw him overboard. He could not swim and was fully uniformed and armed, but he struggled to a ship's ladder, climbed up and, streaming sea-water on to the deck, calmly took up his speech where he had left off. The men's antagonism changed to amused admiration and he won the day.

He did not win the campaign. It became even more fragmented and confusing as the months went by. Finally the British informed him that if the crews of the flotilla, whose loyalties continued to vacillate, did not surrender, the ships would be sunk. They surrendered on his orders, and the men who wished to return to their homes in Russia were allowed to do so. The rest went into exile, among them Voskresensky.

The last glimpse of Colonel Voskresensky of Bicherakov's Cossacks is boarding a train for Batoum in March 1919. The first glimpse of the demobilized Colonel W. de Basil is of his arrival in Paris later that year, with no other possessions than his Cossack uniform and a sable coat.

In a (translated) interview in 1937 he speaks of leaving his wife with friends in Persia (from the south of Russia many exits were made to Near Eastern countries):

My pressing problem was to find some way of earning a living. Paris was full of Russian refugees like myself, looking for work or working at the queerest jobs; I was an unemployed professional soldier with few qualifications that were of any commercial value. I met a friend who told me he was driving a taxi; that gave me an idea. I did not get a taxi, but a few days later I was engaged as driver of an eight-ton lorry.[7]

The lorry belonged to a film studio. De Basil found accommodation at the Porte de Clignancourt, at a grocer's shop. Hubert Griffith saw these lodgings in 1939 when the Colonel drove him to the south of France. Despite a midnight start, de Basil roused the grocer and his wife:

Cries of delight rang through the night! They hauled him inside. A feast was improvised, and wine corks flew, as for a long awaited and festal reunion.[8]

Once settled in Paris, de Basil sent for his wife Nina Leonidova, who arrived with his cousin Valeria Ellanskaya. The two women were theatrical dancers trained at the Moscow Théâtre des Arts. As early as 1911 this theatre was sending abroad small, nameless groups of girls. At the London Hippodrome that year a troupe described as 'The Moscow Aesthetic Dancers' ('Mme Elena Knipper-Rabeneck and 8 Beautiful Russian Girls') had appeared in choreography by the leading lady, and the tradition of non-classical ballet had been continued. To help the de Basil family finances, Leonidova and Ellanskaya began to appear in variety theatres in France, Italy and Egypt. De Basil, for whom lorry-driving was hardly a long-term career, decided to form a small dancing troupe.

He had made friends in Clignancourt with an Italian-Swiss business-man of the name of Trusetta, who lent him money for the venture. De Basil faltered for a moment. Should he put such money into the risky business of running a ballet company or open a Caucasian restaurant in Paris, which would stand a better chance of doing well? He was an addict of his native cuisine. One of his principal pleasures through life was to take over someone's kitchen and spend hours preparing a Caucasian meal, serving it at about eleven at night to guests whose appetites had sometimes waned with waiting.

The ballet company won, and not only because of the existence of his wife and cousin. Ballet had always been one of his enthusiasms.

From my youngest days I knew that when I became a man I would be a soldier. But that did not prevent me from taking an enormous interest in the theatre, the opera and above all the ballet . . . Often I played truant from school and furtively watched a performance at the theatre. Even the thrashings I received when I was found out – as I invariably was – did not deter me.[9]

The theatres were in Tiflis and Rostov, the dancers itinerant stars of the Imperial Ballet.

He had the Cossack's love for and instinctive response to music, song and dance that makes their folk ensembles a stirring experience.

Cossacks express all their feelings in their songs and dances; even now I can mentally hear the barbaric appeal of their music as I heard it in the trenches on the Russian frontier.[10]

Once Haskell was being driven by him through the night to Paris from Monte Carlo. De Basil had a badly injured hand on which a two-hour operation had been performed, but drove as recklessly as he always did, ignoring the pain and disability (again, as he always did). Turning on the car radio, they picked up a concert of Cossack music. The Colonel was delighted, and joined in the songs as they raced through the night.[11]

As a result of M. Trusetta's friendly gamble, early in 1921 a programme for the first time bore the title 'Ballets Russes – dir. W. de Basil', with the qualifying subheading 'Danses Plastiques'. Leonidova and Ellanskaya were joined by a third lady, Galya Gloukariova. Their photographs, of plump and pretty girls in flowing draperies and sculptural or oriental poses, are typical of the period – similar studies pepper the pages of *The Dancing Times* in the 'twenties – and they were greeted with some enthusiasm when they made a debut in Switzerland.

The critics were not so happy. De Basil recorded:

When I read the newspapers the next morning I was disillusioned. Most of the critics thought it a pity I had not stuck to soldiering or lorry-driving . . .[12]

So in Geneva he took stock of the situation, engaged a Swedish maître de ballet called Price, and on returning to Paris added four principals: Elisabeth Gluck, a ballerina from Moscow, Olga Smirnova, her husband Nicholas Tripolitov, and another male dancer, Gretchikine. De Basil himself appeared in mime roles under the name of Chernov. The conductor and pianist was called Doubiagski and the new repertoire, although largely made up of *divertissements,* emphasized classical ballet more and *danse plastique* less. *Danse plastique,* one must remember, was having a considerable vogue in Western Europe at that time.

Bravely, de Basil demoted his wife and cousin from the position of top stars:

My cousin was a constant thorn in my side; it was my first experience of the artistic temperament. I found it difficult to contend against![13]

After she left him, Ellanskaya found a place at the Paris Opéra as a *sujet rhythmique*, of whom there were quite a few at that time. De Basil decided (and no doubt never changed his mind) that directing a ballet company would ideally, need 'the wisdom of a Solomon, the cunning of a serpent, and the tact of a diplomat'.[14] Wisdom and tact were not outstanding attributes of his at any time, but he prided himself on his cunning.

Tripolitov recalls a performance on 25 September 1923 at Belleville which de Basil considered very important because of the people who attended it, and which was a considerable success, yielding quotable notices from *Comoedia Illustré*.[15] For this Theodore Vassiliev, who taught at Egorova's studio, was programmed as maître de ballet, and certainly attended some rehearsals and gave his advice. As a result, the Ballets Russes de W. de Basil began a largely pioneering tour of regional France. Classical ballet was almost a novelty in the cities and towns they visited in the autumn of 1923: Dijon, Dôle, Pontarlier, Chalon-sur-Saône, Besançon, Belfort, Nancy, Verdun. They did many one-night stands, in conditions that ranged from *salles des fêtes* still relying on gas rather than electricity to theatres with good stages and comfortable dressing-rooms. They went on to Belgium, playing Ghent, Louvain, Charleroi, Liège. When they returned to France, at Nantes, they added to the repertoire a little oriental ballet, with a libretto by de Basil, in which he played an old sorcerer. They also danced a version of *Le Lac des cygnes* with Smirnova and Tripolitov and de Basil as von Rothbart.

The dancers renewed their contracts for 1924. They were a trifle reluctant, as they were all tired, but de Basil's persuasiveness won the day. He was now in his early thirties – tall, lean, fairish in colouring, blue-eyed. He was a patient man and to some an inscrutable man. He was also capable of high spirits, sudden rages, disarming charm, warm-hearted generosity. In his own language (and later in French and Spanish) he was eloquent. English he spoke increasingly well as the years went by but never with real facility. All the people who were never paid or who were financially cheated were the victims of his conviction that nothing mattered except to keep the ballet company going and of the necessity for converting whatever money he could lay his hands on to that end. When he had extra money, people had only to ask and he would hand it out. When he had little, he was as grasping and doubtfully honest as an old peasant woman, no matter what scrap of contractual paper was flourished at him by somebody's lawyer. In defence of his company's life he would be devious, untruthful, double-dealing and if necessary ruthless. As many of the managers and impresarios with whom he had to deal were equally devious, double-dealing and ruthless, it is hard to feel much sympathy for their protests when he won a point. Unfortunately for him, in the long run he was the loser.

De Basil's Cossack origins are worth a word of explanation. According to his passport – a stateless one – he was born on 16 September 1888 (it may have been earlier) in the small garrison town of Kovno (Kaunas) in Lithuania. This is contradicted by friends who insist that his birthplace was Baku. Certainly he seems firmly established as a Kuban Cossack who grew up in the south. Outside Russia the term Cossack tends to be incorrectly associated with soldiers of a crack regiment, a Russian equivalent of Hussar or Uhlan. Instead it has a racial connotation. The word, which means something like brigand or adventurer, was adopted centuries ago by people who were settled as freemen on the Russian frontiers on condition that they acted as her defence. A closely linked warrior community with an emphasis on bravery, toughness and fighting ability, and little use for the gentler attributes, resulted. They were also, as Gogol's *Taras Bulba* makes clear, fanatically Christian. The name Voskresensky has links with the Russian Orthodox priesthood, and in fact de Basil was a sincere believer. Interestingly, Prince Peter Lieven wrote of him that he was

the type of Russian, the careful, consecutive worker, which is not well known in the West, but a type which exists and is quite characteristic. In everyday life it can be recognized in the learned types of the old sectarian church, quiet, stubborn and hardworking in the extreme. In art a striking example of the type is to be found in Rimsky-Korsakov . . .[16]

This isolated view of de Basil is scarcely borne out by other evidence. It appears to be the Cossack heredity and training that are the important matters where he is concerned. The complete change of course forced on him by the Revolution in no way nullified his earlier influences. Constantly, in considering his character and the contribution he made to ballet, military parallels emerge.

He was by temperament and talents a campaign leader. His form of soldiering had nothing to do with regular army conventions. It was partisan warfare, for which the virtues are courage, endurance,

opportunism, improvisation, successful bluff. In this the military unit –
frequently augmented by camp-followers – is closer to a guerrilla band
under a chief than any orthodox regiment could be.

Every phase of de Basil's career as a ballet director, but
predominantly the South American years when he was very much on
his own, can be seen in terms of reconnaissance, the establishment of
bridgeheads, their consolidation, the bringing up of supplies (and living
off the land where necessary), billeting, parley, treaty. He was his own
advance guard, reconnoitring the next objective and planning his battle
strategy for the next engagement.

His company was to him the equivalent of a partisan brigade. They
were all dedicated to one object – the preservation and presentation of
Russian ballet. Each had an integral part to play in the campaign. They
were also, to his Cossack outlook, a community, each identified with the
other whatever ructions went on within their limits. He found it quite
natural, if often intensely aggravating, that parents and other relatives
should travel with them. If they could find work to help things along or
contribute money for the general good, that too seemed natural. Non-
performing associates, men he had known for many years, however
much they infuriated him at times, were accepted, as soldiers in a
regiment accept each other. He tolerated their idiosyncrasies and
enjoyed their eccentricities. Hurok might inveigh endlessly against Lidji
or Philippov or Zon but de Basil, whatever his private reactions to them
might be, remained unmoved. They were part of his fighting force. A
non-company associate too had a special place – an uncouth, scarred,
shaven-headed man called Vassily or Vassiliev. He may have derived
from army days, may have been that stock character the privileged
servant or loyal batman, and certainly was never discarded. Hubert
Griffith, on his visit to Sospel, found that Vassiliev's

mouth was never shut. Halfway through serving a meal he would sit down at
table, help himself to wine and cigarettes, and dominate the conversation with
his anecdotes. Nobody minded.[17]

It was primarily for Vassiliev and his wife that the Colonel acquired the
farm at Sospel. This changed when he and Morosova went to live there
in 1938 and he planned to recondition it, retire there eventually and
write his memoirs.

The feeling of family influenced many of the dancers, almost against
their will. Considering the instability of their world, the competition of

173

rival groups, there was surprising loyalty from a hard core of artists, as opposed to the temporary or seasonal members of the company. This was not confined to the Grigorievs, who remained throughout, or the character artists like Psota or Hoyer whose best chances lay with that particular repertoire. There were many long associations and more than a few of those who left were motivated by the need for security. They wanted US or Australian nationality after a stateless existence, they wanted large sums of film money, they wanted rich husbands. Whatever quarrels they had with de Basil – and all dancers have quarrels with their directors – and whatever discomforts and difficulties they had to endure, they felt instinctively that with him and in his ballet company they were in touch with something important where ballet was concerned. Sono Osato is not alone when she writes:

to this day I feel gratitude and love and admiration whenever I think of Vassily Grigorievitch . . . the enormous work he did and the fierce tenacity of spirit that drove him will live as long as ballet and its history survive.[18]

De Basil's character is painted in black, white and every shade of grey. He had a dramatic and larger-than-life personality that impressed, infuriated, outraged or amused those who came in contact with it, according to their own inclinations or the nature of their dealings with him. Hubert Griffith, writing in the London *Observer* in 1935, described him as 'one of the most remarkable characters in Europe': 'All his stories both as a colonel of Cossacks in the war and as the lorry driver after are completely fantastic. All of them when strictly investigated turn out to be completely true.'[19]

His need for the challenge of personal danger and his physical courage, a Cossack inheritance, was visible primarily in an astonishing series of car accidents. At one time he drove a racing car with a specially built steel body. Hairbreadth escapes are recalled, in America, in Australia, in Germany. In Germany the car dropped, somersaulting, from one autobahn to another. In America, Psota sustained a scalp wound in another bad crash. Baronova remembers the car breaking down on a railway crossing somewhere in Europe and the tall figure of the Colonel running down the line waving his arms to stop an oncoming train. Some reports suggest that his eyesight was defective from a wound near one eye and certainly his familiar image was a spectacled one. Hubert Griffith, however, as late as July 1939, watched him target-shooting in the south of France.

Second Company, Australia 1936/7
ABOVE LEFT *L'Oiseau de feu:* Hélène Kirsova and Igor Youskevitch
ABOVE RIGHT *Les Présages:* Tamara Tchinarova
TOP *Prince Igor:* Nina Raievska and Léon Woizikovsky

ABOVE *Protée:* David Lichine with Alexandra Denisova, Natasha Sobinova, Sono Osato, Geneviève Moulin and Marina Svetlova
TOP *Francesca da Rimini:* group including Lubov Tchernicheva and Paul Petrov

ABOVE LEFT *Le Fils prodigue:* Irina Baronova and Anton Dolin
ABOVE RIGHT *Icare:* Roman Jasinsky
TOP *Le Coq d'or:* Irina Baronova and Marc Platov (King Dodon) with Galina Razoumova,
Olga Morosova, Sono Osato, Tamara Grigorieva, Roman Jasinsky and Paul Petrov

ABOVE *Les Femmes de bonne humeur:*
Olga Morosova
TOP *Les Femmes de bonne humeur:*
Tamara Grigorieva and Marian Ladre
RIGHT *Le Beau Danube:* Yura Lazovsky

ABOVE *Graduation Ball:*
Tatiana Riabouchinska
and David Lichine
(INSET) Nicholas Orlov

LEFT *Paganini:* Dimitri
Rostov

THIS PAGE

RIGHT Irina Baronova with her husband Gerry
Sevastianov
BELOW Sir Thomas Beecham with
Danilova and Shabelevsky after premiere
of *Les Dieux mendiants,* Covent Garden, 1937

OPPOSITE

FAR RIGHT Natasha Sobinova, Alexandra Denisova
and June Roper, Vancouver, 1938
NEAR RIGHT Tatiana Riabouchinska, Vera Zorina,
Olga Morosova, Irina Baronova, Alexandra Danilova,
Roman Jasinsky and Yurek Shabelevsky,
Santa Monica, California, 1936
BIG PICTURE Tatiana Riabouchinska, David Lichine,
Vsevolod Grigoriev, Natasha Sobinova, Lubov
Tchernicheva, Galina Razoumova, Tamara Grigorieva,
Maori guide, Alexandra Denisova, Lina Lerina, Irina
Kosmovska and Serge Grigoriev, Rotorua, New
Zealand, 1939

ABOVE Bronislava Nijinska with Baronova
and Lichine after premiere of *Les Cent
Baisers,* Covent Garden, 1935

RIGHT Toumanova,
aronova, Riabouchinska and
Danilova, off stage

ABOVE Serge Grigoriev, Vladimir Dokoudovsky and Colonel W. de Basil,
Covent Garden, 1947
TOP LEFT *Cain and Abel:* Carlota Pereyra, Nancy Milton, April Olrich,
Oleg Tupine and Kenneth Mackenzie
TOP RIGHT *Le Mariage d'Aurore:* Tatiana Stepanova and Oleg Tupine

The Colonel had a small-calibre rifle, and never missed the bulls'-eye. When this was thought to be too tame, the devoted Vassily was instructed to stand thirty yards down the drive and throw his hat up in the air: this the Colonel also riddled with bullets. Vassily was directly under the hat as it descended. He had faith in his master's marksmanship.[20]

There were other perilous exploits, sought in an adolescent spirit of dare-devilry – frontier running or independent smuggling . . .

De Basil was no figurehead director. He took a keen and detailed interest in every aspect of the company's life, in every member of its personnel. He travelled tirelessly on its behalf, in that pre-jet age by sea or rail, road or small propeller aeroplane. Whenever he was with the company he constantly watched performances and rehearsals, noting, as does any devoted balletomane, day-to-day modulations in interpretation. Dokoudovsky recalls him as an 'observer *par excellence*'. One evening in South America, in *Paganini*, Dokoudovsky had the feeling, recognizable to most dancers, that for once everything had gone right. For once, his performance had come together in every particular. It was de Basil who came up to him afterwards and not only complimented him but analysed the special merits of that one occasion in detail.

All directors are accused of favouritism, and some have pushed untalented favourites at the expense of other dancers. This was not a fault of de Basil's. When he parted from Nina Leonidova, remaining on friendly terms when she married Vania Psota, it was to marry Olga Morosova with whom he was deeply in love. This marriage [21] – in Nice Cathedral in 1938 – brought him the happiness of a beautiful and charming wife many years his junior who could act as hostess and partner in his social life. He also greatly admired her as a dancer, and had faith in her ability to extend her range from the one in which she was universally acknowledged to excel – that of a soubrette and comedienne. However, he never built the company or the repertoire around her. Not one single leading role was created for her, nor would she have wished him to insist on this. She was entirely free of cut-throat ambition, sincerely appreciative of other dancers' talents, and unhappy that her status as the director's wife placed her in what she felt was an equivocal position where the company was concerned.

One word that crops up time and again in considering the actions of de Basil is the word 'intrigues'. It emerges as a predominant note in Hurok and Hurok-influenced writings. 'He was a born intriguer and delighted in surrounding himself with scheming characters . . . De Basil and his entire entourage lived in a world of intrigues of their own deliberate making.'[22]

The entourage was of course Lidji, Philippov and Zon, and Hurok is quite specific about the kind of intrigues he means:

He [de Basil] would despatch them abroad in his company simply to stir up trouble, to form cliques; for purposes of *chantage*; he would order them into whispered colloquies in corners alternately wearing knowing looks and glum visages . . .[23]

Very nasty conduct – and there is no real point in trying to decide how much or how little truth lies in the accusations – but by no means unique to de Basil. 'Machinations' – another word that crops up continually and derogatorily – and intrigues were indulged in by each and every one of the organizations involved in what was without doubt a bitter balletic civil war, conducted mainly in the Americas and spread over some twenty years. Wars are not fought ethically. The methods of victors are as questionable as those of the vanquished, but their public statements become more widely disseminated.

Hurok also accused de Basil personally, however, of enjoying the whole thing:

De Basil's unholy joy would come from creating, through these henchmen, a nasty situation and then stepping in to pull a string here, jerk a cord there, he would save the situation, thus becoming the hero of the moment.[24]

This was probably true. Haskell, who liked and admired the Colonel, was certain that he steered a course which deliberately played people off against each other – 'he is expert at gaining results from these jealousies by opposing one to the other'.[25] He described de Basil as a natural psychologist, and this is again a characteristic found in military leaders of guerrilla bands. Certainly he liked the challenge of trouble. He was happier when there were complications in the company than when things were going well.

Along with the reputation of a schemer and intriguer, de Basil has that of a man without culture or artistic knowledge whose business instincts and organizing ability steered the company to success. It is an interesting falsification of this distinctly complex man. Initially the world of ballet tried to compare him with Diaghilev and naturally found him totally wanting in terms of artistic erudition and taste. However, the opposite picture of a clumsy and boorish man is untrue. He spoke a

176

cultured Russian and had an average educated man's appreciation of the theatre, particularly music and the dance. Sadly, in the view of many, he knew none of the people he ought to have known, none of the artistically sophisticated amateurs who mattered – 'not even Mrs Asquith'. Dolin had to point out to him at the Alhambra the various titled and influential people of London who kept ballet companies going.[26] He had no contacts in New York café society nor did he ever move happily among the cultured elite. In less sophisticated society, especially with fellow Russians, he could be excellent company. In personal taste he represented the middle road of his generation, without avant-garde cravings. This meant that he also represented the general public, who were becoming increasingly important. It was his trump card – he liked ballet to be entertaining, exciting, moving, colourful and (always a vital if unadmitted point with the normal male audience) put over by attractive young girls, the younger the better, with beautiful legs. His response to what would now be termed the Lolita age group was not only genuine, it was shared by more respectable men than would ever acknowledge it. Nevertheless he was not unappreciative of older dancers. Julian Braunsweg speaks of him standing in the wings, in 1939, watching Baronova's Swan Queen and saying, 'You'll never see such a moving interpretation as long as you live'.[27] Two years before, he had talked of Danilova as 'dancing better than ever, if that's possible. She is an example to the whole lot of them. She dances – like a cascade of water' (obviously thinking of the brilliance and sparkle of her work).[28]

De Basil's initial attitude to ballet was that of an enthusiastic ballet-goer and, as for any ballet-goer, many years of close association with ballet developed greater understanding. He was astute, and when he talked of his company and plans to reporters his words carried conviction. No doubt what he said was the result of conferences with Grigoriev, with his choreographers, with Sevastianov, Ottley and d'Erlanger. A collaborative background to a speech, though, does not necessarily mean that the speaker is merely a mouthpiece. Vova Grigoriev describes his method of work as consulting with all the experts but always finally deciding for himself, and the decisions, Vova felt, were good ones. De Basil could be difficult and unpredictable but he knew what he was doing. Because of this, Vova admired him and never took offence at anything he said.

The oddest misconception about de Basil is that he was a shrewd businessman who was interested in ballet as a means of making money.

Ballet never made money for him. He was not personally extravagant although he had sudden Cossack moods of expansiveness, and he died a pauper. He had little idea of business and he never cared about money except as the lifeblood of his company, about which he cared absolutely. No shrewd businessman would have allowed Lidji to involve him in constant and endless litigation in which he was almost always the loser. A shrewd businessman would have played a far better hand against Hurok and Denham, and would have appeared to co-operate in order to emerge on top in the end. De Basil could not co-operate with anyone and was unable to camouflage this. It was his downfall. Because of it he antagonized Hurok and later Gallo, which left his company not only without promoters in North America but vulnerable to cleverly contrived destructive propaganda. The lengthy negotiations he carried on were not clever. They were simply the result of his obstinate determination not to abdicate leadership. He did not know otherwise how to deal with these people. He was pitting skills learned as a freebooting soldier against professional showbusiness experts. Helen Dzhermolinska, the editor of *Dance Magazine*, writing his obituary in 1951, made clear how uneven was the duel and how much he realized this:

He was himself the victim of unscrupulous fleecing by more adroit practitioners of ballet management. Bearing his losses gallantly and without theatricalities, he would say "I know he's a crook but I like crooks – they make life so interesting!" – adding wistfully, "if I only had his talent . . .!"[29]

The dimension of the man is revealed in the completely varied ways in which he was seen by those who knew him. Hurok allowed him only minor virtues ('an expert cook', 'simple in tastes'), wrote down his courage as stubbornness or bravado, and decided that he was not so much charming as able to turn on charm at will. Shortcomings, for Hurok, there were in plenty – no gentleness or sensitivity, all the makings of a dictator.[30] For Haskell he was 'a clear thinker of immense courage', someone with taste if not the vast erudition of Diaghilev, a man who could be difficult, who had no tactful phrases and who loved a scrap, but whose achievement he wholeheartedly admired.[31] For Pierre Michaut he had *'la volonté, l'adresse et un don d'intuition sinon peut-être un sens artistique personnel'*.[32] For Prince Peter Lieven he was 'no pyrotechnist, no creator of fairy castles, a stubborn builder, consecutive and intelligent'.[33] For Vladimir Dukelsky (Vernon Duke) he was 'a man devoid of social graces, clumsy in a room' (this might well have been a result of his bad eyesight), 'clever in business, with the sketchiest imaginable knowledge of the arts . . . but with a strongly developed sense of humour and a certain rather winning easy bonhomie'.[34]

Baronova says he had great physical and moral courage, enormous and likeable energy, and he was interested in individuals, keen to probe into their lives and feelings. She remembers him with amusement and affection. Gerald Goode found him a rough-cut Russian, a good disciplinarian but capable of violence. To Dokoudovsky and Stroganova he was a warm, lovable personality, a great and misjudged man. April Olrich found that the artistic side of the company meant far more to him than the business side – people were always cheating him, she thought – and recalls him as a charming, kind and knowledgeable man. Dame Marie Rambert also found him charming, many years before, and thought him an excellent entrepreneur and publicist – as well as someone who sincerely loved ballet, 'and beautiful girls, and their bodies in movement'. Toumanova's 'association with Colonel de Basil was a very strong and deep one . . . I had always a great respect for him as my director and now I have a very great admiration for him and for what he did for the world of art'.[35]

For or against, the evidence on Vassily Grigorievitch adds up to a man of unusual character and vitality, a very human being and a man worth remembering by ballet historians as a tenacious and dedicated campaigner for the Russian ballet heritage. 'An audacious man', Helen Dzhermolinska calls him, 'incurably superstitious' – he would never sign a contract unless he had on his person a tiny pair of scissors given to him by his mother, Julie, when he was a boy – 'incurably hopeful . . . remembered by friends for his zest, his love of sun, wine, good food, good company'.[36] In wine, good food and good company he took particular pleasure. Harold Atkins, an English journalist who lunched with him in London in 1947, recalls that they had especially good Burgundy and steak à la Rossini. When Atkins praised them, the Colonel said: 'Shall we have it all over again?' – and ordered an encore.

3

The Baby Ballerinas

ONE of the most enduring publicity catchphrases in ballet history is 'the baby ballerinas'. Haskell, who may have invented it, says that before the London Alhambra season the company was 'known as the "Babies' Ballet", the principals being anywhere between thirteen and seventeen years in age'.[1] Once coined, whoever the coiner, it was too vivid to die. Toumanova, Baronova and Riabouchinska were forever branded by it. Even now, people who never saw any of them dance bracket them together under the old description. It arrests them in time, a trio of divinities on stage who revert outside the theatre into unsophisticated, chaperoned schoolgirls with shoulder-length hair, innocent of make-up, wearing childish clothes and ankle socks. The time is forever 1933, their ages fourteen (Toumanova and Baronova) and sixteen (Riabouchinska).

It was of course their plurality that was particularly startling. The very young dancer was nothing new; but for so many to appear at once, and all with such exceptional technical skill, was a phenomenon. When he saw them in action at the Alhambra, Philip Richardson, the editor of *The Dancing Times*, wrote (as The Sitter Out):

On Baronova and Riabouchinska it is impossible to bestow too much praise. Their technical work is so brilliant and so effortless that they make the most difficult *pas* look easy;[2]

and this was obviously true, too, of Toumanova, whom he did not see until later.

This was the miracle. In the studios of Preobrajenska and Kschessinska outstanding natural ability had been trained, in the space of a surprisingly short time, to an astonishing height of perfection. The technique of these young girls was as astounding to critics, teachers and dance students in 1933 as to the general audience. Naturally, technique has altered since then. In some areas of work it is stronger, in others weaker, but a majority opinion among members of the dance profession who remember them is that they would probably seem equally impressive today. It has been claimed that all young dancers, given the training and opportunities of these children, would be equally good, but although other dancers have also shown remarkable skill in their early teens (Markova in Diaghilev's *Le Rossignol* at fifteen, Beryl Grey as a Sadler's Wells Ballet Odette-Odile at fourteen), it is still not the norm. Professional schools today offer students of eighteen and over as fledglings, who make a mark with one carefully coached graduating performance and then need seasons of *corps de ballet* and small solo roles in order to develop stamina and stage-consciousness. Baronova and Toumanova, at fourteen, were dancing every night of the week in demanding leading roles and surprising the world by their virtuosity. Even Riabouchinska at seventeen – and probably slightly galled at being classed always with her juniors – was younger than most debutante ballerinas of the 'eighties. Admittedly, none of them had to measure up scholastically to orthodox examination standards.

They were not only virtuoso technicians – they had strong and contrasted personalities. Baronova emerges as the liveliest, a girl of enormous willpower, vitality and intelligence who was influenced primarily by her own thoughts, emotions and developing judgement and never deterred or dismayed by challenges. At twelve, a new pupil at Preobrajenska's studio, her determination was tested. Her contemporary, Toumanova, was turning multiple *fouettés* to right and left with exactness and facility. Baronova, without at that time any dedication to the dance, but with a strong schoolgirl compulsion to compete and excel, made up her mind to do as well. She fell over repeatedly, but mastered her difficulties, and with that mastery gained a lasting commitment to dancing.

Toumanova's was a more gentle and less assertive temperament, dominated by the tremendous personality of her mother. Of the three, she was the one who embodied everyone's idea of a Russian ballerina. Exotic in appearance, a South Russian with large dark eyes, raven wings of hair and magnolia skin, she combined lyricism and virtuosity to a remarkable degree. There was another side to her art – the comedy of the Miller's Wife in *Le Tricorne,* or Swanilda in *Coppélia.* She had the grand manner and this, coupled with youthful grace, was magical.

Her origins were as romantic as her appearance. The tale has often

181

been told of her birth in a cattle wagon occupied by army officers during the hardships of a retreat through Siberia in 1919. Her father was an army colonel, her mother a young woman from the Caucasus of exceptional character and spirit who was to become widely known in the Russian ballet as the most partisan ballet mother of them all. Hers was the drive that more than made up for its lack in Tamara. Mme Toumanova-Khacidovitch now lives in California with her daughter, and everyone who ever met her has a story to tell. In her fierce dedication to Tamara and opposition to Tamara's rivals, she is unlike Tamara herself, whose admiration for other artists and gratitude to the teachers and directors who shaped her career are remarkable and sincere. Mme Toumanova's temperamental extremes, her shrewdness, and her gifts for fortune-telling, faith-healing and poker-playing, are very much part of the Ballets Russes' story.

In 1919 she, her husband and their baby daughter reached Shanghai, but it was not very many years before they made their way to Paris and Tamara began her dance studies with Preobrajenska. She describes Preobrajenska as 'the greatest guide and influence from the very beginning, my complete teacher'.[3] Before many months had gone by she was chosen by Pavlova to dance a Liadov polka choreographed by Preobrajenska at the Trocadéro. This was her first public appearance; the next one, in the children's ballet *L'Eventail de Jeanne*, brought her to the notice of the great critic André Levinson and through him to the ballet world.

L'Eventail de Jeanne was initially conceived and privately presented in 1928 by Mme Jeanne Dubost. It was set to music by ten French composers, and the dances were arranged by Alice Bourgat and Yvonne Franc. Its repetition at the Paris Opéra in March 1929, when Toumanova appeared in it, was even more successful. She danced the polka and valse, and Levinson was amazed at her technical accomplishment. He spoke of '*fouettés en tournant, doubles tours sur la pointe, relevés en arabesque*' which she presented

avec une précoce assurance et une crânerie qui n'est pas de son age. C'est étonnant; c'est aussi effrayant. La plante humaine ne supporte pas sans les plus graves dangers une culture aussi forcée en serre chaude . . .[4]

The production was repeated at Monte Carlo in 1930 when René Blum was greatly impressed by Toumanova's performance. She was signed up for the new Ballets Russes de Monte-Carlo at the end of 1931.

Like Toumanova, Baronova had no memories of Russia. Although she was born in Petrograd, she was taken to Rumania by her parents when she was a year old. Her father, a naval officer, was also an ardent amateur violinist and fled, as she says, 'with his violin under one arm and me under the other'. Mme Baronova, frustrated in her own ambitions to dance, arranged dancing lessons for Irina in Bucharest with Mme Mazhaiskaya, an ex-*corps de ballet* dancer from the Maryinsky. Irina would rather have been tree-climbing. Her facility, if not her vocation, for dancing was almost immediately apparent, and before long a move to Paris and Preobrajenska was advocated. What a marvellous stroke of fate for Preobrajenska – for any teacher – to have two topflight talents to nurture at the same time!

Adorably fair, full of gaiety and tenderness, with a lively sense of humour and a sunny smile, Baronova, like Toumanova, was capable of combining the purist classicism, the most delicious *demi-caractère* work and a deep instinctive understanding for the newer choreographic styles. Like Toumanova, she made her debut early. She and her fellow pupils first earned pin money by appearing at *thé-dansants*, which were in vogue at the time. Then in 1931, she worked (with Balanchine as choreographer) in a production of *Orphée aux enfers* at the Théâtre Mogador. Levinson described her as a '*toute jeune fillette qui enleva son galop culminant en un tourbillon vertiginant avec un natural ingénu et une sûréte magistrale*'.[5]

Toumanova and Baronova were examples of the constantly recurring balletic theme of the twin rivals: Sallé and Camargo, Taglioni and Elssler, Pavlova and Karsavina were their antecedents. Riabouchinska was on her own, something of a maverick. Although she was older, she was perennially the spirit of youth; light, golden, elfin, spiritual. She was a Muscovite, with a wealthy banker father and a dancer mother. Like the other two girls she was trained in Paris, but with Kschessinska. Where they acquired phenomenal turning ability and technical strength from Preobrajenska, she learned Kschessinska's marvellously stylish *port de bras*. Kschessinska herself is quoted as saying: 'I have tried to put part of myself into her – the arms, the rhythm . . .'[6] Her footwork was more suspect, but her equipment for her particular artistic contribution to ballet was complete. Very much a 'performance dancer', she is reputed to have been unable to do in rehearsal technical feats that she accomplished brilliantly once the curtain was up.

In Monte Carlo in early 1932 this trinity of potential stars was far

183

from the blazing galaxy it would eventually become. They were new to each other, to the choreographers and *répétiteurs*, and to the repertoire. They were new, too, to the experienced dancers in their mid- or late twenties who had worked with Diaghilev, and those nearer their own ages who could claim one previous company, usually Ida Rubinstein's. They took each other's measure in class and rehearsal, as did their attendant parents.

The three mothers tend to be talked of as a group. The impression is of a *pas de trois* designed by a choreographer, a triptych, or a three-headed monster termed 'a ballet mother', screaming and gesticulating over its daughters' careers. Of course they were entirely individual and each took up the challenge of her dancing daughter in her own way. They were all young women, in their thirties, expatriates with husbands whose lives and work had been inexorably thrown off course by the Revolution.

Mme Baronova had a firm, quiet determination and a great deal of good sense, which is reflected in Irina's well-adjusted nature. Mme Riabouchinska made many friends (Eglevsky, particularly, remembered her kindness to him as a solitary boy) and, lucky in having more money than most, often tided de Basil over a financial crisis, producing pawnable or saleable jewellery from her underwear at the crucial moment. Mme Toumanova was the emotionally vociferous one, who earned them all a reputation for passionate partisanship.

The first months of 1932 laid the foundations for the three careers. Some of the people in charge – Grigoriev, Tchernicheva, Massine and de Basil – were to be the constant powers in their lives over the next few years. Balanchine, their especial love, would disappear all too soon. Blum, whom Toumanova remembers as 'a most gentle, kind, wonderful person', operated primarily in Monte Carlo. Toumanova, chosen as leading dancer by Balanchine and Massine for their first creations, found Grigoriev initially 'very cold and official'.[7] It was probably, she now feels, a reaction from the enthusiasm other people were showing, but for a sensitive and hardworking 12-year-old, it was upsetting and discouraging.

Relationships would change, perspectives alter, as the dancers grew older and more experienced. Friendships developed, all coloured by rivalry over roles on stage and, inevitably, over the attentions of their young and handsome partners and associates.

The stresses to which these girls were subject make the moans of many contemporary teenagers seem ridiculous. Through their adolescent years they had to work at a totally demanding art. They had to perfect the technique and interpretation of leading roles in a very large repertoire of famous ballets, and learn new ones, to a point that would satisfy their choreographers and teachers, please audiences and outclass their rivals. They danced night after night, travelling widely in Europe and America (Australasia came later for them). They had an increasing number of social engagements, and interviews with press and critics. They were adulated by their public and had to adjust to the exciting and disturbing experience of balletomane attention. They had the usual generation difficulties with parents and those in authority, the physical problems of all young women, the temperamental upheavals of love-affairs, and of gaining or losing boy-friends.

Remarkably, they survived without lasting physical or emotional harm, and without becoming spoilt. Obviously the discipline kept by Grigoriev, and the fact that they shared the limelight fairly equally, were stabilizing factors. Equally important, they had the pressure from above of the great and established ballerina, Danilova. Danilova herself, as reported by Elizabeth Twysden, felt persecuted and threatened by the young dancers and suffered greatly as a result.[8] They themselves on the whole had enough sense and humility to appreciate her quality. Baronova speaks of her as 'a star, with a big S – inimitable in her very special style, elegant, sharp, brisk and gorgeous legs . . . I admired her, I learned a lot from her, and I respected her as an artist very deeply'.[9]

In addition, these children were praised, they were successful, they were loved – and nervous collapse usually happens to the insecure and the unloved.

Of all the enthusiasts of the period, the most famous is Arnold Haskell. He was thirty at the time, and had a very solid background of ballet-going before the advent of the de Basil Ballet. The lean months after Diaghilev's death had driven him to a point where he was ripe for a revelation, and one was vouchsafed on the opening night at the Alhambra. He took the whole company into his loyal affections, but the fervour with which he wrote of the little girls, Toumanova and Baronova, has a marvellously youthful passion.

He was not however blind to their faults. In 1934 he wrote:

Tamara has a dramatic fire and a dominating personality that at its worst turns into overacting and a too keen awareness of the public; Irina a serenity and

185

reserve that may mean loss of contact. Tamara is grave, tragic and dark, Irina gay and fair; between them they divide the emotions, with each one supple enough to challenge the other on her own terrain.[10]

Haskell, like other people, was perennially astounded at the contrast between these little girls in their natural everyday characters and the excitingly expressive artists they became on stage. Certainly the difference savoured of fairytale. It had the mythical, legendary appeal of metamorphosis. Baronova, in particular, continued throughout her career to amaze people. What Haskell calls 'the almost frightening transformation from the person one knows to the stage personality' was felt by everyone who saw this charming, extrovert artist both on stage and off. Even in 1938 an Australian writer found astonishing the difference between her unspoilt character in real life – 'a delightful child in her ways' (she was nineteen at the time) – and her composed and exotic performance in *Coq d'or*.[11] Oleg Tupine, as a boy, arriving in London earlier that year and taken straight to Covent Garden in a taxi by Pierre Vladimirov and Lichine (in make-up) saw *Coq d'or* and immediately fell for the marvellous, glamorous, dark-haired Queen of Shemakhan. Next day in class he could hardly believe that the delightful and unaffected blonde beside him at the *barre* was the same dancer.

It is remarkable, in analysing contemporary accounts, to find that these 14-year-olds had already such subtlety and maturity in performance. Nowadays these are the qualities one frequently pines for in vain from experienced leading dancers. No one, recalling them on stage, discusses the two girls as juveniles. They were compared by critics on the highest level. Back in 1932, Levinson was describing Toumanova's 'oriental languor' that reminded him of Karsavina, declaring that these '*airs penchés et mines dolentes*' hid a technique of a vigour and perfection possessed by none of the Imperial Ballet sylphides of 1909.[12] In September 1934, when Baronova was still only fifteen, Haskell was writing of her as an exceptional mime, able to render the most subtle shades of expression. He added: 'I knew from the first that she shared with Spessiva alone those movements that flow one into the other and that nobility of line that seems to reach into the infinite.'[13]

'Infinity' was a word used (much later) for the third young dancer, Riabouchinska – 'It is the melody in her body which makes her line so perfect and so supple, and gives it a quality of infinity', wrote Beryl de Zoete.[14] Riabouchinska, in retrospect, is seen to have a very independent place and repertoire throughout her long association with de Basil. Included, for good measure, in the 'baby ballerina' category, she was not strictly speaking either a baby or a company prima ballerina. Not for her were Aurora or the lead in *Les Sylphides,* and although she was tried out in *Le Lac des cygnes* this was only briefly. Nowadays, with a far more flexible attitude to casting, when suitability for prima ballerina work is very differently estimated, she would perhaps have established herself as a Swan Queen, but in the more rigid 'thirties she was limited, apart from her creations, to a handful of roles. Her masterpiece was the prelude in *Les Sylphides*, stamped indelibly with her qualities of lightness and musicality. 'In *Les Sylphides*,' says Dame Marie Rambert, 'she did not make an entrance. She was *there...* '[15] Her famous Bluebird *pas de deux* was more argued about, although its flying, fluttering sharpness was exciting.

Massine discovered her unique capacity early, as the Child in *Jeux d'enfants.* Coton delighted in the 'seemingly spontaneous laughs and leaps' with which she conveyed 'the ecstasies of an Alice come at last to a crazy Wonderland'.[16] *Les Présages*, in which Massine exploited the personal idiosyncrasies of his dancers with unerring skill, displayed her as Frivolity, and Adrian Stokes, in one of his less purple passages, conjures up the effect: 'She is gossamer, a feathered particle that travels in sunbeams, floating just above the ground . . .'[17] Speed was one of her attributes. James Monahan terms her 'an embodied scherzo'.[18] Pierre Michaut has a charming phrase: *'parcourir étincelante le plateau.'*[19] Right through the repertoire there are elusive cameo creations, such as the Florentine Beauty in *Paganini*, that celebrate her distinctive individuality. Her perfection of sharpness and brightness as the Golden Cockerel was the ideal complement to Baronova's alluring Queen of Shemakhan.

It was a delight, for both critics and audiences, to watch the steady development of these dancers, year by year, as children became adolescents and adolescents matured into young women. Each season saw differences, in physique and artistry. In 1935 Lillian Moore reported that New York had seen 'a new Baronova – taller, heavier and more mature. She has however developed artistically as well as physically. Her dancing . . . seems more and more a revelation of the classical ballerina's art at its highest development'.[20] The same year *The Dancing Times* in London decided that 'Toumanova has made more progress than any other member of the company . . . She is rapidly developing into the ideal ballerina, both in appearance and technique'.[21] By 1937, Coton was writing that 'Baronova had developed the last finesse of polish to her extensive technique' and that Toumanova – 'surely the loveliest creature in history to dance' – had 'attained the utmost skill of mime and bearing so that one was rarely aware of the individual behind the characterization'.[22]

Baronova and Toumanova overlapped a great deal in their repertoire and the question of priority in creations and first-night performances in various parts of the world was a constantly vexed one. It was usually settled to the accompaniment of tears, protests and passions. For audiences it was marvellous. Balletomanes like nothing better than the chance to take sides, to select favourites, and to talk endlessly about the finer points of alternative interpretations. The rivalry was a whetstone, ensuring a continual fine edge on performance and an intensity of emotional colouring. Critics too, loved to compare and contrast, as did Basil Burdett of the *Melbourne Herald,* who wrote that Toumanova was

a great dancer and fine artist, inclined to be uneven, but that is probably inherent in her style, which is at once extraordinarily controlled yet nervous and sensitive. She lacks the final firm perfection of Baronova's effortless style, but has something many will consider even more precious, which recalls that tremulous birdlike quality of Pavlova.[23]

Wonder children, indeed, these three 'baby ballerinas', who in their brilliant teenage period could command panegyrics. None of these were more perceptive or touching than Prince Peter Lieven's. For him, Baronova, in 1936, was 'an absolutely perfect and finished dancer'. He praises her superb technique and classical style as a true Petipa dancer – and it is sad to think that she never had a chance to get to grips with the Petipa repertoire as it is seen today – her accomplished mime 'lifelike, persuasive and characteristic'. Riabouchinska he saw as an 'inborn' artist, charming, but with her artistic personality not fully developed or defined. This is confirmed later by many writers who found her a slow developer. Toumanova was his 'pet goddess' – 'a perfectly attuned, vibrating string . . .' He speaks of her 'inner fire' and describes her dancing as 'a sort of terpsichorean prayer'.[24]

The early artistic maturity of Toumanova and Baronova, as compared with even older dancers of today, is worth some thought. Did it lie in the quality and methods of their first professional teachers? In the type and content of the mainly *demi-caractère* repertoire they had to learn? In the example of dancers of different ages, background and experience within the company? In the community life, with its opportunities for discussion and analysis of interpretation as well as technique? In the emphasis on interpretation as well as technique, universally accepted in ballet at the time as being the true artistic goal of a dancer? And are we, with all our advances in physical choreography, with its borrowings from acrobatics and gymnastics, possibly the poorer for its loss?

Always with youthful prodigies the question arises as to how they will adapt to their later years. As adults, Toumanova, Baronova and Riabouchinska all added important roles to their repertoires, not necessarily with de Basil, but the full blaze of their glory is now obviously confined within the decade from 1931.

This was undoubtedly because they all suffered very naturally from a reaction against the amount of dancing they had done as children and adolescents. By the time they were in their early twenties, they were veterans. Their mental attitude to ballet had altered and they were looking outside the world they had grown up in for new artistic and emotional experiences. Toumanova and Baronova were tempted away by Hollywood. Baronova made the films *Florian* (1939) and *Yolanda* (1943). Toumanova married the producer Casey Robinson and appeared in many films, including *Tonight We Sing* (1953), *Invitation to the Dance* (1956) and *The Torn Curtain* (1966). Both went back to ballet, but as always happens with dancers the break in continuity made their standards less dependable. Technically they became more erratic, succumbing to the temptation of relying a certain amount on their star reputations. Baronova danced with Ballet Theatre and with Massine's Ballet Russe Highlights and acted in one or two plays before her parting from Sevastianov and marriage to Cecil Tennant in 1946. From then she was, by her own choice, absorbed by family life with her husband and three children. After Tennant's death she re-married Sevastianov, who died in 1974. Toumanova went on dancing longer, creating roles for Balanchine and Lifar at the Paris Opéra and for Wallmann at La Scala and appearing as guest artist all over the world. She was often criticized as producing what seemed to be a mannered caricature of the grand Russian style but she was also often acclaimed, particularly in the Latin countries, for superbly moving performances in *Giselle* and for her creation, in 1952, of Phédre in Jean Cocteau's pantomime-ballet at the Paris Opéra.

Riabouchinska had a less interrupted career. Her marriage to Lichine kept her continuously in ballet and she appeared with other companies after she and Lichine left de Basil – with Ballet Theatre, the Grand Ballet du Marquis de Cuevas, London Festival Ballet and the Ballet des Champs-Elysées.

The three famous 'babies' were not the only young dancers of their generation. Rostova was only seventeen in 1933, as was Grigorieva. Grigorieva's sister, Galina Razoumova, was fifteen, Anna Volkova sixteen. Three young dancers of the Vic-Wells Ballet, Margot Fonteyn, Pamela May and June Brae, were their contemporaries, but were less precocious as technicians and artists.

Once the pattern had been set, it continued. Dancers were regularly engaged in their mid-teens and although only one or two were, strictly speaking, prima ballerinas, de Basil launched many fine soloists.

One who became a prima ballerina was June Roper's pupil, the Canadian Alexandra Denisova (Patricia Denise Meyers). Roper, Preobrajenska-trained, had made her own career in nightclub and revue dancing, but her ability to produce young classical dancers was proved by the fact that ten of her pupils were accepted by the two Ballet Russe companies and Ballet Theatre. Four appeared with the de Basil Ballet: Denisova, Sobinova (Rosemary Deveson), Kira Bounina (Jean Hunt) and Margaret Banks.

Denisova and Sobinova auditioned for the company on 3 February 1938 when they were fifteen. The date has been recorded by Leland Windreich, and the detail too. At Lichine's request, their work was seen at a midnight performance at the Roper studio attended by de Basil and most of the company principals.[25] They were immediately signed up – the formal letter of agreement written out by June Roper and signed by the Colonel specifies that they are accepted as students, 'to take instruction in a course of dancing from the Ballets Russes until April first 1938 while we are travelling in the United States'.[26] They joined the ballet in Portland within the week, and Sobinova began writing home to her mother in a series of letters that reflect charmingly her personality and age and upbringing, and the effect on her of the life and personalities of the company. She was not the first dancer in the family. Her aunt, Doris Nichols, was a well-known ballroom dancer in England in the

190

1930s. Denisova, too, had inherited dance talent – her mother had been a Tiller Girl.

Among Sobinova's first impressions was the firm discipline of the company under Grigoriev. Everything had to be absolutely classical; no 'artistry' was permitted from the *corps de ballet*. She enjoyed the work, and the Vancouver girls made friends gradually, but language was a problem as they found Russian extremely difficult. Osato, on the other hand, had quickly become reasonably fluent. Sobinova was naturally very homesick at times. Lichine was probably the main reason for her persevering with the company – she had adored him from a distance as a dancer, and gazed at his photograph when she was at ballet school. To her delight, as a choreographer he found her the right kind of dancer to work with, and he set many roles on her during her years with de Basil.

The Vancouver girls had led sheltered lives, and Sobinova commented to her mother that there was 'quite a lot of immorality in the company – most of the bigger girls are paired off with boys of the company. Not very nice, is it!!'[27] They were, however, actively cared for by Riabouchinska and Lichine, and other people, like Borovansky, were always ready to advise. Baronova showed them how to make up – it was a special talent of hers. Petrov, who deeply loved pure classical dance, taught Sobinova the Swan Queen quite early (although she never had a chance to dance it) and was a great help over partnering.

Denisova was the one who got the good breaks. After a relatively short time, at Covent Garden in July 1938, she danced the Top in *Jeux d'enfants*. As Danilova and Toumanova had joined the Ballet Russe de Monte Carlo, Baronova was being overworked with Educational Ballets Ltd. Denisova probably owed her selection over other possible contenders to her strong turning ability, a surface resemblance to Baronova, and to Lichine's interest, but she took the chance well.

Sobinova was Denisova's opposite in appearance, with dark hair and lustrous eyes. Haskell regarded her as

exceptionally promising. She is sensitive to a degree, and she has the astonishing gift of becoming beautiful on the stage. Watch her in the corps de ballet, and she stands out for the rare lyrical quality of her movement . . . Her present development is due to Riabouchinska and Lichine. If they can continue to guide her, ballet will not only have a new ballerina, but a lyrical dancer as personal and unusual as Riabouchinska herself.[28]

She never realized her potential, however. For instance, she danced the Cat in *Cendrillon* rather than the leading role, which one imagines she would have suited excellently, and although Lichine used her in composing choreography her only named creation was La Sylphide in the *divertissement* of *Graduation Ball*.

Denisova's great opportunity as a 'baby ballerina' came in Australia. One day in March 1939, in Sydney, Baronova injured her ankle shortly before the performance – the classic situation for 'understudy makes good'. Denisova went on for her, having studied Aurora when she was not on stage in *Choreartium*, and acquitted herself admirably. She repeated the Aurora at Covent Garden the next June, when she was headlined by the popular press as 'Canadian Star of Ballet'.

Beryl de Zoete described her as

enchantingly young. We had already seen her fine quality and particularly neat and effortless style in Baronova's famous role of the Spinning Top in *Jeux d'enfants* . . . Last night her beautiful dancing deserved the applause she received. Her face too is perfect for a ballerina. Are predestined stars always born with features of exactly the right proportions?[29]

A delirious question that needs only one moment's thought to answer in the negative!

The Times was calmer, talking of her

quiet distinction. She has not yet the full measure of the part nor the extra range of expression in the department of her arms that one looks for in the sensational pas de deux, but her correct, cool and easy style and her lightness of poise made a favourable impression.[30]

Cendrillon was her next assignment, but Riabouchinska's roles were always peculiarly difficult to inherit, as they relied on personal qualities that other dancers could neither emulate nor replace. The inexperienced, and probably unsuitable, Denisova inevitably failed to achieve anything magical. Beryl de Zoete, comparing the performance with Riabouchinska's 'fanciful and touching impression' pinpointed the trouble – 'she has not yet attained a certain quality of imagination which adds interest to a formal perfection'.[31] Such a quality of course is usually an instinct rather than an attainment.

The next Australian tour gave Denisova an opportunity to develop a good deal both artistically and emotionally. In Baronova's absence she danced Passion in *Présages, Cent Baisers, Papillons* and, with Geneviève Moulin, created the Competition Dance in *Graduation Ball*. Basil Burdett welcomed the extra authority in her Aurora and praised the 'lovely purity of line that reminds one of Baronova in assurance and control – no greater compliment'.[32]

In Melbourne Denisova married the Cuban dancer Alberto Alonso, and after they left de Basil in 1941 they developed a company in Cuba with a nucleus of Havana-trained dancers. The repertoire included reproductions of Fokine ballets they had danced with de Basil and items of their own choreography. Alonso joined Ballet Theatre in 1944 and at Lichine's suggestion Denisova went into the musical *Rhapsody*, in which he gave her a 'flamboyant solo on a gigantic roulette wheel'.[33] The marriage broke up, and Denisova moved into Hollywood films and television as Patricia Denise, dancing, coaching and acting as choreographic assistant to Michael Kidd and Gene Kelly. She remarried but continued teaching ballet in Los Angeles. Sobinova too left de Basil in 1941, returning to Vancouver to teach, and to marry more than once.

Tatiana Stepanova, the young prima ballerina of the South American years, was first mentioned by Haskell in 1934 in *Balletomania*. In Preobrajenska's studio, he wrote, there was 'a mischievous, apple-cheeked Russian girl, T. Stepanova, who in five years' time may delight us. Already Massine has his eye on her'.[34]

Stepanova's family were Don Cossacks from Rostov who settled initially in Marseilles where she was born. Her father was a White Army sergeant, and when she was a child they all took part in a touring Cossack display group organized to raise funds for emigrés. They appeared in various cities, including London, where Queen Mary made a special gift to the little girl of golden Victorian sovereigns.

The family moved to Paris so that Stepanova could work with Preobrajenska and in 1935 de Basil earmarked her for the company, as he did some other promising youngsters from the Paris studios, and paid for the rest of her tuition. In 1936 she danced the Child in *La Concurrence* in Paris, and in 1937, when she was thirteen, took the Toumanova role in a revival of *L'Eventail de Jeanne* at the Paris Opéra, including the demanding *fouettés en tournant* in the finale. These had to be turned absolutely *sur place*, as they represented the apex of the fan which was shaped on stage by the other dancers. In 1939 she won an important prize at the Concours International de Danse in Brussels and danced a *pas de deux* with Lifar at a performance in honour of Diaghilev in Paris. Then, in December 1939, she and her mother joined the de Basil Ballet – Mme Stepanova later becoming wardrobe mistress – and a long separation from her father began. Reunion came only after Stepanova married and gave up dancing.

The earliest press comment on Stepanova seems to have been on the opening night of the Australasian tour, 30 December 1939, at the Theatre Royal, Sydney. She danced in *Les Sylphides*, again with Lifar, and the critic of the *Sydney Morning Herald*, Ken Wilkinson, wrote next day of her 'floating serenity' and of the 'simple directness of a wonder child'.[35] Her technique was commented on as being strongly developed and fearless, but she featured surprisingly little at that time in leading roles. One of the few was in a revival of *Le Pavillon* which she danced with Lichine and another talented young dancer, Tatiana Leskova. The outsize company allowed her few chances and she progressed less precipitately than her predecessors.

Stepanova appeared in the United States, but an injury to her leg kept her off stage during much of 1941. In South America, however, she began to dance leading roles, inheriting some, like Zobeide, from Grigorieva. On Gollner's sudden departure she was promoted to the long-planned position of prima ballerina.

A tall girl, with the splendid technique and line typical of Preobrajenska's best pupils, she was partnered in the classical leads by Oleg Tupine, whom she found a superb and totally reliable cavalier, rather than by his senior, Jasinsky. De Basil disliked seeing a Prince who was shorter than his Swan Queen or Aurora. *Demi-caractère* leads was different, therefore she danced *Le Fils prodigue* and *Symphonie fantastique* with Jasinsky. *Paganini* was a ballet she particularly loved dancing, either with Rostov or Dokoudovsky, and, like Baronova, she doubled at times in two sections of *Choreartium*. She was principal dancer in some of the operas, and in *divertissement* programmes contributed a popular solo *jota* with castanets – she had made a special study of Spanish dance with Dolores Moreno. Among her creations at that time were the leading roles in *La Isla de los ceibos* and in *Yara*, and in the 1946–7 New York seasons she danced Aurora and *Les Sylphides, L'Oiseau de feu* and the Siren in *Le Fils prodigue*. That spring however she took the decision to give up dancing for marriage, and made her home in Boston.

4
Australia

IN 1940 an Australian writer, T. Essington Breen, contrasted the life-style of the de Basil Ballet in the USA and in Australia.

In the former their movements are peripatetic in the truest sense of the word. There is a constant packing and unpacking of cases as they move from city to city, stopping only for a few nights en route to their ultimate Mecca, New York, where . . .they stay for a season of some three weeks or so only . . . Here, as we all know, we are able to support them for two and three months' seasons in Sydney and Melbourne.[1]

Comparing the populations not only of the cities involved but of the sub-continent of North America and the continent of Australasia, it is illuminating to realize the immense popularity of Russian ballet in the Antipodes. Nor was it one single visit, when a full turnout might be expected out of curiosity. There were three Australian tours: one of nine months by the second company in 1936–7, one of seven months by Educational Ballets Ltd in 1938–9, and the final one of eight months in 1939–40.

Australians have a fallacious reputation – and frequently emphasize it themselves, as Scottish Aberdonians were famous for coining the 'Aberdeen meanness' jokes – for being an uncultured people. Again remembering comparative population statistics, it could be argued that the percentage of Australia's total population interested in the arts is as high as, if not higher than, anywhere else in the world. Certainly, because of the geographical distance which limits the number of visiting theatre companies, concert artists or art exhibitions, there is less art on display at any given time than in the great cities of Europe and North America. This is not always a disadvantage, however, for those interested in the arts. Instead of spreading attention and achieving a wide but possibly shallow area of experience, each exhibit is looked at in depth.

Ballet was not unknown in Australia when the second de Basil Ballet arrived there in October 1936. Local productions had begun in 1835, when a ballet on *The Fair Maid of Perth* was staged at the Theatre Royal, Sydney[2] and after that excerpts from famous European ballets were regularly seen, performed by dancers whose names are not well known in ballet history. *La Sylphide* was produced in full in 1845 and the rest of the century saw a lively amount of dance activity. Ballets such as *Giselle, La Fille mal gardée* and *Le Diable à quatre* were staged, and not only public appreciation but ballet criticism was stimulated.

The Diaghilev Ballet never travelled so far, but Adeline Genée, with Alexander Volinine and a group of Imperial Russian Ballet dancers appeared in 1913, introducing *Coppélia* and Fokine's *Les Sylphides*. The following year the free dance school was exemplified by Maud Allan. World War I then intervened, and it was not until the 'twenties that the next exciting visitors arrived. Pavlova and her company were a great success in 1926 (with Laurent Novikov) and 1929 (with Pierre Vladimirov), while Olga Spessiva and Anatole Vilzak toured with the Levitov-Dandré Russian Ballet in 1934–5.

By this time a local amateur ballet company had started – the First Australian Ballet, founded by Louise Lightfoot and Mischa Burlakov in Sydney. This company staged premieres of various Fokine ballets, although neither of the directors had worked with Fokine and the standard of performance was low.

When the second de Basil Ballet, a company of sixty-two dancers, arrived in 1936 they brought with them a repertoire of twenty-one ballets that had been learnt and rehearsed in a very short time. They sailed from England in August.

'Under a terrific rain,' wrote Olga Philippov in an Australian paper, 'the company left St Pancras Station [London]. Side by side, the Colonel and Mr [Nevin] Tait [of J.C. Williamson Ltd] farewelled the company with chocolates for the girls and cigarettes for the boys, though the last farewell from Europe was given to us by Mr Dandré, the husband of the unforgettable Anna Pavlova, who with tears in his eyes remembered Australia and longed to go back with us. All aboard the packet train and then to Tilbury, where the rush and bustle ended aboard the decks of the *Moldavia*.'[3]

They followed the traditional route that took travellers through the Mediterranean and the Suez Canal, by way of the Red Sea and the

Indian Ocean, to Australia – a marvellous journey that no one who has experienced it is ever likely to forget. Haskell's *Dancing round the World* remains the fullest and most vivid account of the tour. The principal dancers were Woizikovsky, Kirsova, and Blinova with the inevitable Froman. This last partnership was a surviving but stormy one, competent rather than brilliant, particularly effective in lifts because of Froman's height and strength – according to some memories, almost an adagio act. Kirsova had been deservedly upgraded to prima ballerina on her return from the Ballets de Monte-Carlo, where apart from her memorable creation of The Butterfly in *L'Epreuve d'amour* she had been all too little used. Now she gave debut performances in star parts such as the Can-can Dancer in *Boutique* and the Street Dancer in *Beau Danube*. The soloists included Nina Raievska, an excellent character dancer, Nina Youchkevitch, Sonia Woizikovska, Tamara Tchinarova, Igor Youskevitch and Roland Guerard.

For Tchinarova it was a welcome chance to extend her repertoire. She had been trained by Preobrajenska after her family moved to Paris. They were not emigré Russians but from Bessarabia (in eastern Rumania), which meant they could visit their homeland regularly. She worked with Balanchine in *Orphée aux enfers*, as Baronova did, and danced on the Continent with L'Opéra Russe à Paris. She joined the de Basil Ballet during the European tour of 1932 but went with Balanchine – her 'best-ever' teacher – to Les Ballets 1933, returning with Toumanova, Rostova and Grigorieva to the de Basil Ballet in the autumn of 1933.

Another dancer recruited from the Woizikovsky Ballet was the American Thomas Armour. His faithful letter-writing to Margaret Power gave a vivid, dancer's-eye-view of the tour. On 9 September 1936 he wrote:

Since [the Bay of Biscay] we have had lovely weather and perfect seas. I swim daily . . . take a sunbath, play deck tennis, quoits and other games, read, write, dance at night or play Lotto . . . Some of us have already tanned, but most are still in the red stage . . . I get lazier daily, but I suppose we shall start rehearsals after Marseille. If we don't, I shall forget most of the ballets we learned in London before I arrive in Australia. It will be nice to work again, even if it *is* hot . . .

He was right. The rest of the company joined at Marseilles, including the *régisseur* for the tour, Jean Hoyer, who kept the dancers very busy.

We rehearse from 9 to 12 – heat or no heat – but it is all for the good. I do Pierrot and also Poet (in *Carnaval*) – but I lost the Tarantella (*Boutique*) entirely and do the poodle . . . Last night was fancy dress – Léon did Matelot and Farucca, Hélène and Igor waltz from *Sylphides*, Tchinarova and Shaievsky a dance from *Beau Danube*. Raievska did her marvellous Bacchanale and almost wrecked the ship when she fell to the floor . . .

The next letter came from the Arabian Sea:

We don't mind rehearsals now that it is cooler, and it helps to pass the day. Besides that, we need the work to keep in shape and set the ballets. Today we rehearsed *Scuola* and I still dance the Shabelevsky role – but one never knows when a role will be taken away.

The cooler weather was temporary:

Bombay was hot as hell, and from the present temperature Colombo will be hotter . . . I am quite tanned now, as are most of the company. I wanted to cut all my hair off but Hoyer put his foot down, because we do not wear wigs or hats in *Beau Danube*. Such a pity.[4]

The first date was in Adelaide, a city celebrating its centenary, at the Theatre Royal, a charming small theatre that survived until the 1960s. There was no equivalent of Hurok in Australia. The company's impresario was Daphne Deane, who had weathered her litigation troubles with the Colonel and negotiated with the Tait brothers of J.C. Williamson Ltd. Nevin Tait, the London-based brother, had made the contract with de Basil, but the Australian press quickly discovered that the company that had arrived, billed as Colonel W. de Basil's Monte Carlo Russian Ballet direct from Covent Garden Opera, was not quite what it sounded. Some of them were stars, certainly, and most of them had appeared in the de Basil summer season at the Royal Opera House. All the same, E.J. (Ted) Tait was in a grim mood, reflecting a feeling of having been conned, when he went down to Port Adelaide to meet them.

Matters were not helped by the fact that neither Philippov, who was the Colonel's personal representative, nor Lidji, who was managing director, spoke English. Haskell had to act as interpreter in almost every sense. Haskell and Ted Tait got on good terms after initial difficulties, and this made all the difference to the tour. Haskell's gift for liaison work, which made him an inspiring literary ambassador of ballet for countless readers, was of vital importance whenever he travelled with the Russian Ballet. They were all constantly in need of someone to translate not only their words but their attitude to life, and he was brilliant at this.

Tait, to Haskell, was 'a big-hearted man of the theatre with a genius for handling temperamental artists . . . a man of vision, quick to anger, equally quick to forgive.'⁵ Tait, according to his sister-in-law Viola, would later introduce Haskell as 'my friend, Arnold Haskell. I nearly strangled him in Adelaide. Didn't like the look of him at all . . .'⁶

Admittedly it was a tricky situation. Then, even more than now, the Australian public were all too touchy about having second-best artists palmed off on them by people who imagined they would not know any better. It was fortunate for everyone that the company, who had worked hard in London and on board ship, were able to open on 13 October 1936 with an excellent and exciting evening. They danced *Les Sylphides* and three Australian premieres: *Schéhérazade, Spectre* and *Boutique.* John Cargher writes:

What Adelaide and the other Australian cities saw was first-class ballet, of that there was no possible doubt . . . They opened the door to magic of a kind never before seen in Australia. For the first time the emphasis was on the ballets and not on the dancers.⁷

The Australians, once the quality of the company was established, adopted the dancers with that personal warmth of hospitality that their guests never forget. Armour wrote: 'The food is like a dream – only more substantial. We shall all get so fat . . .' He reported on the first performance:

Hélène and Igor danced the pas de deux (*Sylphides*) very well and Dimina was truly lovely in prelude. Léon was excellent in *Schéhérazade* and the can-can, and Nina very good in the former, but not as good as Tchernicheva . . . The poodle dance got a very good laugh here so I won't mind doing it so much now – but I must hurry to the theatre and practise my bark . . .

The reference to Mira Dimina (the American Madeleine Parker) is sad. Hers was the tragedy of the tour – she was already suffering from undiagnosed leukaemia, rapidly became seriously ill, and had to be left behind in Adelaide. She died in a private hospital there on 22 November and was buried two days later in West Terrace Cemetery. The company, who were in Melbourne, asked for a memorial service to be held for her and this was arranged in St Paul's Cathedral. Although it was basically an Anglican evensong, it was attended by members of consulates of countries represented in the company and by the Archimandrites of the Greek and Syrian Orthodox Churches. The Melbourne *Argus* printed a letter of thanks from Philippov, saying that the company had been 'deeply impressed at the tribute paid in Melbourne to an artist who had never appeared before a Melbourne audience.'[8]

Certainly the death of the young dancer deeply stirred Australian sympathies. Haskell wrote:

"I'll send flowers to the grave every week, the white ones she loved", says my friend, the little flowerseller near the Theatre Royal [Adelaide]. And while she was alive they sent her books, flowers and fruit, total strangers moved by the thought of a lonely girl far from home fighting for her life. Not only did the proprietors of my small hotel refrain from grumbling when the telephone rang throughout the twenty-four hours; it was a struggle to pay that phone bill at all. They identified themselves with us in our sorrow.[9]

The dancers had left Adelaide on 28 October in 'a blaze of glory' by special train – 'There were hundreds of our newly-made friends at the station to see us off'.[10] In Melbourne Thomas Armour and the Danish dancer Birger Bartholin (Billy) took a flat in the house of a lady who served them marvellous high teas for a shilling each. The company opened at His Majesty's Theatre on 31 October and stayed until 2 December. They were adored. Armour wrote:

The theatre is filled for every performance even matinees . . . Melbourne has gone ballet mad in a big way – they already have their favourite dancers and ballets and come again and again.

He was in no way exaggerating.

The opening programme was *Sylphides, Schéhérazade* and *Le Mariage d'Aurore* (with Blinova and Froman, but with Kirsova and Guerard in the Bluebird *pas de deux*). The critic of *The Argus* gave Woizikovsky pride of place.

To many Australians this fine dancer is known only by reputation, but all travelled or well read balletomanes hold his work in admiring respect . . . His talent is self-evident, his technical control swift and unerring, his rhythm no affair of mechanical timing but an emotional amplification of the musical phrase . . .

Woizikovsky dominated *Schéhérazade* in spite of an apparently disastrous performance of the score by the orchestra under Jascha

200

Horenstein. Ivan Clayton had trouble with them, too, in *Les Sylphides*. In this ballet 'Hélène Kirsova alone rose superior to the ordeal and floated light as thistledown in the arms of Igor Youskevitch'.[11]

Haskell carried his task of liaison officer into criticism, writing regularly for the journal *Table Talk*. However, he was far from purely adulatory, and his articles are interesting for their descriptions of individual artists' capabilities, a topic on which he was always sensitive, if occasionally over-enthusiastic. He writes of the mazurka in *Sylphides* revealing to the full Kirsova's 'gifts of elevation, strength and precision. Certain flutterings of the hands alone are out of the picture'. Youskevitch is 'that exceedingly rare thing, a natural dancer . . . he combines virility with a true feeling for the romantic.' Raievska as Zobeide 'looks beautiful, exceedingly so, but *à la vie Parisienne* . . . She lacks the grand manner and the dignity that are essentials. She has taken a huge dramatic edifice and fitted frills to it.' Of Guerard's Bluebird he writes 'there is no one today who dances this touchstone of classical virtuosity with greater purity and brilliance.' Blinova's Aurora 'has legs that make her classical work a joy to watch, a body that is light and supple, and great charm of manner . . . Where she fails at times is in her musical sense.'

Two other dancers are specially praised. Tchinarova 'shows a very strong individuality and true artistry' and Woizikovska 'has the most extraordinary gifts as a dancer and an almost unequalled sense of theatre.'[12]

The next programme showed Melbourne two Massine ballets, *Les Présages* and *La Boutique fantasque*. Until this tour no Massine works had been seen in Australia, but *Présages* was as immediate a success there as it had been a failure in New York. The *Argus'* critic called it a 'virile, provocative, iconoclastic ballet'. He goes on:

What with the polite applause of the fashionable audience . . . and the stamping and shouting of the reckless balletomanes under the roof . . . it would seem that much as Melbourne's theatregoers may be charmed by the languors and graces of the traditional story ballet it takes a thorough-going piece of callisthenic abstraction to rouse them to a pitch of frenzy.[13]

Symphonic ballet, to this critic, was 'a new and inviting art form of Miltonic conception'.

Haskell was entranced by Tchinarova as Action: '. . . brilliant. No other word will suffice. With her jet black hair, olive skin and aristocratically energetic movement she called to mind those thorough-bred racehorses I had been watching that afternoon' (presumably at Flemington racecourse).[14]

The season included the first Balanchine and Nijinska works to be seen in Australia – *Cotillon* and *Les Cent Baisers*. Woizikovsky's ballets, *L'Amour sorcier* and *Port Said*, were also given – the latter yet another variant on the sailor-ashore motif that served Massine in *Les Matelots* and Robbins, later, in *Fancy Free*.

Cotillon, programmed with *L'Oiseau de feu* (which scored a tremendous success), was considered

a thoroughly delightful creation, a pictorial study in white, crimson, green and black filled with joys for the eye and ear . . . dances suffused at times with an air of courtly grace, at other times enlivened with the sparkle of wit and surprise of novelty.[15]

Off-stage there was as much activity as on. Hospitality continued. Ballet-goers, delighted and excited by what they saw in the theatre, asked the dancers out every night and all day at the weekends. Cars were put at their disposal, picnics and swimming parties organized, and visits to local beauty spots such as Healesville Wildlife Sanctuary and the Dandenong Mountains were arranged. Daryl Lindsay sketched and painted them, Hugh Hall took countless fine photographs with a miniature camera and one remarkable amateur cameraman, the eye specialist Dr J. Ringland Anderson, took monochrome films from a circle of the theatre. This movie-making was the beginning of a collaboration that was to be resumed on the later tours of the main de Basil Ballet and become an invaluable record of dancers and ballets of the time.

The extraordinary relationship that had been built up between dancers and public resulted in an emotional last night's performance. There were endless curtain calls, a flower-strewn stage, and at last a speech by Woizikovsky:

Flourishing a small leaf of paper, M. Woizikovsky said "Excuse, but I have to read the English!" (laughter and applause). "I wish to thank for your all wonderful appreciation" (Renewed applause). "I hope to come very soon back" (Wild applause) . . .[16]

Next day, when the dancers moved on to Sydney, hundreds of balletomanes thronged Spencer Street Station, showering them with bouquets and streamers.

202

From Sydney, Thomas Armour continued to write to Margaret Power. He and Bartholin found flats at King's Cross where they could go out on the roof and look down on the magnificent many-bayed harbour and its busy traffic. It was another two-month season, one which the *Sydney Morning Herald* found 'one of the most striking and encouraging events in the city's artistic life'.[17] Sydney, like Melbourne, had become 'a city of balletomanes, and the public displayed genuine and spirited enthusiasm'. *Présages* continued as an enormous success. Basil Burdett, the admirable critic of the *Melbourne Herald*, writing in *The Home*, commented on the fact that audiences had accepted its 'choreographic modernity'

not only without question but with enthusiasm. Both capitals have in fact shown a livelier interest in this work than in the more obvious splendours of works like *Schéhérazade.*[18]

This, he felt, proved that there was a receptive and eager public in Australia for new ideas in the arts.

Kirsova was emerging as the ballet-goers' choice of a company star. She was working hard, stimulated by appreciation, and her performances as the Street Dancer, as the Widow in *L'Amour sorcier* and in the Bluebird *pas de deux* made her a firm favourite. The Taits asked that she should dance the Firebird, which was not originally intended. It was given a triumphant premiere on 23 January 1937. She was considered unforgettable and 'absolutely stunning' by people in the audience. Armour wrote: 'She was only half human and with her fine elevation she never seemed to belong to the earth.'

The Sydney season ended on 26 February and the company sailed to New Zealand – Auckland, Wellington, Dunedin and Christchurch. They were becoming very tired, and suffering minor injuries. They went on to Brisbane for two weeks in May. Hoyer and Woizikovsky had not been getting on well together, and Brisbane saw a crisis in their association which resulted in Hoyer's departure. In Brisbane, in contrast to the other Australian cities, audience reaction was cool, but the return to Melbourne on 19 June more than made up for this. 'His Majesty's Theatre, filled with fervent admirers of the dance, resembled an arena bedecked and beflagged to celebrate a famous victory.'[19]

Thadee Slavinsky, a Polish dancer who had been with Diaghilev and Pavlova, was late in reaching Melbourne. He had asked Lidji's permission to stay in Sydney to have treatment for a bone in his foot and used the time to get married to Marie Doran, an Australian actress who had been appearing in variety at Sydney's Tivoli Theatre. Lidji, announcing this to the press, said dryly that 'In producing a wife from a bone in his foot, M. Slavinsky had gone one better than Adam, whose wife had come from a rib'.[20]

Kirsova's Firebird was shown in Melbourne on 23 June. Her dancing was declared to be 'one of the most perfect things seen in this or any other season. The dramatic sense of this versatile ballerina is so convincing that her rare technical accomplishments are scarcely noticed.'[21] Her every performance now was being acclaimed above those of other dancers.

The final programme was given on 6 July, the end of what *The Argus* described as 'the most successful theatrical venture which has ever come to Australia'. The company had been in Australasia for ten months. The season had originally been planned to last four, but 'the capacity of the Australian people to visit and enjoy the ballet night after night had prompted an indefinite extension.'[22]

The only compensation for the adoring Melbourne public was the announcement that there would be a further tour in 1938. Lidji had been to the USA and Europe to see de Basil and the suggestion was that the same company would return with the addition of extra stars. Danilova and Riabouchinska were mentioned as possibilities.

A special train took the dancers to Adelaide immediately after the end of the last Melbourne performance and after a final week's season at the Theatre Royal they sailed for Europe on the *Strathnaver*. Summing up, Armour wrote:

It looks as though any good company coming out now will have a marvellous success – we have paved the way and there is an excellent ballet audience prepared and waiting.

It only had to wait until August 1938. This time, the tour was undertaken by the main company during the Sevastianov-Dandré interregnum. The dancers were led by Baronova, Riabouchinska, Dolin, Lichine and Shabelevsky. Dandré announced the tour at a Covent Garden press conference in July, saying that the company

refused all offers to tour in America this year in view of the conditions that obtained there. The incessant long journeys and one-night stands across the continent and back were bad for the morale and the health of a company of young dancers as well as destructive of good standards of work through the lack of proper facilities for systematic practice and rehearsal. In Australia, as was proved during the season sponsored there last year by Colonel de Basil, there was a great and growing public for ballet of intense but critical enthusiasm, and by giving seasons of some weeks at a time in one centre the company would avoid the over-fatigue of the American tour system.[23]

Of course they were fortunate, having lost the North American connection, to be able to fall back on that waiting audience in Australia for whom the phrase 'intense but critical enthusiasm' is aptly descriptive. Australians are never uncritical. They make keen and detailed judgements and analyses, usually after a show over drinks or coffee. As they are great overseas travellers they are able to compare what is brought to their own doorsteps with performances they have seen in Europe or America. They are, however, heart-warmingly enthusiastic when they enjoy themselves.

This time the company was called the Covent Garden Russian Ballet, presented by Educational Ballets Ltd. Titles never mattered very much – Australians were delighted to renew acquaintances with ballets they had loved and see a dozen others for the first time. Lichine was maître de ballet, Grigoriev *régisseur général* with Hoyer as assistant. Dorati and Vladimir Launitz went as conductors. For Australian dancers, students and teachers one of the biggest thrills was that Fokine was joining the company to supervise his ballets. Opportunities for watching rehearsals were avidly sought.

In the large company one particularly excited 17-year-old was Maria Sanina (Brigitte Kelly, an English girl who had been trained by Marie Rambert and Nicholas Legat). She had taken part with other students in the operas *Prince Igor* and *Orphée* given at Covent Garden in the summer of 1937, and then auditioned for the company. She recalls a panel made up of de Basil, Grigoriev, Borovansky (who had recommended her), Lidji and Haskell. They decided she was hardly ready for the main company, but for experience she was sent to the Lidji-Woizikovsky second company in Europe.

Sanina joined them in Berlin in September 1937. As she was under age to take up paid employment abroad she had to travel on a student's passport. Lidji's secretary was supposed to look after her, but rapidly opted out of the responsibility. She made friends with a South African dancer, Mary Poswolsky, and survived the exhausting but exciting period of touring in Germany, France, Italy and Scandinavia during the winter of 1937–8. When the company disbanded in the summer of 1938, she auditioned again for the main ballet, this time with

205

Sevastianov and Dandré. She had no luck and went away on a family holiday. Suddenly she was called back by telegram, saw Dandré at eleven o'clock at night and signed a contract – de Basil was not the only one to indulge in this practice. With no time at all for shopping or proper packing, she set sail with the others on the *Maloja* for Australia. The ship also carried scenery, costumes and props.

For Dandré it was a happy return to a country he loved. He had been there three times before, twice with Pavlova and once with the Levitov-Dandré. He spoke to *The Argus* on arrival: 'I am proud now to come for the fourth time as the leader of the largest and best company in existence.'[24] Sevastianov announced repertoire and plans, including premieres of Lichine's *Le Fils prodigue* (which happened) and a revival of *Giselle* (which did not). One of the most faithful and assiduous ballet-goers, Ben Arnott, later asked Grigoriev why the *Giselle* project failed and was told that without Danilova to dance the Queen of the Wilis it was not viable.

The opening programme at His Majesty's, Melbourne, on 28 September 1938, was a lightweight affair – *Sylphides* (Baronova and Jasinsky, Riabouchinska and Anna Volkova), *Cendrillon* (Riabouchinska and Petrov) and *Le Mariage d'Aurore* (Baronova and Petrov, with Riabouchinska and Jasinsky in the Bluebird *pas de deux*). Geoffrey Hutton, who had watched and enjoyed ballet in London, was now the bylined, and perceptive, critic of *The Argus*. He wrote of the company as

armed at all points, with at least two superb ballerinas, one of the strongest cohorts of male dancers ever assembled, a wealth of character dancers whose range we have yet to learn, and a corps de ballet which shows the effect of long performance under a firm artistic discipline.[25]

Inevitably, he was not enthusiastic about *Cendrillon* – 'mimed action decorated with dances and comic characterizations'. It was different with the next press night – *Symphonie fantastique* he found to be 'a tremendous choreographic conception'.[26] It contained 'five distinct ballets, each with its own decor and costumes'. Massine 'had explored the range of orthodox and Duncanesque movement to a point which was only guessed at a few years ago'.

Shabelevsky danced the Young Musician, in his first appearance in Australia. Hutton was impressed by his performance and even more by Baronova – 'as complete an actress as she is a classical dancer'. In *Le*

Lac des cygnes she and Dolin excelled any other interpreters seen by him. This was not surprising, perhaps, for Dolin in his *Autobiography* records his pleasure in dancing this ballet with Baronova.

Only with Irina did I ever feel that a Prince Siegfried and Swan Princess were perfectly united . . . She was always as light as a feather in my arms, and her splendid legs used their own strength to fly from the floor.[27]

Dolin had travelled to Sydney by air, leaving England on 19 September in a KNILM Super-Electra airliner, by way of Singapore, Bali, Darwin, and Cloncurry (Queensland). A special aeroplane was chartered to ferry him from Sydney to Melbourne. He was the first person in the theatre world to fly from London to Australia and it was also the first time J.C. Williamson Ltd brought an artist to Australia by air. He was immediately pressed into learning and dancing extra roles, including *Protée* and *Jeux d'enfants*, because a knee injury incurred in London had prevented Lichine from dancing during the entire Melbourne season.

The rest of the repertoire was gradually brought into play. *Concurrence* was greatly appreciated. 'Balanchine's humour does not lie in the incidents of the story but in his freakish sense of the grotesque, his witty burlesques of character and his surprising angular line.'[28] *Choreartium* was considered the most significant of the symphonic ballets: 'It is pure choreography, matching in visual design the auditory design of the music.'[29] *Schéhérazade*, as regulated in London by Fokine himself, was obviously far from the ballet as we see it today. It 'gained very much this season from its rigid adherence to the original choreography'. Osato's chief odalisque was a highlight – 'altogether superior to any which we have seen from any wholly European dancer. Her movements alternate between extreme fluidity and absolute straightness without a trace of effort.'[30] 'Grigorieva's dignified and passionate acting shows a new Zobeide and Shabelevsky, although he does not challenge the physical daring of Woizikovsky, makes the slave a more significant figure.'

The same kind of comparison between these two dancers was made over *Petrouchka*: 'Woizikovsky's dynamic rendering . . . emphasizes the mechanical quality of the puppet. Shabelevsky treated the part with less energy and more pathos, and the result is more moving.'[31]

Présages was as popular as ever, and its performance 'set a standard which we have not before seen approached except by Kirsova as

207

Passion'.[32] *Cotillon* was again admired as having 'the fine polish, the sinister bloom, of decadent art in the hands of a superb craftsman'.[33]

Le Coq d'or was considered a tremendously effective mimed pageant. *Les Sylphides* was given 'perfect performances' by Baronova and Jasinsky, Riabouchinska and Volkova.

The Taits had arranged for Dolin to add his Bolero solo to some programmes, in spite of some opposition from Dandré and Grigoriev. Hutton commented:

This interesting example of the power of a single dancer to hold the stage unaided without high-powered gymnastics was appreciated by the audience. This is significant at a time when there is a tendency for lavish decor and an overweight of literature to substitute for dancing.'[34]

Les Cent Baisers was given with its original leading dancers and the difference was noted: 'We have not previously seen the Princess danced with the technical brilliance and subtle wit given to the part by Baronova.' The ballet itself was now admired: 'Dance flows into dance naturally and inevitably. The conventional exercises of the corps de ballet have been replaced by a complex but expertly woven series of patterns which repeat and develop the line of the solo dancers.'[35]

The company was as great a success off stage as on. Baronova and Riabouchinska were loved for their extrovert charm, and their direct, natural manners appealed enormously to Australians. As in 1936 the dancers were inundated with social engagements and hospitality and had a wonderful, strenuous experience of Australian summer. Again, artists and photographers worked to capture their quality. It can be seen in sketches by Daryl Lindsay and Enid Dickson, in splendid photographs by Hugh Hall and Nanette Kuehn and of course in the Ringland Anderson films. Dr Anderson was now working in colour and photographing from various angles, boxes or wings, or at rehearsal, rather than the continuous full-stage reportage he had adopted for the performances in 1936. His love for dancers and repertoire led him to offer his medical services to them free in return for constant facilities for movie-making.

The Melbourne season ended on 21 November 1938 and the Sydney first night came on 25 November with what the Sydney *Mail* termed 'a classic opening programme' of *Sylphides, Coq d'or* and *Le Mariage d'Aurore*. In a substantial article, their critic wrote

[Ballet] has never been popular in the sense that the unintelligent could spontaneously understand and appreciate it; it is an aristocratic art turned to poetic ends and suited only to the genuinely aesthetic taste. The fact that Australia can support a season prolonged enough to be notable even in a great and sophisticated centre like London implies either a natural curiosity to investigate the unfamiliar or a creditable test for what is so evidently worthwhile.

He was impressed by *Coq d'or*, by the 'sheer poetry of Baronova's virtuosity in the tent scene' and by the 'humour and tenderness of Rostov's King Dodon'.[36]

The Australian press always loves personalities and most of the dancers were depicted in thumbnail sketches by reporters attending rehearsals. Some of these were perceptive and knowledgeable, some not. An editorial in *The Home* poked fun at some 'naive and uninformed writing' in newspapers, instancing one who had been reduced, for want of any real critical ability, to describing Riabouchinska as 'a lively and shapely girl'.[37]

Rehearsals took up a great deal of time. They were called by Grigoriev because many of the company were dancing new roles, and by Dandré, who wanted to stage some of the Pavlova repertoire and was given permission to teach *Paquita* to selected juniors, of whom Sanina was one. They were called by Fokine, who had joined the company in Sydney and who was not only in charge of his own ballets but had begun to plan and work out *Paganini*, and by Lichine, who staged *Le Fils prodigue* in Sydney on 30 December. This, the first world premiere of a Russian ballet in Australia, danced by Grigorieva and Dolin, was an immediate success.

Shabelevsky had left suddenly, for personal reasons, after the Melbourne season and Dolin, already performing Lichine's roles, had to add to his roster the Young Musician in *Symphonie fantastique* and later the Golden Slave in *Schéhérazade*. Lazovsky, emerging as a fine and varied artist, danced the Vagabond in *Concurrence* and, coached by Fokine, the title role in *Petrouchka*, which he made deeply moving. Lichine's Australian debut was in *Choreartium* on 6 January. The *Sydney Morning Herald* was slightly disappointed. Its critic spoke of Lichine's dominating personality but went on: 'his movements had an element of drama in them – a clearcut directness – but they lacked the brilliance which marked the dancing of certain other members of the cast.'[38]

A momentous day for the young Canadian Alexandra Denisova was 11 January, which also gave Australian audiences a splendid 'star-is-born' experience. At the last minute Baronova, scheduled to dance in *Choreartium* and *Le Mariage d'Aurore*, hurt her ankle and Denisova stepped in very creditably.

Geoffrey Hutton went through to Sydney to watch Fokine at work. He described his impressions in the *Argus*:

His hair is grey but the keenness of his eye and the liveliness of his smile rather suggest youth. Fokine in conversation is affable, witty and approachable; Fokine conducting a rehearsal is a despot working with the intense energy of a sculptor in quick-drying clay. In his open-necked shirt he worked through a Sydney heatwave undeterred. He is used to composing all night and rehearsing his composition all day. This concentration gives to his ballets a precision and sparkle which they often lack in other hands. Fokine works like a man who knows exactly what he wants and insists that the dancers shall give it to him.[39]

Seven weeks in New Zealand – Auckland, Hamilton, Wanganui, Palmerston, Wellington, Christchurch and Dunedin – were included in this tour – and New Zealand is by no means next door to Australia. They travelled, of course, by sea. Audiences there were less demonstrative and it needed all the bright and extrovert ideas for offstage propaganda of Baronova, Sevastianov and Dolin to get them really interested. The company danced a smallish repertoire of four triple or quadruple bills, including *Union Pacific* in which Lazovsky was happily cast as the Barman. Lichine was with them, but Shabelevsky was still absent and Dolin's pressure of work resulted, hardly surprisingly, in an injured ankle. He was able to dance only very little for the rest of the tour.

From New Zealand the company went back to ever-loving Melbourne from 25 March to 18 April 1939. It was Fokine's first visit to Melbourne and they were conscious of the honour. He had been rehearsing *Paganini* in New Zealand and the Taits, realizing the interest that would attach to a new Fokine ballet, arranged a stage rehearsal hoping to follow that with a premiere. Nothing had been finalized however with Soudeikine about the designs. Fokine wrote to Rachmaninov:

The ballet was completely choreographed and very well performed in Australia. There was such a demonstration of interest that the management evolved the mad idea of presenting the ballet without costumes and scenery! Knowing that very often the scenery and especially the costumes hamper the dancers, that much that goes well at rehearsals, in practice costumes, gets lost when presented on the stage, I would have welcomed the idea. But in this particular ballet, many dances if given without the necessary masks and props, without the lighting effects, without the platform and so on, could not possibly be understood. Therefore I declined this suggestion . . .[40]

Melbourne audiences now saw Lichine and his popularity there was soon enormous. About *Choreartium* Hutton wrote:

Although he has not yet regained his full technical powers, particularly his elevation, the controlled strength and the musical feeling of his dancing was a revelation. He is not a tall dancer, but he is always the most commanding figure on the stage because of his virility and his complete absorption.[41]

Writing of *Le Fils prodigue*, he found Dolin's performance 'a remarkable one of strength and gymnastic skill with dramatic impulse'[42] but Lichine's 'great sincerity, his sense of guilt and his grief'[43] deeply moved the audience. The ballet he admired. 'It points the way to a new development in the story ballet. It explores new possibilities in the translation of a dramatic situation into movement.'[44]

Fokine's supervision of *Carnaval* resulted in a change of ending, in which Pierrot and Pantalon were cut off from the other dancers by the fall of the curtain 'and the two absurd and pathetic figures are left at the footlights trying to grope their way back'.[45]

The last performance in Melbourne, on 12 April, was thrown open to public ballot to select the programme. 'Anyone who wants to ask for his favourite ballets should write to His Majesty's and his wishes will be taken into consideration.'[46] Whether in fact the result was achieved in this democratic way, the ballets given were *Lac, Symphonie fantastique, Spectre* and *Le Mariage d'Aurore*. This final evening, inevitably emotional, was given a cheerful slant by Frank Tait's announcement from a stage 'heaped with flowers and other tributes including dozens of boomerangs'[47] (Australia's traditional translation of *hasta la vista*) that the company would probably return about the end of October. Sydney said goodbye with a midnight performance on 27 April. The *corps* had already left for Europe after a two-week season in Adelaide, so the programme was made up of excerpts from *Sylphides, Lac, Le Mariage d'Aurore* and *Jeux d'enfants* danced by Baronova, Dolin, Riabouchinska and Lichine. Dolin contributed his Bolero, and Lichine gave a solo performance of *L'Après-midi d'un faune*.

During his time in Australia Dolin, typically, had been taking a keen interest in local schools and dance training, visiting some of them to

211

teach or demonstrate. A publicity story erroneously suggested that he planned to open a summer school during the 1939 Sydney season under the business direction of Alexander Levitov and Arthur Tait in the hope that it would lead to the formation of an Australian company.

Indirectly, however, this de Basil tour did influence the present Australian Ballet. On 12 April 1939 the *Argus* reported that Edouard Borovansky would 'stay behind on the platform when the rest of the company goes on to Adelaide by special midnight train'. Borovansky had decided, in view of the Nazi invasion of his native country Czechoslovakia, that he and his wife (a niece of Dandré's) would settle in Melbourne. Their new school, the Academy of Russian Ballet in Elizabeth Street, would open on 1 May.

Other members of the company who stayed in Australia were Tchinarova, Kousnetsova, Abricossova, Shaevsky, Zeglovsky, Sobichevsky and Bouslov.

The last Australian period of the de Basil Ballet began at the end of December 1939 in the middle of the first winter (by European seasonal thinking), the first summer (by Australian thinking) of World War II. It had been eagerly anticipated from the moment of Frank Tait's announcement in April. The original intention had been for a short season of ten weeks beginning in November before the company went on to the USA. The outbreak of war changed everything.

As the scattered company made its diverse way south, Australian balletomanes had news of them through Geoffrey Hutton and the *Argus*. On 2 December he wrote:

Running the gauntlet of mines and submarines, the flower of the world's dancers, with their priceless stock of scenery and costumes, are somewhere on the high seas bound for Australia.[48]

He went on to list some of the dancers he meant. He had heard from America that Baronova might have a film contract to fulfil there, but most of the others from the earlier tour would return, together with newcomers: Nemtchinova, 'bright star of the Diaghilev Ballet in its last days, who in recent years has been building a national ballet in Lithuania'; Verchinina, 'the model and inspiration of Massine's plastic roles in the symphonic ballets'; 'Most interesting of all is Toumanova, the first of de Basil's famous trio of "babies", who grew up and matured in friendly rivalry with Baronova.'

212

Twelve dancers reached Sydney by 19 December; forty-eight more passed through Melbourne on Christmas Day. With these was the Colonel, saying the right thing – it was the best company he had ever taken on tour 'and they are all so happy to be in Australia where the ballet is so much appreciated'.[49] He visited Borovansky's school in Melbourne and watched the work there. He was delighted that 'his old friend' was spreading the art of ballet in Australia and hoped to find a place for some of his students. Already he had one Australian, Phillida Cooper of Melbourne, dancing in the company as Lydia Couprina. She had made her own way to Preobrajenska in Paris and joined the company from there.

A little later however, in Sydney, the Colonel got into trouble in his press statements. The advent of a very large number of dancers caused concern to some Australians. There had been signs of this in September, when a letter was published in the *Argus* challenging the forthcoming tour:[50] 'Here in Melbourne there is ample material for a permanent ballet company . . . It is time we gave work to our own girls and boys and not a pack of foreigners.'

This routine piece of chauvinism was promptly demolished by letters in defence of the Russian dancers, but it represented a new mood (and one that had its parallel in the USA). The issue surfaced again in December 1939 when Actors' Equity passed a resolution protesting against the employment of as many as 83 foreign artists. They maintained that a company could be formed by importing only ten principals.

According to one report, de Basil countered this by saying that Australians did not as yet have the finesse, the art, to compete – 'footballers yes, ballet dancers no'.[51] Another paper printed a diametrically opposite, and considerably more tactful, interview in which de Basil predicted a great future for Australian ballet, claiming that the men and women were fitted both temperamentally and physically.[52] He was very eager to help the Australian ballet and to that end would see the work of Australian dancers, painters, musicians and writers of libretti. De Basil, defending the favourable report and denying the unfavourable, said, 'It is a terrible distortion. Do they think I am a child, a nitwit or a knave that I change my mind every five minutes and tell one paper one thing and another paper another?'[53] The debate was lived down rather than resolved . . .

The last member of the company to arrive was Lifar, alone, flying in to Darwin from Marseilles. Lodged in a resthouse until he could be registered as an alien, he immediately began rehearsing. Constable Anthony Kenyon of the Northern Territory Police had his questioning 'interspersed with leaps, pirouettes and entrechats by the world famous star'.[54] Kenyon was perhaps specially selected for the job. He was able to tell Lifar he had been a ballet enthusiast 'down south', and was rewarded by an impromptu and unaccompanied solo performance of *Spectre de la rose*.

The tour of the Original Ballet Russe, as it was now called, began at the Theatre Royal, Sydney, on 30 December 1939, with the traditional *Sylphides*, danced by Lifar and the 15-year-old Tatiana Stepanova about whom de Basil had raved to the press. The programme included *Paganini*, which had a mixed reception. Elements in its were liked – the vitality of the score, the stunning designs, the lyrical pastoral scene and, especially, the performances of Riabouchinska and Rostov. The 'cut and dried formulae' however 'looked strangely faded in the harsh, searching light of 1940'.[55]

Toumanova danced *Le Mariage d'Aurore*. She was visiting Australia for the first time and was greatly admired, for her poise and fluency, her deeply romantic appearance, her lovely elegance of line. As well as Aurora, she danced the Swan Queen, the Girl in *Spectre, Sylphides, L'Oiseau de feu* and the three symphonic ballets. She was still very young. She celebrated her 21st birthday in March at a party given for her in his Macquarie Street apartment by an ardent admirer, Fred James. James was a New Zealander who had appeared in silent films in Hollywood and then become Max Factor's manager in Australasia. His devotion to the ballet, and particularly to Toumanova, resulted in a fascinating set of home movies of her performances.

Lifar was in Australia only until 2 March. His greatest success was as dancer and choreographer of *Icare* – here again Australians showed that the unorthodox could command their enthusiasm. The clever set was designed, early in an internationally famous career, by the 23-year-old Sidney Nolan. From the beginning of this tour, de Basil had declared the liveliest interest in Australian art and artists. In this he had no doubt been prompted by Haskell. In *Waltzing Matilda*, Haskell includes an excellent short account of painting in Australia from Conrad Martens onwards. He had made friends with Sydney Ure Smith and Daryl Lindsay, and learnt about the past and present of the graphic arts. Lindsay, Thea Proctor and the 22-year-old Loudon Sainthill had all haunted the Russian ballet, sketching and painting the personalities.

214

Sainthill in fact had gone to England with the returning company in March 1939 and travelled back with the Colonel's party in the December. Nolan, too, was enormously excited by the repertoire and performances. All these artists later acknowledged their debt to the choreography and theatrical design to which they were introduced during their spell of balletomania.

In March 1940 the Colonel announced that he wanted to produce a ballet on an Australian theme. He formed a committee to judge a competition for local designers, who were asked to submit sketches with a brief note of their ideas. On the committee were B.J. Waterhouse, the chairman of the Trustees of the National Art Gallery; Will Ashton, the director of the National Gallery; and Sydney Ure Smith, the president of the Society of Artists. Lichine was to be the choreographer, if the idea appealed to him, and possible subjects were to be drawn from (a) the early period, such as Sydney or Hobart in the days of Macquarie, (b) the gold rush or other early periods or (c) the surf beaches. The winner, a young artist with a future, was Donald Friend with *Hold Up*, featuring the Kelly gang. He was given a prize of £10 and all 76 of the entries were put on exhibition in the National Art Gallery, but there were no funds to stage the ballet. New productions always depended on sponsorship, and sponsorship emerged from the appeal of a theme to someone financially capable of backing it, or the ability of one of the artists concerned to excite enthusiasm for a project in an influential patron.

Australia, although at that time far from the war, was deeply concerned for those who were fighting in Europe. Parcels were organized for Britain and charity galas for various causes. In January 1940 some of the company took part in a matinée at the Conservatorium in Sydney in aid of Czechs who were fighting in France, and there was a special performance in February for the Australian Red Cross. The biggest effort came on 12 February, when a midnight gala was staged for Polish Relief. The programme cover is illustrated with rough drawings by Lazovsky of Polish folk dancers and has handwritten particulars and date, and the entertainment was a *divertissement* of dances contributed by most of the company principals. Toumanova and Jasinsky danced variations from *Raymonda,* Nemtchinova a favourite solo, *Le Vent*, choreographed by Zverev. Algeranov danced one of his Japanese numbers and Schwezov an emotional solo about man's fight for freedom. Verchinina composed *Etude choréographic* for eight girls to Handel music.

215

The Sydney season was crowned, of course, by the world premiere of *Graduation Ball*, immediately popular for what the *Sydney Morning Herald* termed 'its rollicking gaiety, its lilting music, and the comic invention which Lichine had bestowed on the details'.[56] This ballet proved an exception to the local belief that what goes well in Sydney flops in Melbourne and vice versa. When it was shown in Melbourne in April it was acclaimed as sheer delight.

Balletomanes in Melbourne welcomed old and new friends among the dancers. The critic of *The Age* found greater maturity in Riabouchinska and admired the 'nervous, emotional artistry' of Toumanova and the 'feathery lightness of Anna Leontieva who danced the valse in *Sylphides*'.[57] He wrote of Verchinina in *Présages*: 'a real artist in dynamic plasticity and symphonic understanding . . . for the first time here this dominating role was given its true significance.'[58] Nemtchinova and Tchernicheva were probably distressed to be referred to as 'the oldsters' but Nemtchinova provided a 'mystical melancholy' in *Lac* and 'of Tchernicheva's poise and beauty of line and spiritual suggestion one could wax lyrical'.[59]

Hutton continued to write for the *Argus*. He was impressed by Toumanova in *Lac*. 'Blending firmness and fluidity of line, she gave to the part both sincerity and pathos . . .'[60] *Francesca* improved on acquaintance: 'The bold and sweeping rhythm, the dramatic force and the distinctive idiom of this ballet grow more impressive after the first view and its faults seem less important.' *Les Femmes de bonne humeur* had Morosova 'swiftly performing an amazing variety of steps in the mocking mood of Constanza's maid' and Toumanova was a sensation in *Symphonie fantastique*.[61] *The Age* found her equally stunning in *Firebird* – 'an imaginative conception . . . in the pas de deux with Petrov . . . she was a fluttering figure of unearthly beauty and her dance and mime with Köstchei . . . proved her virtuosity in thrillingly dramatic *danse du théâtre*.'[62]

Petrouchka found the two critics united in praise of Lazovsky. They spoke of his 'nervous brilliancy'[63] and 'genuine pathos' and Hutton continued: 'Toumanova brings a magic touch to the Doll. Rigidly mechanical to her fingertips, she yet suggests vanity and fickleness – a brilliant piece of controlled mime.'[64] The production as a whole he found immensely satisfying: 'this company has found a cast which give clarity and force to every detail of a subtle work.' The difference in performance between then and every company's efforts now was never more revealingly stated.

As in Sydney, *Icare* was acclaimed, this time in Jasinsky's performance. Hutton commented: 'For all its apparent modernity this ballet is a return to the clear classical idiom, with an insistent emphasis on elevation . . . Lifar could hardly realize his own creation more completely than Jasinsky, whose representation of the flight of birds was perfect dance mime.'[65]

May was a month for company weddings. Vera Nelidova (Betty Cuff) married an Australian, Angus Tweddle – but there was more publicity for Denisova's wedding to Alberto Alonso ('Cuba' was his company nickname) at the Registrar's Office in Melbourne on 13 May. Denisova danced the lead in *Papillons* that evening and Alonso the Blackamoor in *Petrouchka* and the Colonel gave a party afterwards at the Hotel Windsor.

Lichine was already working on a new ballet to Debussy (never to be staged), which began to be called *Mirage*. This had been projected in the Covent Garden programme in 1939 as *Songe chorégraphique*. Now designs were commissioned from the Australian artist Thea Proctor, and Lichine began rehearsing seriously with his two Canadian protégées, Denisova and Sobinova, with Kosmovska and Moulin. As usual, he told them little about his intentions or the significance of the movements he required from them, except that they were supposed to be 'birds in an enormous tree'.

On 15 June another Australian became a permanent member of the company – Valrene (Valerie) Tweedie from Sydney, who was to be known as Irina Lavrova and tour with them in North and South America. Valrene was a pupil of the fine teacher Leon Kellaway who had danced with Pavlova and the Levitov-Dandré Ballet as Jan Kovsky, and in 1940 Verchinina gave some guest classes at his studio. There was an immediate rapport between the 14-year-old Australian girl and the great freestyle artist, and Verchinina asked her along to the theatre, ostensibly for a class, actually for an audition. Valrene was already greatly in awe of everyone. During the previous season she and her friends had been constant galleryites, watching every performance and getting thoroughly acquainted with the artists and repertoire. That year she, like others, had been on stage as extras – many extras were used wherever the company went, often to fill out the crowd in *Petrouchka* or *Cendrillon*.

Valrene was accepted as a student dancer for the Melbourne season. Almost immediately, Nina Popova fell ill and Valrene was literally pushed on stage – this was a recurring pattern with new recruits – and talked through *Sylphides*. Other replacement roles followed, even small solos, so that her mother had to argue the case with Actors' Equity, whose permission was needed for her to appear at all before the age of fifteen. This range of activity was a bonus for a student dancer – later, when she became a regular member of the company, the hierarchy was brought into operation and she had to 'go up in stages'.

She adored the repertoire, taking special pleasure in the second movements of the three symphonic ballets. Two other Australians were in the company at the time, Phillida Cooper (Lydia Couprina) of Melbourne and Alison Lee (Hélène Lineva) of Perth. Alison Lee remained in Australia when the others went overseas.

The last season in Australia was at the Theatre Royal, Sydney, from 13 July. There were three premieres. The first was Verchinina's *Etude* – confusingly similar in title to her *Etude choréographic* and later known as *Quest* in the USA. Designs by Loudon Sainthill had been announced but in the end it was given in modified practice dress of mauve, buff and blue in front of curtains. The press found Igor Schwezov's *La Lutte eternelle*, to Schumann's *Symphonic Studies*, more interesting. Titles were obviously proving difficult for everybody, and for this ballet some horrific notions were aired. *Thematica* was one, *Struggle for Life*, *Vincit* and *Tantalizing Quest* were others.

The designs were entrusted to a talented pair of sisters from Melbourne, Kathleen and Florence Martin. They had designed various amateur plays, and they produced attractive costumes for their first ballet, in fabrics of shades ranging from warm terracotta to black by way of deep wine, or turquoise and grey-green, against a set of arches. Skibine was the sensation of the work, dancing 'with naturalness and exceptional musical feeling'.[66] The choreography was thought to be 'excellent in the fluid and dramatically effective movements of the corps de ballet, weak in the arrangements of the solos'.

The final novelty was the two-act *Coppélia*, staged by Oboukhov with traditional designs by a great company personality, the wardrobe mistress Olga Larose. Nemtchinova, as well as dancing Swanilda, taught the role to Toumanova and Riabouchinska. Panaiev as Franz and Toumine as Coppélius had both been in the Ballet Russe de Monte-Carlo production in 1938.

The *Sydney Morning Herald* critic found it a delicious period piece, and dissected the three ballerinas' interpretations. Toumanova, on the first night, adopted the 'free and easy comic style of a modern musical comedy – why worry what it used to look like? Let's convert it into a romp'; but by her second performance she had discarded the initial extravagances and gave the part charm and delicacy. Riabouchinska made one think 'how pretty and elegant it all must have been originally'. Nemtchinova approached it from within – nearer the great tradition – 'see how gay, how supple, how simple . . .'[67]

The season ended on 21 August. At midnight on 19 September, however, when some of the leading dancers had already left Australia, a last farewell to the company was said by the Sydney audience. The special short programme began with *Carnaval* and ended with *Le Mariage d'Aurore*, danced by Denisova and Petrov with Moulin and Jasinsky in the Bluebird *pas de deux*. In between these ballets was a set of *divertissements*, mostly selected from the Polish Relief performance but with the addition of a solo, *Dithyramb*, by Verchinina to music by an Australian composer, Margaret Sutherland.

Of these three Australian seasons of the de Basil Ballet companies a remarkable record exists in Dr J. Ringland Anderson's 16mm films. Dr Anderson was an eminent eye specialist. He had served in World War I in the Australian Army and was awarded the M.C. Later he held a Chair in the University of Melbourne. His involvement with ballet was entirely a sideline, and he made his films as a knowledgeable amateur. For him, some of the charm of the de Basil Ballet lay in the exotic Russian character of its personalities and repertoire. The overseas world, the world beyond Australia, had for him, as for so many of his countrymen, an enormous fascination.

During the first visit in 1936–7 he took black-and-white film, mainly from in front and in wonderfully long sequences that are engrossing to watch. Later he took colour (Agfa film of an advanced kind that was not released commercially until after World War II), and occasionally he has spliced together films of different seasons to try to capture a ballet in greater detail. It is less satisfactory, however, to have mixtures of casts, angles, and black-and-white and colour film, running in continuity. There is no sound, of course. For a short edited version containing nineteen excerpts with supplementary material, made by the Australian Broadcasting Commission TV in 1975 and called *Another Beginning*, a music track was dubbed in consultation with Tchinarova.

I was shown the entire set by Adrian Ryan (by courtesy of The Australian Ballet, to whose Archives the films were donated by Dr Ringland Anderson's widow) during many fascinating hours of viewing.

Most ballets and most dancers are represented, and although no ballet is taken right through from beginning to end, there are substantial sequences from many of them. The overall impression is of astounding vitality, energy and commitment. Acting, unashamedly full-blooded and passionate (the brief glimpse of Tchernicheva's Thamar is extraordinarily impressive), is used by every dancer as a natural language. Dance is often untidy in detail compared with current standards of polished technique, but astonishing in its grandeur, its virtuosity in every kind of pirouette and turn, its rapid and complex footwork integrated with head, arms, hands and facial expression in a way that is never now achieved. The intricacy, for instance, of the sections from *Les Femmes de bonne humeur* is remarkable – the combination of every kind of physical movement to depict character and the development of situation.

Among the films are charmingly elusive off-duty and rehearsal shots – fleeting glimpses of nameless ensemble dancers who look familiar but escape identification, arrivals and departures at railway stations with ballerinas grasping bouquets of flowers and balletomanes darting eagerly from group to group, line-ups at curtain calls, the Colonel in and around his large car, the Ringland Anderson swimming-pool and tennis court at Toorak, with dancers dipping into the water, running about with tennis rackets, and dancing excerpts from solos and *pas de deux* in their swimming costumes. At these Sunday parties they were obviously as vigorously intent on leisure as, in the theatre, they were on their performances. Sir Robert Southey, Chairman of The Australian Ballet, is a nephew of Ringland Anderson's wife, and as a boy of fourteen on holiday from boarding school was a delighted guest at the Sunday lunches in 1940 with caviare or red roe (as mysterious in origin in wartime as the Agfa colour film) and bevies of marvellous girls – Toumanova, Riabouchinska, beautiful, green-eyed Grigorieva and the strikingly lovely Osato . . . In the theatre he remembers watching his uncle busily filming from the right-hand box nearest the stage.

The 1940 tour lasted eight months and the company became very much part of the theatre scene. De Basil, talking to a reporter in Los Angeles later, said rather wistfully, 'We had a home in Australia, time to work and study as well as to travel . . .'[68] Artistically it was a mutually profitable time and although J.C. Williamson's financial losses were disturbing the long-term gain to Australian ballet was considerable. In March 1940 a leader in *The Argus* discussed the tours' importance:

220

The ballet has already left appreciable traces on the artistic life of the community. They are to be found not only in the growth of local ballet schools and in art, where Daryl Lindsay and others have found new inspiration, but in the wide circle of those who, from attending ballet performances, have gained fresh interest in music, a wealth of delightful memories, and an additional source of stimulation and pleasure in the many books, pictorial and narrative, which deal with ballet . . . To their credit, Australians have not remained indifferent to the intrinsic artistic richness of ballet and what they grew to appreciate in peace time will seem doubly dear now that war has blotted out so much that was healthy and refreshing.[69]

The influence was not confined to the impact of the company's performances. After each of the Australasian tours dancers were left behind, and their contribution as performers and directors was of the utmost importance in the history of Australian ballet – a subject that is only now being comprehensively researched and written, by archivists such as Edward Pask and critics such as John Cargher. Kirsova settled in Australia after the first tour and opened a studio in Sydney in 1940. Within a year she was staging charity performances and shortly afterwards presented the Kirsova Ballet as the first professional Australian Ballet company. For nearly three years she continued her pioneering work, producing talented Australian dancers and an interesting repertoire, mainly of her own choreography. Borovansky established himself in Melbourne after the second tour and followed the same pattern of a school and initial non-professional performances. In 1944 his company was professionally backed by J.C. Williamson Ltd, built up a great reputation, and after his death furnished the basis for the present Australian Ballet. Other former de Basil dancers who stayed in Australia had considerable influence as performers and teachers: Tchinarova, Kouznetsova, Sobichevsky, Zeglovsky and Shaievsky. Kira Abricossova started the West Australian Ballet, Valrene Tweedie (Irina Lavrova) carried the de Basil tradition into her teaching life in Sydney at her Australian Academy of Ballet. These and other de Basil artists contributed to the firm Russian-British tradition on which native Australian ballet has built its own triumphs. Equally important, the balletomane public created by the tours established a solid backing of private patronage, influential enthusiasm and general interest that ensured continuing support for ballet in the Australian cultural scene.

5

The Company's Influence
on Ballet

THE importance of any ballet company rests in three things: its contribution to choreographic development, the dancers it nurtures and displays, and its value to the audience. As a bonus, there is the long-term influence that its artists exert afterwards as teachers and directors.

The particular value of the de Basil Ballet was as disseminator rather than creator. It was an heir not only to Diaghilev – in the obvious sense of preserving and continuing to present much of his repertoire and allowing his later dancers to offer old and new delights to the public – but to Pavlova, the great travelling ambassador. Where she had blazed the trail, de Basil and his company widened the road and paved the surface.

The de Basil Ballet has often been criticized for the small amount of creative work it fostered. This was limited to one major new development, the symphonic ballet, whose value is debatable, and one home-grown choreographer, Lichine. There were no great discoveries of composers or designers, and of course the principal reason for this relative artistic sterility was the lack of a Diaghilev. The company was never without artistic directors, advisers and consultants but none of them managed to build up a working partnership with the non-artistic director, de Basil.

The difficulty was not that de Basil wanted to rule the artistic roost. He was a man who was willing to listen to the experts and weigh in with a decision of his own primarily to resolve differences and get things moving. He trusted Grigoriev to get on with his work as _régisseur général_. He trusted his choreographers to produce their ballets, although he enjoyed being part of discussions between the creative artists involved. Occasionally he suggested a composer or designer.

222

More often, he pointed out – and controlling the company financially was after all his business – that money would be forthcoming if some particular artist were employed.

There were fruitful associations with Boris Kochno and, later, to a lesser extent, with Henry Clifford, but no one emerged as an overall power where artistic direction was concerned and this, plus unstable funding and a nomadic life, was the main reason for the paucity of original creativity of any high order.

All the same, conclusions of this kind in no way give a true overall picture. There are plenty of present-day companies, particularly in those combining classical and modern dance, with imposing lists of choreographic novelties and launched choreographers, that entirely lack the stimulating vitality of the de Basil repertoire.

Its primary virtue was in range and size. When it settled down for one of its long summer seasons in London, it would present twenty to twenty-five ballets, three of them perhaps new (or new to the repertoire), including works by Petipa, Lev Ivanov, Fokine, Massine, Balanchine, Nijinska, Nijinsky and Lichine. There was plenty of variety of style and period.

New directions were pointed by *Cotillon* and *Jeux d'enfants*, both originating from books by Kochno, but the talking-point of the 'thirties was of course the symphonic ballet. Looking back, it seems almost incredible that passions could run so high, but it was one of the most serious pro and con discussions involving music and ballet critics and devotees that has ever resulted from any choreographic development.

Symphonic ballet was not a totally new notion. Behind every recognized innovator in the arts lie the less publicized experimenters. In 1916, in Leningrad, Fyodor Lopukhov wrote a book, *Paths of the Ballet Master,* which remained unpublished until 1925, in which he expounded the theory of symphonic ballet. He proposed much deeper relationships between dance and music, maintaining that dance steps could parallel and reflect musical structure and tonality. At the same time he demonstrated in a private performance the equation of dancers with instruments of the orchestra.

In 1923, at the Maryinsky Theatre, he choreographed Beethoven's 4th Symphony for eighteen dancers (of whom Balanchine was one) as *Dance Symphony*, taking as his theme 'The Magnificence of the Universe'. The first movement dealt with the birth of light, the second with the triumph of life over death, the third with nature's awakening in the spring, and the fourth movement with the joy of existence.

His pioneer trail was overgrown, and ten years later it was Massine's *Les Présages* that cleared the ground for exploitation. Massine traces the first stirrings of impulse for this to a summer visit he and Delarova made to Sicily in 1931, when he saw the ruined Temple of the Giants in Selinunte:

They immediately suggested to me vast harmonic groupings, and I wondered if it would be possible to create with human bodies a similar feeling of physical grandeur wedded to pure music. I realized that this could only be done by using the symphony of a great composer as the inspiration for my choreography.[1]

With the thoroughness that characterized him as an artist, he went on thinking about this, and by the time he took over as maître de ballet to the Ballets Russes de Monte-Carlo he had decided that the Tchaikovsky 5th Symphony, with its theme of man and his destiny, was the one to use. He had set himself the tremendous task of relating his chosen music to the structural challenge of the Sicilian temples by way of experimental choreography. Always willing to delve into other forms of dance than classical ballet, and to discard traditional or accepted methods of choreographic expression, he applied himself to the problems and came up with striking answers. Not all were appreciated by the critics, but European audiences, so often more receptive than their critics, revelled in the ballet's exciting emotional power and variety.

The great difficulty, from the point of view of A.V. Coton, was 'the exaggerated importance of the quite unnecessary symbolism', but he acknowledged the freshness of the choreographic idiom, the 'inventive technique which went farther away from the classical basis than any previous choreographer's'.[2] Caryl Brahms too decided that 'the ballet is ill at ease with the literary abstracts'.[3] Almost all the music and dance critics hated the designs by André Masson, but it had been a close collaboration with which Massine was pleased, although he allowed a practice-dress staging in London in 1936. Masson complemented the choreography and music by the lines and curves of his backcloth. Massine's subject for the ballet was man's struggle against his destiny. In the first movement he showed human life with its inherent desires and temptations. The second movement introduced love and passion and the personification of fate. In the third movement frivolity was dominant, and the final movement represented war, strife and a final triumph over evil.

224

If *Les Présages* as a whole inspired the spilling of much critical ink, certain sections of it were almost universally admired and forever associated with the dancers who created them. The *pas de deux* for the lovers, danced by Baronova and Lichine, set the direction for countless duets with which other choreographers have later delighted or bored us according to their abilities. It was a very modern concept of smoothly interwoven embraces and inventive lifts, creating an impression of great tenderness.

The other superbly effective role was that of Verchinina as Action. Verchinina's career can be clearly seen now as a bridge between old and new, classical and modern. She was a true innovator – an able, classically trained dancer who could understand and interpret moods and movements far beyond the normal range of ballet at the time. Obviously she was more than an interpreter in the symphonic ballets – she was an inspiration and a collaborating talent. Massine talks of her subtle interpretation of the music:

She curved or straightened her arms in a succession of contrasting positions, using alternatively tremulous flowing movements or sharp close-angled gesture.[4]

Beaumont, too, writes of her arms as

remarkable for their varying quality of movement. Sometimes they described beautiful curves, moving with a gentle rhythm like the ripple of a wave; sometimes they darted forwards or backwards with the sudden swiftness of the flick of a whiplash . . . so dynamic were her movements that she seemed to radiate power.[5]

Massine, like some of his critics, felt that there had been too close a reliance on a theme in *Les Présages*. He now set about an even harder task in *Choreartium*, set to Brahms' 4th Symphony, creating dance that had no purpose other than to parallel or extend the subtleties of the score – a novel approach that has become a commonly accepted definition of choreography. In this latter half of the twentieth century it is theme and story that are the suspect elements of a ballet. Dance, reflecting or developing out of its musical or rhythmic accompaniment is, everyone in the western world agrees, sufficient to make a ballet.

In 1933 however Massine was an experimenter. He abstracted into movement his memories of Italian spires and frescoes or Dresden figurines and produced a work that was widely acclaimed and whose

225

disappearance is often lamented. Dancers who worked on it in its revival at Nervi in 1960 think it would be worthy of resurrection. On another count it was notable. The orchestration of a mass of dancers is far from easy and it was a triumph of co-ordinated production and rehearsal.

There was no programme note or synopsis – a rare state of affairs in ballet at the time. The musical character of the four movements was simply stated, followed by the dancers' names. Toumanova and Lichine led the Allegro non troppo, Verchinina the Andante sostenuto. Riabouchinska and Shabelevksy, Danilova and Jasinsky, carried the Allegro giocoso. All combined in the final Allegro energico e passionato.

One music critic, Ernest Newman, was a total convert to the genre. Of *Choreartium* he wrote:

In a truly extraordinary way Massine has given us a transvaluation into choreographic values of a hundred musical features of the symphony . . . the better we know our Brahms, the more pleasure we derive from *Choreartium* – if only we can put aside all academic prejudices and prepossessions.[6]

There was frequent talk during 1934 and 1935 of other symphonic ballets, principally one to Mozart's Jupiter Symphony. Massine obviously worked concurrently on various projects, including the Beethoven *Seventh Symphony* which was finally presented in 1938 by Denham's Ballet Russe de Monte Carlo. He told a Fleet Street reporter in 1937 that he had begun it three years before, showing him pages from his notebook of 'a long sequence of dots and dashes, scrawls, numbers, diagrams, whorls and spirals which meant everything to him and nothing at all to me'.[7]

There was a gap in stage production of his symphonic ballets, however, from 1933 to 1936 and it is possible that the lack of enthusiasm for *Les Présages* in the USA acted as a deterrent. In 1936 came the Berlioz *Symphonie fantastique*.

In this the first movement established the Young Musician, reflecting his varying moods – gaiety (a *pas de deux* with a small ensemble of three girls), melancholy (a male *pas de trois*), reverie (a female ensemble with a leading dancer), and *passion* (a male ensemble); then, at last, came the entrance of the Beloved. The second movement was a ballroom scene, in which the Musician briefly danced with his Beloved. The third movement began with the duet of the Old and Young Shepherds, and a deer who danced to their piping, and continued with women and

226

children picknicking, and spirits of the wind to parallel the storm motif in the score. The Musician, pursuing the Beloved, saw her flying on wires across the stage – the flight was later omitted. The fourth movement showed a mock trial with judges, executioners and vengeful mob. The fifth movement was a *Walpurgisnacht*, an orgy of monsters, witches, ghouls, vampires, spectres, furies, devils and monks, with the Beloved altered into an evil spirit.

In *A Prejudice for Ballet*, Coton makes an interesting analysis of the choreographic content of the five movements:

(1) An essay in the materia of the earlier symphonic ballets, a troubled fusion of the symbolism and mysteriousness of *Présages* with the architectural structure of *Choreartium*'s fourth movement;
(2) A fine and individualist usage of Maryinskyist bases to produce good ballet from the insipidities of the banal waltz measure;
(3) An episode hallmarked "Massine" on every facet, with an intelligently conceived progression of moves and poses illustrating a romantic evocation already démodé in every other artistic practice;
(4) Melodramatic recitative of Massine's own very individual sort; closely related to *Union Pacific* and tending towards over-emphasis;
(5) A scene which, divorced from the rest of the work, might be Massine's best purely inventive choreography since 1928; as daring a realignment of choreographic material as the first movement of *Choreartium*. [8]

As a lover of *Choreartium*, Coton all the same deplored the new ballet as retrogressive. Massine himself saw it as a progression. In it he 'had to integrate abstract choreographic passages' (particularly in the ensembles of the first movement) 'with a romantic and melodramatic plot'. [9] As with the earlier symphonic works, it was memorably danced by the company and memorably designed by the sensitive and poetic Christian Bérard.

Controversy continued, particularly in London. Another English music critic, Edwin Evans, published an important article in *The Dancing Times* in December 1936 dissecting the various points of view. The question at issue, he felt, concerned

the propriety or otherwise of a choreographer forcing [a balletic] partnership upon the composer of a symphony whose consent could no longer be obtained,

because a symphony is

an organic whole constructed on certain architectonic principles which it was held could not be made visible in terms of choreography.

227

He felt that this would have been wrong if the choreographer had attempted to translate the symphony's meaning wholly and integrally into the language of dance, but that what Massine had done was

to parallel the rhythms, tempi, emotions, conflicts and reconciliations of the symphony with a corresponding sequence of movements in such a manner as to produce an accord between the impressions received through eye and ear.

Interestingly, he cut through the debate about 'absolute' and 'programme' music, which was being fiercely contested, by saying that almost all music proceeds from emotions within its composer 'such as would constitute a "programme" ' if they were put into words. He argued that because of this it is 'not so much a question whether a symphony has a "programme" as whether its programme has been divulged in any other medium but that of music'. As a musician, Evans' own feeling was that Massine had succeeded least well with *Choreartium*, that there the choreography was more episodic and less symphonic than in the other works. Nevertheless he recognized it as an admirable piece of pioneering art.[10]

A reply to the article was inevitable, and it was James Monahan who took up the challenge, with a stimulating personal opinion. He felt that the symphonic ballets were all impressive on first sight but that the more you saw them the less good you thought them. For him, they managed only 'in brief flashes' to become 'a separate yet congruous dancing entity, fulfilling the music and giving it something new'.[11] This view, according to Fernau Hall, was 'wild exaggeration'. More in sympathy with the pioneers than Monahan, he rejoiced in Massine's new discoveries in the field of movement and felt that they were already showing an effect in the work of choreographers such as Antony Tudor and Agnes de Mille.[12]

The importance of the symphonic ballets in choreographic development is largely incalculable. The works themselves are now lost, and even if revived would almost certainly look disastrously dated. This is the penalty exacted from almost all original or avant-garde art, which has a sadly short influential life. Massine was striving for the widest possible freedom of expression for the dance composer *vis-à-vis* the musical score, and countless choreographers of today ought to recognize their debt to his courage and ability.

For many people today, Massine's choreographic reputation is at the lowest possible level. David Vaughan and Dale Harris, in their *Ballet Review* conversation with P.W. Manchester, speak for these:

BR: Well, at that time, Massine seemed to be a great choreographer, and today he seems to be negligible as a choreographer. He has a place in ballet history but we have seen those ballets collapse one after another.

This kind of categorical statement has to be balanced against the excellent points made in reply by Miss Manchester. She is emphatic that, at the time, Massine was 'totally accepted as a great master' and points out how little ever survives from the work of past choreographers acclaimed in their time. Fokine is the one she takes as example but there are others, all the way back to Perrot and Saint Léon. She makes the absolutely vital and relevant point that the ballets of Fokine and Massine were understood by the dancers of the time in a way that no present-day dancers can approach. 'If his things don't work today, it is because our dancers are different today, and they don't know what the earlier dancers knew.'[13] This rings true. When dancers of the future, divorced from the direct influence of Balanchine or Ashton, attempt to perform their ballets, it is very possible that their choreography, which we find so rewarding, will gradually lose its effect. Probably any ballet-goer whose memories go back some time, not necessarily to the 1930s but to the 1940s or 1950s, could list works that were then exciting and moving experiences but which lose immeasurably when attempted by the very different dancers of today. No one can estimate works of the past solely from the standpoint of the present.

The homegrown choreographer David Lichine also had courage, together with persistence, an undoubted talent, and a feeling for new trends that he was for the most part unable to discipline or develop. He created ten works for the company, beginning with *Nocturne* in 1933 and ending with *Cain and Abel* in 1946, darting between a wide variety of styles in an erratic and often brilliant dragonfly flight but consolidating nothing. The principal work that survives to represent him is *Graduation Ball*, a ballet by no means characteristic of his total output. On the ephemeral nature of the art, he himself commented 'Choreography is like moisture in the mouth of an orator.'[14]

A late beginner as a dancer, Lichine was, at 23, a young choreographer. His early influences, obviously, were the men and women he had worked with in the Ida Rubinstein Ballet and the Ballets

Russes de Monte-Carlo. Influences, however, are not what young creative artists want to think about. They are concerned with self-expression, and they rarely see just how much the way they express their thoughts reflects works they have seen and admired.

Nocturne, based on *A Midsummer Night's Dream*, was an idea of Count Etienne de Beaumont. It was given relatively few performances in Paris and London but it had value, particularly in the dances for individuals and minor ensembles which 'had unity of purpose, clarity of expression and sharpness of outline'.[15] Not bad for a novice, but there was nothing sufficiently novel about it to suit an enterprising young man. Lichine tried to startle everyone with his ballet of the following year, *Les Imaginaires*, which earned him mainly ridicule and died almost immediately.

This failure set back his career and it was not until Kochno returned and came up with an idea as simple and orthodox as the geometrical notions of *Les Imaginaires* had been over-complicated that he began again. Staged as *Le Pavillon*, this depiction of romantic love in a garden was admittedly what Horace Horsnell called 'a garnish to the repertory rather than a *pièce de résistance*',[16] but it put Lichine on better terms with the ballet world. Coton, who was no admirer of him as a choreographer, writes that

he put a good deal of thought and design into the conception of the whole pattern of choreography of his *Le Pavillon* . . . and achieved a satisfactory, though by no means perfect, fusion of the main ingredients.[17]

Ernest Newman likened it to 'a triple concerto . . . Lichine's masculine grace and earnestness, the airy-fairy lightness and whimsicality of Riabouchinska, the incomparable balance of Baronova'.[18] Lichine was learning how to use the individual attributes of dancers and how to rely on pure dancing to make an effect. The choreography was technically extremely exacting, harking back more to Petipa than to any more recent master.

The acquisition of the Diaghilev Ballet decors naturally led to plans for re-staging them. Although Massine's version of *Le Bal* (1935) had displeased everyone, including its choreographer, de Basil and Grigoriev hoped for better things from a recension of *Les Dieux mendiants*. This was entrusted to Lichine in 1937. Whether or not he had seen the Balanchine originals of this ballet and *Le Fils prodigue* is something of a mystery. He assured Dolin in 1938 that he had not, but there is evidence that he was in the audience at the Châtelet during the last Diaghilev season in 1928 when he was in Paris and even walked on once in *L'Oiseau de feu*. However, he had never learnt them, and according to Vova Grigoriev the method of production was that Serge Grigoriev described the narrative line of the ballets in conjunction with the score and Lichine then composed his choreography.

Les Dieux mendiants was not a good choice for him and he had very little time to work on it. It was probably decided on principally because Beecham had arranged the score, wanted to conduct it, and was a powerful friend to the company. Lichine, like Balanchine and de Valois in her staging for the Vic-Wells Ballet, had to cope with a very slight story, and he had none of the style and polish which had helped them to embellish it. His only characteristic contribution was the amusing grotesque dance for the black lackeys. As Coton says:

A dancer turned choreographer will almost always be inventive in the genre in which he best dances and with all the goodwill in the world one cannot see Lichine being very much attracted by the delicate and pastoral material which demands as much finesse in construction as it does style in dancing.[19]

Lichine was always very conscious of his need for artistic guidance and willing to profit by it. At this point he came in contact with an important influence, Henry Clifford, who proposed the subject of *Francesca da Rimini* when a wealthy lady offered to back a ballet for Tchernicheva. The cultural education of dancers, so often lacking the more formal disciplines of university or college, greatly depends on whether they meet people who are capable of enlarging their understanding and appreciation of the related arts. This was the real power of the Diaghilev Ballet, and to a large extent the strength of the developing Vic-Wells Ballet which, through Constant Lambert and Frederick Ashton as well as Ninette de Valois, was very much in touch with the writers, artists and composers of the 'twenties and 'thirties. Henry Clifford was Lichine's mentor where painting and sculpture were concerned – and the fact that Lichine had shown, as early as *Nocturne*, a striking sense of design in groupings and tableaux suggests that he had a natural affinity with these arts. Clifford's interest also perhaps inspired Lichine to apply himself more to the choreography, as had Kochno's with *Le Pavillon*. De Basil, in an interview in June 1937, commented that Lichine had been working very hard over *Francesca*:

Up to last season he was often "*un peu vagabond*", inclined to be a bit lazy by the enormously exacting standard of a dancer's life. But he has changed all that . . .[20]

At any rate, *Francesca* was an exciting ballet. As James Monahan put it: 'Like it or not, this was a work that mattered . . . tremendously interesting in its faults as in its achievements.'[21] It had the unevenness and flaws of most full-blooded narrative ballets, but also the merits. A reviewer for the *Boston Monitor* suggested its character:

There is a good deal of rush and fury in the action . . . but there is also some good dance design . . . With a less busy stage, less continuous confusion and excitement, the work might be refined into a tragic ballet of value.[22]

It was always the refinement, the smoothing-out of untidiness, the curbing of excess, that people demanded in Lichine's choreography at this time.

All the same, special personal characteristics were beginning to emerge. The qualities that stamped Lichine's own performances, of dramatic power, vitality, comedy, caricature, were paralleled in his choreography for *Francesca da Rimini* and again, more rigorously controlled by the existing framework, in *Le Fils prodigue*.

By now he was working with more general co-operation from his dancers. The growing child who is taken only half seriously by his family has something in common with the dancer who metamorphoses into a choreographer with his own company. He had persistent problems with some of the senior artists who were not particularly receptive to his fresh but tentative ideas. Even in 1938 he was happiest choreographing for the new young dancers, such as his own Canadian discoveries Denisova and Sobinova in *Protée*. With them he could be as demolishing and authoritative as Fokine, Massine or Nijinska had been in creating choreography. Maria Sanina, working with him as one of the sisters in *Le Fils prodigue*, found that he stripped her confidence right down before he began to build it up again. Denisova and Sobinova felt great sympathy with his creative attitude and saw the potential in his talent.

Between *Francesca* and *Protée* he perpetrated another hurried and disastrous work, *Le Lion amoureux*, but *Protée,* when it came, was obviously a very successful if slight creation. It was greatly loved by many who found it full of delicacy and charm. Instinct suggests that it was the kind of work that would have been more at home in the repertoire of a chamber ballet company like the old Ballet Rambert than with the Ballets Russes. All the same, it continued to be performed, and to be admired, over the years. Like *Le Pavillon*, it had a very slight story: Protée appears from the sea and five temple maidens try in vain to finding out from him what the future holds for them. The Sitter Out in *The Dancing Times* wrote:

With only five danseuses on the stage and making use of a stylized form of classical dancing with occasional suggestions of the Greek convention, he has weaved some beautiful patterns and created some vivid dancing always in complete sympathy with the music . . . Lichine himself makes a striking entry and an equally effective exit – the latter in a flying leap into the sea. His dance on purely classical lines is vigorous and well conceived in contrast with the more peaceful moments which have preceded his coming.[23]

It was *Le Fils prodigue*, however, that established Lichine much more firmly, standing up excellently to comparison with the Balanchine version for Diaghilev. Its quality was relayed to *The Dancing Times* from Australia, where it had its premiere, by Haskell, who referred to its complete success, popular and artistic. He wrote that it showed 'none of the effective superficiality of his popular *Francesca da Rimini* or the childish exuberance of the poor dead *Lion amoureux*', and praised its rich invention and beautiful groupings.[24] Lichine's treatment of the seduction scene was brilliant. While Balanchine's Siren had a long cloak, Lichine's danced within the circle of a hoop – Beryl de Zoete was impressed by her

serpentine dance . . . her passage along the table, handed from upraised arm to arm of the prostrate carousers, the movement in which she is lifted up to crown a pyramid of feasters, the stream of wine out of a channel of hands and the flickering of fingers above the table edge . . .[25]

The *Times* declared that

of all the versions, M. Lichine's is the most distinguished and the most successful. It takes the subject seriously and presents the story in strong stern dances which show considerable powers of invention in their design . . . completely in accord with Rouault's sombre and impressive designs. The ballet has deeply moving as well as greatly exciting moments.[26]

From *Le Fils prodigue* to *Graduation Ball* was a considerable choreographic leap. Lichine had not previously worked in the light comedy vein nor challenged memories of the Massine of *Beau Danube* or *Gaité parisienne*, but he found his own style with spectacular success. In comparison with the Massine works it was direct and unsophisticated, and for that very reason stands up better to countless changes of cast and inflection. It had humanity where the others bordered on caricature, and humour rather than sparkling wit.

Lichine's detailed description of the action, in French, and illustrated by tiny stick-figure sketches, was lodged in the Library of Congress as the first case of registered choreographic copyright in the USA. It is not a notated account of technical matters. It reflects the *demi-caractère* nature of the ballet by setting out much more fully the action and characteristics of the various scenes, reducing the record of dance composition to a minimum. It makes vivid reading, bringing the ballet to life, for anyone who knows it, with astonishing clarity.

A certain amount of revision was done at various times, apart from the loosely programmed title for the Romantic *pas de deux*. This was originally given (correctly) as 'La Sylphide and the Scotsman'; later it became 'Giselle and the Scotsman' or 'Taglioni and the Scotsman'. *La Sylphide* was less familiar in 1940, when the Bournonville production survived only in Copenhagen, than it is now, and it was therefore perhaps natural that confusion set in.

One trio, placed after the Dance Step Competition and before the Perpetuum Mobile, has vanished from the programme. This was the Mathematics and Natural History Lesson, created by Svetlova, Hélène Lineva (Alison Lee) and Maria Azrova (Fay Isaacs). It was an odd little number. Svetlova, sitting at a school desk, was approached by the other two girls dressed as balding professors (slightly reminiscent of the diplomats in *The Green Table*), one carrying an outsize compass, the other a butterfly net. Another variant in the *divertissement* was that for a short time, in Melbourne and Sydney, the Perpetuum Mobile *pas de deux* for Riabouchinska and Lichine was replaced by a 'circus' *pas de deux* in which Lichine was costumed as a Ringmaster and Riabouchinska, in a gold-spangled red costume and a parasol, pretended to walk the tightrope in a rapid medley of brilliant steps.

There is a good deal of evidence that Lichine, who in James Monahan's view suffered mainly from the 'haphazard education' of his life with a 'madly touring company' and needed to be 'curbed without being frustrated',[27] was in many ways ahead of his time choreographically. This was particularly apparent in the type of acrobatic movement and sex-oriented duet with which we are now oversupplied but which were then revolutionary. He was, successfully or otherwise, constantly devising new movement that looked even farther forward than the symphonic ballets – too far ahead, often, to be acceptable at the time. Sobinova recollects that he created dances for her that were similar to Alvin Ailey's Vortex variation in *The River*, and much of the movement in *Cain and Abel*, concentrating on physical interlacing and a great deal of floorwork, would be routine viewing nowadays.

His creations in 1948 for the Ballets des Champs-Elysées – *La Création,* danced in silence, and *La Rencontre* – were experiments to good purpose. Even in 1941 his alarming *Victory* project had anticipated another commonplace of 1970s production. He proposed using the voice of Churchill, with lines from some of his great speeches, because he thought their rhythmical measure was particularly adaptable as an accompaniment to dance.[28] Arthur Franks thought him 'one of the most important figures in post-1945 choreography'. Stability of background, he felt, would allow him to emerge as one of the major choreographers of the century.[29] It was never to be found.

Lincoln Kirstein, in *Blast at Ballet*, wrote (at length) of the de Basil Ballet's complete artistic bankruptcy.[30] Given that he found the symphonic ballets dubiously valuable and heartily disliked Lichine's work both as dancer and choreographer, his view is easily understandable. A special ability is needed to find and launch creative artists and this de Basil lacked. It was not for want of trying. He was always willing to listen to and consider ideas for productions. In 1936, through an interviewer for *Comoedia Illustré*, he made an impassioned plea to young artists:

Je m'adresse à toute la jeunesse impatiente de créer, aux peintres, compositeurs, auteurs, et maîtres-de-ballet. Je les invite à exposer leurs idées, leur promettant qui'ils trouveront en moi un auditeur complaisant et attentif. Tout essai digne d'interêt, toute initiative personnelle, sera accueillie avec joie et examinée avec soin. Les amateurs de la danse, les dilettantes sont priés d'émettre leur avis en qualité des conseilles car ce n'est que par la fusion étroite de nos forces, une collaboration enthousiaste et désinteressé, que nous pourrons infuser aux ballets une vie nouvelle, riche et vibrante.[31]

Whereas Diaghilev could by force of his acknowledged artistic judgement hypnotize people into backing the ballets he wished to do, de Basil generally speaking received backing only for productions that other people wanted done for a variety of reasons. Money was

235

frequently forthcoming only for works that would prove second-rate.

The triumphs of the repertoire were considerable: *Cotillon* and *La Concurrence*; *Jeux d'enfants, Le Beau Danube* and *Scuola di ballo*; *Les Présages, Choreartium* and *Symphonie fantastique*; *Le Coq d'or, Le Fils prodigue* and *Graduation Ball*. Long and reputable lives were lived by *Les Cent Baisers, Protée* and *Francesca da Rimini*; and the revivals from the Diaghilev Ballet, such as *Schéhérazade* and *Good-humoured Ladies*, were carried forward with remarkable vitality into an altered world. It is sad that out of the entire catalogue of creations only *Coq d'or, Le Beau Danube* and *Graduation Ball* are ever now on view, and these in stagings not truly comparable to their original state.

Even if few choreographic advances resulted from the de Basil Ballet, the repertoire in its time looked fresh and stimulating to audiences worldwide, as did the dancers and their performances. Not only the stars were admired. The construction of the company was unlike that of British or American companies of today. It included a group of dancers whose value was that they knew the old repertoire, could guide and teach newcomers, and perform small, but key, roles to perfection. There were one or two purely character dancers but few purely classical dancers – most of the star classicists were also accomplished in *demi-caractère* work. There were sound ensemble dancers who had special soloist contributions to make in specific ballets and there were very young 'apprentice' dancers who learned the ballets with a view to taking over roles in emergencies or to a future as teachers or *répétiteurs*.

De Basil, wrote Haskell, had 'found a formula by which experience and youth can amalgamate to form an exceptional artistic ensemble. He has not only discovered and backed young talent but has also evoked something new in the finished artist.'[32] He had, declared Edwin Evans, replaced a standardized *corps de ballet* with 'a strong ensemble in which each individual artist has the opportunity of showing personality and capabilities'.[33] This is confirmed by the vivid memories of people who saw them, who recall the performances of dancers in minor roles as well as those of the highly-praised stars. Lillian Moore mentions some personal pleasures of this kind, commenting on the by-play or the minor characterization that 'lends a new beauty and meaning to the whole production'. They include Shabelevsky's Groom and Kirsova's Street Dancer in *Petrouchka*. Of Morosova she says: 'Even when she is in the last line of the *corps de ballet* we can marvel at the verve and elan with which Morosova dances.'[34] A cameo such as Borovansky's Athlete in

236

Le Beau Danube was a vital contribution to the ballet's success.

Only a company backed by a permanent and well-staffed school can create dancers from the beginning. Others have to accept dancers from a wide range of early training and do their best to inculcate a company style and character. In the 1930s however the Paris studios of Preobrajenska, Egorova and Kschessinka were a common denominator in the training of the majority of professional dancers. Additionally, the de Basil Ballet had Grigoriev and Tchernicheva, who ensured that successive groups of heterogeneous dancers became identified with Russian ballet. Grigoriev's standards and discipline, his confident expectation that to preserve the Diaghilev heritage and the newer works was a task everyone would recognize to be worth their hardest efforts, created the essential unity of purpose. It ensured that, as Jasinsky and Larkina say, 'even in its less than golden days the de Basil company was a great Ballet Russe'.[35]

It is interesting to try to assess the qualities that made the performances of the emigré Russian dancers so different from anything we see today. They can be analysed, perhaps, under three general headings: technique, theatricality and presentation, and humanity.

Present-day technique is very smooth, very sophisticated, physically arduous (the incidence of serious injuries suffered by artists is disturbing), frequently acrobatic in character. The technique of the Russians was firmly classical with an emphasis on turning and leaping and strong beats. *Caractère* (national) dance and *demi-caractère* (classical dance used to dramatic purpose for character delineation and story-telling) were as important as classical dance. Although there were accepted specialists in the last two categories the classicists (such as Danilova, Baronova and Toumanova) were all able and enthusiastic exponents of *demi-caractère* and *caractère*.

Apart from the symphonic ballets, which heralded the future, technical tricks were used for specific purposes, as in the complex pirouettes for the Top in *Jeux d'enfants*, rather than simply to amaze an audience. The conception of technique was of total physical unification – as much attention was paid to arms, hands, heads and faces as to legs and feet. Feet, in fact, might sometimes look careless by our standards but the expressiveness of hands and faces was infinitely more varied and subtle. No one was capable then of dancing an entire ballet with one rather blank expression, as often happens today.

In presentation, two qualities predominated – nobility and vitality.

The grand manner was native to these dancers and not, in context with each other and with their repertoire, artificial or over-emphatic. Their gestures were generous and fully extended in *adage*. They had more relationship with the boards of the stage, standing firmly and solidly, pushing off into leaps with much more force than is normal today. Their dancing had tremendous vigour; it was a celebration of the life force that George Bernard Shaw would have recognized with delight. They never gave partial or half-hearted performances; they involved themselves fully and with conviction in the ballets they danced.

They were people of the theatre, not of the classroom. They thought in terms of theatrical values, of costume and make-up, of audiences and their reactions, of stages and dressing-rooms, of working with choreographers far more than with teachers, of communicating powerfully across the footlights to other human beings. For them ballet and dance were not matters for academic analysis, for conscious attempts at releasing inhibitions and self-indulgent experiment, but an adored and honoured branch of the theatre that implied pleasure and excitement for dancers and watchers alike.

They matured early, in terms of human understanding. On the whole, international politics concerned them little, but a wide range of emotional responses, including but not confined to sexual experience, gave depth to their work. Through their choreographers and the older artists who were always a feature of the company, their lack of formal schooling was replaced by a wide cultural awareness, a feeling for music and design, and a sharp instinct for varying period and national styles in movement and dance that led them to relate perfectly to such divergent ballets as *Le Beau Danube, Contes russes* and *Choreartium*. They were all actor dancers, capable equally of old-fashioned mime acting and the newer acting-through-complete-body-movement that had begun with Fokine, but they remained classically trained dancers in the true line of succession.

The tally of important artists who made their names with the de Basil Ballet is impressive and the immediate influence of the company in the 'thirties can hardly be overestimated. Wherever they went, in their comprehensive European, North American and Australasian journeys, they became a vital part of the artistic education of a generation. They were glamorous, escapist, amusing, dramatic, poetic, in exactly the way their audiences, frightened by economic collapse and the threat of another war, needed. Just as the movies and the great Hollywood stars supplied a salutory element of sheer enjoyment and relaxation from daily anxieties, the Ballets Russes 'took people out of themselves', and sent them home happier. This is not the mood of dance and ballet after World War II. To entertain is a suspect activity. It was a suspect activity to some people even in 1934. Lillian Moore commented on this:

Surely any theatrical organization which can provide even occasionally such moments of pure poetry as those in which these ballets are so rich is worth its salt whether or not (in the language of the new criticism) it be "fraught with significance" or "expressive of a national consciousness" or "symbolic of the spirit of the age"? . . . great art may also be magnificent entertainment.[36]

In the context of its best years, from 1932 to 1940, the de Basil Ballet was undoubtedly magnificent entertainment.

The artists, not the repertoire, represent the company's long-term influence. They are widely scattered. Some are growing old, some have died. Many are working still for a younger generation and for the future of ballet, teaching, directing, producing. Danilova has spent years at the School of American Ballet, Riabouchinska has a studio in Hollywood, Baronova emerges from Switzerland to give master classes or judge international competitions. Verchinina, in Brazil, teaches her own form of modern dance and choreographs for her dance group. Grigorieva worked as director of ballet at the Colón; Leskova, who teaches in Rio, has staged ballets there as well. Svetlova teaches in Bloomington, Indiana, Jasinsky and Larkina have a regional company and studio in Tulsa, Oklahoma. Ladre and Obidenna teach in Seattle, Dokoudovsky and Stroganova in New York, Tupine in Springfield, Virginia, Anna Adrianova and Lorand Andahazy in Minneapolis. Anna Severskaya (Northcote) and Maria Sanina (Brigitte Kelly) teach in London, Sobinova (Rosemary Deveson) in Vancouver, Valrene Tweedie in Sydney. All of them transmit a valuable tradition to future professional dancers.

Any student of history recognizes that certain areas of bygone activity possess an extraordinary vitality: the court of Elizabeth Tudor, Paris in the French Revolution, the Napoleonic wars, the American Civil War – there are plenty of examples. Research them and you find the present slipping away from you, overpowered by the hypnotic strength of the past. The explanation is that in each case an array of dominant

239

characters, good and bad, who lived and thought with immense egotistical vigour and purpose, came together in co-operation or conflict. The intense and vivid quality of their activity leaps out of the chronicles, and nine-tenths of the current daily round pales into unreality in comparison. In the specialized sphere of the dance, the de Basil Ballet which, by virtue of world war and accelerated social change, seems to be farther back in time than is actually the case, has proved to possess this kind of eternal life.

Notes and References

Any unreferenced quotations from dancers, conductors, etc. derive from conversations with the author

1 *The Company, 1931–52*

JANUARY 1932 TO AUGUST 1934

1 *Lettres de M. Proust à René Blum, 1913–21*, ed. Léon Pierre-Quint, pub. Ed.KRA, Paris, 1930
2 Letter to the author from Tamara Toumanova, 15 August 1977
3 *The Times*, 9 April 1931
4,5 *The Times,* 27 May 1931
6 *Balletomania* by Arnold L. Haskell, pub. Gollancz, 1934
7 *Le Théâtre et la Vie*, journal, pub. Paris, October–November 1931
8 *Balletomania* q.v.
9 *The Complete Book of Ballets* by Cyril W. Beaumont, pub. Putnam, November 1937
10,11 *A Prejudice for Ballet* by A.V. Coton, pub. Methuen, 1938
12 *Invitation to the Ballet* by Ninette de Valois, pub. The Bodley Head, 1937
13 *Tonight the Ballet* by Adrian Stokes, pub. Faber & Faber, 1935
14 *The Complete Book of Ballets* q.v.
15 *A Prejudice for Ballet* q.v.
16 *Ballet – to Poland*, ed. Arnold L. Haskell, pub. A. & C. Black, 1940 ('Three Polish Dancers' by Cyril W. Beaumont)
17 *The Dancing Times*, April 1976 ('Yurek Shabelevsky' by Gordon Anthony)
18 *Le Ballet contemporain, 1929–50* by Pierre Michaut, pub. Ed.Plon, 1950
19 *L'Illustration*, 25 June 1932
20 *The Diaghilev Ballet in London* by Cyril W. Beaumont, pub. Putnam, October 1940
21 *Le Ballet contemporain* q.v.

22 *Balanchine* by Bernard Taper, pub. Harper & Row, 1960

23 *My Life in Ballet* by Leonide Massine, pub. Macmillan, 1968

24 *Balanchine* q.v.

25 *Alexandra Danilova* by A.E. Twysden, pub. Beaumont, 1945

26,27 *A Prejudice for Ballet* q.v.

28 *The Dancing Times,* August 1933 ('Notes on Decor' by G.E. Goodman)

29 *The Dancing Times*, June 1976 ('Alexandra Danilova' by Gordon Anthony)

30 Unpublished diaries, Lionel Bradley Bequest in the Theatre Museum, London

31 *Ballet-go-round* by Anton Dolin, pub. Michael Joseph, 1938

32 Letter from Colonel de Basil, 13 January 1934 (Collection Mme Olga Morosova de Basil)

33 *Balletomania* q.v.

34 Letter to the author from Tamara Toumanova, 15 August 1977

35 *A Prejudice for Ballet* q.v.

36 *Balletomania* q.v.

37 *The Sunday Times*, London, 29 October 1933 (article by Ernest Newman)

38 *Russian Ballet* by Adrian Stokes, pub. Faber & Faber, 1935

39 *Bournemouth Daily Echo*, 27 November 1933

40 *Our Crowd* by Stephen Birmingham, pub. Harper & Row, 1967

41 *Impresario* by Sol Hurok with Ruth Goode, pub. Macdonald, 1947

42 *New York Times,* 31 December 1933 (review by John Martin)

43 *San Francisco Chronicle,* 27 January 1935 (review by Alfred Frankenstein)

44 *New York Times*, 31 December 1933 (review by John Martin)

45 *Bronislava Nijinska: eine Monographie* by Gunhild Schüller, unpub.

46 *Footnotes to the Ballet* ed. Caryl Brahms, pub. Lovat Dickson, 1936 ('The Choreography' by Caryl Brahms)

47 *The Complete Book of Ballets* q.v.

48 *Bagazh* by Nicolas Nabokov, pub. Atheneum, 1975

49 *Henry IV,* Part I, by W. Shakespeare

50 *The Transcript*, Boston, 14 March 1934

51 *The Transcript*, Boston, 10 April 1934

52 *The Boston Globe,* 10 April 1934

53 *The Dancing Times,* July 1934 ('Les Ballets Russes in Paris') by L. Franc Scheuer)

54 *Journey into the Mind's Eye* by Lesley Blanch, pub. Collins, 1968

55 *Evening Standard,* London, 25 March 1952 (interview with Charles Reid)

56 *Nijinsky* by Richard Buckle, pub. Simon & Schuster, 1971
57 *Sunday Referee*, London, 22 July 1934 (review by Constant Lambert)
58 Bradley diaries q.v.
59 *Theatre World*, journal, London, May 1949 (article by Eric Johns)
60 *The Sunday Times,* London, 5 August 1934 (review by Ernest Newman)
61 *Sunday Referee,* 5 August 1934 (review by Constant Lambert)
62 *The Observer,* 12 August 1934 (review by Horace Horsnell)

AUGUST 1934 TO APRIL 1936
1 *Toronto Globe & Mail,* 26 October 1934
2 *The Dancing Times,* January 1935 ('The De Basil Ballet on tour in America' by Lillian Moore)
3,4 *The Boston Post*, 14 November 1934
5 *Dance in Canada,* Summer 1978, No. 16 ('Depression and War but a Golden Age for Dance in Vancouver' by Leland Windreich)
6 *Passport to Paris* by Vernon Duke, pub. Little Brown, 1955
7 *The Sunday Times*, London, 28 July 1936 (review by Ernest Newman)
8 *The Dancing Times,* August 1935 ('Fokine in New York' by Russell Rhodes)
9 Nansen passports were League of Nations Passports issued from 1921 by Fridtjof Nansen, the League's High Commissioner for Russian and Armenian refugees, and were recognized 'in principle' by 53 states
10 *The Times*, London, 30 June 1936
11 *The Riviera News*, Monte Carlo, 23 March 1935
12 *Dance Magazine* (USA), April 1940 (Open Letter from René Blum)
13 Ms. letter in French addressed by René Blum to his business manager, M. Reymond, 26 August 1936 in Dance Collection, New York
14 *Evening Standard,* London, 1 June 1935
15 *The Dancing Times,* July 1935 (review by The Sitter Out)
16 *The Dancing Times*, March 1935 (review by The Sitter Out)
17 *Memoirs of a Ballet Master* by Michel Fokine, trans. by Vitale Fokine, ed. by Anatole Chujoy, pub. Constable, 1961
18 Bradley diaries, q.v.
19 *The Sunday Times*, London, 18 August 1935 (review by Ernest Newman)
20 *The Dancing Times*, February 1976 ('Lubov Tchernicheva' by Gordon Anthony)
21 *Daily Mail*, London, 19 July 1935 (review by Edwin Evans)
22 *The Sunday Times*, London, 21 July 1935 (review by Ernest Newman)
23 *A Prejudice for Ballet,* q.v.
24 *Footnotes to the Ballet*, q.v.

25 *The Complete Book of Ballets,* q.v.
26 Bradley diaries, q.v.
27 *Impresario*, q.v.
28 *The Boston Globe*, 30 October 1935
29 *The Dancing Times,* June 1936 ('Burlesquing the "Ballet Russe" ' by Russell Rhodes)
30 *Looking at the Dance* by Edwin Denby, pub. Pellegrini & Cudahy, 1949
31 *The Dancing Times*, June 1936 ('Nijinska's Productions for the De Basil Ballet' by David C. Maclay)

APRIL 1936 TO APRIL 1937
 1 *Ballet Review* 6 (3), 1977–8, New York, interview with P.W. Manchester by David Vaughan and Dale Harris
 2 *A Prejudice for Ballet*, q.v.
 3 *The Daily Telegraph*, London, 25 July 1936 (review by A.L. Haskell)
 4 *The Daily Telegraph*, London, 31 July 1936 (review by A.L. Haskell)
 5 *Ballet Today*, London, March–April 1946 ('Designing for Ballet' by Cecil Beaton)
 6 Letters to the late Mrs Margaret Power from Thomas Armour, 1936–8, in the Theatre Museum, London
 7 Serge Ismailov's contracts (a) 20 May 1937 with the Ballets Russes du Col. de Basil (b) 9 August 1938 with Educational Ballets Ltd, in Dance Collection, New York
 8 *The Dancing Times,* December 1936 ('De Basil in Berlin' by J. Lewitan)
 9 *The Dancing Times*, December 1936 ('New York Letter' by Russell Rhodes)
10 *A Prejudice for Ballet*, q.v.
11 *Ballet Crusade* by Valentin Zeglovsky, pub. Reed and Harris, Melbourne, 1945

APRIL 1937 TO MARCH 1938
 1 Letter to the author from Tamara Toumanova, 15 August 1977
 2 *Memoirs of a Ballet Master,* q.v.
 3 Letter to the author from Esther Clifford, 27 July 1977
 4 'Canadian Boat Song', authorship disputed
 5 *The Daily Telegraph,* London, 18 June 1937 (review by Richard Capell)
 6 *The Times,* London, 18 June 1937
 7 *Evening News*, London, 18 June 1937 (review by W. McNaught)
 8 *Memoirs of a Ballet Master,* q.v.
 9 *The Sunday Times,* London, 11 July 1937 (review by Ernest Newman)
10 Bradley diaries, q.v.

11 *Memoirs of a Ballet Master,* q.v.
12 *The Times,* London, 21 July 1937
13 *Theatre World,* London, May 1949 (article by Eric Johns)
14 *The Observer,* 18 July 1937 (review by Horace Horsnell)
15 Bradley diaries, q.v.
16 *A Prejudice for Ballet,* q.v.
17 *The Sunday Times,* London, 18 July 1937 (review by Ernest Newman)
18 *A Prejudice for Ballet,* q.v.
19 *Ballet Crusade,* q.v.
20 *The Times,* London, 11 July 1937
21 *The Times,* London, 24 July 1937
22 *The Times,* London 25 September 1937
23 *The Times,* London, 30 September 1937 (letter to the Editor from Michel Fokine)
24 *A Prejudice for Ballet,* q.v.
25 *Memoirs of a Ballet Master,* q.v.
26 *The Times,* London, 15 July 1937
27 Bradley diaries, q.v.
28 *Nikitina* by herself, trans. Baroness Moura Budberg, pub. Allan Wingate, 1959
29 *The Dancing Times,* December 1937 ('New York Letter' by Russell Rhodes)
30 Armour letters, q.v.

MARCH 1938 TO SEPTEMBER 1939

1 *Impresario,* q.v.
2 *Alexandra Danilova,* q.v.
3 *Impresario,* q.v.
4 *Dancing round the World* by Arnold L. Haskell, pub. Gollancz, 1937
5 *The New York City Ballet* by Anatole Chujoy, pub. Knopf, 1953
6 *The Dancing Times,* May 1938
7 *New York Times,* 18 September 1947
8 Ms. memoir by Gerald Sevastianov (Collection Mme Irina Baronova-Tennant-Severn)
9 *Impresario,* q.v.
10 Sevastianov memoir, q.v.
11 *The Times,* London, 18 June 1938
12 Sevastianov memoir, q.v.
13 *The Daily Telegraph,* London, 6 July 1938 (review by Francis Toye)
14 *The Observer,* London, 10 July 1938 (review by Horace Horsnell)
15 *The Sketch,* London, 13 July 1938
16 *St Paul Dispatch,* Minnesota, 12 April 1979 ('Memories of Massine' by Anna Adrianova Andahazy)

17 *Daily Mail*, London, 13 June 1939
18 *The Dancing Times*, June 1938
19 *The Times*, London, 15 July 1938
20 *Covent Garden* by Harold Rosenthal, pub. Michael Joseph, 1976
21 *Sergei Rachmaninov, a lifetime in music*, ed. Sergei Bertensson and Jay Leyda, pub. New York University Press, 1956
  (a) letters from Michel Fokine to Rachmaninov, 23 August 1937
  (b) 29 August 1937
22 *The Daily Telegraph,* London, 24 June 1939 (letter to the Editor from Michel Fokine)
23 *The Daily Telegraph*, London, 30 June 1939 (letter to the Editor from Michel Fokine)
24 *The Daily Telegraph,* London, 1 July 1939 (review by Beryl de Zoete)
25 *The Daily Telegraph*, London, 8 July 1939 (review by Beryl de Zoete)
26 *Supplement to the Complete Book of Ballets* by Cyril W. Beaumont, pub. Beaumont, 1942
27 *The Times*, London, 6 July 1939
28 *The Times,* London, 6 July 1939
29 *The Observer,* London, 16 July 1939 (review by Horace Horsnell)
30 Sevastianov memoir, q.v.

SEPTEMBER 1939 TO SEPTEMBER 1940

1 *Autobiography* by Anton Dolin, pub. Oldbourne, 1960
2 *Sydney Morning Herald,* 23 February 1940
3 *Sydney Morning Herald*, 10 February 1940
4 *Melbourne Herald,* 9 April 1940 (review by Basil Burdett)
5 Letter to the author from Tatiana Leskova, 8 June 1981
6 *The Dancing Times,* February 1936 ('I present a bouquet' by Dennis Stoll)

SEPTEMBER 1940 TO NOVEMBER 1941

1 *Impresario*, q.v.
2 *The Dancing Times*, February 1941 ('New York Letter' by Russell Rhodes)
3 *New York Times*, 17 November 1940 (review by John Martin)
4 *Looking at the Dance*, q.v.
5 *New York Herald Tribune* (review by Walter Terry)
6 *The Dancing Times*, February 1941, q.v.
7 *New York Sun*, 23 January 1941 (review by Irving Kolodin)
8 *New York Times,* 23 January 1941 (review by John Martin)
9 *The Dancing Times*, April 1941 ('Balustrade' by Lillian Moore)
10 Unknown American newspaper (review by R.C.B.)

11 *Looking at the Dance,* q.v.
12 *American Ballet Theatre* by Charles Payne, pub. Knopf, 1977
13 *Toronto Globe and Mail,* 8 February 1941
14 *Toronto Globe and Mail,* 8 February 1941 (article by Thelma Craig)
15 Letter to Colonel de Basil dated 18 March 1941 signed by Boris Runanine, Alexis Vlassov, Lorand Andahazy, Nina Golovina, Kyra Bounina, Sonia Orlova, Anna Adrianova, Serge Ismailov, Narcisse Matouchak, Oleg Tupine, Vladimir Irman, Nicolas Orlov, George Skibine, Vassily Nikolaiev, Marguerite Gontcharova, Ludmila Lvova and Kiril Vassilkovsky
16 *American Ballet Theatre,* q.v.
17 Statement by Col. de Basil, ts. (Fortune Gallo papers, Collection George Verdak)
18 *Impresario,* q.v.
19 Gallo papers, q.v.
20 *American Ballet Theatre,* q.v.
21 Gallo papers, q.v.
22 *American Ballet Theatre,* q.v.
23 Letter to the author from Tatiana Leskova, 8 June 1981, q.v.
24 Letter to Bill McCurdy from Fortune Gallo, 23 June 1941 (Gallo papers, q.v.)
25 Gallo papers, q.v.
26 Statement by Gallo, 10 June 1941 (Gallo papers, q.v.)
27 *Washington Post,* 24 August 1941
28 *Toronto Globe and Mail,* 23 September 1941
29 *The Standard,* Montreal, 11 October 1941
30 Letter to Walter Socolow from Fortune Gallo, 9 October 1941 (Gallo papers, q.v.)
31 Letter to de Basil from Gallo, 21 September 1941 (Gallo papers, q.v.)
32 Letter to Gallo from de Basil, 26 September 1941 (Gallo papers, q.v.)
33 Letter to Lily Laverock from Gallo, 3 December 1941 (Gallo papers, q.v.)
34 Letter to Gallo from Max Schoengold, 18 October 1941 (Gallo papers, q.v.)
35 Letter to Herbert Beeker of Meyer Meyer Austrian and Platt from Gallo, 22 October 1941 (Gallo papers, q.v.)
36 Gallo papers, q.v., 21 October 1941
37 Letter to Max Schoengold from Gallo, 21 October 1941 (Gallo papers, q.v.)
38 Letter to Gallo from de Basil, 28 October 1941 (Gallo papers, q.v.)
39 Letter to Gallo from L.E. Behymer, 7 November 1941 (Gallo papers, q.v.)

40 Document dated 31 October 1941 (Gallo papers, q.v.)

41 Letter to Mary Toye from Gallo, 11 November 1941 (Gallo papers, q.v.)

42 Lettter to Gallo from de Basil, 11 November 1941 (Gallo papers, q.v.)

43 Cable to Gallo from Charles Burke, 11 November 1941 (Gallo papers, q.v.)

44 *Victoria Daily Colonist*, 13 November 1941

45 Letter to Mario Gallo from Charles Burke, 15 November 1941 (Gallo papers, q.v.)

46 Letter to Fortune Gallo from Mario Gallo, 13 December 1941 (Gallo papers, q.v.)

47 Letter from Gallo, 19 November 1941 (Gallo papers, q.v.)

48 Letter to Metropolitan Theatre, Seattle, Mr H.M. Becket from Gallo, 21 November 1941 (Gallo papers, q.v.)

49 Letter to Gallo from de Basil, 29 January 1942 (Gallo papers, q.v.)

NOVEMBER 1941 TO MARCH 1947

1 *Les Balcons du ciel* by Margarita Wallmann, pub. Ed. Robert Laffont, 1977

2 *S. Hurok Presents* by Sol Hurok, pub. Invincible Press, Australia, 1954

3 *Autobiography* by Anton Dolin, q.v.

4 *Les Balcons du ciel,* q.v.

5 *Looking at the Dance*, q.v.

6 *The Dancing Times*, September 1946 ('Lichine creates a ballet' by Gioia Vanni)

7 *S. Hurok Presents,* q.v.

8 *Looking at the Dance,* q.v.

9 *New York Herald Tribune,* 2 October 1946 (review by Walter Terry)

10 *New York Times,* 2 October 1946 (review by John Martin)

11 *The Dancing Times*, May 1947 ('American Notes' by Lillian Moore)

MARCH 1947 TO JANUARY 1952

1 *The Daily Telegraph*, London, 24 March 1947

2 *Braunsweg's Ballet Scandals* by Julian Braunsweg, as told to James Kelsey, pub. Allen & Unwin, 1973

3 *Ballet Review*, New York, Vol. 6 (3) 1977–8, q.v.

4 *Braunsweg's Ballet Scandals,* q.v.

5 *The Daily Telegraph*, London, 15 August 1947 (review by Richard Capell)

6 *New Statesman,* London, 6 September 1947 (review by Beryl de Zoete)

7 *Ballet*, London, September 1947 ('The Original Ballet Russe' by Cyril W. Beaumont)

8 *The Observer,* London, 31 August 1947 (review by Peter Brook)

9 *The Times*, London, 3 August 1947

10 *The Times*, London, 25 July 1947

11 *New Statesman*, London, 6 September 1947 (review by Beryl de Zoete)

12 *Ballet*, London, September 1947 (article by Richard Buckle)

13 *Ballet*, London, October 1947 (article by Doris Langley Moore)

14 *Arts*, Paris, 24 October 1947 (review by Maurice Pourchet)

15 *The Dancing Times*, December 1947 ('De Basil in Paris' by Pierre Tugal)

16 *Borovansky* by Frank Salter, pub. Wildcat Press, Sydney, 1980

17 *Passport to Paris,* q.v.

18 Letter to the author from Deane Schultz, September 1980

19 Letter to the author from Pat Vaughn

20 *El enigma de España en la danza española* by Vicente Mariero, pub. Ed. Rialp, Madrid, 1959

21 *The Sunday Times*, London, 22 February 1952 (review by C.W. Beaumont)

22 Vladimir Dokoudovsky in conversation with the author, October 1977

23 Letter to the author from Tamara Toumanova, 15 August 1977, q.v.

24 Letter to George Kirsta from de Basil, quoted in programme of London season, 1951–2

25 Letter to Tom Bischoff from de Basil, 4 January 1951 (Collection Mme Olga Morosova de Basil)

26 *The Sunday Times*, London, 7 October 1951 (review by C.W. Beaumont)

27 *The Observer*, London, 7 October 1951 (review by Richard Buckle)

28 *The Dancing Times*, November 1951

29 Unknown newspaper (Coventry), 8 October 1951

30 *The Yorkshire Post*, 16 October 1951 (review by Ernest Bradbury)

31 *Manchester Guardian*, 30 October 1951 (review by G.P.)

32 *Newcastle Evening Chronicle*, 24 November 1951

33 *Glasgow Herald*, 11 December 1951

34 *Evening News,* London, 15 September 1951 (article by Duncan Harrison)

35 *The Sunday Times*, London, 6 January 1952 (review by C.W. Beaumont)

36 *The Times,* London, 18 January 1952

37 *Dance and Dancers*, February 1952

38 *Daily Mail*, London, 22 January 1952 (review by Peter Williams)

39 *The Sunday Times*, London, 20 January 1952 (review by C.W. Beaumont)
40 Oscar Beuselinck in conversation with the author, 8 September 1980
41 Sotheby catalogue, 17 July 1968
42 Special resolutions of Russian Ballet Development Company Ltd, 20 November 1964 (Companies House file, London)

2 The Colonel

1 *The Adventures of Dunsterforce* by Major General L.C. Dunsterville, pub. Edward Arnold, 1921
2 The original article appeared in *Sentinelle,* date unknown, a journal published in Paris for the Russian Army in exile. A French translation appeared in *Le Théâtre et la vie*, No. 62 (again, date unknown)
3 *The Adventures of Dunsterforce*, q.v.
4 End-of-year report from the British Flag Captain of the East India Station, Acting Capt. B.J. Washington, RN, to Vice-Admiral A. Cawthorpe, C in c, H.M. Ships and vessels in the Mediterranean, dated 31 December 1918, in the Public Record Office, London
5 *From Whitehall to the Caspian* by Lt. Colonel F.J.E. French, pub. Odhams Press, *c.* 1921
6 End-of-year report, q.v.
7 *Windsor Magazine*, London, January 1937 ('Secrets of the Russian Ballet' by Colonel W. de Basil in an interview with W.S. Meadmore)
8 *Ballet*, London, October 1951, Vol. 11 No. 9 ('Colonel de Basil, a Personal Note' by Hubert Griffith)
9 *Windsor Magazine*, q.v.
10 *Windsor Magazine*, q.v.
11 *The Observer,* London, 2 June 1935 (article by Hubert Griffith)
12 *Windsor Magazine*, q.v.
13 *Windsor Magazine*, q.v.
14 *Windsor Magazine*, q.v.
15 Ms. Memoir in possession of Mme Xenia Tripolitova
16 *The Birth of Ballets-Russes*, q.v.
17 *Ballet*, London, October 1951, q.v.
18 *Distant Dances* by Sono Osato, pub. Knopf, 1980
19 *The Observer*, London, 2 June 1935, q.v.
20 *Ballet*, London, October 1951, q.v.
21 There is thought to have been a first marriage in Russia. The wife died during World War I and de Basil lost touch with their only child, a son
22 *S. Hurok Presents,* q.v.
23 *S. Hurok Presents,* q.v.

24 *S. Hurok Presents*, q.v.
25 *Balletomania*, q.v.
26 *Ballet-go-round*, q.v.
27 *Braunsweg's Ballet Scandals*, q.v.
28 *The Observer,* London, 27 June 1937
29 *Dance Magazine* (USA), September 1951 (obituary of Colonel de Basil by Helen Dzhermolinska)
30 *S. Hurok Presents*, q.v.
31 *Balletomania*, q.v.
32 *Le Ballet contemporain*, q.v.
33 *The Birth of Ballets-Russes,* q.v.
34 *Passport to Paris,* q.v.
35 Letter to the author from Tamara Toumanova, 15 August 1977
36 *Dance Magazine*, September 1951, q.v.

3 *The Baby Ballerinas*

1 *Balletomania*, q.v.
2 *The Dancing Times*, August 1933 (review by The Sitter Out)
3 Letter to the author from Tamara Toumanova, 15 August 1977
4 *Comoedia Illustré*, Paris, 6 March 1929 (review by André Levinson)
5 *Les Visages de la danse* by André Levinson, pub. Ed. Bernard Grasset, 1933
6 *The Dancing Times*, December 1933 ('Two Celebrated Nurseries of Russian Ballet' by L. Franc Scheuer)
7 Letter to the author from Tamara Toumanova, 15 August 1977
8 *Alexandra Danilova*, q.v.
9 Conversation with Irina Baronova
10 *Balletomania*, q.v.
11 *Sydney Mail*, 30 November 1938 (article by Kerwin Maegraith)
12 *Candide*, Paris, 16 June 1932 (review by André Levinson)
13 *Balletomania*, q.v.
14 *The Daily Telegraph*, London, 26 June 1939 (review by Beryl de Zoete)
15 Conversation with Dame Marie Rambert
16 *A Prejudice for Ballet*, q.v.
17 *Russian Ballets*, by Adrian Stokes, pub. Faber & Faber, 1935
18 *The Nature of Ballet* by James Monahan, pub. Pitman, 1976
19 *Le Ballet contemporain*, q.v.
20 *The Dancing Times*, May 1935 (New York Letter by Lillian Moore)
21 *The Dancing Times*, August 1935 (review by The Sitter Out)
22 *A Prejudice for Ballet*, q.v.

23 *Melbourne Herald,* 14 March 1940 (review by Basil Burdett)
24 *The Birth of Ballets-Russes,* q.v.
25 *Vandance,* Canada, May 1978 ('Vancouver Dancers in the Ballet Russe: Three "Canadian Exotics" ' by Leland Windreich)
26 Agreement signed by Colonel de Basil concerning Rosemary Deveson, 4 February 1938
27 Letter from Rosemary Deveson to her mother
28 *Curtain Call,* Canada, December 1940 (article by A.L. Haskell)
29 *The Daily Telegraph,* London, 23 June 1939 (review by Beryl de Zoete)
30 *The Times,* London, 6 July 1939
31 *The Daily Telegraph,* London, 15 July 1939 (review by Beryl de Zoete)
32 *Melbourne Herald,* 14 March 1940 (review by Basil Burdett)
33 *Dance Chronicle,* Vol. 3, No. 1 1979 ('The Career of Alexandra Denisova: Vancouver, de Basil and Cuba' by Leland Windreich)
34 *Balletomania,* q.v.
35 *Sydney Morning Herald,* 21 December 1939 (review by Ken Wilkinson)

4 Australia

1 *Balletomane's Art Book* ed. T. Essington Breen, pub. London Book Publications, Sydney, 1940
2 *Enter the Colonies, Dancing* by Edward Pask, pub. Oxford University Press, 1979
3 *Table Talk,* Melbourne, during 1936 ('Off to Australia' by Olga Philipov)
4 Armour letters, q.v.
5 *Dancing round the World,* q.v.
6 *A Family of Brothers* by Viola Tait, pub. Heinemann, 1971
7 *Opera and Ballet in Australia* by John Cargher, pub. Cassell, 1971
8 *The Argus,* Melbourne, 4 December 1936
9 *Waltzing Matilda* by Arnold L. Haskell, pub. A. & C. Black, 1943
10 *The Argus,* 2 November 1936
11 *The Argus,* 2 November 1936
12 *Table Talk,* Melbourne, during 1936 ('Russian Ballet Premiere' by A.L. Haskell)
13 *The Argus,* 9 November 1936
14 *Table Talk,* during 1936 ('Russian Ballet's Second Programme' by A.L. Haskell)
15 *The Argus,* 30 November 1936

16 *The Argus*, 23 December 1936
17 *Sydney Morning Herald,* 30 January 1937
18 *The Home*, Sydney, ed. Sydney Ure Smith and Leon Gellert, 1 February 1937
19 *The Argus*, 21 June 1937
20 *The Argus*, 24 June 1937
21 *The Argus*, 24 June 1937
22 *The Argus,* 3 July 1937
23 *The Times,* London, 15 July 1938
24 *The Argus,* 27 September 1938
25 *The Argus*, 29 September 1938 (review by Geoffrey Hutton) (N.B. all *Argus* reviews from that date were by Geoffrey Hutton)
26 *The Argus*, 3 October 1938
27 *Autobiography* by Anton Dolin, q.v.
28 *The Argus*, 7 October 1938
29 *The Argus*, 11 October 1938
30 *The Argus*, 1 November 1938
31 *The Argus,* 14 October 1938
32 *The Argus*, 25 October 1938
33 *The Argus*, 25 October 1938
34 *The Argus*, 1 November 1938
35 *The Argus*, 8 November 1938
36 *Sydney Mail,* 30 November 1938
37 *The Home*, Sydney, 3 January 1939
38 *Sydney Morning Herald,* 7 January 1939
39 *The Argus,* 31 January 1939
40 *Memoirs of a Ballet Master,* q.v.
41 *The Argus*, 27 March 1939
42 *The Argus*, 30 March 1939
43 *The Argus*, 31 March 1939
44 *The Argus*, 30 March 1939
45 *The Argus*, 27 March 1939
46 *The Argus,* 31 March 1939
47 *The Argus*, 13 April 1939
48 *The Argus*, 2 December 1939
49 *The Argus*, 25 December 1939
50 *The Argus*, 20 September 1939
51 *Sydney Morning Herald,* 7 January 1940
52 Unknown newspaper
53 *Sydney Morning Herald,* 8 January 1940
54 *The Argus*, 28 December 1939
55 *Sydney Morning Herald,* 1 January 1940

56 *Sydney Morning Herald,* 2 March 1940
57 *The Age,* Melbourne, 15 March 1940
58 *The Age,* 2 April 1940
59 *The Age,* 26 March 1940
60 *The Argus,* 26 March 1940
61 (?) *The Argus*
62 *The Age,* 16 April 1940
63 *The Age,* 7 May 1940
64 *The Argus,* 7 May 1940
65 *The Argus,* 14 May 1940
66 *Sydney Morning Herald,* 26 July 1940
67 *Sydney Morning Herald,* 13 September 1940
68 *Los Angeles Times,* 10 October 1940
69 *The Argus,* 9 March 1940 (leader, 'On with the Ballet')

5 *The Company's Influence on Ballet*

1 *My Life in Ballet,* q.v.
2 *A Prejudice for Ballet,* q.v.
3 *Footnotes to the Ballet,* q.v.
4 *My Life in Ballet,* q.v.
5 *The Complete Book of Ballets,* q.v.
6 *The Sunday Times,* London, during 1936 (review by Ernest Newman)
7 *Evening Standard,* London, during 1936
8 *A Prejudice for Ballet,* q.v.
9 *My Life in Ballet,* q.v.
10 *The Dancing Times,* December 1936 ('The Symphonic Ballet' by Edwin Evans)
11 *The Dancing Times,* July 1937 ('Symphonic Ballet: a Summing Up' by James Kennedy, better known as Monahan)
12 *The Dancing Times,* August 1937 ('Symphonic Ballet: a Reply' by Fernau Hall)
13 *Ballet Review,* New York, 6 (3) 1977–8, q.v.
14 *Ballet,* London, September 1947 ('Thoughts of a Choreographer' by David Lichine)
15 *New Statesman,* London, 5 August 1933
16 *The Observer,* London, 16 August 1936 (review by Horace Horsnell)
17 *A Prejudice for Ballet,* q.v.
18 *The Sunday Times,* London, 16 August 1936 (review by Ernest Newman)
19 *A Prejudice for Ballet,* q.v.
20 *The Observer,* London, 27 June 1937

254

21 *The Dancing Times,* March 1938 ('David Lichine, Choreographer' by James Monahan)
22 *Boston Monitor,* 5 November 1937
23 *The Dancing Times,* August 1938 (review by The Sitter Out)
24 *The Dancing Times,* February 1939 (article by A.L. Haskell)
25 *The Daily Telegraph,* London, 20 June 1939 (review by Beryl de Zoete)
26 *The Times,* London, 8 August 1947
27 *The Dancing Times,* March 1938, q.v.
28 *Curtain Call,* Canada, October 1941 ('This Ballet Business' by Ann Foster)
29 *Twentieth Century Ballet,* by Arthur Franks, pub. Burke, 1954
30 *Blast at Ballet* by Lincoln Kirstein, pub. New York, 1937
31 *Comoedia Illustré,* Paris, 10 June 1936
32 *The Daily Telegraph,* London, 25 August 1936 (review by A.L. Haskell)
33 *Colonel W. de Basil's Ballets Russes,* souvenir book, Royal Opera House, Covent Garden, 1935 (article by Edwin Evans)
34 *The Dancing Times,* May 1934 ('New York Letter' by Lillian Moore)
35 Conversation, Roman Jasinsky and Moscelyne Larkin with Jack Anderson
36 *The Dancing Times,* May 1934, q.v.

PRODUCTIONS

ORIGINAL TITLE AND ALTERNATIVES	CHOREOGRAPHER	BOOK	COMPOSER
L'Amour sorcier (*El Amor brujo*)	Boris Romanov	Martinez Sierra	Falla
L'Amour sorcier	Léon Woizikovsky	Martinez Sierra	Falla
L'Après-midi d'un faune (The Afternoon of a Faun)	Vaslav Nijinsky		Debussy (Prélude à l'après-midi d'un faune)
Le Bal (The Ball)	Leonide Massine	B. Kochno, from a story by V. Sologub, L. Massine	V. Rieti
Balustrade	George Balanchine		Stravinsky (Concerto for Violin and Orchestra)
Beach	Leonide Massine	René Kerdyk	Jean Françaix
Le Beau Danube (The Beautiful [Blue] Danube) (*Le Beau Danube bleu*) (see also *Le Danube bleu*)	Leonide Massine	Leonide Massine	J. Strauss, (plus *Der Schönbrunner* by Josef Lanner) arranged and orchestrated by R. Desormière
Les Biches	Bronislava Nijinska		Poulenc
Bolero	Bronislava Nijinska		Ravel
Le Bourgeois Gentilhomme	George Balanchine	Sobeka (B. Kochno), after Molière	R. Strauss (incidental music for play)
La Boutique fantasque	Leonide Massine	A. Derain	Rossini, arranged by Respighi

DESIGN	THEATRE AND DATE	NOTES
sc. and c. Monte-Carlo 1932, B. Bilinsky	Théâtre de Monte-Carlo, 23 April 1932	Revived from l'Opéra Russe à Paris, 1931
N. Gontcharova	His Majesty's Theatre, Melbourne, 21 November 1936 (II Co)	Revived from Ballets de Léon Woizikovsky
c. Bakst, sc. Prince A. Schervachidze	Alhambra Theatre, London, 2 October 1933; Met., New York, 1 November 1936; Theatre Royal, Adelaide, 20 October 1936 (II Co)	Revived from Diaghilev Ballets Russes, 29 May 1912
G. de Chirico	Auditorium, Chicago, 8 March 1935 (w.p.); Majestic Theatre, New York, 20 March 1935; ROH, Covent Garden, London, 20 June 1935	Given by Diaghilev Ballet with choreography by George Balanchine, 9 May 1929
P. Tchelitchev	51st Street Theatre, New York, 22 January 1941 (w.p.)	
R. Dufy (also curtain), sc. ex. Prince A. Schervachidze	Théâtre de Monte-Carlo, 18 April 1933 (w.p.); Alhambra Theatre, London, 2 August 1933; St James Theatre, New York, 2 January 1934	
c. Count Etienne de Beaumont, sc. V. and E. Polunin, after Constantin Guys. Ladies' costumes ex. Jeanne Lanvin	Théâtre de Monte-Carlo, 7 March 1933; Alhambra Theatre, London, 4 July 1933; St James Theatre, New York, 22 December 1933; Theatre Royal, Adelaide 16 October 1936 (II Co)	Revived and revised into a one-act version from Les Soirées de Paris, Théâtre de la Cigale, 17 May 1924
M. Laurencin (also curtain)	Théâtre de Monte-Carlo, 14 January 1934	Revived from Diaghilev Ballet, 6 January 1924
N. Gontcharova	Théâtre de Monte-Carlo, 7 April 1934	Revived from Théâtre de la Danse Nijinska, 1934 (based on original composition for Ida Rubinstein Ballet, 1928)
A. Benois (also curtain) (ex. Geerts), sc. ex. Prince A. Schervachidze, c. ex. Karinska	Théâtre de Monte-Carlo, 3 May 1932 (w.p.)	
A. Derain (also curtain)	ROH, Covent Garden, London, 16 July 1934; National Theatre. Washington DC, 4 November 1934; Majestic Theatre, New York, 20 March 1935; Theatre Royal, Adelaide, 13 October 1936 (II Co)	Revived from Diaghilev Ballet, 5 June 1919

sc. = scenery, c. = costumes, ex. = executed by, w.p. = world premiere, ROH = Royal Opera House, Met. = Metropolitan Opera House

ORIGINAL TITLE AND ALTERNATIVES	CHOREOGRAPHER	BOOK	COMPOSER
Cain and Abel	David Lichine	David Lichine	Wagner (Rhine Journey from *Götterdämmerung*), arranged by William McDermott
Camille	John Taras	John Taras, after A. Dumas fils	Schubert, arranged by V. Rieti
Carnaval	Michel Fokine	Michel Fokine	Schumann, orchestrated by Rimsky-Korsakov, Glazounov, Liadov and N. Tcherepnine
Cendrillon (Cinderella)	Michel Fokine	Michel Fokine, after Perrault	Frédéric d'Erlanger
Les Cent Baisers (The Hundred Kisses)	Bronislava Nijinska	B. Kochno, after Hans Christian Andersen's *The Swineherd*	Frédéric d'Erlanger
Choreartium	Leonide Massine		Brahms (4th Symphony in E minor)
Chout (*Le Bouffon*)	Boris Romanov		Prokofiev
Cimarosiana (last-act *divertissement* from *Le astuzie femminili*)	Leonide Massine		Cimarosa, arranged by Respighi
Cléopâtra	Michel Fokine		Arensky, Glazounov, Glinka, Moussorgsky, Rimsky-Korsakov, Tanaiev, N. Tcherepnine

DESIGN	THEATRE AND DATE	NOTES
Miguel Prieto	Palacio de las Bellas Artes, Mexico City, 8 March 1946 (w.p.); Met., New York, 2 October 1946	
Cecil Beaton, c. ex. Karinska, sc. ex. E.B. Dunkel Studios	Met., New York, 1 October 1946 (w.p.)	
Bakst	Alhambra Theatre, London, 14 September 1933; Auditorium, Chicago, 20 February 1934; St James Theatre, New York, 16 March 1934; Theatre Royal, Adelaide, 16 October 1936 (II Co)	Revived from Diaghilev Ballet, 20 May 1910 (staged in 1933 by L. Woizikowsky). Earlier version, St Petersburg, 20 February 1910
N. Gontcharova, c. ex. Karinska, sc. ex. Prince A. Schervachidze	ROH, Covent Garden, London, 19 July 1938 (w.p.); Philharmonic Auditorium, Los Angeles, 16 October 1940; 51st Street Theatre, New York, 16 November 1940; His Majesty's Theatre, Melbourne, 28 September 1938	
Jean Hugo, c. ex. Karinska, sc. ex. Prince A. Schervachidze	ROH, Covent Garden, London, 18 July 1935 (w.p.); Met., New York, 18 October 1935; His Majesty's Theatre, Melbourne, 5 December 1936 (II Co)	
C. Terechkovich, Eugène Lourie (curtain, Georges Annenkoff), sc. ex. Elisabeth Polunin	Alhambra Theatre, London, 24 October 1933 (w.p.); Met., New York, 16 October 1935; His Majesty's Theatre, Melbourne, 10 October 1938	
Léon Zack, sc. ex. Kokouchkine	Théâtre de Monte-Carlo, 16 April 1932	Revived from l'Opéra Russe à Paris, 1931
J-M. Sert	Met., New York, 4 November 1936; ROH, Covent Garden, London, 1 July 1937; Theatre Royal, Sydney, 12 January 1940	Revived from Diaghilev Ballet, 27 May 1920 (given on 8 January 1924 as. *Cimarosiana* with added *pas de quatre* by Nijinska)
c. Bakst, sc. Robert Delaunay, c. for Cléôpatra and Amoun by Sophie Delaunay	Academy of Music, Philadelphia, 10 November 1936; ROH, Covent Garden, London, 27 July 1937 (one performance only)	Revived from Diaghilev Ballet, 2 June 1909 (staged as *Une Nuit d'Egypte*, Maryinsky, St Petersburg, 8 March 1908)

ORIGINAL TITLE AND ALTERNATIVES	CHOREOGRAPHER	BOOK	COMPOSER
Les Comédiens jaloux	Bronislava Nijinska	Bronislava Nijinska	A. Cassella, after themes by Scarlatti
La Concurrence (Competition)	George Balanchine	A. Derain	Auric
Constantia	William Dollar		Chopin (Piano Concerto No. 2 in F minor), arranged by Schmidt
Contes russes (Children's Tales)	Leonide Massine		Liadov
Coppélia (2-act version)	A. Oboukhov, after Pétipa	Nuitter and St-Léon	Delibes
Le Coq d'or (The Golden Cockerel)	Michel Fokine	M. Fokine from Bielsky, after Pushkin	Rimsky-Korsakov, adapted by N. Tcherepnine
Cotillon (The Dance)	George Balanchine	B. Kochno	Chabrier, orchestrated by Chabrier, F. Mottl and V. Rieti
Danses slaves et tziganes (Gypsy Dances)	Bronislava Nijinska		Dargomijsky

DESIGN	THEATRE AND DATE	NOTES
G. Annenkov	Théâtre de Monte-Carlo, 24 April 1934	Revived from l'Opéra Russe à Paris
A. Derain (also curtain), sc. ex. Prince A. Schervachidze, c. ex. Karinska	Théâtre de Monte-Carlo, 12 April 1932 (w.p.); Alhambra Theatre, London, 7 July 1933; St James Theatre, New York, 22 December 1933; His Majesty's Theatre, Melbourne, 6 October 1938	
c. Grace Houston, sc. Horace Armistead	Met., New York, 16 October 1946	Revived from Ballet International, 31 October 1944 (a revision of *Classic Ballet*)
M. Larionov	ROH, Covent Garden, London, 7 August 1934; Albany Theatre, Harmanus Bleecker Hall, 2 November 1934 (enlarged and revised); His Majesty's Theatre, Melbourne, 5 December 1936 (II Co)	Revived from Diaghilev Ballet, 11 May 1917 (1st section 25 August 1916, full version 23 December 1918)
c. ex. Olga Larose	Theatre Royal, Sydney, 12 August 1940	Revival
N. Gontcharova (also curtain), c. ex. Karinska, sc. ex. Prince A. Schervachidze (in 1947 Ed Delaney)	Covent Garden, London, 23 September 1937 (w.p.); Met., New York, 23 October 1937; His Majesty's Theatre, Melbourne, 17 October 1938	Opera-ballet version given by Diaghilev Ballet, 21 May 1914
C. Bérard, sc. ex. Prince A. Schervachidze, c. (women) ex. Karinska (men) ex. Lidvall	Théâtre de Monte-Carlo, 17 January 1932 (w.p.); Alhambra Theatre, London, 17 July 1933; St James Theatre, New York, 16 March 1934; His Majesty's Theatre, Melbourne, 28 November 1936 (II Co)	
c. C. Korovine, sc. A. Golovine, c. ex. Hélène Pons	Met., New York, 17 April 1936; ROH, Covent Garden, London, 14 July 1936 (gala performance which included two solos, Danse Russe by L. Sokolova and Danse Boyard by M. Kschessinka); His Majesty's Theatre, Melbourne, 20 October 1938	Revived from dances created by Nijinska for L'Opera Russe à Paris production of *Russalka*, 1931

261

ORIGINAL TITLE AND ALTERNATIVES	CHOREOGRAPHER	BOOK	COMPOSER
Le Danube bleu (The Blue Danube) (printed as *Beau Danube* in London 1947)	scenes and dances arranged by Serge Lifar ('choreography by Serge Lifar', USA, 1946)		J. Strauss, arranged and orchestrated by E. Fuerst
Danzas eslavas	Anatole Joukovsky		J. Gotovac, K. Baranovic and A. Sreckovic
Les Dieux mendiants (The Gods Go A-begging)	David Lichine	Sobeka (B. Kochno)	Handel, arranged by Beecham
Etude	Bronislava Nijinska		J.S. Bach
Etude (The Quest)	Nina Verchinina		J.S. Bach, arranged by A. Dorati
Femmes d'Alger	Vladimir Dokoudovsky	G. Kirsta	Joseph Horowitz
Les Femmes de bonne humeur (The Good-humoured Ladies)	Leonide Massine	Tommasini, after Goldoni	Scarlatti (22 sonatas), arranged and orchestrated by Tommasini
Le Fils prodigue (The Prodigal Son)	David Lichine	B. Kochno	Prokofiev
Francesca da Rimini	David Lichine	Lichine and H. Clifford	Tchaikovsky
Fue una vez . . .	Vania Psota and S. Pueyrredón de Elizalde	Wedebe	Carlos Guastavino

262

DESIGN	THEATRE AND DATE	NOTES
c. Count E. de Beaumont, sc. V. and E. Polunin, after Constantin Guys	Theatre Royal, Sydney, 9 February 1940 (w.p.); Met., New York, 6 October 1946; ROH, Covent Garden, London, 24 July 1947	Re-working by Lifar of *Le Beau Danube* using Count Etienne de Beaumont's original designs
c. W. Jedrinsky	Spanish tour, about September 1948	
c. Juan Gris, sc. Gris after Bakst: the costumes were from *Les Tentations de la bergère* (Diaghilev Ballet) with new designs for the gods; the scenery from *Daphnis and Chloë*	ROH, Covent Garden, London, 17 September 1937 (w.p.); Met., New York, 28 October 1937; His Majesty's Theatre, Melbourne, 6 October 1938	Given by Diaghilev Ballet, 16 July 1928, with choreography by Balanchine
Bilinsky, after A. Exter	Théâtre de Monte-Carlo, 10 April 1934	Revived from L'Opéra Russe à Paris, January 1931 (based on 1925 production of *Holy Etudes*)
(1) c. Olga Larose (2) c. C. Kent, after designs by Cristofanetti	Theatre Royal, Sydney, 25 July 1940 (w.p.); 51st Street Theatre, New York, 11 January 1941 (as *The Quest*)	
George Kirsta, after Delacroix	Royal Festival Hall, London, 3 January 1952 (w.p.)	
Bakst	Academy of Music, Philadelphia, 16 February 1935; ROH, Covent Garden, London, 6 August 1935; Met., New York, 15 October 1935, His Majesty's Theatre, Melbourne, 13 October 1938	Revived from Diaghilev Ballet, 12 April 1917
G. Rouault, c. ex. Mme V. Soudeikine, sc. ex. Prince A. Schervachidze	Theatre Royal, Sydney, 30 December 1938 (w.p.); ROH, Covent Garden, London, 19 June 1939; 51st Street, Theatre, New York, 26 November 1940	Given by Diaghilev Ballet, 21 May 1929, with choreography by Balanchine
Oliver Messel, c. ex. Karinska, sc. ex. Prince A. Schervachidze	ROH, Covent Garden, London, 15 July 1937 (w.p.); Met., New York, 24 October 1937; Theatre Royal, Sydney, 26 January 1940	
Ignacio Pirovano, c. ex. Maria Tcherepennikova, sc. ex. C. Popov	Teatro Colón, Buenos Aires, 27 November 1942 (w.p.)	

263

ORIGINAL TITLE AND ALTERNATIVES	CHOREOGRAPHER	BOOK	COMPOSER
Giselle	Anton Dolin, after Coralli; re-staged by Anton Dolin	Gautier, on a theme by Heinrich Heine	A. Adam, orchestrated by A. Dorati
Graduation Ball	David Lichine		J. Strauss, compiled, arranged and orchestrated by A. Dorati
Icare	Serge Lifar		rhythms by Lifar, orchestrated by A. Dorati
Les Imaginaires (working title *Les Formes*)	David Lichine		Auric
La Isla de los ceibos	Vania Psota	R.V. Barreto	Eduardo Fabini
Jardin public (The Public Gardens)	Leonide Massine	V. Dukelsky and Massine, from A. Gide	V. Dukelsky
Jeux d'enfants (Children's Games)	Leonide Massine	B. Kochno	Bizet
Le Lac des cygnes (The Swan Lake) (one-act version)	after M. Pétipa		Tchaikovsky

DESIGN	THEATRE AND DATE	NOTES
c. E. Berman, ex. Rose Chagall, sc. A. Benois adapted by George Dunkel, ex. E.B. Dunkel Studios	Met., New York, 11 October 1946	Revival
A. Benois, c. ex. Olga Larose	Theatre Royal, Sydney, 1 March 1940 (w.p.); Philharmonic Auditorium, Los Angeles, 10 October 1940; 51st Street Theatre, New York, 6 November 1940; ROH, Covent Garden, London, 22 July 1947	
sc. Sidney Nolan, ex. Jacob Anchutin	Theatre Royal, Sydney, 16 February 1940	Revived from Paris Opéra, 9 July 1935
c. Count E. de Beaumont, sc. Lesley Blanch and Freida Harris, sc. ex. Leon G. Davey	Théâtre des Champs-Elysées, Paris, 11 June 1934 (w.p.); ROH, Covent Garden, London, 31 July 1934	
Jacob Anchutin	Teatro SODRE, Montevideo, Uruguay, 11 February 1944 (w.p.)	
(1) c. and sc. J. Lurçat (1935) (2) c. and sc. Alice Halicka (1936), sc. ex. Eugene Dunkel	Auditorium, Chicago, 8 March 1935 (w.p.); Majestic Theatre, New York, 21 March 1935; ROH, Covent Garden, London, 23 July 1935; Met., New York, 19 April 1936 (revised production); ROH, Covent Garden, London, 29 June 1936	
Joan Miró (also curtain and properties), c. ex. Karinska, sc. ex. Prince A. Schervachidze	Théâtre de Monte-Carlo, 14 April 1932 (w.p.); Alhambra Theatre, London, 5 July 1933; St James Theatre, New York, 26 December 1933; His Majesty's Theatre, Melbourne, 10 October 1938	
sc. Visconti and Geerts, 1932, sc. ex. Prince A. Schervachidze (in Australia, 1940, c. and sc. were credited to C. Korovine, sc. ex. O. Allegri)	Théâtre de Monte-Carlo, 21 April 1932; Alhambra Theatre, London, 11 July 1933; St James Theatre, New York, 9 March 1934; Theatre Royal, Adelaide, 20 October 1936 (II Co)	Revival

ORIGINAL TITLE AND ALTERNATIVES	CHOREOGRAPHER	BOOK	COMPOSER
Le Lion amoureux	David Lichine	Lichine and H. Clifford, from La Fontaine (idea from Kochno)	Karol Rathaus
La Lutte éternelle (The Eternal Struggle)	Igor Schwezov	Schwezov	Schumann, arranged by A. Dorati
El Malón	Vania Psota (consultant for Argentine dance: Antonio R. Barceló)	H.I. Villoud	Hector Iglesias Villoud
Le Mariage d'Aurore (Aurora's Wedding)	after M. Pétipa; choreography for 'The Three Ivans' by Bronislava Nijinska		Tchaikovsky
Les Matelots	Leonide Massine	B. Kochno	Auric
Mute Wife	Antonia Cobos	Cobos, from Anatole France	V. Rieti, ending with *Perpetuum Mobile* by Paganini
Les Noces (The Nuptials)	Bronislava Nijinska	Stravinsky	Stravinsky
Nocturne	David Lichine	Count E. de Beaumont, from Shakespeare's *A Midsummer Night's Dream*	Rameau, arranged by Roger Desormière
L'Oiseau de feu (The Firebird)	Michel Fokine	Fokine	Stravinsky

DESIGN	THEATRE AND DATE	NOTES
Pierre Roy (also curtain), c. ex. Karinska, sc. ex. Prince A. Schervachidze	ROH, Covent Garden, London, 6 October 1937 (w.p.)	
Kathleen and Florence Martin	Theatre Royal, Sydney, 29 July 1940 (w.p.); Philharmonic Auditorium, Los Angeles, 15 October 1940; 51st Street Theatre, New York, 25 November 1940	Revised version of earlier ballet *Etudes choréographiques*
Hector Basaldúa	Teatro Colón, Buenos Aires, 16 July 1943 (w.p.)	
c. A. Benois and Bakst, sc. Bakst, c. for 'Contes de Fée' by N. Gontcharova, others from *Le Pavillon d'Armide* (Diaghilev Ballet)	Academy of Music, Philadelphia, 12 November 1934; Majestic Theatre, New York, 21 March 1935; ROH, Covent Garden, London, 11 June 1935; Theatre Royal, Adelaide, 27 October 1936 (II Co)	Revived from Diaghilev Ballet production, 18 May 1922 In 1936–7 the main company used set for Prologue and II Co that for last act
P. Pruna (also curtains), sc. ex. Prince A. Schervachidze	Théâtre de Monte-Carlo, 22 April 1933; Alhambra Theatre, London, 16 October 1933; St James Theatre, New York, 9 March 1934	Revived from Diaghilev Ballet, 17 June 1925
Rico Lebrun, c. ex. Amalia Fernandez and Eaves, sc. ex. E.B. Dunkel Studios	Met., New York, 4 October 1946	Shortened revival from Ballet International, 22 November 1944
N. Gontcharova	Met., New York, 20 April 1936	Revived from Diaghilev Ballet, 13 June 1923
Count E. de Beaumont	Théâtre du Châtelet, Paris, 30 June 1933 (w.p.); Alhambra Theatre, London, 26 July 1933	
N. Gontcharova Credited to Bakst (II Co) (actually Golovin)	Théâtre de Monte-Carlo, 28 April 1934; ROH, Covent Garden, London 25 June 1934; Auditorium, Chicago, 27 December 1934; Majestic Theatre, New York, 20 March 1935; His Majesty's Theatre, Melbourne, 28 November 1936 (II Co)	Revived from Diaghilev Ballet, 25 June 1910

ORIGINAL TITLE AND ALTERNATIVES	CHOREOGRAPHER	BOOK	COMPOSER
Paganini	Michel Fokine	Fokine and Rachmaninov	Rachmaninov (*Rhapsody on a Theme by Paganini*)
Les Papillons (Butterflies)	Michel Fokine	Fokine	Schumann, orchestrated by N. Tcherepnine
Pas de quatre	Anton Dolin		C. Pugni, transcribed by Leighton Lucas, orchestrated by P. Bowles
Pas de trois	Jerome Robbins		Berlioz
Pavane (Las Meninas)	Serge Lifar		Fauré
Le Pavillon (The Pavilion)	David Lichine	B. Kochno	Borodin, arranged and orchestrated by A. Dorati
Petrouchka	Michel Fokine	Benois and Stravinsky	Stravinsky
Piccoli	Boris Kniasev	Kniasev	Rossini
Pictures at an Exhibition	Bronislava Nijinska		Moussorgsky (orchestrated by I. Boutnikov)
Port Said	Léon Woizikovsky	A. Shaikevitch	K. Konstantinov

DESIGN	THEATRE AND DATE	NOTES
S. Soudeikine, ex. Oreste Allegri	ROH, Covent Garden, London, 30 June 1939 (w.p.); Philharmonic Auditorium, Los Angeles, 12 October 1940; 51st Street Theatre, New York, 8 November 1940; Theatre Royal, Sydney, 30 December 1939	
c. Bakst, sc. M. Doboukinsky (also ex.)	Auditorium, Chicago, 27 December 1936; ROH, Covent Garden, London, 8 July 1937; His Majesty's Theatre, Melbourne, 10 November 1938	Revived from Diaghilev Ballet, 16 April 1914 (earlier, Maryinsky, St Petersburg, 10 March 1912)
after Chalon's lithograph	Met., New York, 7 October 1946	Revived from Ballet Theatre, 16 February 1941
c. John Pratt	Met., New York, 25 March 1947 (w.p.)	
J-M. Sert	Theatre Royal, Sydney, 23 February 1940; 51st Street Theatre, New York, 25 November 1940	Revived from Paris Opéra, 1940 (given by Diaghilev Ballet with choreography by Massine, 21 August 1916)
Cecil Beaton, c. ex. Karinska, sc. ex. Prince A. Schervachidze. In Australia, 1940, sc. Nicholas Benois	ROH, Covent Garden, London, 11 August 1936 (w.p.); Met., New York, 29 October 1936; His Majesty's Theatre, Melbourne, 20 May 1940	
A. Benois (also curtain)	Théâtre de Monte-Carlo, 19 April 1932 (staged by L. Woizikovsky); Alhambra Theatre, London, 19 July 1933; St James Theatre, New York, 8 January 1934; His Majesty's Theatre, Melbourne, 14 November 1936 (II Co)	Revived from Diaghilev Ballet, 13 June 1911. Given by L'Opéra Russe à Paris (1) staged by B. Nijinska with some choreographic alterations (2) staged by L. Woizikovsky
N. Gontcharova	ROH, Covent Garden, London, 12 September 1947	Revived from Théâtre Marigny, Paris, 1940
Boris Aronson	Met., New York, 25 March 1947	Revived from Ballet International, 3 November 1944
M. Larionov	His Majesty's Theatre, Melbourne, 12 December 1936 (II Co)	Revived from Ballets de Léon Woizikovsky, 27 September 1935

ORIGINAL TITLE AND ALTERNATIVES	CHOREOGRAPHER	BOOK	COMPOSER
Les Présages (Destiny)	Leonide Massine		Tchaikovsky (5th Symphony in E minor)
Prince Igor, Polovtsian Dances from	Michel Fokine (The 'first two dances' or 'the first dance' were sometimes credited to Nijinska)		Borodin
Protée	David Lichine	Lichine and H. Clifford	Debussy (Danse Sacrée et Danse Profane)
Pulcinella	Boris Romanov		Stravinsky, after Pergolesi
Schéherazade	Michel Fokine	Fokine and Bakst	Rimsky-Korsakov
Scuola di ballo (The School of Ballet)	Leonide Massine	Massine, from Goldoni	Boccherini, orchestrated by J. Françaix
Sebastian	Edward Caton		Menotti
The Silver Birch	Boris Kniasev	Kniasev	Tchaikovsky

DESIGN	THEATRE AND DATE	NOTES
André Masson, sc. ex. Prince A. Schervachidze	Théâtre de Monte-Carlo, 13 April 1933 (w.p.); Alhambra Theatre, London, 4 July 1933; St James Theatre, New York, 22 December 1933; Theatre Royal, Adelaide, 23 October 1936 (II Co)	
N. Roehrich Korovin, II Co	Théâtre de Monte-Carlo, 11 February 1932; Alhambra, London, 17 August 1933; St James Theatre, New York, 8 January 1934; Theatre Royal, Adelaide, 20 October 1936 (II Co)	Revived from Diaghilev Ballet, 19 May 1909; staged by Nijinska for L'Opéra Russe à Paris, design by Ivan Bilibin
G. de Chirico, c. ex. Karinska, sc. ex. Prince A. Schervachidze	ROH, Covent Garden, London, 5 July 1938 (w.p.); Philharmonic Auditorium, Los Angeles, 12 October 1940; 51st Street Theatre, New York, 8 November 1940; His Majesty's Theatre, Melbourne, 20 October 1938	
G. de Chirico	Théâtre de Monte-Carlo, 30 April 1932	Revived from L'Opéra Russe à Paris, 1931
Bakst	Academy of Music, Philadelphia, 16 February 1935; ROH, Covent Garden, London, 19 June 1935; Met., New York, 9 October 1935; Theatre Royal, Adelaide, 13 October 1936 (II Co)	Revived from Diaghilev Ballet, 4 June 1910
Count E. de Beaumont, sc. ex. Prince A. Schervachidze	Théâtre de Monte-Carlo, 25 April 1933 (w.p.); Alhambra Theatre, London, 10 July 1933; St James Theatre, New York, 28 December 1933; His Majesty's Theatre, Melbourne, 21 November 1936 (II Co)	
C. Milena, sc. Oliver Smith	Met., New York, 13 October 1946	Revived from Ballet International, 31 October 1944
Monique Lancelot	ROH, Covent Garden, London, 11 September 1947	Revived from Paris Théâtre, Marigny, 1940

ORIGINAL TITLE AND ALTERNATIVES	CHOREOGRAPHER	BOOK	COMPOSER
Le Soleil de nuit (Midnight Sun)	Leonide Massine		Rimsky-Korsakov, from *Snegorouchka*
Le Spectre de la rose (The Spirit of the Rose)	Michel Fokine II Co production 'reconstructed' by Woizikovsky	Vaudoyer, after Gautier	Weber
Suite choréographique	Nina Verchinina		Gounod
Suites de danses	George Balanchine		Glinka
Les Sylphides	Michel Fokine		Chopin, orchestrated by V. Rieti
Symphonie fantastique	Leonide Massine	Berlioz	Berlioz
Thamar	Michel Fokine	Fokine, after Lermontov	Balakirev (symphonic poem)
Le Tricorne (The Three-cornered Hat)	Leonide Massine	Martinez Sierra, from a fable by Alarcón	Falla

DESIGN	THEATRE AND DATE	NOTES
M. Larionov	Academy of Music, Philadelphia, 15 February 1935; Met., New York, 16 October 1935; ROH, Covent Garden, London, 19 June 1936; His Majesty's Theatre, Melbourne, 19 December 1936 (II Co)	Revived from Diaghilev Ballet, 20 December 1915
Bakst	ROH, Covent Garden, London, 23 August 1935; Met., New York, 20 October 1935; Theatre Royal, Adelaide, 13 October 1936 (II Co)	Revived from Diaghilev Ballet, 19 April 1911
Odette de Santos, ex. V. Kashouba	Spanish tour, about September 1948	
	Théâtre de Monte-Carlo, 5 May 1932 (w.p.)	
sc. (1) V. Polunin (2) Prince Schervachidze, after Corot (in 1938 c. ex. Olga Larose)	Théâtre de Monte-Carlo, 12 April 1932; Alhambra Theatre, London, 4 July 1933; St James Theatre, New York, 8 January 1934; Theatre Royal, Adelaide, 13 October 1936 (II Co)	Revived from Diaghilev Ballet, 2 June 1909 (earlier *Chopiniana*, Maryinsky, St. Petersburg, 10 February 1907)
C. Bérard, c. for 2nd, 3rd + 4th movements ex. Karinska, for 1st + 5th ex. O. Larose, sc. ex. Prince A. Schervachidze	ROH, Covent Garden, London, 24 July 1936 (w.p.); Met., New York, 29 October 1936; His Majesty's Theatre, Melbourne, 1 October 1938	
Bakst	ROH, Covent Garden, London, 16 August 1935; Met., New York, 11 October 1935; His Majesty's Theatre, Melbourne, 12 December 1936 (II Co)	Revived from Diaghilev Ballet, 20 May 1912
Picasso	Auditorium, Chicago, 20 February 1934; St James Theatre, New York, 9 March 1934; ROH, Covent Garden, London, 19 June 1934	Revived from Diaghilev Ballet, 22 July 1919

ORIGINAL TITLE AND ALTERNATIVES	CHOREOGRAPHER	BOOK	COMPOSER
Union Pacific	Leonide Massine	A. MacLeish	N. Nabokov, based on folksongs of 1860
Valse triste	Nina Verchinina		Sibelius
Variations	Bronislava Nijinska		Beethoven, adapted by Vladimir Pohl
Yara	Vania Psota	G. de Almeida and Psota	Francisco Mignone
Yx-kik	Vania Psota	Maya-Quiché legend	R. and J. Castillo

Opera-ballets

Adriana Lecouvreur	Nijinska		M. Cilea
Aïda	Balanchine		Verdi
Armide	Psota		Gluck
Un Bal masqué	Massine		Verdi
Boris Godunov	Massine		Moussorgsky
Carmen	Balanchine		Bizet

Note: Fokine ballets were credited 'after Fokine' until his association with the de Basil company

DESIGN	THEATRE AND DATE	NOTES
c. I. Sharaff, sc. A. Johnson, c. ex. Valentine Kashuba	Forrest Theatre, Philadelphia, 6 April 1934 (w.p.); St James, New York, 25 April 1934; ROH, Covent Garden, London, 6 July 1934; His Majesty's Theatre, Melbourne, 3 November 1938	
Manuel Muntañola	Madrid, May 1948	Revived from Groupe de danses Nina Verchinina
G. Annenkov	Théâtre de Monte-Carlo, 7 April 1934	Revived from L'Opéra Russe à Paris, 1932
Candido Portinari, sc. ex. Jacob Anchutin	Teatro Municipal, São Paulo, 31 July 1946 (w.p.); Met., New York, 8 October 1946	
	Teatro Lux, Guatemala, December 1945	
	Théâtre de Monte-Carlo, 17 March 1934	Intermède in 3rd act: Amour – Chanova, Palas – Lipkovska, Venus – Corac, Junon – Crofton, Paris – Kochanovsky
	Théâtre de Monte-Carlo, 19 March 1932	Ensembles in 1st and 2nd acts
	Teatro Colón, 2 July 1943	Ensembles in 3rd act led by Moulin, Bechenova, Larkina, Tupine, MacKenzie
	Théâtre de Monte-Carlo, 9 March 1933	Ensemble divertissement in 3rd act
	Théâtre de Monte-Carlo, 18 March 1932	Ensemble polonaise
	Théâtre de Monte-Carlo, 24 March 1932	Ensemble séguedille in 2nd act

ORIGINAL TITLE AND ALTERNATIVES	CHOREOGRAPHER	BOOK	COMPOSER
Carmen	Psota		Bizet
Faust	Balanchine		Gounod
Fay-yen-fah	Balanchine		Joseph Redding
Hérodiade	Balanchine		Massenet
Lakmé	Balanchine		Delibes
Manon	Balanchine		Massenet
Une Nuit à Venise	Balanchine		J. Strauss
Orphée	Lichine and Lizzie Maudrick		Gluck
Patrie	Balanchine		Paladilhe

DESIGN	THEATRE AND DATE	NOTES
	Montevideo, 8 February 1944	Ensemble led by Morosova and Jasinsky
	Théâtre de Monte-Carlo, 13 February 1932	Staged for Goethe's centenary Kermesse ensemble in 2nd act
	Théâtre de Monte-Carlo, 8 March 1932	Ballet *divertissement* in 3rd scene led by Toumanova and Ladre in a Danse Chinoise and including a 'ballet volant'
	Théâtre de Monte-Carlo, 20 February 1932	Ensemble *divertissement* in 3rd act
	Théâtre de Monte-Carlo, 9 February 1932	Ensemble in 2nd act led by Marra
	Théâtre de Monte-Carlo, 28 February 1932	*Divertissement* in 3rd act led by Blinova and Woizikovsky
	Théâtre de Monte-Carlo, 2 February 1932	Ensemble in 1st act; Valse ensemble in 2nd act; in 3rd act, mazurka ensemble and Grand Pas Classique by Blinova, Toumanova, Slavinska, Morosova and Woizikovsky
	ROH, Covent Garden, London, 17 June 1937	Scene 2 of 2nd act by Lichine
	Théâtre de Monte-Carlo, 20 February 1932	Danse Napolitaine: Lipkovska and Guerard. Danse Indienne: *pas de quatre*. Danse Africaine: ensemble. Danse Flamande: *pas de quatre*. Danse Espagnole: Marra and Woizikovsky. *Ballet classique*: Blinova, Toumanova, Froman and ensemble. La Monégasque (music by R. Gunsbourg): ensemble

ORIGINAL TITLE AND ALTERNATIVES	CHOREOGRAPHER	BOOK	COMPOSER
La Périchole	Balanchine		Offenbach
Le Prophète	Balanchine		Meyerbeer
Rigoletto	Balanchine		Verdi
Roméo et Juliette	Balanchine		Gounod
Samson et Dalila	Balanchine		Saint-Saëns
Tales of Hoffmann (*Les Contes d'Hoffmann*)	Balanchine		Offenbach
Tannhäuser	Balanchine		Wagner
La Traviata	Balanchine		Verdi
La Traviata	Psota		Verdi
Turandot	Balanchine		Puccini
Play			
Les Amours du poète	Balanchine		author René Blum

DESIGN	THEATRE AND DATE	NOTES
	Théâtre de Monte-Carlo, 31 March 1932	Ensemble in 3rd act, including Juan Martinez trio of Spanish dancers
	Théâtre de Monte-Carlo, 26 January 1932	Village Dance in 1st act. Skating Ballet in 3rd act led by Marra and Woizikovsky. 'La Neige' (*ballet classique*) led by Blinova and Froman. Ensemble dance of girls with flowers in 4th act. Bacchanale led by Marra in 5th act
	Théâtre de Monte-Carlo, 23 February 1932	Ensemble *divertissement* in 1st act
	Théâtre de Monte-Carlo, 6 March 1932	Ensemble *divertissement* in 1st act
	Théâtre de Monte-Carlo, 11 February 1932	Ensemble in 1st act. Bacchanale led by Marra in 3rd act
	Théâtre de Monte-Carlo, 24 January 1932	Ballet in 2nd scene including Valse, *Pas de deux* by Blinova and Froman, Polka (*pas de deux*) by Marra and Woizikovsky, and ensemble Grande Valse
	Théâtre de Monte-Carlo, 21 January 1932	Paris version with full Venusberg ballet led by Lanina (Blinova) and Woizikovsky
	Théâtre de Monte-Carlo, 3 March 1932	Ensemble in 3rd act led by Lipkovska and Borovsky
	Teatro Colón, Buenos Aires, 28 May 1943	Ensemble led by Stepanova, Mackenzie, Tupine and Dokoudovsky
	Théâtre de Monte-Carlo, 21 February 1932	In 2nd act *Le Ballet Porcelaines de Chine*, ensemble led by Blinova, Toumanova and Woizikovsky
	Théâtre de Monte-Carlo, 5 January 1932	Scene with song 'Le Pauvre Pierre'

279

Divertissements

ch. = choreography, *mus.* = music; names of dancers appear in brackets

Waltz in D flat ch. Shabelevsky, *mus.* Chopin, costume Olga Larose (Baronova) Union House Theatre, Melbourne, 24 October 1938

Bolero ch. Dolin, *mus.* Ravel (Dolin) His Majesty's Theatre, Melbourne, 29 October 1938

Etude ch. Jasinsky, *mus.* Chopin (Etude Op. 10, No. 9) (Osato/Jasinsky) Polish Relief Gala, Theatre Royal, Sydney, 12 March 1940

Danse classique ch. Lifar, *mus.* Glinka (Stepanova) Polish Relief Gala, Theatre Royal, Sydney, 12 March 1940

Raymonda two variations, *mus.* Glazounov (Toumanova) Polish Relief Gala, Theatre Royal, Sydney, 12 March 1940

Raymonda variation, arr. Oboukhov, *mus.* Glazounov (Jasinsky) Polish Relief Gala, Theatre Royal, Sydney, 12 March 1940

Mazurka ch. Lifar, *mus.* J. Strauss (probably from *Le Danube bleu*) (Riabouchinska/Lichine) Polish Relief Gala, Theatre Royal, Sydney, 12 March 1940

Le Vent ch. Zverev, *mus.* Rimsky-Korsakov (probably from *Tsar Saltan*) (Nemtchinova) Polish Relief Gala, Theatre Royal, Sydney, 12 March 1940

Etude choreographic ch. Verchinina, *mus.* Handel (from *The Messiah*) (ensemble of eight girls) Polish Relief Gala, Theatre Royal, Sydney, 12 March 1940

Danse russe ch. Oboukhov, *mus.* Tchaikovsky (Grigorieva) Polish Relief Gala, Theatre Royal, Sydney, 12 March 1940

Rendezvous ch. George Gue, *mus.* Moskovsky (Svetlova/Panaiev) Polish Relief Gala, Theatre Royal, Sydney, 12 March 1940

Spanish Dance ch. Morena, *mus.* Jota de Aragonese (Stepanova) Polish Relief Gala, Theatre Royal, Sydney, 12 March 1940

Etude ch. Schwezov, *mus.* Chopin (Etude ?Op. 10, No. 12) (Schwezov) Polish Relief Gala, Theatre Royal, Sydney, 12 March 1940

Japanese Comic Dance ch. Yasoya Kineya, *mus.* Yakko San (Algeranov) Polish Relief Gala, Theatre Royal, Sydney, 12 March 1940

Capriccio ch. Zverev, *mus.* Saint-Saëns (probably Rondo Capriccioso) (Nemtchinova/Orlov) Polish Relief Gala, Theatre Royal, Sydney, 12 March 1940

Mazurka ch. Lazovsky, *mus.* Levandovsky (Morosova/Ladre/Lazovsky) Polish Relief Gala, Theatre Royal, Sydney, 12 March 1940

Snow Maiden solo *ch.* Massine, *mus.* Rimsky-Korsakov (Verchinina) (from *Soleil de nuit)* Charity gala, Sydney Conservatorium, 12 January 1940

Mazurka ch. Belsky, *mus.* Grovlez (Belsky) Gala Farewell, Theatre Royal, Sydney, 19 September 1940

O Men Futatsu original Japanese music (Algeranov) Gala Farewell,
Theatre Royal, Sydney, 19 September 1940

Dithyramb ch. Verchinina, *mus.* Margaret Sutherland (Verchinina) Gala
Farewell, Theatre Royal, Sydney, 19 September 1940

Offenbach Can-can ch. Dokoudovsky (Stroganova/Dokoudovsky)
S. America, 1943

Pas de trois ch. Dokoudovsky, *mus.* Shostakovich S. America, 1943

The Nutcracker pas de deux (Markova/Dolin) 51st Street Theatre, New York,
29 September 1946

Don Quixote pas de deux (Hightower/Eglevsky) 3 October 1946, (Hightower,
Skibine) 19 October 1946, 51st Street Theatre, New York

Black Swan pas de deux (Hightower/Eglevsky) 5 October 1946
(Stepanova/Tupine) another date, 51st Street Theatre, New York

Ballets projected but never staged by the company

1934
Rebus (Massine-Markevitch-H. Dimier)

Mozart *Symphony in G Minor* and Beethoven *Seventh Symphony*
(Massine)

1936
Le Baiser de la fée (Nijinska-Stravinsky)

Esquisse de musique (Lichine-Glazounov 'Four Seasons') (in rehearsal)

Les Fâcheux (Nijinska-Auric-Braque)

A ballet to music by John Field

Pulcinella (Massine-Stravinsky/Pergolesi-Picasso)

1937
La Chatte (no choreographer mentioned)

Le Triomphe de Neptune (Ashton-Berners)

Les Espiègleries d'Arlequin (Fokine)

1938
Le Triomphe de Neptune

La Foire Sorotchine (Lichine-Moussorgsky)

La Nymphe endormie (Fokine-Couperin-Derain)

A ballet on Polish national dances to Chabrier

Paquita (Petipa-Minkus) (in rehearsal)

1939
Les Fâcheux

Fairy Doll (Clustine-Bayer)

Le Train bleu (Nijinska-Milhaud)

Bacchanale (Fokine-Wagner)

281

1940
Mirage (Lichine-Debussy) (in rehearsal)

1941
V – for Victory (Lichine)

1948
The Abyss (Dokoudovsky-A. Tcherepnine) (completed but not staged)
Niobe (3 acts, designs completed by de Chirico)

1947
Theme and Variations (Taras-Tchaikovsky)

1949
Istar (Dokoudovsky)
Celestina (Dokoudovsky-Pedrell)

Dancers

Dancers who appeared with de Basil's Ballets Russes

f. = female, *m.* = male, where no first name is known, except in the case of a Russian name that is indicative of sex

'Aus II Co' and *'Eur II Co'* indicate the second company in Australia and Europe

Where a territory is indicated, there is no evidence that the dancer appeared elsewhere with the company, although he or she may have done

r.n. = real name, where this differs from a stage name

Where a dancer is better known by a later name (e.g. Tamara Grigorieva who danced originally as Tamara Sidorenko), full particulars are under that entry with a cross-reference from the earlier name

g.a. = guest artist

Name(s)	*Dates with the company*
Abricossova, Kira	1934–9
Adama, Richard	April 1948–9 (Spain, etc.)
r.n. Holt	
Adjemova, Sirène	1946–7 (USA)
Adrianova, Anna	January 1934–38
r.n. Bridge, Shirley	1941
Alexandrov, Gregory, Grisha	1933–43 (asst. *régisseur* Australia 1940)
r.n. Roscupkin	
Algeranov, H.	1933–4
r.n. Essex, Algernon Harcourt	1937–42
Alonso, Alberto	1935–December 1940
r.n. Alonso y Rayneri	1941 (Cuba) *g.a.*
Andahazy, Lorand	1936–41
Andreiev, Savva	1936–7 (*Aus II Co*)
	1937–8 (*Eur II Co*)
	1940–2
Angelova, Nada	1947

Antonova, Hélène	1936–7 (*Aus II Co*)
	1937–8 (*Eur II Co*)
Arapov, Vladimir	1947–9
Armour, Thomas	1936–7 (*Aus II Co*)
	1937–8 (*Eur II Co*)
Arova, Sonia	1951–2 (UK)
r.n. Errio	
Artois, Jeanne	1948–9 (Spain etc.)
r.n. Beazley	
Assenkova, Katia	1938–9
r.n. Stevenson, Dorothy	
Azrova, Maria	1939–41
r.n. Isaacs, Fay	
Balanchine, George	1932 (Monte Carlo, one performance
r.n. Balanchivadze	only 17 January)
Baline, Valentin	1936–7 (*Aus II Co*)
	1937–8 (*Eur II Co*)
Banks, Margaret	1946–7 (USA)
Barlow, Ann	1946–7
Barnett, Robert	April 1948–9 (Spain etc.)
Barneva, Olga	1947–9
Baronova, Irina	1932–9
	November 1940–41
	1946 (S. America, *g.a.*)
Barkova, Dorothy, Lee, Lina	1941–3
r.n. Buckridge	
Bartholin, Birger	1936–7 (*Aus II Co*)
Beatty, Biddy	1951–2 (UK)
Bechenova, Tatiana	1939–47
Bell, Robert – see Belsky, Boris	
Belsky, Boris	1935–41
r.n. Bell, Robert	1947 (programmed as Bell, Robert)
	(asst. to *régisseur général*)
Beltchenko *f*	1937–8 (*Eur II Co*)
Bentley, Patricia	1951–2 (UK)
Berry, Joyce	1933
r.n. Thornton-Berry, Joyce	
Blanc, Kyra	1932
Blinova, Valentina	1932 (programmed as Lanina-Blinova,
r.n. Lanina-Blinova	Valentina, at times)
	1936–7 (*Aus II Co*)
	1937–8 (*Eur II Co*)

Bobek, S. *m*	1947
Bogardis, Dominie	1934
Bolin, Marianne	1948–9 (Spain etc.)
Bondireva, Irina	1936–7 (*Aus II Co*)
	1937–8 (*Eur II Co*)
Bordes, Salvador	1946–7
Borovansky, Edouard	1933–9
r.n. Screcek-Borovansky	
Borovsky, Metek	1932
Bounina, Kira	1939–41
r.n. Hunt, Jean	
Bouslov, Serge	1934–9
Boyer, Monique	1948–9 (Spain etc.)
Branitska, Nathalie	1932–6
	1936–7 (*Aus II Co*)
Britneva, Maria	1933, 1934, 1937 (London)
Bronley, Noël *f*	1951–2 (UK)
Burke, Anthony	1951–2 (UK)
Candael, Marina	1948–9 (Spain etc.)
Canonov, Thomas	1934
r.n. Cannon	
Carter, Jack, Jak	1951–2 (UK)
Carter, Mela – see Kalinovska, Xenia	
Celada, Raul, Raoul	1946–7
Chabelska, Galina	1932–8
Chamié, Tatiana	1932–7
Chanova, Ruth	1934 (Monte Carlo)
	1937–8 (*Eur II Co*)
Charaska, Adèle	1946–7
Chatalova	1937–8 (*Eur II Co*)
Chaurand *m*	1947
Christie, Elizabeth	1951–2 (UK)
Clark, Cherry	1947
Claus, Jack	1947
Clausen, Bergljot	1947
Cobos, Antonia	1946–7 (USA) *g.a.*
r.n. Nahl, Phyllis	
Coenca *f*	1948–9 (Spain etc.)
Conlon, Natalie	1942–7
(alternative name Clare, Natalie)	

Constantine, Hélène	1941 (as Muselle)
r.n. Muselle (or Musil)	1947
Coudine, Dimitri	1934
r.n. Coudy, Douglas	
(alternative name Kydine)	
Couprina, Lydia	1939–43
r.n. Cooper, Phillida	
Damon, Joan	1948–9 (Spain etc.)
Danielian, Leon	1941
Danilova, Alexandra	1933–8
Deacon, Olive	1937–8 (*Eur II Co*)
Delarova, Eugénie	1933–8
Denisova, Alexandra	1938–December 1940
r.n. Meyers, Patricia Denise	1941 (Cuba) *g.a.*
(alternative name Denise,	
Patricia)	
Diakonova	1937–8 (*Eur II Co*)
Dieken, Sandra	1948–9 (Spain etc.)
Dimidova, Mona	1936–7 (*Aus II Co*) (as Ducret)
r.n. Ducret, Mouna	1937–8 (*Eur II Co*) (as Dimidova)
(alternative name Ducrailova,	
Hélène)	
Dimina, Mira	1935–36
r.n. Parker, Madeleine	1936 (*Aus II Co*)
Dokoudovska, Tatiana	1947
Dokoudovsky, Vladimir	1942–52
Dolin, Anton	1933
(original name Healey-Kay,	1938–9
Patrick)	1946–7 (USA) *g.a.*
Dolotine, Jashf	1932–4
r.n. Crandall, Joseph	1936–7 (*Aus II Co*)
	1937–8 (*Eur II Co*)
Dorina	1937
Doubrovska, Felia	1932
r.n. Dluzhnevska	1937 (London) *g.a.*
Ducret, Mouna – see Dimidova,	
Mona	
Dukassova	1937–8 (*Eur II Co*)
Dunaev, Oleg	1941
Dwyer *f*	1946–7
Dzikovsky, Edouard	1937–9
Eglevsky, André	1933–4

	1946–7 (USA) *g.a.*
Evans, Jane	1951–2 (UK)
Facer, Michael	1951–2 (UK)
Farmer *f*	1946–7
Farrell, Raymond	1948–9 (Spain etc.)
Fedorova, Anna	1932
Ferguson, Mildred	1946–7
Fernandez, Royes	1946–7
Ferran, José	1948–9 (Spain etc.)
Francis, Gillian	1951–2 (UK)
Franco, Marilia	1944–7
r.n. Ferraz	
Frank, Alexis	1936–7 (*Aus II Co*)
Froman, Valentin	1932
	1936–7 (*Aus II Co*)
	1937–8 (*Eur II Co*)
Fuentes *m*	1948–9 (Spain etc.)
Garina, Mary	1936–7 (*Aus II Co*)
(alternative name Guerard,	
Margot)	
Gavrovsky	1937–8 (*Eur II Co*)
Gay, Anna	1946–7
Gehrig *f*	1946–7
Georgieva, E.	1936–7 (*Aus II Co*)
Gewurtz, Mattlyn	1946–7
(alternative names Gavers,	
Gevaertz)	
Gnatt, Poul	1951–2 (UK)
Gollner, Nana	1936
	1942–3
Golovina, Alexandra	1943–7
r.n. Galvez, Elsa Garcia	
Golovina, Nina	1936
r.n. Godby, Gladys	1936–7 (*Aus II Co*)
	1939–41
Gontcharova, Marguerite	1939–42
Gordon, Iain	1951–2 (UK)
Gordon, William, Glen	1947–9
r.n. Stott-Williams, Gordon	1951–2 (UK)
Gordova	1937
Gould, Diana	1935 (London)
Gregory, John	1947

287

Gregory, Tony	1951–2 (UK)
Grieg, Leon	1951–2 (UK)
Grigoriev, Serge	1935–40
Grigorieva, Tamara	1933–44 (programmed as Sidorenko
r.n. Sidorenko	before 1935)
Grinwis, Paul	1947–9
Grossen, Vanda	1936
	1936–7 (*Aus II Co*)
	1937–8 (*Eur II Co*)
	1938–9
Gueneva, Willy *f*	1933
Guerard, Margot – see Garina,	
Mary	
Guerard, Roland	1932–6
	1936–7 (*Aus II Co*)
Gutierrez, Carmen	1946–7
Harvey, Robert	1951–2 (UK)
Hawkins *f*	1948–9 (Spain etc.)
Herklots, Silvia	1951–2 (UK)
Herrera *f*	1946–7 (USA)
Herrera, Reynaldo	1946–7 (USA)
Hiden, Georgia	1946–7 (USA)
Hightower, Rosella	1946–7 (USA)
Hinton, Paula	1951–2 (UK) *g.a.*
Holt, Iris	1946–52
Hosking, Loveday	1951–2 (UK)
Howard, Andrée	1933 (Monte Carlo)
r.n. Barton, Louise	
Howard, Mary Jane	1951–2 (UK)
Hoyer, Jean, Jan	1932–6
	1936–7 (*Aus II Co*)
	1938–9
	1947
Ignatov, Vladimir	1939
Inglesby, Mona	1939 (London)
r.n. Kimberley	
Irman, Vladimir	1939–43
r.n. Snaksarev	
Ismailov, Serge	October 1933–41
r.n. Berlinraout	1946–7 (USA)
Ivangin, Nicolas	1939–40

Ivanov	1937–8 (*Eur II Co*)
	1938–41
Jasinsky, Roman	1932
	October 1933–47
Jeanmaire, Renée, Zizi	1947
Joukovska, Jania	1948–9 (Spain etc.)
Joukovsky, Anatole	1948–9 (Spain etc.)
Kalichevsky, Vladimir	1947
Kalinovska, Xenia	1936–7 (*Aus II Co*)
r.n. Carter, Pamela Mela	1937–8 (*Eur II Co*)
	1947 (London *g.a.* as Carter, Mela)
Karina, Elena	1947–9
Katcharov, Michel	1932–7
Katchourovsky, Leonide	1932
Kauflin, Jack	1946–7 (USA)
Kschessinska, Mathilde	1936 (London *g.a.* one performance only, 14 July)
Kelepovska, Nathalie	1935
Kern, Marita	1947–9
Kervily, Irène	1932
King, June	1951–2 (UK)
Kirsova, Hélène, Lena	1932–4
r.n. Wittrup, Ellen	1936–7 (*Aus II Co*)
Klausen, Werner	1951–2 (UK)
Klimov, Pierre	1947
Kobseva, Olga	1933–4
Komarova, Hélène	1947
Koon, Alpheus	1946–7 (USA)
Korjinska, Marija	1936
	1936–7 (*Aus II Co*)
Koslov, Alexis	1935–8
Koslovsky	1937–8 (*Eur II Co*)
Kosmovska, Irina	1937–9
r.n. Popov	
Koumani, Maya	1951–2 (UK)
Kouznetsova, Raisse, Raya	1937–9
r.n. Hirsch, Raisse	
Krassnova, A.	1933
	1936
Ladre, Marian	1932–47
	(1945–7 *régisseur*)

289

Lander, Toni	1951–2 (UK, *g.a.*)
r.n. Pihl Petersen, Toni	
Lanese, Lillian	1946–7 (USA)
Lanina-Blinova, Valentina – see	
Blinova	
Larina, Hélène	1933–4
Larkina, Moussia	1941–7
r.n. Larkin, Moscelyne	
Larsen, Irene	1946–7
Laurence, Kenneth	1948–9 (Spain etc.)
Lavrov, Mischa	1937
Lavrova, Dora	1935–6
Lavrova, Irina	1939–42
r.n. Tweedie, Valrene	
Lazovsky, Yura	1935–41
Lendrum, Anna, Joan	1951–2 (UK)
Lenska	1937–8 (*Eur II Co*)
Leonov	1937–8 (*Eur II Co*)
Leontieva, Anna	1936–41
Lerina, Lina	1938–9
r.n. Leri, Jacqueline	
Leskova, Tatiana	1939–43
Lesprilova, Duscha	1934
r.n. Bamberger, Helen	
(alternative name Stuart, Helen)	
Lewenhaupt, Karen	1951–2 (UK)
Lichine, David	1932–41
r.n. Lichtenstein	1947 (London)
	1948 (Spain)
Lifar, Serge	1939–March 1940 (Australia)
Lineva, Hélène	1939–40 (Australia)
r.n. Lee, Alison	
Lipatov, Serge	1932–8
Lipkovska, Tatiana	1932–7
Lipska, Vera	1936–7 (*Aus II Co*)
	1937–8 (*Eur II Co*)
Lloyd, Barbara	1947–9
Lorrain, Roland	1946–7
Loubert, Gladys	1947
Lunina, L.	1934
r.n. Rothney, Lorna	
Luthi *m*	1948–9 (Spain etc.)

Lvova, Ludmila	1936–41
r.n. Low, Betty	
Lyman, Louise	1932
Lynova, Beatrice	1941–3
McBride, Pat	1946–7 (USA)
(N.B. this is not the better-known Patricia McBride of New York City Ballet)	
McDowell, Norman	1951–2 (UK)
MacKenzie, Kenneth	1940–7
Makaiev, Ivan	1941
Mann, Grace	1947
Mannechez, Jacqueline	1951–2 (UK)
Markova, Alicia	1946–7 (USA) *g.a.*
r.n. Marks, Lilian Alicia	
Marra, Eleonora	1932–7
Massine, Leonide	1933–January 1938
Matouchak, Narcisse – see Matouchevsky	
Matouchevsky, Narcisse	1933–43 (programmed as
(alternative name Matouchak)	Matouchak from 1938)
May, Herida	1951–2 (UK)
r.n. Cammish, Ivy	
Mayne, Olgalita	1947
Melnikova, Natasha	1939–42
r.n. Moulin, Thérèse	
Mestre, Gloria	1946–7
Meyer *f*	1946–7 (USA)
Michel, Lola	1936
Michkovitch, Milorad	1947
Milenko, Serge	1946–7
Miltonova, Anna	1942–7
Moncion, Francisco	1946–7 (USA) *g.a.*
Monson, Helga	1947
Morosova, Olga	1932–8
r.n. Verchinina, Olga	end 1939–49
Morris, June	1946–7
Moulin, Geneviève	1939–47
(briefly given stage name of Zlatina, Lubov)	
Mounsey, Yvonne – see Zarova, Irina	

Mouravieva, Tatiana	1936–7 (*Aus II Co*)
Muselle, Hélène – see Constantine	
Natova, Nina	1936–7 (*Aust II Co*)
Nelidova, Vera	December 1933–40
r.n. Cuff, Betty	
Nemtchinova, Vera	1937–8 (*Eur II Co*)
	1938
	1939–40 (Australia)
	1940–1 *g.a.*
Newstead, June	1948–9 (Spain etc.)
Nicolaiev, Vassily	1939–42
r.n. Tupine, Vassily	
Nikitina, Alice	1937 (London) *g.a.*
Novikova, Marina	1937–8
Nygren, James	1946–7
Obidenna, Lara, Illaria	1932–47
Olena, Yvonne	1947
Olrich, April	1945–7
r.n. Oelrichs	
Orlov, Nicholas	1939–41
	1947–9
Orlova, Sonia	1937–41
r.n. Gronau, Sonia	
Orskov, Anker	1951–2 (UK)
Osato, Sono	1934–41
Oxvig *f*	1948–9 (Spain etc.)
Ozoline, Arved	1936
Paget, John	1951–2 (UK)
Panaiev, Michel	1939–41
Patterson, Yvonne	1946–7
Pereyra, Carlota	1946–7
Petersen, Kenneth	1947
Petrov, Paul	1932–43
r.n. Pedersen	
Platov, Marc	1935–8
r.n. le Plat, Marcel	
(alternative name Platt, Marc)	
Polouchina, Hélène	1936–7 (*Aus II Co*)
Popova, Nina	1939–41
Poswolsky, Mary	1937–8 (*Eur II Co*)
Powers, Regis	1946–7
Priour, Ted	1947

Psota, Vania	1933–6
	1942–7
Radova, Nina	1935–7
r.n. Smith/Schmidt,	
Vivian/Vivienne)	
Raievska, Nina	1933–4
	1936–7 (*Aus II Co*)
	1937–8 (*Eur II Co*)
Razoumova, Galina	1933–41
r.n. Sidorenko	
Reznikov, Michel	1947
Riabouchinska, Tatiana	1932–41
	1947 (London)
	1948 (Spain)
Ristic, Milos	1936–7 (*Aus II Co*)
	1937–8 (*Eur II Co*)
	1939
Roberts, Olga	1947
Roje, Ana	1938–9
(alternative name Roy)	
Rollatsch, Janice	1946–7 (USA)
Rörvig, Xenia, Vibeke	1937–8 (*Eur II Co*)
Ross, David	1951–2 (UK)
Rostov, Dimitri	1936–42
r.n. Kulcizky	
Rostova, Lubov	1932–7
r.n. Kylberg, Lucienne	
Roudin, Pennie	1946–7 (USA)
Roussova, Lelia	1935–6
r.n. Russell	1936–7 (*Aus II Co*)
	1937–9
Rovida, Enrique	1942
Roy, Ana – see Roje	
Rueda, Nivardo	1946–7 (USA)
Runanine, Borislav	1937–41
Rupe, Marjorie	1946–7 (USA)
Russon, Janet	1951–2 (UK)
Rykov, Ivan, Vania, Jean	1934 (Monte Carlo)
	1936–7 (*Aus II Co*)
Sabo, Rozsika	1946–7 (USA)
(alternative name Szabo)	
Sand, Inge	1951–2 (UK)

Sanina, Maria	1938 (*Eur. II Co*)
r.n. Kelly, Brigitte	1938–9
Savitska	1933
Scarpa, Anna Tina	1936–7 (*Aus II Co*)
(alternative name Scarpova)	1937–8 (*Eur II Co*)
Schwezov, Igor	1939–41
Scorer, Betty – see Souvorova,	
Elizabeth	
Scott, Betty	1948–9 (Spain etc.)
Scott, Brian	1951–2 (UK)
Seibert, Wallace	1946–7 (USA)
Semenov, Simon	1935–6
	1938–9
	1947
Semenova, Tatiana	1933–4
Sergava, Katherine	1941
Sergievsky, Orest	1941
	1946–7 (USA)
Serov	1946–7 (USA)
Serova, Lisa	1934–9
r.n. Ruxton, Elizabeth	
Serova, Olga	1941
Severskaya, Anna	1936–7 (*Aus II Co*)
r.n. Stafford-Northcote	
Shabelevsky, Yurek	1932–November 38
	1941 *g.a.*
	1943 *g.a.*
Shaievsky, Valery	1936–7 (*Aus II Co*)
	1937–8 (*Eur II Co*)
	1938–9
Sharova, Kira	1941–2
Shea, Mary Jane	1948–9 (Spain etc.)
Sidorenko, Galina – see	
Razoumova, Galina	
Sidorenko, Tamara – see	
Grigorieva, Tamara	
Sidorova, Felia	1939
r.n. Finklea, Tula Ellice	
(alternative names Charisse,	
Cyd and Istomina, Maria)	
Silva, Ricardo	1946–7 (USA)

Skibine, George	1939–41
	1946–7 (USA)
Skouratov, Vladimir	1947
Slavinska, Hélène, Helia	1932
Slavinsky, Thadee, Tadeo	1936–7 (*Aus II Co*)
Smirnov	1948–9 (Spain etc.)
Smirnov, Anatole	1934–5
Smirnova, Nadia	1937
	1939–40
	1947
Sobichevsky, Edouard	1937–9
Sobinova, Natasha	1938–40
r.n. Deveson, Rosemary	
Sokolova, Lydia	1936 (London) *g.a.* one
r.n. Munnings, Hilda	performance only 14 July)
Solis, Jose	1946–7 (USA)
Sonne, Doris	1932
Sorina	1933–4
Souverbie *f*	1948–9 (Spain etc.)
Souvorova, Elizabeth	1936–7 (*Aus II Co*)
r.n. Scorer, Betty	1937–8 (*Eur II Co*) occasionally
	programmed as Scorer
Spirka, Arnold	1936–7 (*Aus II Co*)
Spurgeon, Jack	1937–8 (*Eur II Co*)
(alternative name Spur, Jan)	1951–2 (UK)
Stambaugh, Guy	1947–9
Starr, Dolores	1948–9 (Spain etc.)
Steele, Barbara	1941–3
Stemmler, Lee *f*	1951–2 (UK)
Stepanova, Alexandra	1936–7 (*Aus II Co*)
	1937–8 (*Eur II Co*)
Stepanova, Irène	1932, 1933 (Monte Carlo)
Stepanova, Tatiana	1937–47
Strakhova, Kira	1935–9
r.n. Thal, Patricia	
Strakhova, Natalie	1932
Stroganova, Nina	1942–7
r.n. Ström, Nina Rigmor	1948–52
Strogova, Paulina	1934–5
r.n. Hythe, Prudence	
(alternative name Hyman,	
Prudence)	

Svetlova, Marina	1939–41
r.n. Hartmann, Yvette	
Swatzel, William	1946–7 (USA)
(alternative name Glenn, William)	
Talina	1935
Tallchief, Marjorie	1946–7 (USA)
Tarakanova, Nina	1933–4
	1947 (London) *g.a.*
Taras, John	1946–7 (*régisseur*, ballet master)
Tchernicheva, Lubov	1935–48 (teacher, 1932–52)
Tchinarova, Tamara	1932
	September 1933–6
	1936–7 (*Aus II Co*)
	1937–8 (*Eur II Co*)
	1938–9
Terekov, Miguel	1944–7
Thiel *f*	1947
Thomas, Grace	1947
Tibor, Yvonne	1941
Torina	1932
Toumanova, Tamara	1932
r.n. Khacidovitch	September 1933–7
	1939–41
Toumine, Sviatoslav	1939–41
Tovarov, Dimitri	1935–6
	1936–7 (*Aus II Co*)
	1937–8 (*Eur II Co*)
Trefilov, Louis	1941–3
r.n. Trapaga, Luis	
Tresahar, Edna	1932–9
Tripolitov, Nicolas	1948–9 (Spain etc.)
Tripolitova, Xenia	1948–9 (Spain etc.)
Tucker, Dorothy	1946–7 (USA)
Tucker, Joan	1951–2 (UK)
Tupine, Vassily – see Nikolaiev	
Tupine, Oleg	1938–47
Tweedie, Valrene – see Lavrova, Irina	
Unguer, Serge	1936–7 (*Aus II Co*)
	1937–8 (*Eur II Co*)
	1939–41
Valenska	1932

Valevska, Olga	1936–7 (*Aus II Co*)
r.n. Williams, Audrey Wilson	
Van Alen *m*	1948–9 (Spain etc.)
Varicchio, Adelaide	1946–7 (USA)
Vassilevsky	1951–2 (UK)
Vassiliev	1948–9 (Spain etc.)
	1951–2 (UK)
Vassilkovsky, Kiril	1939–52
r.n. Vernstam, Cyril	
Vecchio, Alberto	1946–7 (USA)
Verchinina, Nina	1932–7
	1939–41
	1946–7 *g.a.*
	1948–9 (Spain etc.)
Vernon *f*	1947
Vernova	1939
Vicary, Rosalind	1951–2 (UK)
Vickers, Frederick	1951–2 (UK)
Vladimirov, Serge	1936–7 (*Aus II Co*)
	1937–8 (*Eur II Co*)
Vlassov, Anton	1937–41
r.n. Weisser, Robert	
(alternative name Pagent, Robert)	
Volkova, Anna	1933–43
Voronova, Hélène	1948–9 (Spain etc.)
Vostriakov	1937
Warwick, Stephen	1947
Wassilieva, Irina	1936–7 (*Aus II Co*)
	1938–9
West *m*	1946–7 (USA)
Winter, Marjan	1936–7 (*Aus II Co*)
	1937–8 (*Eur II Co*)
Woizikovska, Sonia	1936–7 (*Aus II Co*)
	1937–8 (*Eur II Co*)
Woizikovsky, Léon	1932–4
	1936–7 (*Aus II Co*)
	1937–8 (*Eur II Co*)
Wolff, Robert	1941–3
Wolska, Hélène	1938–9
r.n. Forbes-Jones, Bessie	
Worrall, Olga	1946–7 (USA)

297

Wust, Waldemar	1937
Yavorska	1935
Youchkevitch, Nina	1934 (Monte Carlo)
	1936
	1936–7 (*Aus II Co*)
Young, Leo	1936–7 (*Aus II Co*)
Youskevitch, Igor	1936–7 (*Aus II Co*)
	1937–8 (*Eur II Co*)
Zalipskaya, Lolla, Lila	1941 (USA)
alternative name Zali	
Zarevsky	1946–7 (USA)
Zarova, Irina	1939–41
r.n. Leiberandt, Yvonne	
(alternative stage name	
Mounsey, Yvonne)	
Zeglovsky, Valentin	1936–9
Zlatina, Lubov – see Moulin,	
Geneviève	
Zonova, Cecily	1937 (*Eur II Co*)
r.n. Robinson	
Zorina, Vera	1934–6
r.n. Hartwig, Eva Brigitte	
Zoritch, George	1935–8

Dancers who appeared with L'Opéra Russe à Paris
(* indicates those who later appeared with the de Basil Ballet)

(F)

Adamian, C. Baudier, *Joyce Berry, Bolotina, *Tatiana Chamie, Cherbatcheva, *Diakonova, *Felia Doubrovska, Ficher, M. Filippova, Irene Gjebina, Lya Gjebina, Jureneva, Klemetzkaya, Leff, *Tatiana Lipkovska(ya), *Eleonora Marra, Matvjeva, *Lola Michel, Miklachevskaya, *Vera Nemtchinova (*g.a.*), Bronislava Nijinska, Panatchevskaya (or Panatchevnaya), Claudia Pavlova, Lidia Pavlova, L. Polesskaya, Savelieva, Ludmilla Schollar, *Tatiana Semenova, Mona Stal, Tchistiakova, Thoressen, N. Tichonova, *Edna Tresahar, Vorobieva, Z. Will

(M)

*H. Algeranov, Archambault, Bologovsky, *Anton Dolin (*g.a.*), *Valentin Froman, Grey, *Serge Grigoriev, Aubrey Hitchins, *Jean Hoyer, *Serge Ignatov, *Leonid Katchourovsky, Korvsky, Eugene Lapitzkij, *David Lichtenstein (Lichine), Lissanevitch, Grant Mouradov, N. Moysenko, Anatole Oboukhov, Boris Romanov, Roudine, Schwetzov, Sergueev,

298

*Smirnov, Tchigrine, Thariat, *Serge Unger, Anatole Vilzak, *Léon Woizikovsky (*g.a.*)

Dancers who appeared with the de Basil Ballet only in the special Nijinska season in Monte Carlo in 1934

(F)

Choukina, Mia Corac (Slavenska), Kathleen Crofton, M. Filippova, Anna Istomina (N.B. not Audree Thomas who was known by this name from 1940 with other companies)

(M)

Rollo Gamble, M. Geier, V. Karnetsky, Boris Kniasev, Vadim Kochanovsky, Valdemar Kostenko, Savitsky, Alfred Suterov, Arthur Sutherland, Vijanek

The role of the Child in *La Concurrence* was danced in various countries by the following dancers, some of whom had only the one named role and so do not appear on the main list of dancers. The year quoted is the first known appearance:
Irène Stepanova (Monte Carlo 1932); Maria Britneva (London 1933); Tatiana Stepanova (Paris 1936); T. Tcharova (Joy Camden-Pratt) (London 1936); Patience Ditchfield (Diana Field) (London 1938); June Mackay (Melbourne 1938); Leona Paddison (Sydney 1938); Pamela Bromley-Smith (Australia 1938); Bunty Kelly (London 1939)

Dancers of the Teatro Colón, Buenos Aires, or the Montevideo theatre or others who appeared with the de Basil Ballet only in Central and South America between 1942 and 1946

(F)

COLÓN Isabel Admetlla, Esmeralda Agoglia, Mura Astrova, Julia Barreiros, Catalina Cresto, Nelida Cendra, Dora Del Grande, Leticia de la Vega, Maria Della Garcia, Estela (?) Deporte, Esther de la Zerda, Beatriz Ferrari, Amelia Fanstein, Esther Gnavi, Victoria Garabato, Adela (or Teresa) Goldkuhl, Gloria Kazda, Amalia Lozano, Katherine Levers, Lilia (or Maria L.) Lemos, Milena, Josefina Molino, Lida Martinoli, Elena Peréz, Maria Ruanova, Angeles Ruanova, Matilde Ruanova, Maria Schein, Eugenia Szapoval, Ana (Hilda) Yussem, Blanca Zirmaya
MONTEVIDEO Alvarez, Banegas, Balbi, Brotska, Cuschnir, Casella, Chalinska, de la Sierra, Demichelli, Galvan, Grondona (two), Gubitosi (two), Larenska, Sagrera
OTHERS Leda Yuqui (Rivas), Nelly Hawtrey, Kyra Nelidova (Nelly Laport), Diana Markova, Eva Serova, Marie-Jeanne, Anna Leonidova, Irinova

(M)

COLÓN Roberto Campos, Alberto Castaño, Julio Deporte, ?Eduardo

Deporte, Eugenio Gonzales Diaz, Angel Eleta, Wilfred Fedorov, Victor Ferrari, David Grey, Emilio Heyberger, Louis Le Bercher, Carlos Leite, Roy Milton, Manuel Molina, Francisco Pinter, Elbio Reyes, Alberto Siccardi, Armando Varela, Cesar Yurekov
MONTEVIDEO Dante Fantini, Hery Thomson, Sulevich, Vasques
OTHERS Fernando Alonso (*g.a.*), James Upshaw, Oriansky, Adrian Orlov

Dancers who are said to have appeared temporarily with the de Basil Ballet in the 1934 New York season and possibly on tour at that time

(F)

Clausina (Stella Clausen), Dorothy Cutler, Elena de Rivas, Dolova, Duncan, Farina, Fonareva (?Nina Fonarov), Ruth Haidt, Irinova, Klassova, Levina, Magova, Martinova, Noskova, Petrova, Tatianova, Nina (Tatiana) Vitneva, Vodova, Vortova, Voudina, Nina Whitney

(M)

Baratov, Leon Barté, Nicolas Daks, Dollarov (?William Dollar), Nicolas Gelikhovsky, Val Gueral, Hal Haskins, George Kiddon, Leon (Anatole) Livov (Leon Fokine), Nikov, Povich, Robinov, Robel, Val Strechnev, P. Weine (Allan Wayne)

Dancers reported to have appeared briefly with the de Basil Ballet, mostly in the *corps de ballet* or as extras in various parts of the world

(F)

Marilyn Burn (Australia 1938–9), Joanna Bowers (UK), Jean Brandon (Australia), Edna Busse (Australia), Cherlova (Melbourne 1937), Chelska (London 1934), Roy Currie (Melbourne 1940), Peggy Chauncey (Petrova) (Australia 1936–7), Ludmilla Chiriaev (1936–7), Patricia Cape (Australia), Maria de Baroncelli (Europe 1947), Jean Edwards (Australia), Ann Horn (Paris 1949), Joan Hope (Australia), Angela Hellas (London 1939), Anna Ivanova (London 1934), Delysia Jacobs (London 1947), Diana Kelly (King) (Paris 1949), Nancy Knott (USA 1934–5), Catherine and Dorothie Littlefield, Marie Mack (Australia 1938–9), Anne Mackintosh (Anne Chloe Elder) (Australia), Marianne Martin (Australia), Sheila Meyers (London 1939), Delfina Morales (Paris 1935), Nina Minakova (USA 1937), Sandra Molostvova (London 1933), Mourova (Australia 1936–7), Maia Nievska, Kyra Nijinska (London 1933), Poida (London 1934), Christine Rosslyn (Paris 1949), Winifred Sharpe (Australia 1938–9), Lindsay Shaw (Australia), Pat Vaughn (Paris 1949), Natasha Withall (Australia 1938–9), Alta Warshavska (Chicago 1935), Juliana Yenakieva (1942), Maria Valeska

(M)

Angelo Andes, Bryan Ashbridge (Melbourne 1940), Igor Barczinsky (1939), John Byron (London 1934), Juan Corelli (Barcelona 1947–8), Georges

Fostikov (Tomin), Dennis Grey (Nelson Rodrigues), Paul Granitch (Paris 1949), Fernau Hall (London 1947), Travis Kemp, Lesterov (London 1934), Yeichi Nimura (1935), Philippe Perottet (Australia 1940), Rex Reid (Australia 1938), Vassilie Trunov (Australia 1936–7), Vladimir Valentinov (Paul Valentine/William Daixel) (USA 1934–5), Trafford Whitelock (Australia 1938–9)

Conductors

1932   Marc-César Scotto (Monte Carlo only), Roger Desormière, Pierre Kolpikov

1933   Desormière (Paris and Monte Carlo), Kolpikov, Efrem Kurtz (from the Alhambra London season), Antal Dorati (from November)

1934   Kurtz, Dorati

1935   Kurtz, Dorati, Rudolf Kwasnica (asst. at Covent Garden); Sir Thomas Beecham conducted the opera *Prince Igor* and the revival of *Thamar* at Covent Garde; in Philadelphia, Leopold Stokowsky was guest conductor

1936   Kurtz, Dorati. With II Co in Australia, Jascha Horenstein and Ivan Clayton

1937   With II Co in Europe, Ivan Clayton; Kurtz, Dorati; Beecham conducted *Les Dieux mendiants* at Covent Garden in San Francisco, Pierre Monteux was guest conductor

1938   Dorati: in London, also Georg Solti, Franz Allers, Ivan Clayton; in Philadelphia, Eugene Ormandy and Saul Caston as guest conductors; in Australia, Dorati and Vladimir Launitz

1939   Dorati, Launitz

1939–40 In Australia, Dorati and Max Goberman

1941   Dorati; in New York, also Mois Zlatin; Stravinsky as guest conductor for *Balustrade*; in Washington, Alexander Smallens; in Chicago, Eugene Fuerst

1942   Fuerst; Hector Iglesias Villoud as guest conductor for *El Malón*

1943   Fuerst; at the Colón, Juan Jose Castro, Roberto Kinsky, Albert Wolff, Cesar de Mendoza; William McDermott; Walter Duclos

1944   Fuerst, McDermott, Carlos Zozaya

1945   McDermott

1946   McDermott; in New York also Mois Zlatin, Dorati, Cesar de Mendoza and Robert Zeller as guest conductors.

302

CONDUCTORS

1947   In New York, Mendoza and Zeller; in London, Anatole Fistoulari
and Richard Beck; in Paris, Walter Duclos, Rudolf Kwasnica

1948   In Spain etc. Joaquin Gasca, Steven Candael, Janis Suchovs

1951–2 In the UK, Joseph Horowitz, Colin Davis, Alfred Barker

Books and Periodicals

other than those listed under Notes and References

Amberg, George, *Ballet: The Emergence of an American Art*, pub. Mentor Books, New York, 1949

Ambrose, Kay, *Balletomane's Sketchbook*, pub. A. & C. Black, London, 1941

Anderson, Jack, *The One and Only: the Ballet Russe de Monte Carlo,* pub. Dance Horizons, New York, 1981

Anthony, Gordon, *Russian Ballet*, pub. Geoffrey Bles, London, 1939

Anthony, Gordon and Haskell, Arnold L., *Ballet*, pub. Geoffrey Bles, London, 1937

Anthony, Gordon and Sitwell, Sacheverell, *Massine*, pub. Routledge, London, 1939

Beaumont, Cyril W., *The Monte Carlo Russian Ballet*, pub. Beaumont, London, 1934

Beaumont, Cyril W., *The Ballet Called Swan Lake*, pub. Beaumont, London, 1952

Beaumont, Cyril W., *Michel Fokine and His Ballets,* pub. Beaumont, London, 1945

Brodovitch, Alexey and Denby, Edwin, *Ballet*, pub. J.J. Augustin, New York, 1945

Chujoy, Anatole, *The Symphonic Ballet,* pub. Kamin, New York, 1937

Chujoy, Anatole and Manchester, P.W., *The Dance Encyclopedia*, pub. Simon & Schuster, New York 1967 (also 1949 edition)

Crosland, Margaret, *The Memoirs of Giorgio de Chirico*, pub. Peter Owen, London, 1971

Deakin, Irving, *To the Ballet*, pub. Allen & Unwin, London, 1936

Détaille, Georges, *Les Ballets de Monte Carlo, 1911–44*, pub. Arc-en-Ciel, Paris, 1954

Dorati, Antal, *Notes of Seven Decades,* pub. Hodder & Stoughton, London, 1979

Gard, Alexis, *Ballet Laughs*, pub. Greystone Press, New York, 1941

Gunsbourg, Raoul, *Cent Ans de souvenirs . . . ou presque*, pub. Ed. du Rocher, Monaco, 1959

Haskell, Arnold L., *Balletomane's Scrapbook*, pub. A. & C. Black, London, 1936

Haskell, Arnold L., *Balletomane's Album*, pub. A. & C. Black, London, 1939

Haskell, Arnold L., *Ballet Panorama,* pub. Batsford, London, 1938

Jackson, Stanley, *Inside Monte Carlo*, pub. W.H. Allen, London, 1975

Koegler, Horst, *Concise Oxford Dictionary of Ballet*, pub. Oxford University Press, London, 1977 (also German edition, pub. Friedrich Verlag, 1973)

Kochno, Boris, *Le Ballet*, pub. Hachette, Paris, 1934

Krokover, Rosalyn, *The New Borzoi Book of Ballets,* pub. Knopf, New York, 1956

Lifar, Serge (trans. James Holman Mason), *Ma Vie from Kiev to Kiev*, pub. Hutchinson, London, 1970

Lynham, Deryck, *Ballet Then and Now*, pub. Sylvan Press, London, 1947

Matamoro, Blas, *La Historia del Teatro Colòn 1908–68*, pub. Buenos Aires, 1972

Manchester, P.W., *Vic Wells: A Ballet Progress*, pub. Gollancz, London, 1942

Obolensky, Prince Serge, *One Man in his Time*, pub. Hutchinson, London, 1942

Severn, Merlyn and Haskell, Arnold L., *Ballet in Action,* pub. The Bodley Head, London, 1938

Swinson, Cyril (ed.), *Dancers and Critics* (Alexandra Danilova by Joan Lawson, Tamara Toumanova by Leandre Vaillat), pub. A. & C. Black, London, 1950

Victorica, Victoria Garcia, *El Original Ballet Russe en America Latina*, pub. Ed. Arturo Jacinto Alvarez, Buenos Aires, 1948

Walsh, Dr T.J., *Monte Carlo Opera 1879–1909*, pub. Gill & Macmillan, London, 1975

Williamson, Audrey, *The Art of Ballet*, pub. Paul Elek, London, 1950

Wilson, G.B.L., *Dictionary of Ballet*, pub. A. & C. Black, London, 1974

Dance Chronicle, Vol. 3, No. 1, 1979 ('The Career of Alexandra Denisova' by Leland Windreich)

Ballet Annual, pub. A. & C. Black, London, 1947–51

The American Dancer

Ellis, C.H., *The Transcaspian Episode, 1918–19*, pub. Hutchinson, London, 1963

Luckett, Richard, *The White Generals*, pub. Longman, London, 1971

Norris, CB, RN, Captain David, *Royal Central Asian Journal, 1923* (Caspian Naval Expedition 1918–19, Lecture to the Society)

Norris, Admiral D.T., *Papers of Admiral D.T. Norris 1875–1937*, Vol. 4, in the National Maritime Museum

The Solicitors' Journal, 14 August 1937 and 26 February 1938 (Massine *v.* de Basil)

The Law Reports, London, 1936–45 (Massine *v.* de Basil)

Index

307

315

Kathrine Sorley Walker has been the London *Daily Mail*'s ballet critic for a dozen years, and writes articles on dance for most of the specialist journals. She frequently provides program notes for such companies as the Royal Ballet and the London Festival Ballet, and contributes articles on dance to many major encyclopedias. This is her ninth published book on the dance.